A History of the
Brewing Industry in Scotland

And there will be Lang-kail and Pottage,
And Bannocks of Barley-meal;
And there will be good sawt Herring,
To relish a Cog of good Ale.

A History of the Brewing Industry in Scotland

IAN DONNACHIE

JOHN DONALD PUBLISHERS LTD
EDINBURGH

Paperback edition 1998

ISBN 0 84976 496 6

·Printed in Great Britain by Bell & Bain Ltd., Glasgow

Introduction

Scottish Brewing History since 1980

It is twenty years since the first edition of this book and nearly thirty since I began to research the history of the brewing industry. I have had cause to reflect on the fact that I came to this project by chance: moving permanently to Edinburgh I was casting around for a suitable doctoral research topic, and having just taken a flat in the Canongate almost directly opposite the old Holyrood Brewery, the choice was obvious. What started out as a study of one of the capital's most important industries soon expanded, indeed, almost spun out of control, into a study of the wider Scottish industry. I certainly did not realise the enormity of the project nor its implications: what had begun as an Edinburgh-based study would take me not only to breweries, archives and libraries all over Scotland, but also further afield in search of relevant brewing records in Newcastle, London and Dublin. However, I did quickly realise that despite the apparent extent of surviving material I had come to this study just in time, for in the 1950s and 1960s a wave of take-overs, amalgamations and closures (described here in Chapter 12) had changed the face of the industry, whose history and heritage were all too rapidly finding their way on to the scrap heap. It was obviously only a matter of time before the records which had escaped the waste-paper drives of an earlier generation ended up on the bonfire. But there were enthusiasts in almost all of the surviving breweries who not only assisted me with my research but also ultimately helped to rescue and preserve the surviving records.

When I embarked on research into the history of the industry in Scotland I had as a model Peter Mathias's magisterial work on English brewing. As soon became apparent Mathias had very sensibly cut short his study at 1830, for such was the complexity of the later nineteenth and twentieth century industry and so daunting (and patchy) the records that even the most dedicated scholar would have felt intimidated. However, thanks to the company papers I was able to access and what was then pioneering work in legal records, I was able to piece together the story of the industry's growth during the eighteenth and nineteenth centuries. As readers will find out for themselves in the pages of the book, this happened along parallel paths, in that as well as generating large urban enterprises, growth in demand brought into being numerous smaller breweries, the micro-breweries of the early industrialisation era, which sprang up in smaller towns. Thereafter the major transport developments of the Victorian era started the long process of concentration and rationalisation, common to Britain as a whole, and superbly documented in Gourvish and Wilson's comprehensive study of the industry from 1830–1980. This happened later in Scotland than in England and the mechanics of the process revealed in my final chapter here, with the exception of a few company histories, remain to be unravelled in greater detail.

Gourvish and Wilson set a new standard in the business history of the industry and their book was a benchmark against which any future work will be measured. They wisely recognised from the outset that they could not match the detail of Mathias, given the huge weight of source material available. Firms grew in size, the industry generated a mass of statistics, and company law forced firms to keep proper records. After the 1870s specialist brewing journals (some of which can be found in the Scottish Brewing Archive) provided a wealth of detail covering every aspect of the trade, from raw materials through to a diversity of products. Moreover, as I myself found, the industry itself is difficult to confine since it runs in so many directions. It encompassed hundreds of firms of various sizes across Britain, retailing beer through thousands of outlets. The industry is pervasive in other respects. Through its raw material supplies it retains close links with agriculture and an important related activity, malting; it has always been conspicuously taxed, hence linking it closely to fiscal policy; and the sale of beer is enmeshed in complex licensing laws, always different in Scotland for good historical reasons. In all these areas, especially when the Temperance Movement was active during the nineteenth and early twentieth centuries, the industry was forced into the forefront of national politics.

The British Brewing Industry managed to keep a balance between these many themes by sticking to the essential developments, economic and social, within the brewing industry itself, and thus provided the first extended account of brewing in the modern period. Thoroughly based on research in the archives (including those in Scotland), it traced the development of the industry from one in which there were hundreds of firms producing beer to one dominated by half a dozen large companies. It carried the reader from the porters, ales and stouts, the vast vats, drays and numerous pubs of Victorian Britain, to the draught lagers, giant computer-controlled fermenters, beer tankers and theme pubs of the late twentieth century.

A wide range of topics was investigated by Gourvish and Wilson, many with important implications for the history of the Scottish industry. They discussed the free trade in beer, the impact of temperance, and the emergence of the great Victorian breweries together with their acquisition of public houses and company status. In the twentieth century their book examined the significant impact of the two World Wars, the movement for improved public houses, the relative sobriety of the inter-war period, and the revolutionary changes in the industry since the 1950s. A huge amount of new ground was covered with the different experiences of hundreds of breweries, large and small, traced across a century and a half. The history of the Scottish industry and much that I wrote here can thus be seen in context: expansion partly explained by buoyant home markets and exports; the contraction caused by progressive loss of markets, especially abroad; and the late rationalisation in the 1950s and 60s brought about by the dominance of family firms reluctant to relinquish control. The book is thus an important starting point for anyone interested in the business and social history of Scottish brewing. It tells us a great deal more about developments north of the border than Mathias's pioneering work, with its inevitable emphasis on the English industry. But it does not discount a growing volume of other useful studies specifically concerned with Scotland.

Apart from this major study which shows how the Scottish industry relates to the wider scene there are two important finding aids which have proved invaluable to the researcher, one covering mainly primary sources, the other secondary literature. The first by Lesley Richmond and Alison Turton provides a detailed and comprehensive guide to sources for the industry's long and complex history by presenting the results of the first national survey of brewing archives. It provides brief histories of nearly 650 breweries throughout Britain, including most of those still brewing today, along with lists of archival records. Nearly all the Scottish breweries with surviving records are documented; others for which material has subsequently come to light can readily be checked in the Scottish Brewing Archive. Local historians can easily use this aid to find out about the history of some long forgotten brewery or family associations with a firm or public house.

The second reference tool to which attention should be drawn is David Gutzke's annotated bibliography on alcohol in the British Isles. This provides a detailed guide to publications on the drink industries since Roman times, a large majority of over 2,000 citations being devoted to the brewing industry and its products. In addition to books and articles, the volume lists unpublished manuscripts, essays in edited works, and dissertations. Detailed annotations provide the user with information about a work's thesis or theme, the use of primary materials, relationship to other studies, and also give a critical evaluation and the location of sources. Works that use some primary sources such as autobiographies, diaries and memoirs are also included.

Since this book was first published there have been several useful surveys of the development of Scottish brewing. Two papers published in the Proceedings of the Royal Society of Edinburgh describe the history of the industry so far as it affected brewing science and provide insights into the evolution of the processes since the days of Roberts's *Scottish Ale Brewer and Practical Maltster*. In the more historical of the two Anna MacLeod surveys the contribution of Scots to brewing science, much of it originating from Heriot-Watt College/University. Biological science, she maintains, has always been fundamental to the modern industry, but a history of brewing could well be written from the viewpoint of the chemical engineer who is expert in separation procedures and in materials science. Colin Slaughter, in describing the techniques of brewing, could point to the fact that in 1986 there were 15 commercial brewing operations, representing a range of productive capacities ranging from under 100 barrels a year for the smallest one-person operations to over 2.5 million barrels a year from the largest plant. All the main beer types, ale, lager and stout, were produced with lager remaining a more important component of the total than for the UK generally. There was one Scottish-based UK national brewer and production was carried on by three other UK national firms. These four accounted for most of the beer produced with the rest contributed by two wholly Scottish enterprises and one then owned by an English regional brewer. There is a useful and splendidly illustrated account of the industry in the *Scottish Drink Book*, while many interesting facts about the industry in Scotland can also be obtained from *The Beer Drinker's Companion*, which also illustrates the huge range of marketing materials brewing has generated historically.

Given the concentration of the industry in Scotland much of the recent historiography has a focus on Edinburgh and Glasgow, but most of the studies have been general rather than specifically concerned with individual enterprises. It is therefore surprising that there is as yet no detailed history either of the constituent Scottish enterprises that make up Scottish & Newcastle or the many other important firms that were swallowed up in the various amalgamation of the fifties and sixties. Certainly as far as William Younger is concerned David Keir's now very dated volume merely scraped the surface and this old and distinguished business, the Scottish equivalent of Whitbread south of the border, deserves a thorough-going business history. In Glasgow Tennent and its numerous constituent enterprises have perhaps fared better, though the history of the parent firm with its dynamic and innovative management under Hugh Tennent and distinctive trust ownership and operation needs to be investigated. Fortunately the visitor can gain a good impression of the company's history and products in the innovative museum and visitor centre that has been developed at Wellpark Brewery in the East End of Glasgow.

Outside Edinburgh and Glasgow the only study of urban concentration is Charles McMaster's study of the brewing industry in Alloa. As he points out, next to Edinburgh and Leith, it probably had the best advantages of anywhere in the east of Scotland for successful enterprise in brewing: raw materials supplies on its doorstep, ease of shipping, and potentially lucrative outlets in nearby colliery and textile communities. Alloa quickly became a major centre of the industry with several large firms, notably George Younger, Arroll and Calder, dominating the market. But McMaster suggests that over-capacity was already evident by the 1890s and that it was for this reason, combined with the competition coming from Edinburgh and Glasgow brewers, that the major Alloa firms turned with such enthusiasm to the export trade — an important development I discussed elsewhere in a study of the Scottish overseas trade. Subsequent to McMaster's study, sadly, the brewing industry of Alloa has shrunk still further. So Maclay's Thistle Brewery, a doggedly independent enterprise with a history going back to the nineteenth century, deserves to be researched for its survival tactics alone.

We are still lacking a detailed study of the industry in other quite significant centres, notably in Falkirk (where distilling was also important), and further north, Perth (another distilling centre), Dundee and Aberdeen. In all four the industry was quite large, and with several important firms surviving to the 1950s or 1960s, deserves to be researched fully. Unfortunately experience has shown that the longer breweries stayed in business the less likely it was that historic records of any worth have survived and the gaps are difficult to fill. Both Aitken and Ballingall, briefly discussed here, are good cases in point.

The firm of James Aitken & Co in Falkirk was a large and important one, but like so many in the 1950s and 60s fell victim to the squeeze exerted by Edinburgh and Glasgow rivals. The Scottish Brewing Archive holds some of the records which have survived on this firm and has also published in its newsletter a fascinating account by a former employee, showing how valuable this sort of testimony can be in reconstructing business as well as personal histories in the industry. Much could certainly be done on the oral history of the industry generally as the generation connected with the industry from the time of the closures and amalgamations is now in old age.

As far as the Fair City is concerned the *SBA Newsletter* of Autumn 1992 reprinted a most interesting article from the 1950s on Wrights of Perth, a firm which dated back to the eighteenth century and was typical of the medium-scale breweries developed in the larger burghs. What this article showed was that as late as the 1950s this was quite a progressive enterprise, having restructured itself several times and acquired the only other remaining brewery in Perth, Muir and Martin's South Inch Brewery, as well as an aerated water factory and bottling business in nearby Dunkeld. During the 1950s a whole range of new equipment had been installed and the firm could boast proudly that it was 'almost self-sufficient, making its own malt, brewing beer to suit a variety of tastes, importing beer for those of foreign palate, making its own soft drinks, owning its own trade outlets'. But like so many others the firm succumber to takeover, in this instance by Vaux in 1961. Nearby Blackford had no fewer than three breweries and was more important than the place suggests, especially since malting survived there long after brewing ceased in the 1920s.

Dundee also had a significant brewing history that remains to be fully documented. There were several firms active during the nineteenth and early twentieth centuries, the most prominent being Ballingall. The Park and Pleasance Breweries dated back to the eighteenth century, but were enlarged and modernised after the Ballingall family became sole proprietors in 1852. Hugh Ballingall was a typical Victorian entrepreneur and under his dynamic leadership a large and successful business was created. Apart from an extensive local trade, Ballingall also sold in England and overseas. The firm's products were famous for their quality and won a succession of awards at exhibitions in Edinburgh and Paris. Unfortunately after the death of Hugh Ballingall the business seems to have suffered from 'entrepreneurial failure' and increasing competition from larger brewers elsewhere. As in practically every other case of amalgamation or closure during the first half of the twentieth century the major brewers in the central belt had the advantages of economies of scale and better transport working in their favour. However, 'Bally's' saw through the depression, the Second World War, and survived long enough to market some of its products in cans. Brewing ceased at Dundee in 1964, with Drybrough first continuing to brew on the firm's behalf for some time and then supplying, another typical series of events, leading to the ultimate demise of what remained of the Ballingall brewing enterprise.

There are numerous other instances of a similar cycle in the history of other doomed breweries, some of which can be traced in Chapter 12.

Dunbar is unique in the survival there of a long-established brewery, Belhaven, whose origins date back to the eighteenth century, and whose products and markets remained essentially local until quite recently. One of the reasons this enterprise survived was judicious family management and a range of traditional products targeted at a clearly defined and loyal market — the magic ingredients for a successful small brewery. Other towns, like Haddington and Cupar, had important malting and brewing industries which would repay investigation partly because their activities were often integral to much larger and more complex agricultural and commercial operations. There have been studies of breweries in even smaller towns, notably Irvine and Catrine in Ayrshire. The persistence of small town enterprises, many of which are mentioned in the pages here, is as remarkable as the list and data assembled by Arie de Groot on hundreds of individually named firms. This is an invaluable aid to the local as well as the brewing historian and can be consulted in the Scottish Brewing Archive. Local historians interested in the industry in their own community can readily follow up the many references cited here, perhaps using local directories, newspapers, maps and plans to chart its history.

Another topic which has attracted considerable attention is the brewers themselves. This is highly appropriate given the on-going historical debate about the nature and role of entrepreneurship in later nineteenth and early twentieth century Britain. Briefly this thesis suggests that 'entrepreneurial failure' became increasingly evident in family enterprises as the founding generation passed control on to their descendants. William McEwan, Hugh Tennent and George Younger among others represent different aspects of this debate. All three had brewing connections, in Tennent's and Younger's cases going back several generations. In McEwan's the link was through his brother-in-law, one of the Alloa Youngers, and an uncle, John Jeffrey, the Edinburgh brewer. His father was a ship owner, possibly carrying in his cargo, barrels of Alloa ale.

There was no evidence of entrepreneurial failure among this group, indeed McEwan rapidly built up a business to rival that of the other two and of the major Scottish brewing dynasty, the Edinburgh Youngers. The question is, how did McEwan do it? Work on his early life proves that in a series of apparently mundane commercial jobs he acquired the critical skills necessary to be successful in business. After a thorough training with Jeffrey and using family and borrowed capital he set up the Fountain Brewery. This development came at a judicious time and making much greater use of railway transport than had hitherto been the case in the industry McEwan opened up an extensive market for his products in central Scotland and beyond. McEwan soon found himself riding high on the brewing boom and within ten or fifteen years headed a business almost as large as his nearest, and much longer established rival, William Younger.

Like Hugh Ballingall, Hugh Tennent was a young man when he entered the industry and was another illustration of the fact that in innovation Scottish brewers were well ahead in the technology and science of the industry. While there will probably always be controversy about the origins of lager in Scotland, there can be no doubt that it was Tennent who realised the potential of the product. His connections with German brewers put him ahead of the field, with the first custom built plant in Glasgow. In producing lager, Tennent and other Scottish brewers, were continuing a long tradition of innovation evidenced in their early adoption of mechanisation, refrigeration, and bottling. The science of brewing was also widely recognised and adopted, with important implications for quality control. We might just note that Scottish emigrants were actively involved in the development of breweries in many countries overseas, notably in Australia, New Zealand and India, but this remains to be investigated in any detail.

After the brewing boom of the late nineteenth century and particularly the surge in exports to the early 1900s there is some evidence that brewers sat back on their laurels, and maybe the period immediately before 1914 could be characterised as one of 'entrepreneurial failure'. But as Peter Payne pointed out about the late nineteenth century Scottish ironmasters, for what seemed to them very sound reasons they stuck with what they knew, rather than invest at that stage in the new steel making technology. So the brewers were not that different and for much of the period, we must remember, had the added threat of temperance — even prohibition — hovering above their heads. The idea that the successful brewing families just sat back and took it easy was certainly not true of George Younger of Alloa, who at that period, probably realising the difficulties that might lie ahead for the industry on the domestic front, became one of the leading British exporters. After World War One realism is increasingly evident in the board minutes and quite dynamic and innovative efforts were made in both home and overseas markets and with new products, especially bottled beers and lagers. For the latter product there was a growing market, led by Tennent, so the early entry into lager brewing by that firm proved a judicious decision. It later led the field in the canned trade, first in the stubby 'Brasso'-style tins and later in more conventional cans. Some of these have now become art forms, particularly those displaying the more exotic — or should it be erotic — poses of the 'Lager Lovelies', sadly missed in these politically correct times.

The final chapter of this book describes the complex web of take-overs and mergers which by the 1970s had turned the Scottish industry into a microcosm of the British, dominated as it then was by six major brewers. While the names may have changed, as they seem to do constantly, the UK structure in the late 1990s, taking account of further amalgamations and acquisitions, remains much the same. Five of the key players, Bass, Scottish & Newcastle, Guinness, Allied Domecq, and Whitbread, rank among the top 100 companies in the UK, while the sixth, Carlsberg, is 399th in Europe's top 1000. The industry in Scotland is now concentrated in two major enterprises in Edinburgh and Glasgow, another of the UK nationals having ceased production at its Alloa plant. However, brewing continues at the Thistle Brewery in Alloa, as it does with great success at Belhaven in Dunbar and at the Caledonian Brewery in Slateford. The performance of the industry remains an important barometer of the economy hence corporate and financial dealings attract regular comment in the business sections of newspapers and periodicals, which provide very useful up-to-date information on what remains a dynamic but fast moving sector.

In 1979 when keg beer had a virtual monopoly everywhere, cask conditioned products were hard to come by. But thanks to the Campaign For Real Ale, certainly one of the most successful consumer movements of modern times, and to the sensible response of the industry, an enormous range of real ales (including many from England) can now be found in all but the most remote locations. While the history of CAMRA in Scotland remains to be written, there is no doubt that some of its key personnel and most enthusiastic members exercised considerable influence on the industry since the 1970s. Apart from goading the brewery giants into action the demand for cask conditioned ales has spawned a whole generation of micro-breweries, whose history also remains to be documented and recorded in any detail. Unfortunately, as McMaster pointed out, although twenty small breweries were started up between 1965 and 1990, many of them proved transitory. One of the earliest was also the most ancient, the Traquair House brewery, revived in 1965 by the late laird, Peter Maxwell-Stuart, in cellar premises dating back at least to the eighteenth century. Its output was initially designed for consumption by visitors to the historic house, but while production remains modest the products are now more widely available.

The first new brewery was established in 1978 at Bothwell, where I recall sampling some of its first products. It survived, with a change in ownership, until 1987. Another early entrant to micro-brewing, albeit much more highly capitalised and on a larger scale, was the Broughton Brewery, which started out in 1979 with one ale, then gradually broadening its product range and widening its market. No doubt the idea that such an enterprise could prove a success encouraged others with the result that the early 1980s saw several other micros dedicated to fulfilling the demand for traditional cask beers in their own localities. That at Alford revived the name of Devanha, an old Aberdeen brewery, while others included the Alice Brewery in Inverness, the Strathalbyn Brewery in Clydebank and the Leith Brewery. If some of these brewers had read this book more closely they would perhaps have re-thought their business strategies, but even if the breweries did not survive they contributed substantially to the revival of traditional ale brewing and made their products better known locally. Several of the later ventures, including the revived Caledonian Brewery at Slateford, although on a much larger scale than any of the others, proved highly successful. There are presently over twenty micro-breweries in production, geographically scattered from Orkney to Dumfries and Galloway. These produce a wide range of ales, one of the most innovative being Fraoch, a heather ale, first brewed by the Celts and their ancestors. A rediscovered recipe was the basis of Fraoch, launched in 1993.

It will be obvious to the user of the references and bibliography that information about the history of the brewing industry is to be found in a great variety of locations. One of the most important ones, the Scottish Record Office, has added significantly to the list of archives dealing with brewing. Many of these holdings lay undiscovered in legal and business records, such as those dealing with dissolved companies or sequestration proceedings, and can now be accessed with ease thanks to careful indexing. Local archives and local history libraries can also provide information on breweries using such sources as valuation rolls, directories, street plans, newspapers and photographs.

The major repository of the industry's history and heritage is the Scottish Brewing Archive located in the Business Records Centre, University of Glasgow. Prior to its amalgamation with this, the largest business archive in Scotland, it was housed at Heriot-Watt University, where the International Centre for Brewing and Distilling maintains a distinguished record for its teaching and research. Through the work of the archive and its trustees close links are maintained between the two institutions. Since 1982, and thanks to the enthusiasm of the archivists and their supporters, the SBA has augmented a major library of historic brewing literature and an impressive archive of records representative of the industry in Scotland. Most of the major firms and many of the smaller ones are represented. The records are described at length in the archive's own listings and in Richmond and Turton, already mentioned. The records include major collections of trade and marketing material, posters, display cards, labels, bottles, cans, and other brewing ephemera, including modern and current items, one of the largest collections of its kind. It also holds film, video and sound recordings relating to the industry and related activities. The SBA publishes a newsletter and journal and is the logical starting place for the many studies that remain to be undertaken in the national and local history of this complex but fascinating industry, its many breweries, and its varied products.

REFERENCES

J. Alexander, *Dundee Pubs. Past and Present* (Dundee, 1992)

B.R. Bennison and J.P. Merrington, *The Centenary History of the Newcastle Breweries Ltd*, (Edinburgh, 1990).

E. Bevan, 'Men of Brewing: George Lorimer (1846–1939)', *SBA Newsletter*, vol 22, Winter 1993, pp.18–22.

M. Black, 'The Fort Bar', *SBA Newsletter*, vol 22, Winter 1993, pp.12–15.

R. Close, 'Catrine Brewery' *SBA Newsletter*, vol 27, Summer 1996, pp. 15–21.

R. Close, 'Irvine Brewery', *SBA Newsletter*, vol 28, Spring 1997, pp.11–15.

J. Dallas and C.McMaster, *The Beer Drinker's Companion* (Edinburgh, 1993).

I. Donnachie, 'Drink and Society 1750–1850: Some Aspects of the Scottish Experience', *Scottish Journal of Labour History*, no. 13, 1979, pp.5–22.

I. Donnachie, 'World War One and the Drink Question: State Control of the Drink Trade', *Scottish Journal of Labour History*, no.17, 1982, pp.19–26.

I. Donnachie, 'Hugh Tennent', 'William McEwan', 'George Younger, Viscount Younger of Leckie' and others in A. Slaven and S.G. Checkland (eds.) *Dictionary of Scottish Business Biography*, vol. 2 (Aberdeen, 1990).

I. Donnachie, 'Following the Flag: Scottish Brewers and Beers in Imperial and International Markets, 1850–1939', in R.G.Wilson and T.R.Gourvish (eds.), *The Dynamics of the International Brewing Industry Since 1800* (London, 1998), pp.123–141.

T.R. Gourvish and R.G. Wilson, *The British Brewing Industry 1830–1980* (Cambridge, 1994).

D. Gutzke, *Protecting the Pub. Brewers and Publicans Against Temperance* (Royal Historical Society Studies in History 58) (London, 1989).

D. Gutzke, *Alcohol in the British Isles from Roman Times to 1996. An Annotated Bibliography* (Westport, CT, 1996).

D.I.H. Johnstone, ' History of the Beer Can' *SBA Newsletter*, vol 23, Summer 1994, pp.13–18.

D.I.H. Johnstone, ' History of the Beer Can. Part 2' *SBA Newsletter*, vol 25, Summer 1995, pp.10–14.

E. King, *Scotland Sober and Free. The Temperance Movement 1829–1979* (Glasgow, 1979).

A.M. MacLeod, 'Brewing', *Proceedings of the Royal Society of Edinburgh*, 84B, pp. 37–64, 1983.

C. McMaster, *Alloa Ale. A History of the Brewing Industry in Alloa* (Alloa, 1984).

C. McMaster, 'The Breweries of Blackford', SBA Newsletter, no 7, Summer 1986, pp. 7–12.

C. McMaster, 'Ballingall & Co Ltd', *SBA Newsletter* no 11, Summer 1988, pp. 16–18.

C. McMaster, 'Porter Brewing in Scotland', SBA Newsletter, no 12, Autumn 1988, pp.4–7.

C. McMaster, 'Ballingall's of Dundee: Part Two. 1897–1968', *SBA Newsletter*, no 12, Autumn 1988, pp. 13–15.

C. McMaster, 'Scotland's Forgotten Breweries: Mark Binnie & Co, The Nungate Brewery, Haddington, East Lothian', *SBA Newsletter,* no 12, Autumn 1988, pp. 8–9.

C. McMaster, 'Scotland's Other National Drink? A Short History of Lager Brewing in Scotland', *SBA Newsletter*, no 14, Spring 1989, pp.10–13.

C. McMaster, 'Beer — A Proud Tradition' in *Chambers Scottish Drink Book* (Edinburgh, 1990), pp. 45–71.

C. McMaster, 'Gordon & Blair Ltd: The Craigwell Brewery, Edinburgh, and the Home Brewery, Glasgow', *SBA Newsletter*, no 17, Summer 1990, pp. 3–5.

C. McMaster, 'Robert Deuchar Ltd: The Sandyford Brewery, Newcastle and the Duddingston Brewery, Edinburgh', *SBA Newsletter*, no 18, Winter 1990–91, pp.6–8.

C. McMaster, 'Scotland's New Breweries', *SBA Newsletter*, no 18, Winter 1990–91, pp.9–10.

C. McMaster and T. Rutherford, *The Tennent Caledonian Breweries*, Scottish Brewing Archive (Edinburgh, 1985).

C. McMaster and T. Rutherford, *A History of the Belhaven Brewery*, Scottish Brewing Archive (Edinburgh, 1985).

G.J. Noonan, *Scotch Ale*, (Brewers Publications 1993).

L. Richmond and A. Turton, *The Brewing Industry. A Guide to Historical Records* (Manchester, 1990).

T. Rutherford, 'Prohibition: The Brewers' Response', *SBA Newsletter* no 6, Winter 1985, pp.8–10.

C. Schofield and A.Kamm, *Lager Lovelies. The Story Behind the Glamour* (Glasgow, 1984).

J.C. Slaughter, 'The Brewing Industry', *Proceedings of the Royal Society of Edinburgh*, 87B, pp. 269–283, 1986.

A. Topen (ed.) 'Andrew Smith's Brewing Notebook', *SBA Newsletter*, Spring 1993, pp. 14–16.

A. Topen, 'William McEwan: The Early Years', *SBA Newsletter*, vol 23, Summer 1994, pp.31–39.

A. Topen (ed.), 'James Fleming's Scrapbook', *SBA Newsletter*, vol 24, Winter 1994–5, pp. 25–27.

K. Wilbraham, 'Impost, Ale and Relief: Sources for Brewing History at Edinburgh City Archives', *SBA Newsletter*, vol 28, Spring 1997, pp. 26–31.

R.B. Weir, 'The Drink Trades', in R. Church (ed.) *The Dynamics of Victorian Business* (London, 1980).

A. Young, 'Reminiscences of Aitken of Falkirk', *SBA Newsletter*, vol 23, Summer 1994, pp.24–27.

Preface

IN a country so justifiably proud of its many fine whiskies, it is not really surprising that the distilling industry has held the limelight for so long—and been the subject of myriad books. Now at last it is the turn of Scotland's other drink—and I do not refer to the product so loved by Billy Connolly and others as a miracle pick-me-up—but to beer and the Scottish brewing industry. There is no history of this long important activity—only the odd passing reference in more general works and a handful of company histories mostly published privately and difficult to come by.

Writing this book has given me a great deal of pleasure. I sincerely hope that the end product will be enjoyed by the countless people who have been intrigued by the subject of my research in recent years. The result may not appeal to everyone, for I have tried to write a serious economic and social history of brewing in Scotland, and make no apologies for this. I suppose fellow-academics will disagree with a lot of my ideas and conclusions—and I would be the first to admit that there is still plenty of scope for more detailed research on many aspects of the industry.

A substantial section of this book started life as a doctoral thesis in the Department of History, University of Strathclyde. Much has been retained and new material added, particularly on the more recent history of the industry in Scotland. Part of a chapter appeared as an article entitled 'Sources of Capital and Capitalization in the Scottish Brewing Industry, c. 1750—1830' and published in the *Economic History Review*. I am grateful to the editors of that journal for allowing publication here.

In the course of research and writing I have incurred many debts. First I would like to thank Professor John Butt for his constant encouragement and helpful advice. Other former Strathclyde colleagues who have helped in various ways include Dr. Tom Devine, Dr. W. Hamish Fraser, John Hume (who also supplied some illustrations), and Dr. James Treble. Professor Peter Payne of the University of Aberdeen was good enough to make a number of helpful suggestions on improvements to early drafts. In this—as in other ventures over the years—Professor Sidney and Mrs. Olive Checkland of the University of Glasgow have provided cheerful encouragement. The Open University was kind enough to grant an extended period of study leave and I would like to thank Professor Arthur Marwick and Professor John Ferguson for making this possible. Professor Anna Macleod of Heriot-Watt University kindly gave me some advice on sources for scientific and technical developments in brewing.

The management and staff of the major Scottish breweries have been courteous and helpful in making available their business records: Scottish & Newcastle Breweries Ltd (who hold the records of both William Younger and William McEwan); Tennent-Caledonian Breweries Ltd, now part of Bass Charrington (for the records of Tennent); and Whitbread (Scotland) Ltd (for material on Archibald Campbell Hope and King Ltd). In particular, thanks are due to George Bertram and Peter Dundas of Scottish and Newcastle, D.I. Macleod and C.K. Mills of Tennent-Caledonian, and T.C. Ferguson of Whitbread.

I wish also to thank the staff of the following libraries and archives for their patient help in the course of my research: the Scottish Record Office, Register House; the National Library of Scotland; the Signet Library of the Court of Session; Edinburgh University Library; Andersonian Library, University of Strathclyde; Glasgow University Library; the Mitchell Library, Glasgow; Aberdeen City Library; Newcastle City Archives; Durham University Library; Bodleian Library, Oxford; the Jennie Lee Library at The Open University; Public Record Office, London; Guildhall Library, London; and, the British Library.

A multitude of other thanks are due to friends and colleagues whose ideas I shared over a congenial pint including—in no particular order—Ian Wood, Henry Cowper, Jean Jordan, Dennis Walder, Colin Luckhurst, Dr. Christopher Harvie, Dr. Ronnie Watson, Gordon Young, John McKay, Graham Cummings, Dr. Wray Vamplew, and John Tuckwell of John Donald Publishers. No fewer than four secretaries, Patricia Slater, Susan Spencer, Susan Haggis and Aileen Arnot coped admirably to produce the typescript.

1979.   Ian Donnachie.

Contents

List of Tables

1
Prelude to Growth

THE development of the brewing industry in Scotland since the mid-eighteenth century has been more a reflection of economic growth than a cause of it. Yet, like the other great drink industry of distilling in the Highlands, brewing was—and remains—very important in certain areas of the Lowlands in terms of the extent of output and size of business units. Throughout most of the period under review the brewing industry provides a useful barometer of economic progress, or the lack of it. Prior to the seventeenth century brewing was a widespread domestic activity, though some formal business organisation was just discernible in the larger burghs, like Edinburgh, an early centre of the trade. Later, in the eighteenth century, brewing was one of several important primary processing industries which developed rapidly in response to growing population and rising incomes—others being trades like grain milling, tanning, leatherworking, soap making and distilling. During the classic Industrial Revolution period, the brewing industry in Scotland expanded rapidly along parallel paths: numerous breweries were built in country towns, while in the cities much larger units began to emerge. The size of brewery more often than not reflected the size of its local market.

As the nineteenth century progressed the Scottish industry became increasingly exposed to national influences, particularly in regard to techniques of production and company organisation. But although Scotland shared the experience of the Brewery Boom in the period 1885-1900, and was open to many other external forces, the industry retained many characteristic features. For example, on the retail side there were many differences from south of the Border. The tied-house system—which restricted the sale of beers to those supplied by the brewer to whom the pub was 'tied'—had only limited development, mainly because of differences in the licensing laws. The twentieth century has seen many dramatic changes in the structure of the industry. As a result of amalgamations all but a handful of the smaller breweries have disappeared and the industry is almost wholly dominated by multi-national brewing giants. One of the so-called 'Big Six' is Scottish and Newcastle Breweries, a group with a long and interesting history, reaching back to the middle of the eighteenth century. To trace something of the prelude to these developments, however, we must look back beyond the Industrial Revolution to the seventeenth and early part of the eighteenth centuries.

The Seventeenth Century

The main developments in Scottish brewing before 1700 include the emergence

1

of a considerable brewing interest in Edinburgh organised in a powerful Society of Brewers, the expansion of the trade in other towns throughout the Lowlands, and—the most significant episode—the establishment of a large brewery in Leith by an English capitalist. These and other elements of growth probably reflected a new impetus towards industrial and commercial development in seventeenth century Scotland.

It is certainly no accident that Edinburgh became the focal point of the Scottish brewing industry at such an early date. The rich agricultural hinterland of Lothian was the city's granary, supplying both mills and breweries. Excellent supplies of pure, fresh water could readily be obtained from wells in and around Holyrood, Canongate and Cowgate. Coal for heating and boiling could easily be supplied from nearby collieries. Finally, a large and ready market existed in the city, port, and immediate environs for the various products of the breweries. By the beginning of the seventeenth century Edinburgh was already the leading centre of brewing. The brewers were among the leading burgesses and the Brewers' Craft one of several influential trades. Certain brewers in 1596 had established a Society of Brewers to concern itself with all aspects of the trade, including grain supply, malt and water for brewing, marketing and pricing policies, and protection against outside competition and foreign imports. The Society of Brewers established a large plant near the Cowgate, this and other breweries being supplied with water from a specially constructed reservoir, which stored water pumped by a windmill from the Burgh Loch.[1] Later, in the 1630s the 'common brew-house' of Edinburgh supplied a large proportion of the local market for ale and beer, being described by one observer, Sir William Brereton, as having 'the greatest, vastest leads, boiling keeves (or vats), cisterns and combs (or tubs)' he had ever seen. 'The leads to cool the liquor in,' he added, 'were as large as the whole house.'[2]

Outside the capital the brewing trade by the mid-seventeenth century was also beginning to concentrate itself in key areas of production, the dominant districts being Lothian, Fife, and the coastal ports of Angus. In agriculturally rich Lothian, brewing was carried on in Prestonpans (already, as its name indicates, a minor industrial centre), Haddington (also important for its maltings), and the port of Dunbar in East Lothian; while in West Lothian, Linlithgow (another milling and malting centre) and Bo'ness on the Forth estuary were of more than local significance. Further west, on the upper reaches of the River Forth, Stirling had established itself at an early date as a leading centre of both malting and brewing, while nearby Alloa (later an important rival of Edinburgh) served a colliery and salt-panning district.[3] Fife was a significant brewing county by the seventeenth century: all the Forth ports, from Culross in the west to Crail in the east, had breweries, and larger burghs, like Dunfermline, Anstruther, Cupar and St. Andrews, all had substantial brewing trades.[4] Further north, the two Tayside ports of Perth and Dundee were close rivals, the latter recording at least six brewers of consequence in 1627.[5] Burghs of the north-east with brewing trades included Aberdeen, Fraserburgh and Banff, while Elgin in Moray was the natural centre of an extensive milling, tanning, malting and brewing industry in a rich arable district.[6]

In the west of Scotland the most important centre of brewing was Glasgow, where the Tennent family were already established as innkeepers and ale brewers by the close of the sixteenth century.[7] Other Clyde ports, like Dumbarton, Greenock (by the latter half of the seventeenth century a growing harbour), Ayr, and Irvine were of secondary and more local significance. Southern Scotland had several towns with well-established brewing trades, including Duns and Kelso in the Merse and the vital port of Berwick at the mouth of the River Tweed.[8] In the western Borders and Galloway, Dumfries was the only centre of any consequence, with the exception of small Solway ports, like Kirkcudbright. During the seventeenth century Dumfries was becoming established as an important centre of agricultural processing, including both malting and brewing.[9]

Throughout the seventeenth century there are increasing numbers of references to brewing and malting in the Reports of the Privy Council of Scotland and the Acts of the Parliament of Scotland, two valuable sources of data relating to the economic development of Scotland before the Union of 1707. Some references from the mid-1620s are typical. In 1625 we find the Scottish Parliament passing legislation forbidding the sale of imported English ale and the Baltic equivalent called 'sowens.' Under this Act the 'hamebringing of foreyne beir' was made an offence, but despite this large numbers of east coast merchants (especially in Dundee, St. Andrews and Kirkcaldy) seem to have imported and sold considerable quantities of imported ale.[10] Scots ale was notoriously poor in both flavour and general quality. Hops were little used, being an expensive, luxury import from England or the Continent. Few contemporary observers had much good to say of the Scots pint: Fynes Moryson wrote in 1598 that the ale drunk by 'the better sort of citizens' was so bad that it would 'distemper a stranger's body.'[11] If this sort of comment was typical, it is perhaps not surprising that the Scottish Parliament was worried. Some evidence indicates that the growing challenge to the Scottish domestic product from imported ales was growing throughout the century. In 1627 it was reported that there existed 'a great disproportion between the prices of English beer and the ale of this Kingdom.' It was inadvisable, the Parliament argued, that foreign imports should be sold at twice the price 'of the like produced at home,' especially when (they considered) Scots ales were in no way inferior. Legislation fixed the price of imported liquor at not more than £6 per tun retail, and similar enactments revising import prices continued to be placed on the statute book throughout the remaining years of the Scottish Parliament's existence.[12]

The Scottish brewing trade thus required some measure of protection against foreign competition, especially at the 'luxury' end of the market, though cost and distance must clearly have been major disincentives to importers. The ordinary Scot buying publicly brewed ale, however, had to stomach a fairly inferior commodity, manufactured from raw materials of poor quality. With the possible exception of major centres, like Edinburgh, Glasgow and Dundee, the industry was organised on traditional craft lines, catering for limited local markets. Modes of production were old-established and like most other crafts brewing was hidebound with constricting and often ancient customs, the majority of which stifled innovation and expansion.

Yet in the years after 1660, brewing was only one of several important consumer industries to expand under the aegis of Parliamentary and Crown encouragement. These included soap, glass and sugar manufacture, salt boiling, coal and lead mining, textiles and fishing.[13] Acts of the Scottish Parliament provided (at least on paper) a wide range of incentives to merchants and entrepreneurs in the development of the export trade and home-based manufactures. Numerous joint-stock and chartered enterprises were established in Scotland, the majority concerned with processing primary products and thus closely related to the land and agriculture.[14] One remarkable example of large-scale entrepreneurship and business organisation in this period was the brewery concern established at Leith about 1670, probably the largest integrated unit in Scotland before the Industrial Revolution.

The Leith brewery was associated with a remarkable English entrepreneur, Sir James Stansfield, a former colonel in Scottish Cromwellian forces who apparently settled in Scotland in the late 1650s. At a time when the Scottish Parliament was so actively promoting manufactures and industry of all kinds, and attempting to attract by a variety of concessions foreign (mainly English) capital and skill, Stansfield and his partners were responsible for the development of a wide range of business enterprises, including metal mining, woollen textile manufacture, glass making and brewing.[15] Stansfield's earliest activities seem to have been in the field of mineral exploitation, for he was associated for some time with the Duke of Buccleuch's lead mines at Wanlockhead in Dumfriesshire. Although lead was the most important mineral worked, others, including silver and gold, were mined. Lead was partly processed at Wanlockhead and partly at Leith, where the Stansfield enterprises owned extensive property near the Shore. Stansfield was extremely active in Edinburgh and seems to have made continuous representations to Parliament on the potential of numerous industrial developments. By the late 1660s, however, he had settled on an estate near Haddington in East Lothian and diversified his interests to include agricultural improvement and wool manufacture. As so many landowners in the eighteenth century were later to realise, it was an obvious step from raising the products of the land to further processing them for the growing urban market in nearby Edinburgh.[16]

Although there are many gaps in the source material, the Stansfield Manuscripts do contain several immensely useful documents, including 'Accompts' and 'Abbreviates of Accompt'[17] relating to the breweries during the years 1671-76. A statement of profit and loss during these years is given in Table 1. The accounts show only a marginal profit of £2000 Scots over six years' trading and various degrees of loss in two years out of every three. When the company was finally wound up, however, it was stated to have uncollected debts amounting to a total of £54,000 Scots, and another 'Abbreviate' for 1671-76 credits the concern with a profit of nearly £70,000 Scots during its six years of operation.[18] Looking at these data, it would not be unreasonable to conclude that a contemporary brewery might sustain a loss two years in every three, largely because of exposure to

Table 1

Financial Statement of the Leith Breweries 1671/76

Year	Receipts (£ Scots)	Issues
1671-2	37,351	34,229
1672-3	44,699	51,959
1673-4	37,306	41,276
1674-5	42,343	28,604
1675-6	17,444	18,411
1676	28,456	31,179
Totals	207,599	205,658

short-term fluctuations in the price of grain. Certainly, two-thirds of the Leith brewery outlays were represented by grain, as the following entries from a 'Balance of the First Book' for 1671-72 indicate:

	£ Scots
Beir (3,008 bushels)	18,773
Servants' Wages	2,444
Hops	1,198
Coals	1,501
Total	£23,916

Other financial and market considerations were clearly of equal or greater importance, but it is evident from the business papers and accounts of many later brewery concerns that injudicious grain purchase and over-capitalising on unsold ale stocks in situations of short-term price fluctuation were the two main causes of business failure. Undoubtedly, the latter half of the seventeenth century was even more prone to unpredictable harvests and erratic primary product prices than occurred during most of the subsequent century.[19]

Although the Leith brewery concern continued to operate until the mid-1680s, the last surviving business record is a ledger of 1677-78. It shows that the Yardhead breweries, under Cockburn's management, produced a range of ales and small beers for local customers (including many merchants in Leith and some Edinburgh nobility) and inns. They probably also supplied ships in the ports of the Forth, either by direct sale or through merchants. The privileges granted to the company by the Scottish Parliament were thus of considerable value, though they must have upset the brewers of Edinburgh, who were staunch defenders of their monopoly within the city. The brewery also had an interest in another of Stansfield's projects, a glass and bottle works, erected in nearby North Leith (glass works were to become an associated feature of several later breweries, including those at Alloa and Dumbarton). Stansfield established a company of 'adventurers' to finance the glass works, including such prestigious partners as the Earl of Argyll (1/8th share), Sir Robert Gordon of Gordonstoun (1/8th), James Sinclair of Roslin (5/16ths) and the Earl of Balcarres (1/8th), leaving 5/16ths of the business in his own hands. Two foreign artisans, Moses Henzell and Joseph Damian (presumably Germans) were brought to Scotland to supervise the erection of the works and train local personnel. One of Stansfield's English associates described the two foreigners as 'very haughty and spirited men,' perhaps some indication of the degree of financial coercion needed to attract them to Scotland. The glassworks was in operation by 1679, its main product being glass bottles for the brewing trade.[20] Obviously the whole brewery complex at Leith was a large and well integrated production unit for its time and was certainly unparalleled in Scotland until the latter half of the eighteenth century.

The large breweries developed in Edinburgh under the aegis of the Society of Brewers and in Leith by Sir James Stansfield and partners were clearly atypical. Much more familiar was the sole female brewer, the burgess brewer, or the innkeeper brewing for direct public sale. The city of Aberdeen had no fewer than 144 brewers in 1693, many being either burgesses with other trades, or female domestic brewers.[21] A few years later, in 1700, when brewers in the county of Fife presented a memorial complaining about wrongful imposition of excise duties on their beer and ale, an amazing 522 signatures were appended to the document.[22] As Table 2 shows, the largest groups were in the old coastal ports and in market towns, like Falkland and Cupar (no figures are given for Dunfermline):

Table 2

Distribution of Brewers in Fife 1700

Centre	No.	Centre	No.
St. Andrews	70	Pittenweem	23
Dysart	41	Elie	17
Wemyss	37	Leven	16
Cupar	36	Kennoway	15
Anstruther	29	Auchtermuchty	15
Kinghorn	27	Ferryport	15
Falkland	25	Strathmiglo	13
Crail	24	St. Monance	11

Further north in the fertile grain district of Moray, Elgin had a public brewery at Oldmills on the River Lossie, but despite its presence over 80 licensed brewers were operating at the close of the seventeenth century.[23] Assuming Aberdeen and Elgin were fairly typical burghs, and Fife a typical county (albeit with a long established brewing tradition and with many environmental advantages), the extent of small-scale domestic brewing about 1700 must have been very great.

Early Eighteenth Century Developments

The years 1700 to 1750 were a critical and formative period in the development of the Scottish brewing industry. They saw for the first time on any scale the growth of more formal business organisation, within what had been until that time little more than a domestic craft. Private brewing and brewing by inns remained widespread (and may actually have increased with rising population, especially in the Central Lowlands), but there was a significant growth of public breweries in most of the major centres. Four important brewing firms were established during these years, and several others had their origins in the first half of the eighteenth century. However, there were still a number of constraints on expansion. First, lack of transport limited the scale of developments, for the sheer physical difficulty of transporting beer in bulk largely restricted delivery to customers within easy reach of the brewery. Second, although many burgh privileges had begun to die out in the later seventeenth century, some old-established practices still hampered commercial and industrial development. These included general civic interference, craft rights, ancient monopolies, multure dues and local licensing controls. Third, there were newer challenges from other quarters (often imposing even greater constraints on the expansion of the industry in the first half of the century), most notably the extension of national taxation and excise on malt, beer and ale, and associated with this development the appearance on the scene of the notoriously scrupulous and incorruptible Exciseman. Fourth, there was the challenge of competition in a slowly expanding market—mainly from rival drinks and the spirituous liquors, brandy, gin and whisky. The years after 1730 saw the growth of a modest export trade, mostly the result of demand by expatriate Scots (mainly merchants and planters in the West Indies and North American Colonies) with a palate accustomed to Scottish brewed ales.

It is extremely difficult to arrive at any meaningful estimate of ale production or more general rates of growth for the brewing industry in Scotland much before the middle of the eighteenth century. The only indicator of any real value is that provided by the excise revenue returns for ale and malt, available after 1707 in unbroken series.[24] A full tabular statement of these revenues is provided in the Appendix, but summary data for the years 1707-50, sufficient for our purposes here, appear in Table 3.

Table 3

Gross and Nett Revenues of Excise (Ale and Malt) 1707-50 (£ Sterling)

Year	Beer & Ale (gross) £000s	Malt (nett) £000s
1707	44	—
1710	54	—
1715	50	—
1720	57	—
1725	49	22
1730	53	26
1735	48	20
1740	33	7
1745	37	14
1750	42	21

Source: SRO, E 904/3 Gross and Nett Produce of the Excise.

The statistical information provided by Excise data is of considerable value in building up some sort of picture of changes in the brewing craft before the

Industrial Revolution. The crude summary data above record substantial growth in revenue from beer and ale excise between 1707 and 1720 and decline thereafter (with some revival in 1730) up to 1750. Fig. 1 shows the picture in greater detail, and emphasises particularly the peaks and troughs in revenue receipts over the period as a whole. Despite all appearances, the trend over the years 1707-50 is upwards, indicative of modest but nevertheless perceptible growth. If the data are considered at face value, then it is possible to conclude that the brewing industry (while undergoing substantial structural change towards the middle of the century) was largely stagnant, and that this situation simply reflects the general course of the Scottish economy during this half-century. Certainly the only other reliable statistical indicator of the progress of the economy at that time, annual grain prices, demonstrates only too clearly the relative stability of agriculture in the years before 1750. If official statistics on the revenues of malt and ale excise are to be believed, the only conclusion to be drawn is that public, licensed (or common) brewing remained relatively static. Perhaps this situation existed because of the newly introduced malt tax and ale excise, which acted as considerable disincentives to brewers. Given slow population increase, growing competition from other beverages, narrow profit margins, and perhaps even a revival of private brewing (thus avoiding taxation), the stagnant condition of the trade until 1750 occasions little surprise.

There is some reason to suppose that increasing control on the part of national and local authorities was primarily responsible for the slow development of public breweries in Scotland. Certainly the regulation and supervision of the brewing process by officers of Excise was greatly facilitated in larger, more concentrated units of production. It was virtually impossible to regulate and tax an industry organised on essentially domestic lines—the figures of brewers in Fife about 1700 make this patently clear. A second factor critical to the emergence of an industrial organisation in the brewing trade was the slow growth of demand for consistently good and wholesome ales and beers. The number of formally organised brewery businesses was still small, and even these did not appear until the 1740s. Three important firms had their origins in that decade: Archibald Campbell, Argyll Brewery, Cowgate in Edinburgh (1740); John and Robert Tennent of Wellpark Brewery, Glasgow (c. 1745); and William Younger of Abbey Brewery, Holyrood, Edinburgh (1749). Significantly, all four founders had established family connections with brewing (Tennents, for example, had been innkeepers and brewers in Glasgow since the late sixteenth century), farming or general merchanting, and at least one, William Younger, had extensive Excise experience. From the outset these three firms were brewers of consequence, and the two great breweries of Youngers and Tennents ultimately came to dominate the Scottish industry during the early decades of the nineteenth century.[25]   Many restrictive practices continued to hamper the growth of the brewing industry until late in the eighteenth century and even after, but in the formative period 1700 to 1750 they were particularly prevalent in the old burghs, where craft and merchant privileges were still adhered to. There local authorities continued to be dominated by merchant interests generally unsympathetic and even antagonistic toward external businessmen. Thus a well-meaning entrepreneur establishing a brewery, distillery, mill or tannery either in or within the environs of one of Scotland's older towns would be likely to meet with hostility from the established burghal and merchant interest. Alexander Clunie and some fellow merchants, for example, clashed with the magistrates and council of Perth in 1741 following the opening of their brewery and distillery at South Inch just beyond the city boundary. In this case the city authorities sought to impose an age-old multure on the malt made by Clunie and his partners, as well as a local excise on the finished products—ale and spirits.[26]

Another typical complaint against local taxation was that contained in a contemporary broadsheet of 1710, *The Brewers Farewell, to the Magistrates, Heritors, Merchants and Crafts of Edinburgh*. The brewers complained of excessive supervision and tax burdens, including the ale impost and multure payments. They maintained that such taxes had led to an expansion of brewing beyond the city boundaries and had given cost advantages to country brewers at their expense.[27] It is indeed significant that many of the new breweries established in the period were located in the environs of existing centres—and not in the towns themselves. The problems in Edinburgh and Perth might have been extreme—but they were typical.

Robert Tennent, co-founder of the great brewing firm of Tennents, was 'harrassed by lawsuits' instigated against him by the Incorporated Trades of Glasgow, despite the fact that he was a respected burgess and freeman of the Malt Craft. In his petition to Lord Drummore of the Court of Session in 1749, Tennent stated that he had kept a large inn 'for several years past' where he had carried on his own malting and brewing. Tired of repeated fines by the Incorporated Trades for brewing without paying local taxes, he had been forced to resort to the courts. The fact that the judge found in Tennent's favour in this instance is a good indication of a slowly changing attitude to monopoly and burghal privilege by the middle of the eighteenth century.[28]

Landowners often reacted similarly: in 1746 the brothers George and James Shaws, proprietors of a successful brew-house and maltings in the Linlithgow-shire village of Bathgate, found themselves prosecuted by John, Earl of Hopetoun for back-payment of ten years' multures, because they ground their own malt in the brewery (in steel mills) rather than at the mill to which by age-old custom the people of Bathgate were thirled.[29]

In some areas the burghal revenue from malting and brewing was put to good use. Although Charles Addison, a brewer and merchant in Bo'ness, resented the tax imposed locally since the Union of 1707 on 'ale and beer brewed or vended in the Town and Parish of Bo'ness,' he recognised the value of the harbour improvements on which the revenue had been expended. Addison's main quarrel on this occasion was not with the burghal authorities but with the local land-holder, the Duke of Hamilton, who had been imposing tolls and duties on ships using Bo'ness harbour, with the result that trade declined badly.[30]

The control of drunkenness had always been a concern of both civic and church authorities, as an examination of any burgh or presbytery records will clearly indicate. By the late seventeenth century (far in advance of national legislation) local licensing of malt houses, brewing premises, inns and drinking houses was becoming a common feature in most Scottish towns. An example of early civic interest in the brewing and sale of beer was St. Andrews, an old-established centre of malting and brewing in the prosperous agricultural district of East Fife. The rules of the Malt Craft in 1730 make it clear that both the craft and its sales outlets were to be closely supervised by 'experienced men' who would periodically inspect malt barns, breweries and drinking houses under the authority of the Burgh Council.[31] By the middle of the eighteenth century the quality of the beer was probably as much a concern as the price. In other towns where malting and brewing were of growing economic importance, for example, Edinburgh, Stirling, Ayr, Dunbar and Glasgow, burghal authorities exerted increasing control over both the quality and sale of beer, though the nature of supervision certainly varied greatly from place to place.[32]

Next to the survival of old-established practices and monopoly privilege, the major challenge to the growth of large-scale mass production brewing in Scotland during the first half of the eighteenth century was the extension of national taxation on malt and beer. By the 1707 Treaty of Union the duty on malt (6d per bushel in England) was not to be applied in Scotland for the duration of the War of Spanish Succession, if that period were longer than the proposed seven year exemption, but in 1713 came the attempt to extend the Malt Tax to Scotland. Scottish members of the Union Parliament put forward numerous objections: Scotland could not afford to pay the tax; it was an intolerable burden on Scottish landowners, as rents were paid in kind and barley was a considerable part of the Scottish crop; and, lastly, it would significantly increase the price of ale. The Scots proposed an amended tax of 3d per bushel and pointed out that Scottish malt generally sold at a third of the price of English and was of much inferior strength. Despite support for the Socts from the north of England and Wales, the bill extending Malt Tax to Scotland became law in 1713.[33]

There is some evidence to indicate that enforcement was limited before 1725: in the *Journal of the House of Commons* there is no division between the English and Scottish Malt Tax returns until 1722, and from that year to 1725 the net produce of the Malt Tax in Scotland is simply recorded as 'nil.'[34] Contemporary Excise Returns are equally unhelpful, for the Malt Tax revenues are included with other items and the data for 1713-26 are combined to give a net produce of £56,838, an average for the twelve years of just over £4,736.[35] Thus even before 1720 the modest revenues derived from Scottish excise were causing concern and this led eventually to pressure for more efficient collection and further extension of duties. Meanwhile a great deal of antagonism built up in Scotland against the Malt Tax and its extension to ale and beer at a rate of 6d per barrel brewed for sale.[36]

Petitions flooded the House of Commons from all over Scotland about the Malt Tax.[37] All were concerned with the effects of the compromise 3d duty per bushel on malt or gloomy forecasts about the effects of the newly proposed 6d duty on each barrel of ale. Typical of the more general economic arguments presented were those of 'the Heritors and Freeholders of the Shire of Murray' (an important barley-growing and malting district) in a petition of 28 February 1725. They argued that it was impossible for Scotland to pay the duties because of the poor quality of barley (or bigg) and the 'decay of trade and the poverty of the people.' 'The people,' they said, 'are disabled from consuming ale or beer except at so low a price as renders it impossible for the brewers to sell it at so low a price and at the same time answer the Malt Tax and other duties of Excise with which the produce of Barley or Bigg in Scotland is charged, except they can buy it at so low a rate as to ruin the Rents and Estates of the Heritors of Land.' They went on to maintain that with the weaker strength of ale brewed in Scotland and the 2d impost per pint of beer in many of the older burghs (dating from pre-Union), the resulting excise was higher in proportion than in England.

The amended Malt Tax bill was finally approved in March 1725, the new duties to take effect from June of that year.[38] Despite widespread protest (especially in Glasgow and Edinburgh) the excise on malt and beer was implemented, apparently with little force and considerable inefficiency. Certainly, evasion of duty amongst brewers and maltsters was both considerable and widespread: the introduction of excise merely intensified long-established practice! At the same time it probably slowed down the emergence of organised public breweries, a phenomenon best illustrated by the fact that no important commercial breweries, apart from the Edinburgh and Leith enterprises, were established until the 1740s.

The domestic market for ale before the middle of the eighteenth century grew only slowly: Scotland's population rose from somewhat less than a million in 1700 to little more than 1¼ million in 1755. However, much of the growth was concentrated in the towns, creating an enlarged urban market for the products of a slowly developing countryside and adding momentum to the rise of consumer industries like milling, tanning and brewing.[39] If the evidence of contemporary social commentators and surviving local authority records is to be relied upon, beer and ale were undoubtedly the dominant drinks of the masses in early eighteenth century Scotland.[40] Earlier, Thomas Kirke, an English traveller had written:

> Their drink is ale, made of beer malt, and tunned up in a small vessel, called a cogue; after it has stood a few hours, they drink it out of the cogue, yest and all; the better sort brew it in large quantities, and drink it in wooden queighs, but it is sorry stuff . . .

Wine, however, was much preferred by the gentry, drunk in huge glasses, filled to the brim.[41]

The later evidence of contributors to Sir John Sinclair's *Statistical Account* reflects changed habits since earlier in the century. Whereas the day-labourer or mechanic of the mid-1790s drank a small bottle of unmixed whisky at one sitting, his forebear of the 1740s would be more likely to have drunk 'a Scots pint of 2d ale or small beer.' According to another commentator, 'good two-penny' was always the most popular drink amongst the working class, even a generation before the compilation of the *Statistical Account*.[42]

Rivals to beer began to appear on the scene during the first half of the eighteenth century. With increasing affluence, wine (and later spirit) drinking spread from the upper class nobility and gentry to the new, rising bourgeois merchants of places like Glasgow and Leith. Scotland did have a long-established wine import trade, mainly from France (to ports of the Clyde, like Ayr and Irvine) or the Low Countries (to the East Coast ports), and this trade grew substantially during the century. By the latter half of the eighteenth century most Scottish towns of consequence had at least a handful of wine merchants, and the major ports like Greenock, Glasgow and Leith could muster many wine and spirit importers. What holds for wines was also true of the imported spirits, mainly brandy and rum, whether legally traded or smuggled.[43] Whisky—because of its relative cheapness—increased greatly in popularity. It was an important drink amongst most classes of society in the Lowlands long before the waves of immigration from the Highlands and Ireland contributed to its more general consumption amongst the working class.[44]

It is, of course, exceptionally difficult to estimate the level of spirit consumption in Scotland at any time before the nineteenth century, because of the widespread evasion of excise and the extensive smuggling from the Continent, Ireland and the Isle of Man.[45] Table 4 gives some indication of the level of legal spirit imports towards the middle of the century.

Historians of eighteenth century smuggling estimate that about the same quantity of spirits entered the country illegally—although it is more difficult to gauge just how much was for domestic consumption and how much for re-export elsewhere.[46] Imported tea and coffee, though still expensive, were beginning to make inroads into the lower middle-class market, as the recollections of contributors to the *Statistical Account* bear out. Thus by 1750 some challenge to ale and beer was already present, although the effects of widespread spirit drinking in a society undergoing increasingly dramatic change were still to be felt.

Before the middle of the eighteenth century the export of beer and ale from Scotland was negligible. There can be little doubt that Scottish merchant émigrés in Europe, the North American Colonies and the West Indies carried to those

Table 4

Account of Spirits made from Corn & Molasses/Quantity of Foreign Brandy Imported:
Scotland 1738-44

| Year | Spirits (tons) | | Brandy (gallons) |
	Corn	Molasses	
1739	629	202	1351
1740	636	190	1028
1741	399	132	—
1742	590	112	205
1743	686	80	873
1744	842	—	2181

Source: PRO, T64/257, Account of Spirits made from Corn & Molasses and the Quantity of Foreign Brandy Imported to Scotland, 1738-45.

foreign climes a taste for local ales, so that Scots ale was clearly being imported to these spheres in small quantities, probably from the 1720s. In 1765 (as a later chapter indicates) beer export was described as 'a very material article of commerce for Scotland,' but unfortunately there are no reliable statistical indicators before 1755, and even these are insufficiently detailed to show actual destinations of exports, showing merely the countries to which beer was being sent.[47]The data for 1755 are shown in Table 5.

Table 5

Scottish Beer and Ale Exports from Official Excise Data 1755

Destination	Gallons	£ Value (st.)
America	1288	64
Germany	96	5
Holland	256	13
Poland	192	10
Spain	242	12
Total	2074	104

Source: PRO, CUST 14/1A Scotch Exportation, Ale and Beer, 1755-6.

America (presumably including both British North America and the West Indies) thus accounted for 62 per cent of Scottish exports, while European markets absorbed the rest (exports to other areas, such as Ireland, were too modest to warrant inclusion). Significantly, more than three-quarters of the exports to Europe were directed at long-established spheres of Scottish trade, notably Holland and the Baltic Sea ports of Poland.[48]

By the middle of the eighteenth century the modest brewing industry of Scotland was poised for a period of substantial growth, although there were many significant obstacles in the way of progress. A framework for expansion already existed: a growing domestic market and spheres of influence amongst expatriate Scots in the mercantile colonies of North America and the West Indies; a basic business structure and some brewing firms of considerable potential in the key centres of the industry; fundamental commercial and entrepreneurial skills; and, established links with a rapidly developing agriculture and with the landed interest. Transport was a problem, but markets adjacent to many breweries in urban districts already presented considerable potential thanks to population growth and increasing incomes. So brewing in Scotland shared with other contemporary primary processing activities, like milling, tanning, soap-boiling and distilling, an optimistic environment for growth in the consumer revolution which was to accompany the classic Industrial Revolution during the years between 1780 and 1820.

NOTES

1 J. Grant, *Old and new Edinburgh* (1882), vol II, 268, 346.
2. P. Hume Brown, *Early travellers in Scotland* (1891), 141-2.
3 For Stirling see R. Renwick, *Charters relating to the royal burgh of Stirling* (1884).
4. J. Thomson, *GVA Fife* (1800), 302; for St. Andrews, SRO, B 65/18/3 Records of St. Andrews Trades: Maltmen's Records.

5 J. Mclaren, *The history of Dundee* (1874), 344; RPCS 2nd Series, vol II (1627-8), 174.

6 For Elgin see H.B. Mackintosh, *Elgin: past and present* (1914), 127-8, 130.

7 R. Reid, *Glasgow: past and present* (1884) has many refs; see also J. and R. Tennent, *Wellpark Brewery*, Glasgow (1966) and SRO, COS, 1st Div. Inglis M 2/27, Maltmen of Glasgow v Robert Tennent, 1749.

8 For Ayr see A.I. Dunlop, *The royal burgh of Ayr* (1953), 179.

9 W. Singer, *GVA Dumfries* (1812), 422-3.

10 RPCS 2nd Series, vol I, xxxi, 170-1; ibid, vol II, 116, 289.

11 Hume Brown, 89.

12 RPCS 2nd Series, vol II (1627-8), 289.

13 T.C. Smout, *Scottish trade on the eve of Union* (1963); also his articles on 'The lead mines at Wanlockhead,' *TDGHNAS*, 39 (1960-1) and 'The early Scottish sugar houses 1660-1720,' *EHR*, 14 (1961); B.F. Duckham, *A history of the Scottish coal industry* (1970), 14-23; J. Butt, *The industrial archaeology of Scotland* (1967), 132-5.

14 Scott, vol I, 327-8; vol II, 189-92.

15 /W.R. Scott, *The records of a Scottish cloth manufacturer at New Mills, Haddingtonshire 1681-1703* (1905); SRO, MP 279, Papers of Sir James Stansfield, re Newmilns, Wanlockhead and Leith. (RH 9/18).

16 T.C. Smout, 'Scottish landowners and economic growth 1650-1850,' *SJPE*, 11 (1964).

17 SRO RH 9/18/279, Abbreviate of Comptes 1671-76.

18 Ibid, Accompt Courant in the Company of Brewery 1671-76; Accompt Debit and Credit of James Cockburn's First Book.

19 Ibid, Accompt of the Brewhouses in Leith and the Balance of the First Book, 1671-72; R. Mitchison, 'The movement of Scottish corn prices in the seventeenth and eighteenth centuries,' ECHR, 18 (1965).

20 SRO RH 9/18/279, Papers re the Glasshouses of North Leith 1678-87.

21 RH 15/1/113, Ane List of the brewers . . . within the Town of Aberdeen, 1696.

22 SRO COS, UP McNeill A 1/19, Auchmouty & Veitch v the Brewers of Fife, 1700.

23 Mackintosh, op.cit., 129.

24 SRO, E 904/3, Account of the gross and nett produce of the excise for Scotland, 1707-1807: Produce of the duties on beer, ale, malt, etc.

25 SRO, GD 241, Thomson, Dickson & Shaw Mss. Papers of Archibald Campbell, brewers in Edinburgh; James Aitken & Co. *Two hundred years of progress* (Falkirk, 1940); Records of J. & R. Tennent; Records of William Younger & Co.

26 SL, SP 40/9, Walter Millar v Alexander Clunie, Merchant in Perth and others, 1751.

27. NLS, ALP, *The Brewers Farewell*, 1710.

28 SRO, COS, 1st Div. Inglis M 2/27, Maltmen of Glasgow v Robert Tennent, 1749.

29 SL, SP 4215, John, Earl of Hopetoun, Proprieter of the Mill of Bathgate and John and James Bells, Tacksmen v George and James Shaws, Brewers, 1752.

30 SRO, COS, BCP Group I 69/628, Petition of Charles Addison, Brewer & Merchant in Bo'ness, 1812.

31 SRO, B 65/18/3, St Andrews Trades: Maltmen's Books, 1762-1849, 2 vols.

32 SRO, B6, Ayr Burgh Records; B66, Stirling Burghs Records; B18, Dunbar Burgh Records; GCA B8/4, Licensing Records.

33 P.W.J. Riley, *The English ministers and Scotland* (1964); J. Mackinnon, *The union of Scotland and England* (1896). NLS, ALP, *A letter from a Brewer... concerning the Malt Tax* (1713), *Scotland's complaint against the Malt Tax* (1713) and *Memorial concerning the Malt Tax* (nd) are typical of the many pamphlets complaining about the tax.

34 *Journal of the House of Commons*, vol 20, 563, 774. Gross receipts were the critical variable. It seems probable that administrative charges were initially heavy and therefore swallowed any accruals.

35 SRO, E 904/3, Account of... the Produce of Excise, 1707-1807.

36 Journal of the House of Commons, vol 20, 359.

37 Ibid., 469 (from Renfrew), 594 (from Moray), 598 (from Elgin) are typical.

38 NLS, ALP, *The Act of Parliament upon the Malt Tax* (1724). Other pamphlets on the 1725 Act include *Copy of a letter from a Gentleman in Edinburgh to his Friend in the Country upon the subject of the Malt Tax* and *Some thoughts concerning the Malt Tax... to the consideration of the Landed Interest of Scotland*. On the Malt Tax riots in Glasgow see *Letter from a Gentleman in Glasgow to his friend in the Country concerning the late Tummults which happened in that City* (1725).

39. J.G. Kyd, *Scottish Population Statistics* (Edinburgh, 1952), xv.
40. Hamilton, op. cit., 104-5.
41. P. Hume Brown, (ed), *Early travellers in Scotland* (Edinburgh, 1891), 263-4.
42. *OSA*, 1, 286-7; ibid, 2, 113-4.
43. Hamilton, op. cit., 252, 283.
44. The evidence of numerous entries in the *Statistical Account* of the 1790s bears this out.
45. See, for example, L.M. Cullen, *Anglo-Irish trade 1660-1800* (Manchester, 1968), 150-1.
46. Cullen, op. cit., 137-54; W.A. Cole, 'Trends in eighteenth century smuggling', *EHR*, 10 (1958).
47. PRO, CUST 14/1A. The Scotch Exportation of Goods and Merchandise, 1755-63.
48. PRO, CUST 3/1 and 10, Ledgers of Imports and Exports, 1697-1707; T64/241, Accounts of Exports of British Manufactures from Scotland to Holland, Germany and Russia, 1732-72.

2
Growth and Fluctuations
1750-1850

THE Scottish brewing industry, like other sectors of the economy, was subject to fluctuating fortunes during the century 1750-1850. In common with so many other primary processing industries, its progress (or lack of it) was partly regulated by the natural cycle. As Ashton indicated, the influence of harvests, at least in the eighteenth century, was very great.[1] Indeed this occasions little surprise in an economy which, even at the beginning of the nineteenth century, was still largely dominated by agriculture. The close relationship of the brewing industry to agriculture (discussed at length in Chapter Three) is borne out by an examination of excise returns and grain prices for the period 1710 to 1830. The fluctuations in agricultural prices were directly reflected in statistics of beer and malt excise and those of beer output: a year of poor harvest and high grain prices resulted in a severe cutback in malt and beer output and hence a reduction in the revenue of excise, with the converse situation recorded in a year of abundant harvest and low prices.[2] The attitude of the state was also significant. In years of high grain prices malting was often prohibited, hence a fall in the revenue, like that which occurred at the opening of the nineteenth century. Any increase in the level of excise was likely to affect the consumption of beer. Even if grain prices remained stable, any increase in the level of excise would affect demand for beer, particularly if a decline in standard of the product took place. The inverse relationship of grain prices and excise revenues is clearly illustrated in Figures 1 and 2. The onset of the Revolutionary and Napoleonic Wars produced severe distortion in the agricultural economy of Britain, and this was particularly felt in marginal farming areas in the Lowlands of Scotland. Yet despite these difficulties the industry maintained considerable progress throughout the war and was also apparently little affected by post-war depression. Complete recovery had been effected by 1820, although export markets suffered badly and did not recover their former buoyancy until the early thirties. Throughout, brewing to a large extent shared the fortunes of agriculture.

These trends in the Scottish brewing industry broadly reflected the level of economic activity in Britain as a whole throughout the latter half of the eighteenth and early part of the nineteenth centuries. The business cycle for Scotland may have been different from that of Britain, but on the whole the evidence (from Court of Session minute books and other records) of business difficulties and bankruptcies before 1830 indicates a close parallel. Using the analysis presented in the seminal work of Gayer, Rostow and Schwarts, it is possible to relate move-

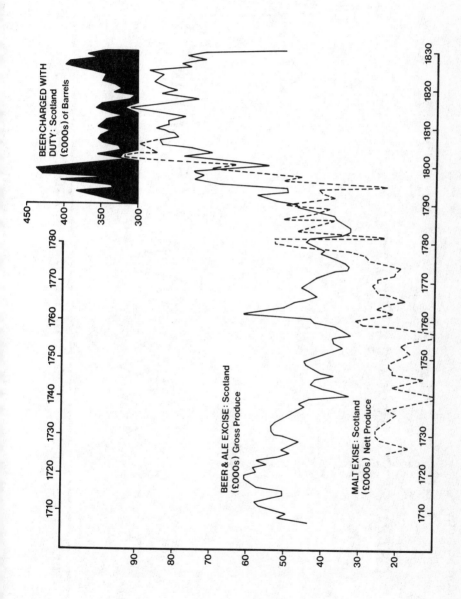

Fig. 1

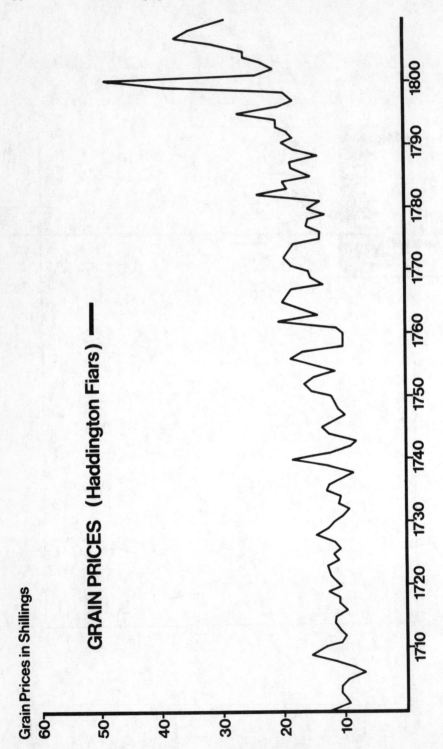

Grain Prices in Shillings

GRAIN PRICES (Haddington Fiars) ——

Fig. 2

ments in the statistics of beer output to cyclical trends in the economy as a whole.[3] The following summary shows the 'reference dates' of peaks and troughs in the graphs of beer production, set against the turning points of the business cycle between 1790 and 1830:

Beer Production (Scotland)		Business Cycle (Britain)	
Peak	Trough	Peak	Trough
1793	1794	1792	1793
1796	1797	1796	1797
1799	1802	1800	1801
1803	1804	1802	1803
1807	1809	1806	1808
1810	1813	1810	1811
1815	1818	1815	1816
1819	1820	1818	1819
1822	1824	1825	1826
1826	1828	1828	1829
1829	1830	1831	1832[4]

Sources: derived from Table 12 and A.D. Gayer et al, *The growth and fluctuation of the British economy, 1790-1850*, Vol. I, 27-9, 211-3, 342-3, 349-51.

As already indicated, it would appear that in the majority of instances a downturn in general economic activity, associated with a poor harvest and a rise in agricultural prices, led to a slump in beer sales, if only because real wages were likely to fall in these circumstances. But because it was relatively difficult to transfer to the consumer the full effect of increased costs—as indicated by the general stability of beer prices—the brewer was faced with two possibilities: either to accept erosion of profit margins or to lower the quality of his product. This latter course had obvious limitations if markets were to be retained. This was probably the case in 1793-4, 1801-02, 1803-04, 1808-09, 1813, and 1819-20, although one must bear in mind that grain and malt could be stored in years of surplus. In other years the picture is less straightforward, but in many cases special circumstances prevailed. For example, in the period 1795-97 there were remarkable fluctuations in the price of grain. Because of a poor harvest in 1794 there was no surplus the following year, and even a good harvest failed to bring about price reductions. There were consequently severe shortages in 1796, although an abundant harvest made possible a fall in grain prices towards the close of the year. A surplus from this harvest counteracted a mediocre crop in 1797—a crisis year in the economy—and one of slump in the Scottish brewing industry.[5] At the close of the period covered by statistics of beer output, the years 1827-32 saw fluctuations in the British domestic price index, the general trend being downward. The harvest was poor in 1828, but recovery took place in 1829.[6] The circumstances are clearly reflected in the trend of beer production (see Table 12). There are many limitations in such a simple analysis of dates and trends, but for a critical period of the Industrial Revolution at least it is possible to see something of the relationship between general economic trends and those of the industry under study.

Although agriculture was the source of supply of all the major raw materials of brewing, it had much greater influence on the fortunes of the industry. It was an important source of capital, entrepreneurship and labour. Surplus capital and some of the profits of successful agricultural improvement gravitated naturally into primary processing industries like brewing. Just as the brewery provided a useful and profitable outlet for the farmer's barley, so it presented him with an interesting investment opportunity. Some landowners and farmers even started their own breweries, hence reducing the bulk of their produce and raising its value many times over. Such country breweries often served an important need in the community, especially if problems of transport isolated it from more distant sources of supply. The farmer turned brewer never lost his contact with the countryside: even the urban brewer was in constant touch with the land through his dealings with grain merchants, farmers and country maltsters. This was also true of the workforce, modest though it was. Many brewery labourers had probably drifted into country villages and towns from the land, and the tasks they undertook in the brewhouse were similar to those on the farm. Even the brewing 'season' was at first regulated by the natural cycle.[7]

The transformation of brewing from a domestic craft into a mass-production consumer industry was essentially a response to the rising living standards of a growing population. Scotland's population rose from 1.2 million in 1755, when the Rev. Alexander Webster carried out his census, to 2.8 million in 1851.[8] More significant was the fact that a growing proportion of the population slowly gravitated to the new industrial districts of the Central Lowlands, creating a concentrated urban market for the products of agriculture, particularly the drink industries.

The following sections of this chapter attempt to present an overview of growth and fluctuation in the Scottish brewing industry between 1750 and 1850, from two related viewpoints. Firstly, there is an examination of excise and related production statistics which tries to indicate the main trends in the trade, with special reference to the period before 1830 (the Beer Excise was abandoned after this date, though malt continued to be taxed as before). Secondly, there is an assessment of some other indicators of trends in brewing, with particular emphasis on the numbers and size of breweries operating at different periods, changes in business organisation, markets and workforce.

Excise and Related Data

Throughout most of the period of this study, excise duty represented nearly half the breweries' costs, and so requires considerable attention in any examination of growth and fluctuation in the trade between 1750 and 1850.[9] Additionally, the great dependence of the public revenue on the brewing and malting industries meant that both were subject to much greater scrutiny and regulation than other excisable manufactures.[10] The result is a voluminous and often baffling archive of statistical and other material (mainly housed in the Scottish Record Office and the National Library of Scotland), which provides a valuable profile of growth and fluctuation in the industry during this period, particularly between 1750 and 1830. However, before examining the excise data in detail it is necessary to describe briefly the nature of the excise system in Scotland, its operation, collections and regulations as they relate specifically to the brewing and malting industries.

Table 6

Gross Produce of the Revenues of Excise 1710-1810 £(00s)

Item	1710	1720	1730	1740	1750	1760	1770	1780	1790	1800	1810
Beer	535	570	531	328	422	536	434	450	481	580	830
Malt	—	—	319	143	278	396	333	655	673	803	1850
Spirits (D)	36	15	50	36	140	80	65	400	565	520	8770
Spirits (I)	—	—	10	—	24	57	168	226	320	296	2270
Leather	—	43	58	70	95	88	90	107	187	246	380
Soap						25	60	175	454	720	1025
Linen/Printed Textiles						21	35	165	697	922	3180
Glass							26	77	210	325	760
Salt										610	980
Candles						70	59	95	170	145	—
Paper							9	—	56	240	444
Tobacco									382	260	1305
Totals	571	628	968	577	959	1263	12791	2350	4195	5667	21794

Notes
(1) All figures rounded to nearest hundred.
(2) Does not include excise fines and random excise revenues.
(3) D:Home distilled spirits.
     I :Imported foreign spirits.
(4) Statistics for 1810 include Temporary or War Duties imposed 1802-03.

Sources: SRO, E904/3, Account of the Gross Produce of the Revenues of Excise for Scotland, 1707-1807; E 904/4, General Account of All Duties of Excise (Scotland), 1808-32.

During most of the eighteenth and early nineteenth centuries the customs and excise system in Scotland was entirely separate from that of England. At the time of the Union Scottish Commissioners were appointed by the Crown, the Boards of Customs and Excise being administered essentially as departments of the Scottish Exchequer based in Edinburgh.[11] After 1707, as we have seen, brewing and malting became increasingly subject to regulation and taxation according to English practice, and by the 1720s the customs and excise system in Scotland was probably at least as efficient as that beyond the metropolis in the provinces of England and Wales. Excise duty extended to the same commodities as south of the Border: in the first half of the eighteenth century the most important excisable items were beer, malt, spirits (either home distilled or imported), leather and printed fabrics (see Table 6). The major difference from the English excise system lay in the rates of duty: Scottish products, and especially malt made from local grain, were often inferior to those manufactured in the south, and therefore subject to lower duties (see Table 22).[12]

The organisation of the Scottish customs and excise system followed closely that described by Hoon in England, although here we are concerned only with the excise of beer and to a lesser degree of malt.[13] Unlike whisky (both Irish and

Scottish varieties) and imported foreign spirits, beer was not a commodity likely to be 'run' on any significant scale. It was thus of only passing interest to the customs officer. Below the Board of Commissioners of Excise for Scotland and the central administration were a series of collections each headed by an official known as a collector. By 1775 there were fifteen collections: from north to south these were Orkney, Caithness, Inverness, Aberdeen, North Argyll, South Argyll, Perth, Fife, Glasgow, Ayr, Linlithgow, Edinburgh, Haddington, Teviotdale and Dumfries.[14] The boundaries were always rather ill-defined (especially in far-flung collections like Inverness or Dumfries) and there seems to have been some degree of overlap in certain collections. Undoubtedly the efficiency of the excise was at its greatest in Edinburgh and neighbouring collections, where central supervision was relatively easy. It was perhaps fortunate for the excise that such a large proportion of the brewing and malting industries was concentrated in three or four collections close to the capital, for evasion and fraud in the untamed regions of distant collections were rife. In 1775-76 the four collections of Haddington, Edinburgh, Linlithgow and Fife accounted for 47.5 per cent of all malt excise revenue.[15]

From each individual collection 'States of Account' would be returned to Edinburgh on a regular basis. These showed the gross produce of the different duties according to returns made by officers and gaugers in the collection, with deductions for legal allowances, such as bounties on exports. Many of the Collectors' States of Account survive—major sources of local statistical information for a wide range of industries apart from brewing and malting.[16] From the individual States of Account half yearly and annual summary statements were prepared for examination and approval of the Board of Commissioners. They are extremely detailed, providing statements of the gross produce of excise on all dutiable commodities, together with details of sums expended in gauging, collection, general administration and allowances. Where appropriate, information on additional and consolidated duties is given, though unfortunately (as is the case with malt and tobacco duties) it is sometimes unclear to which commodities they apply, particularly during the war years 1793 to 1815, when a massive extension of taxation on all consumer goods took place. Yet the data on general revenues of excise provide a useful statistical profile of fiscal response to industrialisation, related population growth and increased living standards in a rapidly developing economy.[17]

An examination of the revenues of excise for the period 1710 to 1810 provides a useful indication of the increasing importance of primary production and consumer goods during the eighteenth and early nineteenth centuries. Table 6 indicates the gross produce of the revenues of excise each decade between 1710 and 1810, for main dutiable commodities, including beer and malt. No data are available for malt in the years before 1726-27. At the beginning of the period covered by this table the total revenue of excise was of the order of £60,000, nearly 90 per cent being accounted for by beer and ale excise. It is quite probable that this figure included some revenue from malt excise, which like the tax on ale was so resisted by the population at large. It is therefore difficult to estimate how accurate the returns are before the mid-1720s. Certainly by 1730-31, the first year in which it is possible to relate all of the excisable items (including malt) to the total revenue of excise for that particular period, beer represented around 50 per cent of gross revenue, while malt accounted for 30 per cent of the total. These proportions were roughly maintained in the three subsequent decades, and as reference to Table 6 shows, by 1760-71 beer revenue accounted for 45 per cent of the total, £135,800. Significantly, beer revenue was almost exactly the same in 1760 as it had been fifty years before, and malt excise, although fluctuating violently in intervening years, had shown little overall increase. However, there had been a notable increase in the revenue derived from taxation of other drinks, especially imported wines, brandies and home distilled spirits, as well as an extension of taxation of other consumer products. By 1760 nearly two-fifths of the gross revenue of excise in Scotland derived from taxes on leather, soap, candles, linen and printed textiles.

Yet the massive extension of taxation on drink and consumer products came only after the 1760s. The statement of excise revenue for 1770-71, shown in detail in Table 7, gives a good indication of the range of chargeable goods and their relative value to the exchequer. Malt revenue was exceeded by the total revenue from miscellaneous excisable commodities, although beer (30 per cent of the total) remained the single most important source of taxation. During the course of the Revolutionary and Napoleonic Wars the range of dutiable commodities was greatly extended and rates of duty further raised. By 1803, for example, the malt tax on Scottish barley was 3s 9½d (19p) per bushel, whereas its pre-war level had been just over 8d (3½p).[18] In order to raise additional revenue for the war effort, temporary duties were extended to malt, home distilled spirits, imported wines and brandies, tobacco and snuff. Table 7 also shows that excise revenue in 1810-11 reached a total of £2,283,000, the duty on beer and ale amounting to £83,000, a mere 3½ per cent of the total. Following the close hostilities and the difficult post-war years, most duties were lowered, though few returned to their pre-war level. Ultimately a number of items ceased to be excisable: the excise on beer was abandoned in 1830, after much pressure on the part of brewers and temperance advocates. Malt continued to be taxed as before, although by the 1830s perhaps less than a fifth of malt made in Scotland was used by brewers.[19]

Having examined the excise of beer and malt in the context of the general revenue of excise, it is important now to discuss the statistical series for both commodities separately in an attempt to assess growth and fluctuations in the Scottish brewing industry. It is worth emphasising at this point the assertion made by Mathias with respect to England that reported annual production of beer and malt during the eighteenth and early nineteenth centuries may have underestimated the actual quantities produced and consumed by as much as a quarter. The efficiency of surveying and gauging certainly rose with the passing years, but so too did the incentives for fraud and evasion in circumstances of escalating rates of duty. This was especially true of Scotland (in Highland collections and in country districts throughout the Lowlands), where the inclination and opportunities for evasion were higher.[20]

Excise statistics for beer and ale are available in unbroken series from 1707-08, when national duties were introduced under the Act of Union, until 1830-31, the last complete year before repeal of taxation. New duties were introduced in 1709-10 and returns made separately under the heads 'Old Duty' and 'New Duty,' until both were amalgamated in a single return in 1750-51. The 'Additional Duty,' introduced by Act of Parliament in 1760, first appears in the following year's return, 1761-62, and returns continued to be made under the heads of 'Old Duty' and 'Additional Duty' until these were co-ordinated into one tax during 1787-8. The war years saw a dramatic increase in beer excise duties, there being two increases in 1802 and 1803. The returns for 1801-02 and 1802-03 are entered under the headings 'Consolidated Duty' and 'New Duty' (i.e. that of 1802). Thereafter there is no differentiation between the two, and a single consolidated figure is returned until 1830-31, when the duty was repealed.[21]

Table 7

Revenues of Excise 1770-71 and 1810-11

Item	£	1770-71 £	%	1810-11 £	%
Beer and Ale	29331 (O) 14109 (A)	43440	30.05	83149	3.64
Spirits (I)		16785	11.61	227412	9.96
Spirits (HD)		6526	4.51	876961	38.41
Candles	5949			—	
Leather	9052	21070	14.57	38032	1.66
Soap	6069			102506	4.48
Paper	946			44372	
Linen	3581			197980	13.93
Starch	304	7445	5.15	—	
Glass	2614			75781	
Others		6764	4.67		9.83
Fines		9198	6.36	223415	
Malt	33924		23.03	184879	8.09
Salt				97970	4.29
Tobacco & Snuff				130529	5.71
Totals	144546		99.95	2282986	100.00

I : Imported   HD : Home distilled
O : Old Duty   A : Additional Duty
Source: as Table 6.

Malt excise data are less useful than those for beer and ale, particularly at the beginning and end of the series. Statistical information is widely scattered in various customs and excise records, separate States of Accounts for duties on malt being prepared between 1756 and 1776, when for some reason this practice was discontinued. Problems of administration and enforcement meant that no post-Union excise was gathered until 1713. Unfortunately, the excise duties were lumped together in one sum covering the period 1713-26, individual entries appearing year by year only after 1726-27. Additional duties were introduced on 8 February 1760, and a new duty (almost double that of 1760) was enforced on 31 May 1780. During the Napoleonic Wars two increases in malt duty took place in

1802 and 1803, although the real impact of these is masked by the fact that after 1799 the malt return includes revenue from temporary excise duties on certain categories of manufactured tobaccos and snuff. Further confusion results from the incorporation into the revenues of unpaid duties from earlier years. During the rest of the war the returns are equally unreliable, often incorporating duties on other random consumer products, not apparently classified elsewhere. Finally, one beneficial point about the malt revenues, in common with those of beer, was that the excise year generally ran from 5 July in any one year to the same date the following year—a period which to some extent corresponded with the brewing and malting cycle.[22]

The excise of beer and ale 1707 to 1831 appears in full in the Tabular Appendix, while Table 8 provides a five-year summary of the same statistics. As previously

Table 8

Beer and Ale Excise 1710-1830
Gross Produce (£)

1710	53551	1775	35047
1715	50353	1780	45766
1720	57305	1785	35373
1725	48623	1790	48176
1730	53197	1795	69849
1735	48277	1800	54723
1740	32931	1805	84005
1745	35663	1810	83149
1750	42206	1815	86814
1755	37787	1820	84891
1760	43627	1825	76524
1765	44942	1830	51353
1770	43440		

Source: SRO. E904/3 + 4.

indicated, there were marked fluctuations in the curve of revenue receipts in the period before the middle of the century, varying from a peak of over £60,000 in 1718-20 to a trough of around £32,000 in the excise year 1740-41. The overall trend, however, was upward. Throughout the period after 1750 considerable fluctuations recur, movement from peak to trough being in roughly four or five-year cycles, corresponding to the influence of harvests both on the brewing industry itself and the economy as a whole. As Ashton explained, there is a tendency for the figures of beer excise to move in short waves, with an upward trend for two or three years followed by a downward trend of about the same duration. One reason for this is that both good harvests and dearths tended to cluster. Furthermore, the fact that barley and malt could be stored meant that the effects of a glut or a shortage were often spread over a longer period than a single excise year.[23] This is best demonstrated by comparing the general movement of Scottish grain prices with excise data. Figures 1 and 2 show not only the close parallels between the trends of beer and malt excise revenues, but also a significant relationship between both these series, the statistics of beer production (given in Table 12) and the trend of grain prices. In the period 1758 to 1761 harvest yields were high, and this resulted in lower than average grain prices. Maltsters and brewers probably bought in more grain than usual, holding some in store as well as producing more malt and beer. Reflecting this situation, beer and malt excise returns rose dramatically, reaching a peak in 1760-61 in the case of malt and 1761-62 in that of beer. Some proportion of the increase in these years could be accounted for by new duties, but the same phenomenon can be observed at regular intervals until the beginning of the nineteenth century, notably in 1780-81, 1788-89, 1796-98 and 1802-03. In the last instance, however, temporary war duties substantially distorted the picture. Corresponding relationships are seen in years of poor harvests and high grain prices, for example, in 1782-3, 1794-5, 1799-1800 and 1807-8.

A more detailed profile of beer excise returns during the vitally important period 1780 to 1830 is provided in Table 9, while Table 10 gives a series of related growth rates which can readily be compared with those for beer production set out in Tables 13 and 14. Beer excise averaged around £40,000 per annum in the period 1750 to 1790. The excise fluctuated considerably according to the natural cycle of good or bad harvest, but at no time exceeded the figure returned in 1760-61, or just over £61,000 (partly the result of the newly imposed duty of that year). The 1790s saw a rapid increase in excise revenue, indicated clearly in Table 9. Despite the

Table 9
Beer and Ale Excise 1780-1830
Gross Produce £(000s)

1780	46	1807	81
1781	44	1808	81
1782	26	1809	86
1783	23	1810	83
1784	24	1811	83
1785	35	1812	78
1786	37	1813	87
1787	38	1814	94
1788	42	1815	87
1789	48	1816	79
1790	48	1817	75
1791	55	1818	85
1792	58	1819	81
1793	50	1820	85
1794	51	1821	87
1795	70	1822	87
1796	75	1823	85
1797	73	1824	88
1798	76	1825	77
1799	67	1826	80
1800	55	1827	73
1801	65	1828	78
1802	80	1829	73
1803	71	1830	51
1804	76		
1805	84		
1806	85		

Source: SRO, E904/3 + 4.

setback at the turn of the century in the 'dear years' of 1799 and 1800, this growth was maintained throughout the early 1800s. The annual average excise return between 1805 and 1825 was £85,000 and production 350,000 barrels (see Table 12). The overall growth rate between 1790 and 1810, shown in Table 10, was four per cent per annum. Over the thirty years 1780 to 1810 the rate of growth per annum was 2.0 per cent and in the period 1780-1820 1.5 per cent.

Table 10

Growth Rates of Data in Table 9
Beer Excise 1780- 1830

	Terminal Years	Length of Period	% Growth p.a.
A.	1790-1795	5	7.8
	1790-1800	10	2.4
	1790-1805	15	3.9
	1790-1810	20	4.0
	1790-1820	30	1.9
	1790-1830	40	0.1
B.	1787-1800	13	2.8
	1787-1810	23	3.5
	1787-1820	33	2.4
C.	1780-1800	20	0.9
	1780-1810	30	2.0
	1780-1820	40	1.5

Source: derived from data in Table 9.

The malt excise revenue provides a less reliable indicator of trends in brewing. The statistics themselves are exceedingly complex, and in the period before 1800 it is difficult to estimate how much gauged malt was used by distillers rather than brewers. But despite many problems of analysis, the figures of malt revenue follow roughly those of beer. Returns fluctuated wildly in the years after 1779, particularly in the 1780s; and the imposition of heavy war duties resulted in even greater extremes within the four-five year natural cycle. A detailed profile of the net revenue from malt excise between 1780 and 1805 is provided in Table 11, but it should be noted that these figures included miscellaneous duties on other commodities after 1799. In the years 1780-89 average annual net produce was £42,000 and in the nineties it was around £48,000. By 1807-08 the revenue from temporary or 'war' duties greatly exceeded that of the established excise: the gross total for that year was £154,000, almost two-thirds derived from temporary taxes. At the end of the war the gross revenue of malt excise was £192,000. After the post-war recession recovery was rapid, the return for 1820-21 being £159,000 gross in malt duty and an additional £65,000 in temporary duties and unpaid excise from earlier years. A large proportion of the post-war increase reflected the growth of distilling. Gross revenue exceeded £½ million in 1830-31, perhaps less than a quarter being derived from the brewing trade. Certainly by the middle of the century nearly four-fifths of all malt made in Scotland was absorbed by distilleries. In 1848-49 Scottish maltings produced 518,000 quarters of malt, only 108,000 quarters being used to produce beer.[24]

Perhaps the most reliable indicator of growth and fluctuation in the Scottish

Table 11

A. *Malt Excise 1780-1805*
Nett Produce (£ 000s)

1780	54	1793	41
1781	54	1794	42
1782	24	1795	22
1783	48	1796	51
1784	44	1797	46
1785	40	1798	60
1786	53	1799	71
1787	45	1800	62
1788	42	1801	97
1789	38	1802	102
1790	51	1803	86
1791	54	1804	87
1792	38	1805	94

Note: includes miscellaneous duties on tobacco etc. after 1799.

B. *Growth Rates of Malt Excise*

Terminal Years	Duration	% Growth Rates p.a.
1780-1800	20	0.7
1770-1790	20	3.4
1770-1800	30	2.9

Source: SRO, E904/30.

brewing industry is provided by output statistics, which are available for the years 1787 to 1830 inclusive. Table 12 provides a detailed analysis of Scottish beer and ale production, data being derived from excise and parliamentary returns. Returns for strong beer were made throughout the whole period. Separate returns for small beer and the traditional '2d Ale' were recorded before 1802, afterwards being amalgamated in production figures for table beer. As the table indicates, total production rose from 246,000 barrels in 1787 to 437,000 in 1799, the year of highest recorded output. Thereafter production fluctuated at around an annual average of 330,000 barrels. In 1830, the last year of beer excise, the output of the Scottish industry was 340,000 barrels. Table 13 shows the annual rates of growth of beer charged with duty for various periods between 1787 and 1830, the highest overall rate of growth being 3.5 per cent per annum during the years 1787 to 1800. In the years 1787 to 1810, an era which seems from other points of view to have been one of the most dynamic in the history of the Scottish brewing industry before 1850, the overall annual growth rate was a more modest 1.4 per cent.

The statistics of strong beer output over this period as a whole also merit close analysis. Strong beer was perhaps the most important drink produced by Scottish brewers, popular not only at home but also in England and other more distant markets. The measure of its popularity and success is seen in the growth shown by the figures in Tables 12 and 14. In the thirteen years between 1787 and 1800, as Table 14 shows, production of strong beer rose at a rate of over 9.0 per cent per

Table 12

Beer Charged with Duty: Scotland 1787-1830 (000s of Barrels)

Year	Strong Beer	Small Beer	Table Beer	2d Ale	Total
1787	24	108		114	246
88	23	115		119	257
89	34	121		116	271
1790	43	136		122	301
91	43	139		124	316
92	47	160		145	352
93	48	172		158	378
94	40	154		139	333
95	40	156		139	335
96	78	178		150	406
97	88	168		165	321
98	77	179		171	427
99	84	184		169	437
1800	75	161		150	386
01	73	162		102	337
02	94	95	41	89	319
03	106		249		355
04	93		230		323
05	105		221		326
06	119		230		349
07	121		234		355
08	114		234		348
09	118		221		339
1810	127		227		354
11	120		230		350
12	121		222		343
13	116		199		315
14	133		206		339
15	135		222		357
16	127		222		349
17	111		206		317
18	109		192		301
19	124		209		333
1820	116		207		323
21	123		206		329
22	125		224		349
23	124		222		346
24	114		229		343
25	124		244		368
26(a)	132		275		407
26(b)	134		264		398
27	122		271		393
28	112		241		353
29	119		247		366
1830	111		229		340

Note: figures given are for years ended 5 July except:
    (a)   three-quarters of the year from 5 July 1826;
    (b)   three-quarters of the year to 5 April 1827.
Sources: PP 1826-27 XVII A & P Account of the Quantity of Different Sorts of Beer made in each Kingdom 1786-1826; PP 1828 XVIII A & P Account of the Number of Barrels of Strong Table and Intermediate beer brewed in England, Scotland and Wales 1827-28; PP 1830 A & P Five Accounts re Beer and Brewers.

Table 13

Growth Rates Per Annum of Beer charged with Duty 1787-1830

	Terminal Years	Length of Period (Years)	% Growth Rate Per Annum
A.	1790-1795	5	2.3
	1790-1800	10	2.5
	1790-1805	15	0.6
	1790-1810	20	0.8
	1790-1820	30	0.2
	1790-1830	40	0.3
B.	1787-1800	13	3.5
	1787-1810	23	1.4
	1787-1820	33	0.8
C.	1805-1815	10	0.9
	1805-1825	20	0.6
	1805-1830	25	0.2

Source: derived from data in Table 12.

annum, and was almost 5 per cent per annum over the period to 1820. In 1787 strong beer output was only 24,000 barrels, but production surged ahead rapidly after 1790 to reach 75,000 barrels in 1800. Thereafter annual average output was 120,000 barrels. Strong beer was the mainstay of the Scottish export market: by 1815 exports reached the modest figure of 14,000 barrels, a large proportion being strong beer sent coastwise to the ports of Newcastle, London, Bristol and Liverpool.

Table 14

Growth Rates Per Annum of Strong Beer charged with Duty 1787-1830

Terminal Years	Length of Period	% Growth Rate Per Annum
1787-1800	13	9.1
1787-1810	23	7.5
1787-1820	33	4.9
1787-1830	43	3.6

Source: derived from data in Table 12.

Other Indicators

The actual numbers of breweries operating at different times provide some guide to the course of the industry between 1750 and 1850, although such an analysis cannot fail to take account of business size. There were probably fewer than fifty public breweries in Scotland about the middle of the eighteenth century, largely a reflection of the circumstances described in Chapter One. Outside the larger cities and towns the craft was essentially dominated by domestic operatives and brewing victuallers manufacturing ale for limited local consumption. The number of breweries increased dramatically in the 70s and 80s and by the time the first *Statistical Account* was published in the mid-1790s there were around 150 firms, some very small (see Table 15). About the same period the Sun Fire Insurance Office of London was extending its business north of the Border and had 120 Scottish breweries on its books. These probably represented an estimated two-thirds of the whole industry. As Table 15 demonstrates, further expansion took place in the twenty years after 1800: by 1820 there were 240 firms at work, the largest recorded number at any period. Five years later *Pigot's Commercial Directory of Scotland* (1825-26) provides a detailed picture of a widespread industry organised in 233 units, scattered from Kirkwall in the north to Stranraer in the south. Most towns of any size had at least one brewery, and it follows that many firms were small affairs—modest country enterprises manufacturing local grain into ale for sale to strictly local markets. Some country brewers were more ambitious, however, developing their businesses with enterprise and seeking out markets more distant than those reached by the brewery cart-horse and waggon in an hour's haul. At the same time the industry was becoming increasingly an urban phenomenon organised in larger, mass-production plants: Edinburgh had 29 breweries, Glasgow 27 and Aberdeen 13. Elsewhere the industry had begun noticeably to concentrate itself in other centres like Greenock, Alloa, Falkirk, Stirling and Perth. The mid-1820s were the heyday of country brewing in Scotland, but soon the tentacles of the larger and more competitive businesses with cost advantages began to reach out and absorb the weaker country firms. Rationalisation had clearly begun by the beginning of the 30s as urban brewers sought out country trade at the expense of smaller competitors, and by 1840 there were fewer than 200 breweries. More small-town breweries succumbed in the subsequent decade, leaving 150 firms in 1850. In simple numerical terms the industry had turned full circle within sixty-odd years.

Table 15

Numbers of Breweries in Scotland 1790-1850

Year	No.	Sources
c 1790	150	Statistical Account
c 1800	180	Sun Fire Office Policies
1822	241	PP 1822 XXI A&P Account of No. of Brewers
1825	233	Pigot's Commercial Directory of Scotland
1832	216	PP 1833 XXXIII A&P No. of Brewers
1841	197	PP 1841 XXVI A&P No. of Brewers
1850	154	PP 1850 LII A&P No. of Licensed Brewers

The general structure of the Scottish brewing industry, particularly business size and organisation, changed greatly in the century 1750-1850. This reflected the evolution of the trade from what was little more than a craft organised on domestic lines to a large-scale production industry catering for a mass market. The majority of breweries active at the time the first *Statistical Account* was compiled were small: many may in fact have been little more than brewing victuallers or innkeepers and publicans brewing for sale to their own customers. It is difficult to imagine, for example, how a town the size of Dunfermline (population 5,200 in 1801) could consume the output of ten breweries, given the long-established tradition of sobriety among the handloom weavers there. At any rate, the experience of Dunfermline was typical of many other towns, for during the Industrial Revolution the number of breweries was reduced to three. By 1825 they dominated the trade of the town and district.[25] Even these must have been modest by the standard of city plants, like those of Archibald Campbell or William Younger in Edinburgh and Robert Cowan or John and Robert Tennent in Glasgow. Yet the three breweries in Dunfermline were probably typical of dozens elsewhere in Scotland at the time.

By the mid-1790s the Sun Fire Insurance Office had issued a total of 120 policies to Scottish breweries: small firms with a fixed capital valuation of less than £500 represented 75 per cent of the total. Half the insured fixed capital (nearly £50,000 was tied up in 14 large businesses, mainly located in the established brewing centres. Rather incongruously, the period 1795-1825 saw both an extension of country brewing and a parallel expansion of larger, urban breweries in centres of rapid population growth, such as the industrial districts of the west of Scotland. Both country brewing and town breweries expanded at the expense of the brewing victuallers or domestic brewers, who were gradually forced out of business by increased taxation, rising costs and changing tastes. The parallel growth of country breweries in small market or harbour towns, like Brechin or Banff, and that of larger, more integrated plants in Alloa, Edinburgh, Glasgow and other major centres, should occasion little surprise, when one remembers the limitations imposed on movement by high transport costs and the bulkiness of barrels full of ale and beer. Breweries were developed to serve essentially local markets and generally the size of the market was reflected in the size of the plant. At one end of the scale was the small Dunbar brewery operated by A.M. Bruce, whose sales were confined to the town and immediate locality, and at the other, Archibald Campbell of Argyll Brewery in Edinburgh's Cowgate, who sold his beer and porter in Glasgow and the west of Scotland as well as in Edinburgh.[26]

There were exceptions to the rule, for the enterprising country brewer often made good and expanded his business both at the cost of his less dynamic country colleagues and that of the urban brewer. William Ainslie of Duns, Charles Dudgeon and Company of Belhaven Brewery, Dunbar, and the Brechin Brewery Company are three good cases in point. They achieved success by attacking urban markets or by specialising in the production of strong beer or porter, which commanded a better price than ordinary ale and beer, and could stand higher transport costs.[27] Others again tried their fortunes in more distant markets, not the exclusive sphere of the city brewers. The coastal trade contributed substantially to the success during the period 1785-1825 of breweries in harbour towns like Berwick, Kirkcaldy, Arbroath, Montrose and Banff. Landward transport costs severely limited the range and market of all but the large brewers, but the relative cheapness of shipping or movement by canal greatly extended outlets for those brewers able to take advantage of them.[28]

Throughout the first half of the nineteenth century general transport improvements, particularly the growth of coastal shipping services and the rapid expansion of the railway network, gave still more advantages to the large, urban brewer in and around Edinburgh, Alloa and Glasgow. Brewers there were ideally located to develop the highly concentrated market of the Central Lowlands, and after the end of the 1820s they came to have increasing influence over the industry as a whole. City brewers could tackle distant markets, which at the turn of the century would have proved extremely hazardous and generally unprofitable. The result was a gradual erosion of the competitiveness of local breweries in small country towns and villages, many of which had either succumbed or been bought out by the beginning of the forties.

There is considerable evidence of expansion on the part of urban breweries in the 1830s and 1840s, a direct response to growing market opportunities both at home and abroad. George Younger and Sons of Alloa, a firm with an established reputation in the domestic, London and overseas markets, began an expansion programme at their Meadow Brewery in 1832, purchasing adjoining property as it fell vacant. The firm was thus able to extend its brewery and maltings and by 1850 it produced around 25,000 barrels per annum.[29] Another case in point is provided by William Younger and Company's Abbey Brewery in Edinburgh. It was also extended in the early 1830s by the energetic William Younger II's acquisition of adjoining breweries, maltings and vaults in the Canongate. Younger also built new maltings nearby at Abbey Hill.[30] Alexander Campbell, alive to the opportunities of increasing business in the English market, particularly in London, greatly expanded the capacity of the Argyll Brewery in the late 1830s.[31] As both David Bremner and Alfred Barnard clearly demonstrate, the expansion of the thirties and forties which these examples typify was further reflected in more general growth in business size after the middle of the century.[32] The Scottish brewing industry, more so than that of England, pointed the way to future developments in other consumer industries. Local markets for locally produced goods had already been wholly or partly absorbed by a growing national market for a mass consumption product. A large proportion of this new market was dominated by urban brewers. They gradually consolidated their grip on particular localities by the extension of loans to public houses, although it is worth emphasising that this system was not a feature of the Scottish industry before the later Victorian era.

The fluctuating fortunes of the modest non-domestic trade over the century 1750 to 1850 also provide some measure of the growing maturity of the Scottish brewing industry. In 1780, when production was about 220,000 barrels per annum, the domestic market absorbed all but 1½ per cent of the total. The situation had changed little by 1800, although production had grown to 386,000 barrels. In that year exports were a mere 4,600 barrels, 2,000 of which were sent coastwise to English markets, mainly in London.[33] The export trade was certainly extremely hazardous, dogged as it was by problems of communication, shipping, large-scale breakages and credit—the more distant the market, the greater were the problems. Perhaps for this reason brewers who ventured into distant trading looked at the outset to English markets, where after 1790 there was growing enthusiasm for Scottish strong ales and even for porter manufactured north of the Border. By 1815 Scottish exports were 13,700 barrels, over 60 per cent being consigned to England, and a further 30 per cent to customers in North America and the West Indies.[34] So small was the volume of Scottish beer exports before the middle of the nineteenth century that one is forced to the conclusion that barrels were often simply consigned by optimistic brewers or their agents to make up cargo—rather, as Mathias suggests, like bricks. Yet Scottish brewers were doggedly persistent in their efforts to develop the export trade, and this suggests that the long-term gains were worth the trouble and frustration involved. Between 1815 and 1835 there was a fall in exports, possibly offset to some extent by trade with English markets—though unfortunately no statistics exist to support this view. From the late 1830s, there are tentative indications of the expansion of foreign trade forthcoming in mid-century. In 1850 exports were 21,000 barrels, worth more than £62,000. Scottish beer and ale had followed the flag to Asia, Australasia and Africa, which together accounted for nearly half the total. By this time Scottish brewers alive to the possibilities presented by the foreign trade had successfully developed good 'keeping beers' which would travel well and maintain their quality in the most extreme climate: hence brews like 'Export' beer and 'India' pale ale. It may be added that the latter was first brewed for sale to émigré Scots in the West Indies and only later found its way to India to quench the thirst of expatriate Scottish soldiers, merchants and civil servants.[35]

The brewing industry was no great employer of labour, for wages often represented less than a tenth of overall costs. Brewing tended to be essentially qualitative in its labour requirements: a modest number of skilled craftsmen were supported by a force of unskilled labourers. Sir John Sinclair, in his *Analysis of the Statistical Account of Scotland*, estimated that 4,390 persons were employed in the drink industries (see Table 16), principally brewing and distilling. Of this

Table 16

Industrial Employment in Selected Sectors c 1795

Nos employed manufacturing	Scotland domestic	Export to England	For foreign export	Total
Liquors, fermented and distilled	3,695	530	165	4,390
Glass	725	190	325	1,140
Cooper Work	1,900	30	680	2,610
Leather	2,000	100	300	2,400
Soap	740	—	70	810
Wool				24,800
Linen				76,600

Source: J. Sinclair, *Analysis of SA* (1825), I, 321.

number, perhaps 2,500 worked in breweries, almost the same numbers being employed in cooperages or in tanneries and leather works. Sinclair was probably quite wide of the mark, because he based his calculation on the returns from the questionnaire sent to ministers and other compilers of parish accounts, not all of whom were particularly attentive to statistical detail. The *Statistical Account* reported fewer than 100 breweries in the mid-1790s, when in fact there were at least 150. Admittedly many were very small, each employing a mere handful of labourers. In 1800 the Scottish brewing industry probably employed about 3,000 persons, and in addition provided work for others in related trades like malting, coopering, millwrighting and haulage. After the early nineteenth century peak of production was reached in the mid-1820s, brewing became increasingly concentrated in larger units of production, mostly in the old-established centres of the trade, like Edinburgh, Falkirk, Stirling, Alloa, Glasgow, Dundee and Aberdeen. However, the labour requirements seem to have been little affected by these developments, which were essentially capital rather than labour intensive. When the occupational census of 1841 was taken, 1,085 persons in Scotland were designated brewers. Of course, this modest figure cannot take account of everyone directly employed in the trade at that period, for example the many labourers, coopers and draymen classified elsewhere in the census returns. There were 498 maltsters, although by this time nearly four-fifths of their output was being used in distilleries rather than breweries. Nevertheless, some proportion of maltsters and their labourers were dependent on the brewers for employment. Table 17

Table 17

Brewers and Maltsters 1841, by County

County	Brewers	Maltsters	County	Brewers	Maltsters
Aberdeen	58	36	Kinross	1	-
Argyll	26	63	Kirkcudbright	8	-
Ayr	14	6	Lanark	117	81
Banff	16	7	Linlithgow	5	12
Berwick	14	1	Nairn	1	1
Caithness	3	3	Orkney & Shetland	2	1
Clackmannan	27	26	Peebles	2	-
Dumbarton	4	7	Perth	48	23
Dumfries	14	1	Renfrew	28	28
Edinburgh	193	82	Ross & Cromarty	8	7
Elgin	18	10	Roxburgh	20	2
Fife	62	22	Selkirk	1	-
Forfar	146	10	Stirling	198	41
Haddington	20	16	Sutherland	1	-
Inverness	17	5	Wigtown	8	4
Kincardine	5	3			
			TOTALS	1085	498

Source: PP 1844 XXVII Population (Occupation Abstract), 1841, Part II Scotland.

indicates the distribution of those giving their occupations as brewers and maltsters in 1841. The most interesting feature is the concentration of brewers in the historic centres of the craft, almost half the total being employed in the Lothians, Fife, Stirling and Clackmannnan. Lanark, Angus, Perth and Aberdeen counties were also important, but elsewhere brewers were thin on the ground. It is clearly difficult to estimate with any real accuracy how many people were employed either directly or indirectly in breweries. It was probably about 4,500 - 5,500 because many of the 197 breweries at work in 1841 must have been modest affairs run by a single brewer with the help of a couple of labourers, perhaps just employed for the season. On the other hand, some of the urban breweries, particularly in Edinburgh and Glasgow, were already quite large, with a labour force of a hundred or more.

This survey leaves many unanswered questions (for example, those of capital structure after 1800 and production after 1830) and raises not a few others. Yet most of the available indicators confirm the view that the Scottish brewing industry, after a slow start in the 1760s and 1770s, expanded rapidly between 1780 and 1800. It maintained slow progress throughout the remainder of the Napoleonic Wars and, following a short post-war slump, recovered its former fortunes. There was some limited expansion in the 1820s, and thereafter the industry seems to have maintained a steady course until the middle of the century. By 1850 the Scottish brewing industry had undergone a major transformation in business organisation, many country breweries having been absorbed by former urban competitors. The latter largely dominated the trade. However, much of the character of a past era survived. Many a small brewery was still at work producing ale in the traditional way for sale in a limited, local market. The ultimate demise of the Scottish country brewery lay in the future—for by the end of the nineteenth century the surviving brewery giants were battling one against the other for the remainder of the domestic market.

NOTES

1 T.S.Ashton, *Economic fluctuations in England, 1700-1800* (Oxford, 1959), 27-8.
2 Ibid., 37-8.
3 A.D.Gayer et al., *The Growth and Fluctuation of the British Economy 1790-1850* (1953).
4 Ibid., Vol II, 348; P.Mathias, *The Brewing Industry in England, 1700-1830* (1959), 376.
5 Gayer, op.cit., Vol. I, 27-9, 349, 351.
6 Ibid., 211-13.
7 Ashton, op.cit., 6-7.
8 J.G.Kyd, (ed.), *Scottish population statistics* (Edinburgh, 1952), 8-9, 83.
9 Mathias, op.cit., 339-40; SRO, RH 15/1705-23, Misc. Cash and Day Books of Patrick Murison, 1792-6.
10 PP 1821 VIII, Report on Petitions Complaining of the Additional Malt Duty in Scotland.
11 I am grateful to Dr A.Murray of the Scottish Record Office for his help in the use of Treasury and Exchequer records on Customs and Excise.
12 Mathias, op.cit. 400.
13 E.E.Hoon, *The Organisation of the English Customs System 1696-1786* (new ed. 1968), 56-7.
14 SRO, E906/51 Collectors States of Accounts 1775-6.
15 Ibid.
16 SRO, Exchequer Records, formerly E906 series have recently been re-indexed and are now classified as E555. The former class number is retained here.
17 SRO, E904/3, Account of the Gross Produce of the Revenues of Excise for Scotland, 1707-1807; E904/4, General Account of All Duties of Excise (Scotland), 1808-32.
18 PP 1803-4, IV, Report on . . . Scotch, Barley and Malt, 3-5, 17.
19 PP 1850, LII, A + P, Accounts re Brewers and Beer: Bushels of Malt Used (Scotland).
20 Mathias, op.cit. 342, 345.
21 SRO, E904/3 + 4.
22 Ashton, op.cit. 6-7.
23 Ibid. 37-8.
24 PP 1850 LII, A + P. Accounts re Brewers and Beer: Bushels of Malt Used (Scotland).
25 *OSA*, 13, 438-9; *Pigot's Commercial Directory of Scotland* (1825-6).
26 SRO, RH15/642 A.M.Bruce's Cash Book 1784-5; SRO COS UP Currie Dal C 18/2 Archibald Campbell & Co. v McLaren & Shields, 1851.
27 SRO RH15/731 Seq. of Wm Ainslie 1802; *OSA*, 5, 461.

28 *OSA*, 5, 38; *OSA*, 20, 357.

29 *A short history of George Younger & Son Ltd, Alloa 1762-1925*, 7.

30 D.Keir, *The Younger Centuries* (1951), 39-40.

31 SRO COS Currie Dal C 18/2 Archibald Campbell & Co. v McLaren & Shields 1851, Print of Documents.

32 D.Bremner, *The Industries of Scotland* (1869), 436-43; A.Barnard, *Noted Breweries of Great Britain and Ireland* (1889-91), 4 vols.

33 PRO CUST 14/3 & CUST 1313/4 Exports from Scotland, 1780-1 and 1800-01.

34 PRO CUST 8/3, Exports from Scotland 1815.

35. PRO CUST 9/39, Produce of the UK Exports 1850; W.H.Roberts, *The Scottish ale brewer* (1837), 3rd ed. 1847, 158.

3
Agriculture and Brewing : the raw materials of an industry

THE relationship between agriculture and the drink industries of brewing and distilling was close, each sector being to a high degree dependent on the other. In a cereal-growing district the landowner or farmer, the maltster or brewer, and the middleman grain merchant shared a mutual interest in the annual harvest and to a lesser or greater extent their separate fortunes were regulated by it. Grain yield, quality and price were of critical importance to all three. Yet the relationship between the land and brewing was not simply based on the dependence of the latter on raw materials supplied by the farm. Numerous farmers and landowners themselves turned to brewing, for it was both a potentially profitable sideline and a logical extension of barley cultivation. Many more invested surplus capital in the brewing industry: the financial interests of these landowners, farmers and grain merchants is further explored in Chapter Four. Naturally, there was a less noticeable reverse flow, when the profits of success in brewing were ploughed into landed estates, farms and agriculture. Another link lay in the trade in brewers' waste (known in Scotland as 'draff'), which was sent back to the farm for cattle and pig fattening. Although this branch never assumed the proportions of a similar reverse flow from distilling, it was nevertheless quite a significant feature of the brewing industry in, for example, Fife, the Lothians and Stirling. The relationships between farmers, grain merchants, maltmen, brewers and a whole host of other groups with related interests (such as bankers and general merchants) were often complex, and in many cases their businesses were linked by close family ties or by interlocking partnerships.[1] Indeed it was commonplace by the late eighteenth century to find one or more of these separate functions performed by a single individual, family firm or partnership—with no particular designation other than that of 'brewer.'

The natural cycle of the farmer's year very much regulated activities at the brewery. Like other primary processing industries, brewing tended to be slack in summer and relatively active in autumn and winter. The busiest period for malting was after Michaelmas, when the new crops of barley had been gathered and the weather was neither too warm nor too cold.[2] The brewing season in Scotland generally also coincided with the winter months of October through to March. William Black, in his *Practical Treatise on Brewing*, notes that October could never be regarded as a good brewing month (particularly for what he describes as 'keeping beers'), though this does not seem to have been so in Scotland, possibly because of the noticeable climatic differences from the South. 'Keeping beers' should be brewed, says Black, 'in frosty, or at all events cool, open weather, which may be expected in December, January, February and March.' For 'running beers' (beers for immediate sale) seasonal climatic variations were of less importance, although according to Black 'very few brewers possessed of capital brew in summer.' Before the invention of artificial cooling devices (such as fans and water-cooled refrigerators) the brewers' activities had to be fairly heavily concentrated in the winter months. Brewers in Scotland clearly had some marginal advantage over English counterparts, although, as Black indicates, Scottish preference for slow fermentation may have cancelled environmental advantages. By the late eighteenth century both production and consumption of beer were carried on the year round in larger breweries, although most country brewers seem to have suspended operations in June and resumed them only in October.[3] So, during most of the period with which this study is concerned, brewing was essentially a seasonal activity: the onset of harvest would occasion a flurry of activity at the brewery involving last minute maintenance and cleaning, ready for the first brew of the new season.

It is no accident that even before the period of rapid growth during the Industrial Revolution the Scottish brewing industry had already begun to concentrate itself in the good barley lands of the Lothians, Fife and Angus. A valuable statistical indicator is provided by the malt returns for Scottish excise collections during 1752-3—a period when most of the malt made would almost certainly have been wholly absorbed by brewing, except in a few northern collections where commercial distillation was in its infancy.[4] The data presented in Table 18 indicate a marked concentration of malting in the Lothians—representing more than one

Table 18

Malt Revenue by Excise Collection 1752-3

Collection	Value (£)	% of Total
Aberdeen	2640	3.80
Ayr	2564	7.39
Argyll N.	791	2.28
Argyll S.	685	1.97
Caithness	313	.90
Dumfries	1114	3.21
Fife	4169	12.02
Glasgow	3727	10.47
Haddington	3837	11.06
Inverness	1182	3.40
Linlithgow	3147	9.07
Perth	4484	12.93
Orkney	57	—
Lewis & Skye	3	—
Zetland	12	—
Islay	8	—
Edinburgh	4906	14.15
Teviotdale	1021	2.94
Total	34670	

Source: SRO, E905/46, Accompt of Duties 1752-3.

third of the Scottish malt revenue, while Fife and Perth together return another quarter. Population density was clearly an important locational factor, though unfortunately the boundaries of the excise collections do not bear direct comparison with the county by county demographic data provided by Webster's census in 1755. The brewing industry was above all an essentially Lowland industry, with the largest concentration of breweries on the eastern seaboard, in burghs stretching from Berwick in the south to Aberdeen in the north. This critical and important concentration in the east was further intensified by the early decades of the nineteenth century, when barley imports from English cereal districts, like Norfolk became increasingly important.[5] This gave distinct and obvious advantages to the east coast ports, like Edinburgh, Alloa and Aberdeen, although breweries in Glasgow and the west of Scotland had the benefit of ready

Table 19

Distribution of Breweries by County 1825 (Ranked Order)

County	No.	Pop. 1821 000s
Midlothian	34	191
Lanark	30	244
Angus	20	113
Fife	19	114
Aberdeen	16	155
Perth	14	138
Stirling	14	65
East Lothian	11	35
Dumfries	10	70
Berwick	8	33
Roxburgh	7	40
Clackmannan	6	13
Ayr	5	127
Kincardine	5	29
Renfrew	5	112
West Lothian	4	22
Wigtown	4	33
Kirkcudbright	3	38
Banff	2	43
Moray	2	31
Orkney	2	26
Peebles	2	10
Ross & Cromarty	2	68
Selkirk	2	6
Argyll	1	97
Caithness	1	29
Dumbarton	1	27
Inverness	1	89
Total	233	

Source: *Pigot's Commercial Directory of Scotland 1825-6;* Kyd, 83.

barley supplies from Galloway and Ireland. The nature and extent of the trade in grain is discussed later in this chapter. Nevertheless the brewing industry during the Industrial Revolution proper was much more widely dispersed than this summary analysis would indicate. Barley or its derivatives was widely grown in the Scottish Lowlands, from Berwick to Caithness, and breweries were developed during the period 1770-1830 wherever a potential market existed and raw materials were readily available in the locality. By 1825 (as the data in Table 19 show), despite the dominance of the brewing industry in the eastern counties, there was hardly a market town of any consequence in the Lowlands not possessed of at least one brewery.[6] In many country towns of north-east and south-west Scotland, for example Elgin and Dumfries, brewing was a significant trade processing locally grown barley.[7] Numbers in themselves, of course, do not give an adequate picture, nor can they be in any way directly related to population density, because the ten breweries in Dumfries were probably equal in size and capital to one in Edinburgh or Glasgow.

Barley Cultivation and the Cereal Districts

Two main types of barley were used in the malting and brewing processes as practised in Scotland during the eighteenth and early part of the nineteenth centuries. The first and most significant was common barley, generally grown in most of southern Scotland, particularly in Angus, Fife and the Lothians. The second was generally known in the southern Lowlands as 'bear,' and in Aberdeenshire, Buchan and elsewhere in the North as 'bigg' or 'big.' Bear or bigg was by far the hardier of the two, could ripen in a short season, and thus was extensively cultivated as a food and rent crop in the North, the Borders, Galloway, and on marginal barley-growing land elsewhere in the upland districts of Scotland.[8] Scottish grains were generally inferior to English, a fact widely recognised both by the brewing/malting trade and by the Excise. The lower level of excise duty on malt which reflected this difference dated back to the days of the hated Malt Tax introduced after the Union, and although the gap between English and Scottish duties narrowed later in the eighteenth century (see Table 22), Scottish brewers would reluctantly admit that the more expensive English barley was superior even to the best that East Lothian could produce.[9] Yet despite this, there were many important barley-growing regions in Scotland, and many other districts in the country where significant quantities of barley, bear or bigg were cultivated. On these supplies the Scottish brewing industry primarily relied.

By the middle of the eighteenth century the rich arable counties of the Lothians and Fife adjoining the Firth of Forth had already established themselves as the granary of Scotland. The Agricultural Revolution north of the Border had begun there earlier in the century. The emphasis was firmly on cereal production, commonly wheat or barley on all but the poorer upland soils, where oats would be planted. Typical of the early 'improvers' in East Lothian was the renowned John Cockburn, who built a planned village on his estate at Ormiston and created his own local market for barley by the erection of a brewery, managed by one of his most progressive tenants, Alexander Wight.[10] Cereal cultivation expanded considerably after the 1770s, barley being the most important crop, supplied to maltings and breweries in production centres at Dunbar, Haddington, Edinburgh,

Dalkeith, Bo'ness, Dunfermline and elsewhere. John Thomson in his *General View of the agriculture of Fife*, published in 1800, summarised concisely the more general market opportunities presented to the farmers of the area:

A circumstance tending to encourage and promote agricultural improvement in this country, is, that the farmer can always find a ready market for the produce of his farm. The great population of Fife, and the extent and flourishing state of its manufactures, must require a large and constant supply of provisions . . . and a constant demand upon the farmer for every article of that kind which he can furnish. And as the market is ready, so it is convenient. He can never be exposed to any considerable expense or loss of time in carrying his victual to market. Besides having the advantage of large demands for home consumption, he can find a ready and profitable market for his surplus produce to any amount.[11]

All of this undoubtedly could have been said of the close relationship between Lothian and Fife farmers and the important brewing trade of the region during the period 1770 to 1830. Although brewing in this region was overwhelmingly an urban trade, the connexion with the surrounding countryside was omnipresent, for the Edinburgh brewers, maltmen and grain merchants were invariably linked by ties of kinship with the farmers and landowners—even if this was not so, all shared a common concern about the barley harvest.

Several districts within this important cereal area produced the best and most sought after barley in Scotland. East Lothian (especially around Haddington, East Linton and Dunbar) and the East Neuk of Fife grew the finest malting barley anywhere in Scotland; several brewers in evidence to the *Report on Petitions Complaining of the Additional Malt Duty in Scotland* (1821) attested to the excellence of East Lothian barley. James Meiklejohn, the Alloa brewer, described it as 'the best in Scotland,' while William Berwick, an Edinburgh maltster and brewer, said it was five per cent better than any in Scotland and in good years a lot more.[12] Somerville, in his *General View of the Agriculture of East Lothian*, reported that East Lothian barley was 'preferred by most brewers and distillers to the English kinds,' but all the evidence would seem to indicate that although this may have been true in the first decade of the nineteenth century, it was decreasingly so at larger urban breweries producing porters or strong ales for export in competition with English rivals, and thus requiring the best available barley.[13] The relative quality and price of Scottish and English barley naturally varied from season to season and, as we discuss later in this chapter, these two variables had a considerable influence on the brewer's preference for one or the other. Often, in fact, he would use a mixture of English and Scottish grains in malting—depending on price and quality in any particular brewing year.[14] Despite the challenge of English imports and a resulting decline in barley acreage throughout the region after the early 1800s, the Lothians and Fife remained the principal source of barley for the breweries of south-east Scotland.[15]

Elsewhere in the east of Scotland were several important barley-growing districts. To the south were Berwickshire and the Merse district of the lower Tweed valley, which with adjacent Northumberland were important sources of supply for local country brewers on both sides of the Border, as well as those in Edinburgh and Newcastle. Thomas Jopland, farmer, brewer and maltman with a business established at Coldstream in 1800, records that Berwick and Northumberland barley were very alike. The varieties grown there tended (like bear or bigg) to have thicker husks than English or Lothian barleys and thus required longer steeping to make malt.[16] The development of an important malting industry, associated at first with brewing and later with distilling, likewise resulted in a great extension of acreages under barley in the fertile lands of the Carse of Stirling along the upper shores of the Firth of Forth and including much of the better arable land of Clackmannan and West Lothian, the latter county having more in common with Stirling than the more fertile East Lothian. A contemporary describes barley cultivation in this district during the early nineteenth century as follows:

The time of sowing barley is from the beginning of April until the middle of May. The seed in use is a kind which has long been naturalised to the climate. Little if any big is now sown, although in upland and late soils, it is more suitable and better adapted to the climate, as it ripens at least two weeks earlier than barley. The quantity of seed per acre is from 8 to 14 pecks, according to the soils. After the seed is sown, the ground receives no further culture, except the clearing from it of thistles or other tall weeds.

Barley is cut with a sickle. It is often laid down in single sheaves and spread a little on the middle of the ridge, in which state it remains for a day or two, in order to its being dried more speedily. After this it is bound and set up in shocks of ten sheaves. It is then left to stand till it is completely dried and ready to be stacked. This commonly requires 14 days unless the weather is very favourable.[17]

The barley harvest came as early as the first week of August in a good year, or in an unfavourable one or on poorer soils, in mid-October. Here, as everywhere, the activities of brewer and maltman were regulated by the barley harvest.

Angus and adjoining parts of Perthshire in the lower Tay valley were another significant barley-producing area, supplying breweries in Perth, Brechin, and the coastal ports of Dundee, Arbroath and Montrose, as well as having a substantial export trade to Edinburgh and Glasgow.[18] Angus barley was also much favoured by Aberdeen brewers: William Black of the Devanha Brewery there observed that it 'answered very well and produced a fair profit.' In some years it was as good as the grain from East Lothian and often matched even English barley, which because of transport costs was much more expensive.[19] Bear or bigg was also grown extensively in the upland farming districts of Angus and the Mearns, usually as a rent crop. The land use pattern in a typical parish, Logie Pert, shows barley as the second cereal crop, occupying about a quarter of the arable acreage:

Crop etc.	Acres
Oats	740
Barley and Common Bear	420
Pease	144

Wheat	70
Flax	46
Fallow, turnips, potatoes	160
Hay for cutting	270
Pasture, including Waste	890
Moor, uncultivated	350
Woodland	770
	3860

Most of the barley and bear from this particular parish was sold for malting to breweries in nearby Brechin and Montrose.[20]

There were several important barley areas in the north-east of Scotland, especially Buchan, Moray and Easter Ross. Here distilling was always a much more significant industry than brewing, although in Aberdeen, Elgin, Banff and other centres there were a number of important breweries. Undoubtedly the drink industries greatly encouraged the cultivation of barley, as one piece of evidence given to a parliamentary committee in 1804 made clear:

Before the introduction of the Turnip Husbandry in this County (Aberdeen), which cannot be traced back farther than forty years, and was not general until twenty years ago—we had probably 14,000 or 15,000 Scots acres of what were termed our *Infield* lands, annually sown with Bear or Big . . . Ten years ago, when there was a liberal competition between the Brewers in the Towns and the numerous licensed distillers who were scattered over the County (which occasioned a great demand for Bear or Bigg) the great wide Balks or Pieces of barren land, between the ridges of our Infield . . . were ploughed up, the distinction between the Infield and the Outfield ground was gradually abolished, and a great proportion of the latter was limed, and manured for a Crop of Turnips, and then laid down with Bear and Grass Seeds. Our agriculture at this time was rapidly advancing towards Perfection.[21]

Aberdeen was the focal point of an important grain trade, the outlet for cereal exports by sea to the urban markets of central Scotland, with meal and barley the most important elements. The same was true of Banff, Inverness and other ports in the north-east, though in most of Buchan and Lower Speyside it was the development of commercial distilling which had initially brought about the extension of barley acreages. In the neighbourhood of Huntly, for example, little barley had been grown locally until distilleries created a substantial and conveniently close market for the crop.[22] Elgin was a long-established centre of malting and brewing in the rich barley lands of Moray. At the beginning of the eighteenth century malting was the most important local industry, with thirty malt barns 'always employed,' although the imposition of the Malt Tax resulted in decline. Later developments in both distilling and brewing, however, revived barley cultivation and the barley trade, and by the 1780s Elgin had at least one large brewery malting 1,500 bolls of barley per annum.[23] Easter Ross, and particularly the area known as the Black Isle, was another important cereal district supplying local distilleries and a handful of country breweries in Inverness, Cromarty and Tain.[24] At Cromarty, a substantial brewery (remains of which can still be seen) was established by George and Alexander Ross, the local landed proprietors—as much to combat the evils of whisky drinking as to support a ready market for barley from their Black Isle estates.[25] The Agricultural Revolution brought great changes to two other locally important cereal districts in the far north, Caithness and Orkney, but as far as brewing was concerned supplies of barley from these districts were of relatively little significance to all but a few brewers in Wick, Thurso and Kirkwall.[26]

In several areas of the west of Scotland barley cultivation for the brewing trade was of considerable importance by the middle of the eighteenth century. After a period of relative buoyancy between 1760 and 1790 imports from Ireland and the Lothians contributed to a net decline in barley cultivation in this region, the only exception being Dumfries and Galloway in the south-west.[27] Glasgow, Greenock, Kilmarnock and Ayr were the main centres of malting and brewing in the rapidly developing industrial districts of central Scotland, while Dumfries was the dominant centre in the relatively isolated south-west. The best barley came from Lower Clydesdale, Ayr and Galloway, while upland districts everywhere produced the inferior variety, bear, again mainly as a rent crop.[28]

Barley, in its various forms, was a versatile crop and could be grown in most Lowland districts of Scotland, but there can be little question that rising demand from the liquor industries greatly stimulated barley growing and production. This was widely recognised by the writers of the various *General Views of Agriculture* covering the areas which we have just described. Unfortunately, there are few reliable estimates of either acreages or yields of barley in Scotland during the eighteenth and early nineteenth centuries. The best information is that provided in the pages of the *Statistical Account* and the *General Views* for the various key barley-producing counties. Sir John Sinclair, in his *Analysis of the Statistical Account*, estimated that of 1.6 million acres under cereals 280,000 acres were devoted to barley, worth, in 1814, £2.2 million:

Table 20

Crop Acreage and Value, 1814

Crop	Acres (000s)	Value per Acre (£)	Total Value (£ 000s)
Grass	2489	2	4979
Wheat	140	11	1541
Barley	280	8	2241
Oats	1260	7	8822
Rye	½	6	3
Beans & peas	118	6	708
Potatoes	80	8	640
Turnips	407	4	1628
Flax	16	8	132
Gardens	32	15	480
	4824		21176

Source: J. Sinclair, *Analysis of SA*, I, Appendix, 17.

As a point of comparison, the barley acreage of England c1800 was estimated at slightly less than 1 million, a high proportion of the crop being used in malting and brewing.[29] Barley was certainly a specialist crop in some of the farming districts we have described, and in these areas at least, most of production found its way to maltings, breweries and distilleries. By the beginning of the nineteenth century the Scottish brewing and distilling industries probably absorbed equal proportions of domestic barley, while certain sectors of brewing came increasingly to rely on superior English grain imported coastwise from the barley lands of East Anglia. Changes or developments in the drink industries, as Mathias notes, had a widespread and intimate connexion with farming, and this is very obviously seen in the response of agriculture to demands for barley in certain regions of Scotland during the period 1770-1850.[30]

Barley and Malting

Although it is generally held that barley production had greatly increased in Scotland throughout the latter half of the eighteenth and early part of the nine-teenth centuries, this might, in fact, seem very unlikely if the excise data for malt production are taken at face value; but, as indicated elsewhere, this particular series has to be treated with extreme caution. Fluctuating levels of taxation and enforcement make customs and excise data much less valuable than they might otherwise be. Nevertheless, the available data from the excise returns on malt provide some measure of the expansion of barley cultivation, malting, brewing and indirectly of barley imports in the period before 1810.[31] The data in Table 21 show a modest increase between 1730 and 1775, and a much more rapid rise thereafter, due essentially to the imposition of new duties. The duty (see Table 22) was raised by ½d per bushel in 1760, but this modest increase had little effect on

Table 21

Nett Produce of Excise on Malt 1730-1805 (Rounded)

	£
1730-1	26,000
35-6	20,500
40-1	7,250
45-6	14,100
50-1	21,000
55-6	16,500
60-1	32,200
65-6	18,500
70-1	26,100
75-6	25,000
80-1	53,500
85-6	40,300
90-1	51,000
95-6	22,500
1800-1	62,000
05-6	94,500

Source: SRO, E904/3 Gross & Nett Produce of Excise 1707-1807.

the overall trend: although the near doubling of malt duty on 31 May 1780 certainly did so.[32] Any examination of malt revenues, therefore, ought to take account of these changes, and it is probably best to regard the years 1725-60, 1761-80 and 1781 onwards as separate periods, bearing in mind also the massive increase in rates of duty during the Napoleonic Wars. Taken over the period 1725-1810 as a whole, the figures show only a slight increase if allowance is made for changes in rates of duty. This feature of the malt excise data has already been examined by Mathias with regard to the English experience. He emphasises the importance of an increasingly efficient excise, pointing out that this might lead to the conclusion 'that the later figures relate more exactly to the total malt manufacture and barley production than earlier' and thus to the natural inference that a greater proportion of barley was actually being made into malt in 1730 than in 1780.[33]

Other factors which clearly have to be taken into account are the increasing use of malt and, later, raw grain by distillers (especially towards the end of the eighteenth century), and the qualitative improvements in malting and brewing which took place throughout the period.[34] Although it seems doubtful that barley cultivation rose much in England, in Scotland (as in Ireland) there was a considerable extension of barley cultivation in the regions described after the 1770s, coinciding to some degree with the large-scale expansion of the drink industries. Taken at face value, and even allowing for changes in rates of duty, the Scottish malt excise data generally bear this out.[35]

Table 22

Rates of Malt Tax: England and Scotland, Per Bushel

Year	England	Scotland		Bigg
		Barley		
1713	6-16/21d	6-16/21d		as barley
1725	6-16/21d	3-8/21d		as barley
1760	9¼d + 2/21d	4½ + 12/21d		as barley
1780	1s4¼d	8-1/3d		as barley
1802	2s5d	1s8¾d		as barley
1803	4s5¾d	3s9½d		3s 1¼d
1817	2s5d	1s8¾d		1s 8¾d
1819	3s7¼d	3s7¼d		3s 7¼d
1822	2s7d	2s7d		2s 0d

Source: PP 1803-4 IV Report on Scotch Barley and Malt, 3-5, 15-17.

The surveys of malt in excise collections do provide some indicators of the importance of barley-growing and malting in the respective districts of Scotland, and this can be tested against other data. It must be emphasised, however, that precise conclusions are difficult. Much barley was not malted in its place of growth, the boundaries of excise collections are not known with any accuracy, and it is impossible to translate revenue totals back into quantities because of the wide range of excise rates over the period as a whole, and, more critically, because of the lack of standard weights and measures throughout Scotland.[36] With these caveats in mind, Table 23 (similar to Table 18) shows the relative concentration of malting in Fife, the Lothians and Perthshire—a pattern firmly established by the mid-eighteenth century and still true in 1820. This pattern is also borne out by figures for total malt production during 1794-1803, shown in Table 24, where the leading collections are Fife, Perth, Ayr, Edinburgh and Linlithgow, with the first two being the key districts malting superior quality barley. The picture had changed very little by 1830 (see Table 25), although Glasgow had by this time established itself as an important malting centre, much of the production being absorbed by distilleries in and around the city. The Lothians, Fife and Stirling, however, remained the most significant malting districts, accounting for nearly £150,000 in revenue. This pattern was clearly reflected in the concentration of formally designated maltsters in and around Alloa, Stirling and Falkirk about the same period, as indicated in Table 26.[37] The conclusion which can be drawn from the malt excise data as a whole is that regional specialisation in malting increased throughout the period and that by the early decades of the nineteenth century it was overwhelmingly concentrated in the old-established centres of eastern Scotland and, like brewing and lowland distilling, had become an essentially urban industry.

Table 23

Malt Revenue by Collection 1775-6

Collection	Value (£)	% of Total
Aberdeen	2412	5.4
Ayr	1575	
	1975	8.0
Argyll N.	823	
Argyll S.	1424	5.1
Caithness	850	1.9
Dumfries	1089	2.4
Fife	6191	14.0
Glasgow	4912	11.1
Haddington	5000	11.3
Inverness	1828	4.1
Perth	4995	11.3
Linlithgow	5153	11.7
Teviotdale	989	2.2
Orkney	134	—
Edinburgh	4640	10.5
Total	43990	

Source: SRO, E 906/51 Collectors' States of Accompts: Malt, 1775-76.

Table 24

Total Malt Manufactured by Collection 1794-1803

Collection		000s bushels		
		Total	from barley	from bigg
Aberdeen		1201	—	1201
Ayr		2014	797	1217
Argyll		223	4	219
Caithness		90	—	90
Dumfries		364	279	85
Fife		2896	2894	2
Glasgow	1656	1656	1531	125
Haddington		1098	1041	57
Inverness		392	81	311
Linlithgow		1785	1580	205
Perth		2251	2230	21
Teviotdale		337	337	—
Orkney		27	—	27
Edinburgh		1902	1898	4

Source: PP 1803-4 IV Report on Scotch Malt and Barley, 88-9.

Yet, as Mathias notes (again in the context of the English malting trade), this may in turn have reflected the greater specialisation in the growth of barley, but the malting figures themselves are not adequate evidence for this suggestion.[38]

Table 25

Beer and Malt Revenue by Collection 1830-1

Collection	Beer (£)	Malt (£)
Aberdeen	4299	23920
Ayr	4502	30562
Argyll N.	—	2988
Argyll S.	—	926
Caithness	407	6781
Dumfries	2350	6432
Edinburgh	15662	60167
Elgin	599	22444
Fife	2507	25941
Glasgow	8454	79904
Haddington	2832	37002
Inverness	277	18019
Linlithgow	1970	26271
Montrose	3627	14411
Perth	1029	31729
Stirling	2817	96723
Totals	51732	484220

Source: SRO, E905/124 Malt and Beer Excise Revenues 1830-31.

Table 26

Corn Merchants and Maltsters by Centre 1825

Centre	Corn Merchants	Maltsters
Edinburgh	103	—
Glasgow	41	2
Leith	18	—
Aberdeen	17	—
Dundee	11	—
Montrose	11	—
Dunbar	10	—
Berwick	9	—
Kelso	6	—
Kilmarnock	6	2
Perth	6	—
Haddington	5	—
Cupar	4	—
Ayr	3	3
Dumfries	3	10
Falkirk	3	5
Inverness	3	—
Kirkcaldy	3	—
Stirling	2	7
Greenock	1	—
Alloa	—	10
Paisley	—	1

Source: *Pigot's Commercial Directory of Scotland, 1825-6.*

Malting had always been something of an intermediary between the farmer and the brewer, though commonly in Scotland brewers made their own malt. Before brewing expanded during the 1770s, malting had been a separate trade (for example in old centres of the industry, like Dunbar, Stirling and Elgin), but it became increasingly associated with brewers during the Industrial Revolution, re-emerging as an important industry in its own right in the opening years of the nineteenth century with the rise of commercial distilling.[39] Nevertheless, the malting trade remained an expanding and viable entity throughout the period, with the largest proportion of the industry concentrated in Alloa, Stirling and Falkirk by 1825 (see Table 26).[40] Even if brewers undertook their own malting, the malt barns and kilns tended to be separate from the brewery. Aitken's of Falkirk had their maltings at Linlithgow near good barley supplies from West Lothian farms, while several Edinburgh brewers had premises in Haddington and Dunbar. This arrangement made much more sense than would at first appear: maltings inevitably took up a great deal of space (Aitken's Mains Maltings at Linlithgow had a frontage of nearly 200 ft), and certainly few urban brewers in Edinburgh or Glasgow had opportunities for anything but vertical expansion.[41] Premises located in or near the countryside were more conveniently located for essential supplies of barley, the storage of which also took up a great deal of space. In the majority of situations land and grain costs probably offset those of trans-port from country to town. Even before the expansion of malting as an independent trade there were some extensive maltings: the Alloa premises of William Welsh were valued at £1,000 in 1801 and those of Adam Dawson in Linlithgow at the same amount.[42]

The Grain Trade

Throughout the eighteenth and into the nineteenth centuries Scottish brewers and maltsters generally used local barleys, being driven further afield only in the occasional years of shortage affecting their traditional and natural sources of supply. But by the end of the eighteenth century, apart from the obvious local and regional markets (for example Buchan, supplying the brewers of Aberdeenshire and the distillers of Speyside), there was a growing national market within Scotland for high quality malting barley and this led to the emergence of specially significant barley areas attracting the attention of middlemen grain merchants. Such was the growth in the drink industries after 1770 that marginal cereal lands (like Galloway, as we have seen) were often made profitable by non-local demand for barley, and in such areas the crop became a significant element not only in the rotation pattern but in the economics of farming.[43]

The grain trade was concentrated in the key barley-producing areas of Berwick, the Lothians, Fife, Angus and Buchan, and it was in these districts that the main groups of corn merchants were based (see Table 26). Edinburgh and Leith naturally dominated the trade, having 121 merchants in 1825, while elsewhere in the Lothians the malting and brewing towns of Haddington and Dunbar were of secondary importance. The grain trade of Fife was essentially dominated by Edinburgh merchants from across the Firth of Forth, though both Cupar and Kirkcaldy provided more local outlets for the agriculturally rich heartland of the county. These towns had important primary processing industries using grain as their basic raw material, including not only malting, but also brewing, distilling and milling, and the majority of businessmen in these trades also acted as corn factors or merchants. Further north, Dundee and Montrose dominated the important Angus grain trade with 22 merchants between them (Perth was also an important centre in the upper Tay valley), while Aberdeen was the focal point of activity in a wide area of north-east Scotland. Practically all of the market towns and coastal harbours of Buchan and Moray exported grain to the south after the 1770s, the main centres being Elgin, Banff and Inverness. Falkirk and Stirling, two important centres of the drink industries, had between them five grain merchants in 1825, though here many local brewers, maltsters and distillers also had substantial interests in the business. Glasgow, however, dominated the grain trade of the west, having 41 factors or merchants, with Kilmarnock and Ayr acting as lesser centres. Much of the coastal import trade from Dumfries and Galloway and from Ireland was also controlled from Glasgow.[44]

Before the emergence of such a substantial and formalised structure linking, through corn factors or merchants, the farmer, maltster and brewer, many brewers would deal directly with the farmer. This certainly was the case at most country breweries, which, as we have seen, would normally receive their barley supplies from neighbouring farms.[45] Even larger breweries had their own (often long-established) contacts with the countryside, sometimes at a considerable distance, as was the case in Tennents' business relationship with farmers and corn merchants in Dumfries and Galloway during the 1780s. The informal relationships were certainly maintained at almost all levels of the trade, emphasising yet again the close mutual interest of farmer, maltster, brewer and distiller in the success of the harvest. Even after the 1790s, when the grain trade was increasingly concentrated in the hands of merchants in urban centres, bargains were still struck directly between farmer and brewer, especially so where the latter operated a meal or grain business as a side-line.[46]

The largest market for grain anywhere in Scotland was undoubtedly the Lothians. Edinburgh and Leith together dominated the Scottish trade, exerting considerable influence in areas as far afield as Berwickshire and Angus. In the mid-1790s barley was supplied to the Lothian and Edinburgh markets from all over the Merse and lower Tweed valley, being either carted overland or exported coastwise via the ports of Eyemouth and Berwick. Similarly, grain was shipped south from the ports of Angus, and even modest harbours there, such as Gourdon, exported substantial quantities of grain each year to the Firth of Forth and even onwards from Bo'ness and Grangemouth to Glasgow by the newly constructed Forth & Clyde Canal.[47] In the Lothians themselves the existence of such a ready market had a profound influence on the development of agriculture during much of the eighteenth and nineteenth centuries. In the *General Views of Agriculture* and the majority of entries in both *Statistical Accounts* the importance of the barley market is duly acknowledged: Dunbar, for example, had a very important corn and malt trade in the 1790s, and the town was famous for the quality of its malt, 'being remarkably well made'; while the consumption of barley at local breweries and distilleries in Linlithgow was 'very considerable' and the porter and small beer produced could 'vie with any in Scotland.'[48]

Further west, Falkirk, Stirling and Alloa absorbed barley from a wide district: Airth, in the lower Carse of Forth, was a particularly well-favoured area supplying local brewers; and the barley bought from the farmers of Clackmannan was considered 'equal to any.' John Thomson estimated that the quantity of malt used by brewers in Fife alone amounted to nearly 20,000 bolls per annum in 1800, discounting large quantities of malt and raw barley sent outwith the county to breweries around Edinburgh, Alloa and Falkirk. One country brewery at Dysart (a coal-mining and salt-panning burgh) malted 1,000 bolls per annum in 1794, most of the barley being grown in the surrounding countryside. Production was 2,500 barrels, most of it sold in Kirkcaldy and neighbouring colliery villages.[49] Alloa breweries and maltings imported large shipments of barley from a wide area in sloops and boats which docked at its own harbour and that of the nearby village of Cambus, where there was a brewery, mills and a large distillery.[50]

The malting and brewing industries of Perth and Angus relied heavily on local barley supplies, which were always large enough to fulfil regional demand and contribute to the development of a coastwise export trade by the 1780s. The inland market was dominated by Perth, which had an extensive range of primary processing industries by the 1770s, including milling, malting, brewing and distilling, supplied with raw materials from the surrounding countryside. Brechin and Montrose both had important brewing industries, and the latter port was also the focus with Dundee of a significant grain trade.[51] The marginal barley lands of the Mearns and Kincardine mostly marketed their produce in Aberdeen, which was the dominant centre for the grain trade in the north-east. The sphere of influence of the Aberdeen grain factors and merchants stretched throughout Buchan, Moray, Inverness and even as far as Easter Ross and Caithness, a point which again emphasises the importance of local harbours and coastwise shipping to farmers and merchants alike.[52] Much of Strathdon was good barley countryside, especially around Inverurie and Alford, and the local grain trade greatly benefited from the construction of the Aberdeenshire Canal, opened from Aberdeen harbour to Port Elphinstone near Inverurie in 1805.[53] Banff had an important export trade both in grain and beer, because there was a well-established brewery there before 1775; and Inverness in the inner Moray Firth was similarly an important centre for a wide area of the eastern Highlands, which included the Black Isle of Easter Ross (Fortrose and Cromarty were important harbours there) and much of the fertile countryside surrounding the Beauly Firth. Inverness had three corn merchants so designated in 1825.[54] As in Galloway, the impact of cereal farming on the landscape of Easter Ross and Caithness during the years 1790-1820 was truly dramatic, as the surviving remains of country grain mills in both areas so clearly show.[55]

The corn market of the west of Scotland was dominated by Glasgow, and the merchants there had widespread contacts in Ayrshire, Dumfries and Galloway, Angus and the Lothians; Glasgow and Edinburgh merchants were always close rivals—no doubt seen in open competition at many an auction during harvest time in the grain markets of Haddington and Dunbar.[56] In the south-west too they would find themselves competing for the farmers' grain with factors from Cumberland and Lancashire across the Solway Firth. The Irish trade too was of growing importance after the 1780s, and Glasgow merchants were conveniently placed to develop this through the Clyde ports. Glasgow itself had a significant brewing and malting industry throughout most of the period, while other important centres included Greenock, Paisley, Kilmarnock and Ayr (see Tables 19 and 26).[57] All but the larger breweries drew their barley from the surrounding countryside.

Between 1770 and 1850 Galloway was an important grain-exporting district, with its main markets in Cumberland, Lancashire, Ireland and the west of Scotland. Barley was always a significant rent crop and its cultivation played a vital part in the regional farming economy of both Dumfries and Galloway. The area was typical of many in Scotland where cereal growing was widely extended in marginal land, particularly during the period of high primary product prices during the war years 1793-1815, in what is essentially a pastoral district. The present-day landscape preserves evidence in abundance of large-scale enclosure, with the traditional stone dykes dividing fields which have probably never been ploughed since the early nineteenth century. Broken-down ruins of water-driven grain mills, often on the very margin of cultivation, testify to the prosperity of oats and barley growing in the late eighteenth and early nineteenth centuries.[58]

There is plenty of documentary evidence in estate records and the *Statistical Accounts* of the nature and extent of the barley trade in Galloway. Between 1784 and 1790 over 40,000 quarters of grain (most of it barley) were exported from Stranraer, an average of nearly 6,000 quarters per annum. Surrounding parishes in the Rhins of Galloway had seen a massive extension of cereal production during the preceding twenty years. Sorbie, an important agricultural parish in the Machers district of Wigtownshire, shared a similar experience. Following extensive improvements and enclosure by the Earls of Galloway after 1760, it exported substantial quantities of barley through its new planned village and harbour of Garlieston, mainly to Liverpool, Dublin and the west of Scotland. An even more isolated parish, Colvend and Southwick in the Stewartry of Kirkcudbright, exported 2,500 bushels of barley per annum in the 1790s, practically all destined for ports beyond the Solway Firth, Whitehaven, Lancaster and Liverpool.[59] Many farmers and grain merchants in the area had established contacts with brewers and distillers in both Scotland and England, the best example being the close relationship between the Glasgow brewers, Tennents, and corn factors in Dumfries, Kirkcudbright and Whithorn. This pattern, once firmly established, remained important well into the nineteenth century.

Tennents combined brewing with grain dealing, and their surviving letter books from the 1780s provide an invaluable insight into the operation of the grain trade in the west of Scotland and the closely related mutual interests of brewer and farmer. It is clear that Tennents already had well-established links with farmers and grain merchants in Dumfries and Galloway before the 1780s, mainly with contacts in Dumfries, Kirkcudbright and Whithorn. Most of the correspondence in the Rough Letter Copy Book of 1785-89 deals with business between them. The majority of the transactions were concluded on bills of accommodation or credit by Tennents to the sellers, payable in two or three months—though the shorter period was apparently preferred. Bills were endorsed on Tennents' behalf by, among other bankers, Sir William Forbes and Company and Patrick Millar and Company, which is interesting because both were Edinburgh houses, although they did have substantial interests in the south-west.[60] Here is some typical correspondence. Tennents write to John Hannay of Kirkcudbright on 11 February 1786 saying, 'your prices are too high for this market; when they come lower, deliver a cargo of your best barley fit for malting to Greenock.'[61] The autumn of the same year produces a flurry of correspondence with farmers and merchants throughout the south-west. Tennents write as follows to James Mackenzie and Company of Dumfries on 2 September 1786:

> It is now some time since we had any favour of you. On account of this please advise the state of the markets; and if your harvest is over and how your crops are succeeded. If new barley can be purchased any way reasonable, we would take a cargo of it provided it's dry as to be shipped with safety, not to heat or spoil in the passage. If it is soft, could it be got kiln dried, and at what expense? Should the quality be fine and the price not to exceed 20 to 22 shillings per quarter, you may purchase for us 4-5,000 quarters if the price answers. Could

the quantity be procured and in readiness for shipping in two or three weeks after receipt of this. As we have a vessel of our own about the burden that we could send round for it about that time: indeed, if it's not got soon, it would not answer us so well.[62]

November finds them buying barley from John Milroy of Whithorn, and placing an order with James Beck of Kirkcudbright for a cargo of barley to be delivered to them in two months' time.[63] The correspondence starts up again in spring the following year and always the concern is with quality. To John Carruthers of Dumfries they write:

> The skipper says the cargo is just a little heated. However, the sample seems meaner in quality than the other cargoes. But we shall be glad if the other stock turns out better. We approve you shifting part of the cargoe, otherwise it must have been much damaged. If you procure another cargoe, could you get part or the whole of it kiln dried?[64]

Again, they write to James Dunsmore of Garlieston in the Machers of Wigtownshire, asking him to deliver a cargo of 'your best bear or barley' and also 'send some of your best meal' which they could sell in the Glasgow markets.[65] The remaining correspondence during the period 1787-9 maintains the same level of concern with harvests and barley quality, and even finds Tennents buying grain further afield in Leith and Dundee.[66]

One final area in the south of Scotland remains to be considered, Berwickshire and the eastern Border country, which although ostensibly an extension of the Lothians was isolated enough to have similar characteristics to Dumfries and Galloway. There, Kelso was an important regional centre, with several corn merchants and two breweries producing 2,500 barrels of beer annually in 1794. Indeed, the two counties of Roxburgh and Selkirk (in places like Melrose, Jedburgh and Ednam where there were quite large country breweries) had a substantial local malting and brewing industry, with a total production of over 10,000 barrels in 1794-5 paying £2,000 in malt and beer excise.[67]

Nearby Berwick, at the mouth of the Tweed, also had an important grain trade (with nine merchants in 1825) serving three or four local breweries and one in Duns, where William Ainslie developed a large brewery with a wide trade in the years before 1800. The Berwick factors were also involved in the coastal trade to ports of the Forth and Tyne.[68]

Tennents' dealings with the farmers and merchants of the south-west show just one aspect of a considerable coastal trade in grain—particularly barley for breweries and distilleries—which developed in Scotland during the latter half of the eighteenth century. For just as Dumfries and Galloway and to a lesser extent Argyll supplied Glasgow and the Clyde ports of Ayr, Irvine, Greenock and Port Glasgow, so there was also an extensive trade on the east coast. Bulk grain movements overland became increasingly feasible with the development of turnpike roads, and we can see something of this in the inland trade from Berwickshire to the markets of Dalkeith and Edinburgh during the 1790s.[69] The majority of barley-growing districts were within easy reach of a harbour, so that the growth of a coastwise grain trade was readily facilitated. Thus Berwickshire grain (and some from Roxburgh and Northumberland) found its way north to Edinburgh, Leith and Alloa through the ports of Eyemouth and Berwick, and almost as much East Lothian barley was sent coastwise to Leith by Dunbar and North Berwick as went by cart overland.[70] The Angus ports of Dundee, Arbroath and Montrose also supplied Edinburgh and Glasgow: Montrose had a considerable trade, exporting 7,000 quarters of barley and 8,000 quarters of malt in 1789.[71] Exports from the north-east found their way south by sea from ports like Aberdeen, Peterhead, Fraserburgh, Banff, Lossiemouth and Inverness, trade being well-established by the 1780s. The Rev. Dr. George Skene, in evidence to the parliamentary committee on Scottish barley and malt (1804), estimated that Aberdeenshire alone exported 20,000 quarters of barley per annum in the 1790s, although later changes in the rate of duty on bear or bigg severely affected the trade.

Table 27

Exports of Bigg/Barley from Aberdeen 1798-1804

Year ending 5 January	Coastal Quts.	Foreign Quts.
1798	15,200	—
1799	14,500	—
1800	23,900	4,800
1801	2,900	—
1802	5,700	—
1803	8,200	—
1804	2,500	750

Source: PP 1803-4 IV Report ... on Scotch Barley & Malt, 20-21.

At the very least the figures in Table 27 indicate that the coastal trade from Aberdeen and its outports was of considerable importance at the close of the eighteenth century.[72] Barley exports from the north-east almost certainly declined after 1800 when commercial distilling began to absorb most local production and brewers in and around Edinburgh were seeking supplies of superior English barley rather than the inferior varieties from the north. As we have already noted, Dumfries and Galloway was a relatively unique area supplying large quantities of grain (and especially barley) to England as well as Scotland through the Solway ports, like Dumfries, Kirkcudbright, Wigtown and Stranraer.

With the continued expansion of the Scottish drink industries after the 1780s imports of English and Irish barley became increasingly significant. Quality and price were, as always, the main determinants—and the nature of the harvest largely controlled these. The grain import trade from England was at first very much influenced by relative differences in taxation (see Table 22), but as the gap between English and Scottish duties narrowed during the Napoleonic Wars, Scottish brewers had increased incentives to use better quality English barley, particularly if they were brewing porter or selling in English and overseas markets. The demand for inferior bear or bigg was similarly affected by relative differentials in excise rates, with a resulting increase in demand for marginal cereal districts producing this inferior grain. There was a two-way flow between Scotland and England in barley as well as beer, and, as Mathias noted, 'differences between the state of the harvest in the two countries, or price differentials changing within a single year, could give obvious reasons for a double flow of the same commodity—but often the basis of trade was exactly the difference between the two different sorts of barley.'[73]

The trade in grain was well established by the closing decades of the eighteenth century. Alexander Bald estimated that between 1760 and 1780 nearly 60,000 quarters of barley were imported to Scotland (mostly in the 70s) mainly from England, Ireland and the Baltic. Barley exports, he thought, were more substantial (perhaps 10 - 15,000 quarters per annum), particularly in years of good harvest.[74] As the data in Table 28 indicate, the flow of barley from England to Scotland began in the 1780s, and all the evidence suggests that the importers tended to be the large, urban brewers in places like Edinburgh, Alloa, Dundee and Aberdeen. William Black of Gilcomston Brewery in Aberdeen, for example, imported Norfolk barley in the years after 1807, and despite heavy transport and shipping costs, found it to his advantage.[75] This and other evidence before parliamentary commissions on the Malt Tax during the early part of the nineteenth century suggests that English barley was increasingly used by Scottish brewers in the search for quality. Barley was often bought directly from English grain factors in London, Norfolk, Lincoln or Cambridge, and imported coastwise from the ports of Yarmouth, Wells, King's Lynn and Boston. Other brewers bought from the Leith and Edinburgh grain merchants.[76] Coastal imports from England were thought in 1808 to be about 100,000 quarters per annum, about a quarter of which was probably used by brewers. Trade from Ireland to the ports of the Clyde was also considerable, especially in years of bad harvest, but this is much more difficult to quantify. Barley imports from Ireland certainly came to Ayr, Irvine, Saltcoats and Greenock after 1780—and in all four places malting and brewing were of more than local importance by the early 1800s.[77] It is likely that increasing quantities of inferior Irish grain were absorbed after this period by the distilling trade in the west of Scotland. The English barley trade grew considerably during the first few decades of the nineteenth century: nearly 40,000 quarters of English barley were imported to Leith alone in 1820-21.[78]

Table 28

Exports and Imports of Barley etc. 1771-1804

Year	Exports		Imports
	Barley	Bear	Barley
	(000s Quarters)		
1771	—	2.4	—
2	—	2.8	—
3	—	0.2	0.8
4	—	—	12.7
5	—	0.5	16.3

Exports and Imports of Barley etc. 1771-1804 (Cont.)

| Year | Exports | | Imports |
	Barley	Bear	Barley
	(000s Quarters)		
1776	—	—	8.1
7	—	4.4	0.5
8	—	6.0	—
9	—	0.8	0.2
1780	—	0.8	—
1	—	18.3	—
2	—	15.6	—
3	—	13.0	1.6
4	—	1.4	57.0
5	—	2.7	33.4
6	12.0	4.7	3.5
7	9.3	10.1	12.2
8	1.5	3.6	25.4
9	0.8	2.1	0.7
1790	19.1	10.9	2.4
1	—	—	5.8
2	—	—	17.4
3	1.0	—	30.6
4	—	—	29.7
5	—	—	6.4
6	—	—	—
7	—	—	2.2
8	—	—	11.3
9	—	—	23.8
1800	22.5	—	1.5
1	—	—	8.0
2	—	—	9.0
3	1.0	—	3.4
4	3.5	—	4.4

Source: A. Bald, *The farmer & corn dealers' assistant* (1807), 438-42.

The Trade in Draff

The reverse flow of brewers' and distillers' spent grains (or draff) to the farm was the final element in the simple cycle linking the drink industries and the land. The earliest instance of the draff trade in Scotland is recorded in the business books of John Wilson and Company of Stirling, where 'An Account of Draff Sold' shows the sale of 1,423 bolls (value £52) between January and November 1749.[79] The draff trade was an established feature of most breweries in town and country by the middle of the eighteenth century, and as the brewing and later the distilling industries grew during the Industrial Revolution period, so the reverse flow of spent grain to the countryside increased.[80] Cattle and hog feeding became a natural appendage of many country breweries, distilleries and starch works, and seems to have been an expanding business by the time the first *Statistical Account* was compiled in the 1790s. At Inveresk, for example, cattle and hogs were fattened at local soap works, a brewery and a distillery; while at Linlithgow 180 black cattle fed off the draff supplied from local breweries and distilleries. Near Clackmannan no fewer than 7,000 black cattle and 2,000 swine for sale in urban markets were being fed from the distilleries and breweries around Alloa, and in nearby Dunfermline 200 swine produced £300 per annum.[81]

Hog feeding seems to have been a specialist activity in Dumfries and Galloway, East Lothian and Berwickshire. Robert Somerville, in his *General View of the Agriculture of East Lothian*, provides an interesting description of pig raising and feeding about 1805:

Upon the ordinary farms the number of hogs bred is so small as to require very little accommodation. The price of grain and other articles has lately been such as to prevent farmers from either breeding or keeping more than are necessary picking up the scattered grains, or offal, that would otherwise be lost about every farm.

A low building called a *cruive*, sometimes divided, is the only accommodation thought necessary for them: but where distilleries, starch works etc. are carried on, the breeding and fattening of hogs are particularly attended to, and form no inconsiderable part of the profits arising from these manufactures, as in their maintenance many things are consumed that would otherwise be lost. At all the principal distilleries, starch works etc. there are separate buildings for the hogs, with every requisite accommodation for breeding, rearing and fattening them.[82]

Somerville says that hogs were at that time 'kept in considerable numbers' in the county, 'though the flesh does not form a general article of food here.' The main markets were in Leith and Berwick, where swine were sold for victualling ships. The same was true during the 1790s of the fattening trade in the south-west, the main outlets being in Liverpool, Newcastle or the ports of the Clyde, and in this district pig breeding and fattening remained an important and growing industry into the 1840s.[83]

A number of brewers owned farms, and animal feeding would therefore be regarded by them as a logical extension of their main activity. This was specially so at the large country breweries, and even urban brewers owned and ran farms as a sideline.[84] The Tennent family were typical, with their farm on the outskirts of Glasgow: miscellaneous cash accounts for the period 1776-1806 indicate an extensive business in corn, meal, potatoes, dairy cows and pigs, the last no doubt fattened profitably with draff from the Wellpark Brewery.[85]

Agriculture and brewing were therefore linked in a complex cycle of activities— the majority dictated to a lesser or greater extent by the harvest. The prosperity of the Scottish drink industries after the middle of the eighteenth century was the result of subtle and unquantifiable changes in taste throughout a growing and essentially urban population. Yet without the agricultural response, growth would have been impossible, and, for brewing at least, the intimate connexion with the countryside was vital to success.

NOTES

1 Mathias, op.cit. 316, 463.

2 T.S.Ashton, *Economic fluctuations in England 1700-1800* (1959), 6-7.
3 W.Black, *A practical treatise on brewing* (1835), 60-3.
4 SRO, E 905/46, Accompt of Duties under the Management of the Comm. of Excise 1752-53.
5 Mathias, op.cit. 399-401, 435.
6 Data from *Pigot's commercial directory of Scotland 1825-6.*
7 Mackintosh (1914), 115, 129-30; I.Donnachie, *The industrial archaeology of Galloway* (1971), 51-2, 55.
8 J.A.Symon, *Scottish farming: past and present* (1959), 10, 98, 123, 127-9.
9 PP 1821 VIII Report ... on Malt in Scotland, 7-13, 25-30, 34-5, 64-5.
10 J.Handley, *Scottish farming in the eighteenth century* (1953), 145-9.
11 J.Thomson, *GVA Fife* (1800), 386.
12 PP 1821 VIII Report on Malt in Scotland, 25-6.
13 G.Somerville, *GVA East Lothian* (1805), 120.
14 PP 1821 VIII Report on Malt in Scotland, 27.
15 SRO E 905/124, Malt and Beer Excise Revenues 1830-31, see Table 3.8.
16 PP 1821 VIII Report on Malt in Scotland, 34-5.
17 J. Trotter, *GVA West Lothian* (1811), 96.
18 *OSA*, 7, 202; ibid, 13, 6-7, 110-12, 504.
19 PP 1821 VIII, Report on Malt in Scotland, 7-9.
20 *OSA*, 9, 44-5.
21 PP 1803-4 IV, Report on Scotch Barley and Malt, 18-19.
22 G.Keith *GVA Aberdeenshire* (1811), 587; OSA, 11, 471-3.
23 OSA, 5, 8-9, 11; Mackintosh (1914), 115, 129-30.
24 SRO, GD 23/14/198, Bught Papers, Papers re Brewery Co. of Inverness 1771-84; *Pigot's commercial directory of Scotland 1825-6.*
25 *OSA*, 12, 255; J.Sinclair, *GVA Northern Counties* (1795), 65.
26 J.E.Donaldson, *Caithness in the eighteenth century* (1938) describes in detail the barley and grain trade of Caithness; P. Bailey, *Orkney* (1971) has much useful material on agricultural improvement there.
27 *OSA*, 2, 185-6.
28 Ibid, 12, 33.
29 Mathias, op.cit. 390.
30 Ibid, 391.
31 SRO, E 904/3 General accompt for All Duties under the Management of the Comm. of Excise: Malt.
32 PP 1803-4 IV Report on Scotch Barley and Malt, 3-5, 15-17, 20.
33 Mathias, op.cit. 391-2.
34 In PP 1803-4 IV cited above, evidence of Rev. Dr. George Skene Smith indicates that two-thirds of barley cultivated was actually being absorbed by distillers at that period.
35 SRO, E 904/3 Gross Produce of the Revenues of Excise indicates that malt tax represented 23 per cent of total revenue in 1770, but this had fallen to 9 per cent by 1810, largely the result of a massive extension of duties on consumer goods generally.
36 Comparison of data in SRO E 905/46 and E 905/124 shows how much the excise districts had changed between 1750 and 1830. PP 1803-4 IV Report on Scotch Barley and Malt, 88-9 defines the boundaries of the collections in the early 1800s, but even this leads to confusion. Linlithgow is defined as 'the whole of the County of Linlithgow and Stirling, Part of Perthshire, and Part of the County of Edinburgh.' The need for books like A. Bald's *The farmer and corn dealer's assistant* (1807) is a good indication of the problems presented by Scottish weights and measures.
37 *Pigot's commercial directory of Scotland 1825-6.*
38 Mathias, op. cit., 391-2.
39 For Dunbar see *OSA*, 5, 480-1; for Stirling an early example of business activity is John McKellan, Maltster in SRO, RH15/2018; for Elgin see note 7 above.
40 *Pigot's commercial directory of Scotland, 1825-6; NSA Clackmannan*, 49-51; *NSA 8 Stirling*, 20.
41 *Two hundred years of progress: James Aitken & Co Ltd 1740-1940* (1940), 8-11. Mains Maltings still survive and went out of use only recently. They are illustrated in J.Butt, I.Donnachie and J.Hume, *Industrial History: Scotland* (1968), 21.
42 GH 11937/31 Sun CD Series 714518, 26/1/1801; ibid 11937/31 Sun CD Series 699203, 14/2./800.
43 Hamilton (1963), 103-10; R.Mitchison, 'The movements of Scottish corn prices in the seventeenth and eighteenth centuries,' *EcHR* 18 (1965), 278-91.

44   *Pigot's commercial directory of Scotland, 1825-6;* A.Bald, *The farmer and corn dealer's assistant* (1807), 438-9; GVAs for East Lothian, West Lothian, Fife, Aberdeenshire, Banff and Inverness.
45   See for example SRO, RH 15/731 Seq. of Wm. Ainslie, Duns, 1802; RH 15/2048 Sq. of John Irving, Langholm, 1809-11; COS, Currie Dal Seq. R1/18, Archibald Richardson, Newton Douglas, 1799.
46   Tennent Mss. Letter Books.
47   *OSA,* 5, 92-4; 10, 206, 210; 13, 6-7; 14, 13-4, 37-9; 15, 177.
48   *OSA,* 5, 480-1; ibid, 14, 552, 556.
49   *OSA,* 3, 490; ibid, 15, 193; *GVA Fife,* 303; *OSA,* 12, 515.
50   *OSA,* 8, 599; SL, SP 293/14 Pet. of Alloa Brewing Co. and Andrew Roy, Manager, 1815.
51   *OSA,* 8, 468; ibid, 13, 110-12, 504; J.Butt, *Industrial archaeology of Scotland* (1967), 42, 296; Butt, Donnachie & Hume (1968), 15.
52   PP   1803-4   IV   Report   on   Scotch   Barley   and   Malt,   17-34;   *OSA,*   7,   202.
53   J.Lindsay, *The canals of Scotland* (1968), 99-112.
54   *OSA,* 11, 403-4; D. Scouter, *GVA Banff* (1812), 304; SRO, COS, CMS C1/31, Seq, Alex Cowrie, Brewer, Banff, 1809.
55   Clearly this can only be tested by field evidence. The evidence I have gathered from such surveys in Easter Ross, Caithness and Orkney leads to the conclusion that the expansion of cereal farming during the war years 1793-1815 was of considerable magnitude.
56   *OSA,* 10, 165.
57   *Pigot's Commercial directory of Scotland, 1825-6;* PP 1831 VII Report from SC on Use of Molasses in Breweries and Distilleries, 123.
58   Donnachie (1971), 30-1, 184-5; I.Donnachie, *War and economic growth in Britain 1793-1815* (1973), 154-5.
59   Donnachie (1971), 184-7; *OSA,* 1, 361; ibid; 250; ibid, 17, 103.
60   Tennent Mss. Rough Letter Copy Book 1785-9, T.-Sir Wm. Forbes & Co. 14 Aug. 1788 and T.-Patrick Millar & Co. 22 Aug. 1789 are typical.
61   Ibid, T.-J. Hannay 11 Feb. 1786.
62   Ibid, T.-J.Mackenzie & Co 2 Sept. 1786.
63   Ibid, T.-J.Milroy 20 Nov. 1786; T.-J.Beck 20 Nov. 1786.
64   Ibid, T.-J.Carruthers 22 March 1787.
65   Ibid, T.-J.Dunsmore 7 April 1787.
66   Ibid, T.-J.Wilson, Dundee 26 July, 1788. To James Murrison of Leith they write in the same month saying, 'the market is filled with barley and meal from Dumfries and Galloway.'
67   *GVA Roxburgh & Selkirk* (1813), 216; *OSA,* 10, 590.
68   Pigot 1825-6; *OSA,* 14, 13-14; SRO, RH 15/731 Seq. of Wm. Ainslie 1802.
69   *OSA,* 14, 506.
70   *OSA,* 5, 480-1; ibid, 10, 165-6; R.Somerville, *GVA East Lothian,* 124.
71   *OSA,* 5, 40; ibid, 12, 179.
72   PP 1803-4, IV, Report on Scotch Barley and Malt, 20-21.
73   Mathias, op.cit. 399-401.
74   A.Bald, *The farmer and corn dealer's assistant* (1807), 438-42.
75   PP 1821 VIII Report on ... Additional Duty on Malt in Scotland, 7-9.
76   Ibid, 26-30. It took eight days' sailing from East Anglia, according to the evidence of William Berwick, and this was about the same time as grain imported to Leith from the Moray Firth.
77   *OSA,* 7, 22-3, 173, 175; A.I.Dunlop, *The royal burgh of Ayr* (1953), 179.
78   PP 1821 VIII, 28.
79   SRO RH15/2215 J.Wilson & Co. Cash, Day & Account Books, 1740-57.
80   P.Mathias, 'Agriculture and the brewing and distilling industries in the eighteenth century,' *EHR,* 5 (1952).
81   *OSA,* 13, 465; ibid, 14, 556, 625-6; ibid, 16, 14-15.
82   R.Somerville, *GVA East Lothian,* 46-7.
83   *OSA,* 2, 27-8; *NSA 4 Dumfries,* 163. In the parish of Clackmannan 400 cattle were fed with the draff from 8 local breweries and 2 distilleries c1840, according to *NSA 8 Clackmannan,* 49-51.
84   PP 1831 VII, Report from SC on Use of Molasses in Breweries & Distilleries, 69, 79-80, 83. George Dunlop, an East Lothian distiller, said, 'brewers and distillers in the country all wish to have farms.' He himself had large farms and fed 'a great deal of cattle' both on the farms and at the distillery.
85   Tennent Mss. Misc. Cash Accounts 1776-1806.

4

Entrepreneurship and Capital

ENTREPRENEURSHIP, entry to the brewing trade, business organisation and capital structure in the Scottish brewing industry between 1750 and 1850 very much reflected the close relationship between the landed and commercial interests. Although brewing was well established as a formal industry in its own right on the eve of the Industrial Revolution, few brewers, great or small, lost sight of their origins or their informal links with the countryside.

Entrepreneurship and Business Organisation

Many entrepreneurs in Scottish brewing had modest and often humble origins, for the establishment of a small brewery required only nominal capital. A great many brewers undoubtedly started life in related trades, as publicans, innkeepers, victuallers, maltsters, grain merchants, or even as their servants. A cursory glance at the major brewers' business records provides two examples of just this: Robert Tennent started out as a publican in Glasgow, while James Yates, who started a brewery in Edinburgh about 1765, had been a tenant farmer and waggoner with Archibald Campbell of Argyll Brewery there.[1] Family connexions with related trades were always important, and often the accumulated profits of farming, malting, milling or distilling could be used to finance a move into brewing: William Younger's father was a successful farmer at West Linton and helped to establish his son's Edinburgh business in 1749.[2] Yet the origins of all but the most prominent Scottish brewers in the Industrial Revolution period are obscure. The majority appear to have had connexions with either lesser merchanting or with farming. An examination of twenty brewers' testaments and wills registered in the Commissariats of Edinburgh, Linlithgow and Haddington (covering the prominent brewing counties of the Lothians) shows that eighteen had modest landed or business interests before entering the trade, while the remaining two had been innkeepers or ale and porter dealers. William Scott (died 1821), a brewer in Leith, seems typical, for, having started out in life as a general merchant, he turned to brewing after marrying into an East Lothian farming family. Another merchant, Robert Aitken of Fisherrow, near Musselburgh, (died 1818) also became a brewer c1800, no doubt selling his ale and beer to local seamen, fisherfolk and colliers.[3]

Movement within the main primary processing trades might occur at any level, as the survey of capital formation described below makes all too clear. Many men of business in related trades might find themselves in brewing by accident of circumstance, such as a brewer's debt or bankruptcy: so publicans, maltmen and farmers might enter the trade with only limited technical knowledge or skill. Sometimes they would retain the services of the bankrupt brewer as a paid manager. Many brewers, however, entered the trade as apprentices, without having previous connexions with it. Some (the younger sons of farmers) would bring with them a modest amount of capital, others (like the sons of artisans) might have only their strong arm and an eye for a potentially lucrative trade.[4]

Business organisation in the Scottish brewing industry was generally straight-forward, indeed much simpler than the complexity of vested interest might suggest. The majority of businesses were either owned by individual master brewers, or were family and other partnerships. Most country brewers and the majority of smaller urban brewers were owner-occupiers, either brewers by trade, or farmers, merchants, maltsters and others, turned brewers. There were exceptions to this rule, for some country breweries (for example, those in Inverness and Brechin) were large and the risk was spread amongst a group of partners. In a few cases even small breweries were run by a partnership (usually the brewer, joined by local farmers and merchants), the Auchtermuchty Brewing Company being a good example (see Table 29).[5] Most of the larger urban breweries in Edinburgh, Glasgow, Alloa and elsewhere were family businesses or partnerships, begun by an individual brewer. For all, growth came gradually out of profits and if the brewer were successful very large businesses could be built up under family ownership or partnerships. There are numerous examples of especially long-lived and successful family businesses in Scottish brewing: John and Robert Tennent of Glasgow, James Aitken of Falkirk, George Younger and Robert Meiklejohn (both Alloa), Andrew Drybrough and William Younger (both Edinburgh), John Fowler of Prestonpans, and Charles Dudgeon of Dunbar.[6]

The partnership structure and capital (where known) of eight Scottish breweries are shown in Table 29. Three were large city companies, the remainder

Table 29

Partnership Structure 1753-1820

Brewery		Date	Partners	Total Capital (£)
Anderston Brewery Co.	(1)	1763	6	6,000
	(2)	1765	10	10,000
	(3)	1774	10	—
	(4)	1800	4	18,000
Pleasance Brewery Co.	(1)	1809	4	9,000
(Dundee)	(2)	1819	5	9,000
Aberdeen Brewery		1820	6	6,000
Inverness Brewery Co.	(1)	1771	5	1,000
	(2)	1782	3	1,000
Auchtermuchty Brewery Co.		1809	7	500
Brechin Brewery Co.		c1790	2	—
R. McMurdo & Co.		1765	4	—
Carlyle, McKinnel & Co.		1772	5	—
J. White & Sons		c1800	2	—

Sources: SRO, Court of Session Cases; Signet Library, Session Papers.

modest country partnerships, with a capital of £1,000 or less. In all but three of the eight, surviving business records provide much interesting and valuable information on the history and operation of the various partnerships, and also throw some light on management practice (examined in Chapter Five) in Scottish brewing. The Anderston Brewery Company of Glasgow (later variously known as John and William Cunningham and Company, and Robert Cowan and Sons) was one of the largest partnership concerns in Scotland during the Industrial Revolution period. It provides a remarkable example of the bond which united diverse interests in the business of brewing, and, although a Glasgow-based concern, it had partners drawn from the merchant community of both Edinburgh and the west of Scotland. The original partnership was established in 1763, its contract reading as follows:

> It is agreed and finally concluded by and amongst ... John Glassford, William Bogle, Peter Mudoch, merchants in Glasgow, Patrick Millar, merchant in Edinburgh and John and William Cunningham, brewers in Edinburgh, in manner and to the effect following, that is to say, the said partners agree to be in Company and Partnership together in prosecuting and carrying on a joint trade in the business of Brewing Strong Beer, Strong Ale and Small Beer in a Brewhouse and Office-Houses which the said parties have now agreed to erect with all convenient speed near to the town of Anderston, upon that piece of ground belonging to the said partners, and which was lately the property of Robert Finlay, merchant in Glasgow, and in vending and selling the said Ale and Beer; and that for the whole space of 21 years complete and after the 1st August 1763.[7]

Glassford, Bogle, Murdoch and Millar would each hold a 1/6th share, the two Cunningham brothers, 1/6th between them, the remaining 1/6th being held by Robert and John Cowan. The capital was £6,000 and the partners agreed 'that whatever further sums shall be found necessary to carry on the business, shall be borrowed on the joint security of the partners.' There must have been few worries on this point: Glassford, Bogle and Murdoch were successful colonial merchants in Glasgow, while Patrick Millar had established an important merchant and finance house in Edinburgh. All four were later to become significant landowners in the west and south-west of Scotland.[8] The individuals participated in the second partnership of 1765, raising the capital to £10,000, and including Robert and John Cowan (merchants in Bo'ness and Carron), and Thomas Hopkirk, John McCall, James Gordon and James Warroch, all colonial merchants in Glasgow (£1,000 each). The Cunningham brothers were again retained as joint managers. Over the succeeding decade the business grew substantially, the brewing of ales and porters for the domestic and export market proving 'extremely lucrative.' In 1774, management passed to James Warroch when John Cunningham withdrew from the business (William having previously sold out in 1771).[9] The 72 shares in the company (with the 1765 figures in brackets) were held by the following partners:

John Glassford	13	(12)
William Bogle	9	(8)
Peter Murdoch	9	(8)
Thomas Hopkirk	9	(8)

John McCall	9	(8)
John & Robert Cowan	9	(8)
Patrick Millar	5	(4)
James Gordon	5	(4)
James Warroch	4	(3)
John Cunningham	—	(9)

A subsequent partnership resulted in the withdrawal of all but three of the original partners (John Hopkirk, son of Thomas, and the Cowans), while George Munro, son-in-law of Peter Murdoch, joined as fourth partner. The 1800 partnership was to run for 15 years, and with a capital of £18,000 the business had tripled in value since its original establishment. Munro came of another Glasgow merchant family and his share in the Anderston Brewery Company (by then trading under the name of Robert Cowan and Sons) was only one of many industrial interests, including the Shotts Iron Company (associated with Hugh and Robert Baird) and the Banton Coal Company (another Baird enterprise).[10] The Cowans had clearly done very well out of their initial enterprise and investment, for by 1800 their assets in the company were worth £9,000, over and above which John Cowan was made manager for the duration of the new partnership.

The next largest concern in this survey was the partnership of Dundee merchants who established the Pleasance Brewery Company there in 1809. Ebenezer Anderson, a local merchant, and his son James, were joined by two other merchants, William Lindsay and David Jobson Jr (later agent at Forfar for the Dundee Banking Company), the capital being £9,000. Shortly after the concern got underway the elder Anderson died, his son fell into ill-health, and Jobson became insolvent, but despite these adversities the brewery seemed to prosper under its manager, Patrick Millar. The new partnership was formed in 1819 and had a capital of £9,000, Patrick Millar and his son holding three shares, William Lindsay and his son three, and Patrick Scott, a newly assumed partner, three. The contract of copartnership agreed to balance the books annually and to borrow any additional working capital on bonds or bills 'signed by all partners.'[11]

The Aberdeen Brewery Company provides a later, if slightly more informal, example of a brewery partnership, linking the landed interest on the one hand and the commercial on the other. Established in 1820, the North Street Brewery Company of Aberdeen had a capital of £6,000 and six partners: James Milne of Esslemont, William Hay of Craigie and George Hay of Tullihilt (all substantial local farmers); James Muir (an Aberdeen lawyer); Thomas Baird (a coppersmith there); and Thomas Aitken (a brewer). In the original contract of copartnery it was stated that the business was to be managed by a committee of three partners, elected annually at a general meeting. This quorum was 'to have sole and exclusive power of binding the Company in all transactions; subscribing all bonds, Bills and other Writings, in which the Company might be concerned; and acting in all matters.' Here was a striking illustration of the dangers involved in sleeping partnerships lacking stringent articles of agreement and formally designated management. In reality the management of the brewery was left to Aitken and 'such of the partners as had leisure to attend to it.' Yet, on the face of it the partners were well matched. The three country farmers had ample surplus capital and a good knowledge of barley, harvests, and the local grain market; while the lawyer, coppersmith and brewer could contribute financial and technical expertise. Most of the initial working capital was raised 'on Bills and Accommodation Bills,' and three banks, including the Aberdeen Banking Company, were apparently only too anxious to provide loans. Baird, the coppersmith, constructed the equipment and machinery in the brewery. A year after opening, the North Street Brewery was already being described as 'a most important concern'—as it might have remained had not Aitken foolishly obtained personal advances by forging his partners' signatures on promissory notes in his own favour. Aitken, in his way, represents a general business problem—the technical man does not always make a competent or honest manager. Perhaps this fly-by-night partnership was doomed from the outset, merely one example of the tendency for failure to concentrate around infant firms, especially at this later stage in the development of the Scottish brewing industry: a crude operation of the 'last in, first out' rule. By the same token, well-established firms were relatively immune.[12]

The other partnership concerns in this survey were altogether more modest country breweries in which the risk was spread amongst several individuals. Partnerships like those of the Inverness Brewery Company and the Auchtermuchty Brewery Company (see Table 29) do illustrate the point, however, that sophisticated partnerships were not confined to large urban breweries. The Inverness Brewery Company originated in 1771 and was therefore a creation of the important period of expansion in Scottish brewing which preceded the Industrial Revolution—and in this case, accompanied the first wave of agricultural change in the eastern Highlands. A typical country brewery, it was developed by William Scott and William Cuthbert, merchants, Duncan Grant, a lawyer, and William Fraser, tacksman of Kingsmills, all 'gentlemen of property and enterprise,' and had an initial capital of £1,000. They set up what they described as a 'central stock' of £400 to get the brewery started: for 'purchasing Uttensills, Bear, Hopps, Paying the Rents, Maltman, Brewer and Clerks Wages and such other Charges necessary for carrying on the Trade.' James Scott, William's brother, joined as a fifth partner some time after the concern got going. Grant rented a malt barn and erected the brewery. Each partner, according to the articles of agreement, had to 'supervise the company and keep proper books,' so in the early stages no one seems to have been designated as manager. The surviving records provide some insight into the operations of a country brewery partnership: raw materials of barley and malt were obtained locally, generally it would seem from friends of the partners; hops and bottles came from London and Leith in the holds of local shipmaster acquaintances; a local millwright maintained the brewery utensils and machinery. By 1782, when the second partnership was brought into being, the Inverness Brewery Company had a resident manager, John Gilzean, and an annual turnover of about £1,000.[13] The company continued successfully until the mid-1790s when its assets were acquired by a new partnership trading under the name of Imray, Young, Frazer and Company, consisting of three merchants (one of them also agent for the Bank of Scotland in Inverness), two local farmers, a miller, and a brewer.[14]

Strikingly similar in structure was the more modest Auchtermuchty Brewery Company, established at the later (and more commercially dangerous) date of 1809. It consisted of seven local merchants and had a capital of £500, although the partners were committed to providing as much cash as might be needed to set up the brewery. The company immediately obtained a cash credit of £500 from the British Linen Bank, appointed Thomas Adamson as manager and bought 'a considerable quantity of malt and barley ... at high prices.' Inevitably this led to difficulties because the value of the barley and beer stocks fell with prices, and by midsummer 1811 the partners had determined to sell up and cut their losses. Although production was maintained until 1812, this ill-fated and badly run enterprise finally collapsed the following year.[15]

The three remaining partnerships were also country breweries: the Brechin Brewery Company; Robert McMurdo and Company of Dumfries; and John White and Son of Penicuik, Midlothian. All three represented a unity of merchant and other interests. The Brechin Brewery Company, established c1790 by William Gillies and David Dakers, two local merchants, had a long and successful life, soon establishing a wide trade in porter as well as ale.[16] Robert McMurdo and Company of Dumfries was an earlier example of a country brewery partnership established in 1765, and reconstituted in 1772 as Carlyle and McKinnel, with the original manager, John McKinnel of Midglen, as principal shareholder. This later became one of several important malting and brewing businesses in Dumfries and Maxwelltown, the most significant centres of the industry in south-west Scotland.[17] The family partnership of John White and Son was interesting because it was a joint enterprise in cotton, paper making and brewing, as well as having strong family connexions with the distilling industry through marriage to the Haigs. The Whites' Haughhead brewery, near Penicuik, was probably a much larger concern than its £1,500 valuation in 1814-15 would indicate, having not only an extensive trade in the Lothians, but also numerous customers as far afield as Berwickshire, Dumfriesshire and Perthshire.[18]

Capital

'The industrialisation of a predominantly rural society,' writes E.L. Jones, 'will understandably draw where possible on agrarian sources of capital, entrepreneurial talent and technical skill. If these do not originate in agriculture proper, they will come from its penumbra of servicing and processing trades.'[19] On the other hand we should remember clearly the view presented by Mathias that commerce was the most important source of external capital and entrepreneurship in the English brewing industry.[20] These two views are by no means mutually exclusive, and indeed, in the context of the discussion about the financing of primary processing industries in the consumer revolution of the eighteenth century, they are perhaps directly complementary. Certainly, one can assert with confidence that investment in primary processing industries, like malting and brewing, proved an attractive financial proposition to many groups within the emergent Scottish agricultural and commercial community during the latter half of the eighteenth and early part of the nineteenth centuries.[21]

The result was a complex series of inter-relationships and financial interests linking primary producers, financiers, processors and distributors. Farmers, landed gentry, grain merchants, lawyers, industrialists, merchants, banks and excise officers provided for the brewing industry what we would describe as 'external' capital. The brewers, victuallers and innkeepers likewise provided capital from within the industry itself, capital already present when expansion got underway.[22] In addition to these groups, there were other miscellaneous interests, including other primary processors, like millers, bakers and distillers, or groups representing special technical skills, such as coopers, millwrights, coppersmiths and glass bottle makers.

Clearly the landed and farming groups held mutual interests, and often relied heavily on the merchants, lawyers and banks for working capital to develop their estates or advance the cause of agricultural 'improvement.' For these two groups a brewery interest was a logical extension of cereal production, particularly in good barley areas like those of Fife and the Lothians. Grain merchants occupied an important position in the structure, acting as intermediaries between the landed interest and the brewer, and at the same time closely allied with the merchant, legal and banking groups. The others, including the brewers themselves, were linked in mutual self-interest with farmers, grain merchants, and, above all, with the banks. Banks clearly had a critical role and although there is some evidence of direct investment, their function as mobilisers of credit to the brewers was of much greater significance. Complex though this picture of inter-relationships may already appear, it is worth emphasising that important two-way linkages often existed between breweries and most of the other investing groups. Firstly, for example, farmers often became maltsters and brewers (if they did not invest directly in someone else's maltings or brewery) in their own right, while many successful brewers bought land and farms with the profits of their brewery (and often as an extension of brewing, as we have seen).[23] Secondly, at the opposite end of the brewing 'cycle' innkeepers and victuallers soon found a reverse flow of capital from the larger breweries—inns supported by brewers' capital already existed by the closing decades of the eighteenth century.[24] Thirdly, the inter-relationships between the various groups of 'external' and 'internal' investors emphasise above all the subtle but important seasonal cycle of economic activity which linked the farmer, grain merchants, maltster and brewer—a phenomenon characteristic of brewing more than any other consumer industry.

Investment in brewing was seen by the majority of 'external' interests as a logical extension of their main activities (for example, the farmers, grain merchants or innkeepers). For others, such investment would no doubt be regarded much as speculation in any other industrial or commercial enterprise. Yet brewing, like other consumer industries of this period (especially grain milling, leather tanning and whisky distilling), almost certainly represented a safer investment than many manufacturing activities, for example cotton spinning or iron manufacture. Despite the vagaries of seasonal activity, and fluctuations in grain yield and price (which so influenced profit potential), beer and ale were at least assured of an expanding domestic consumer market even in troubled times. The artisan or day-labourer might go without a new cotton shirt in times of hardship—but not his ale! After the 1770s the foreign market for Scottish ales also held potential and this was widely recognised.[25] Obviously there were numerous casualties in the Scottish brewing industry during the years 1780 to 1830, just as in all commercial activities caught up in the maelstrom of an economic revolution. But the casualty rate was probably lower than in other industries and many seem to have survived short-term adversity. Business casualties in Scottish brewing often resulted from a failure to anticipate future trends in grain prices: a brewer able to produce a palatable ale and sensitive to the seasonal turn of the grain market was likely to be successful.

Investment in the Scottish brewing industry was dominated by four main characteristics. Firstly, there was a preponderance of brewers' capital. Secondly, capital migrated to the industry from the landed and merchant interests. Thirdly, the banks were involved in the discounting of bills and the extension of credit to brewers. Fourthly, there was an expansion of the industry on two broad fronts: the emergence of large urban production units (in, for example, Edinburgh, Glasgow and Alloa); and a parallel development until the mid-1820s of numerous country breweries. Table 30 (derived from a survey of brewery insurance valuations, described later in this chapter) shows something of the origins of investment in 120 brewing and related businesses c1795.[26] It can be seen that 75 per cent of total insured capital at that period was represented by persons designated as brewers or maltsters, while 25 per cent of total valuation in this survey was in the hands of principal partners otherwise designated, mainly farmers and merchants. Of this 25 per cent about 10 per cent was composed of miscellaneous groups, including members of the omnipresent legal fraternity, distillers, grain millers and merchants, innkeepers and porter dealers.

Table 30

Designations of Partners of 120 Scottish Breweries c1795

	No. of Firms	Insured Capital (£)	%
Maltster & Brewer	8	10,250	9
Brewer	59	63,550	61
Farmer & Brewer/ Maltster	13	7,800	7
Maltster	20	6,000	5
Merchant	9	13,700	12
Others	11	6,900	6
TOTALS	120	108,200	100

Source: GH, Sun Fire Insurance Office Policies.

A similar picture is provided by an analysis of ten brewery sequestrations from

Court of Session papers during the period 1795 to 1826.[27] This shows the dominance of merchant creditors (certainly a generic category, which must be treated with some caution) and the involvement of other groups (especially country banks, lawyers and farmers) in extending credit to the breweries concerned or discounting bills on the brewers' behalf. Of the ten brewers in this sample, Thomas Monteath and Alexander Hedderwick are typical. Monteath, a country brewer in Stenhousemuir, found himself 'failing in his circumstances' in 1801, his largest debt being to a grain merchant in Dunbar (from whom no doubt he obtained his supplies of East Lothian barley) for just over £100 advanced on security in 1799. Other creditors included John Aitken, the Falkirk brewer, and William Ballantyne, a local farmer. If this is representative of a small country brewer, the Hedderwick sequestration provides a good example of a more extensive urban brewery. Alexander Hedderwick, proprietor of a brewery in the Gorbals, Glasgow (who was also a porter dealer) was declared bankrupt in that specially bad year 1826, owing debts to three major banks that had advanced him credit: the British Linen, the Royal Bank of Scotland, and the Commercial Bank, amounting in all to about £500.[28]

Table 31

Creditors of Ten Random Brewery Sequestrations 1795-1826

Brewer	Date	F	B	V	M	Bk	L
Alexander	1795	-	4	-	2	1	-
Watson	?	-	-	-	2	-	2
Richardson	1799	-	-	-	2	1	-
Henry	1800	-	1	-	3	-	1
Monteath	1801	1	1	-	2	-	-
Cowie	1809	-	-	-	-	4	1
Bowman	1811	2	-	-	-	-	-
Murray	1822	-	-	-	2	-	2
Gellatly	1823	1	1	-	2	-	-
Hedderwick	1826	-	-	1	-	3	-
TOTALS		4	7	1	15	9	6

F - Farmers   M - Merchants   Bk - Banks
B - Brewers   V - Vintners   L - Lawyers
Source: SRO, Court of Session Records.

If the evidence of the insurance valuations is to be believed, internal capital dominated the Scottish brewing industry in the mid-1790s, although the figures in Table 30 give us little indication of just how much of this capital was in reality derived from 'external' sources. Many of the firms were probably recent in origin and this must have been particularly true of the majority of small, country breweries (for example, Andrew Beveridge of Pathhead in Fife and William Johnston of Kirkcudbright), which usually derived investment and working capital on bills or bonds from local merchants, farmers or country banks. However, several of the firms included in this group were old-established, especially important being the larger businesses, like Youngers (Edinburgh), Cowans of Anderston

(Glasgow) and Tennents (also Glasgow). Charles Addison's brewery in Bo'ness was one of the largest in Scotland, having fixed a capital valuation of £3,000 (and stock worth nearly £4,000 on hand), making a total value far in excess of most contemporary urban breweries, even in Edinburgh and Glasgow.[29] But the majority of self-financed businesses were small. The Scottish brewing industry was thus dominated (at least in numerical terms) by country brewers who had invested their modest savings of a few hundred pounds to buy and equip a simple brewhouse. A detailed analysis of the size and structure of the Scottish brewing industry is provided later in this chapter.

Perhaps the most significant of all external groups financing the rise of the Scottish brewing industry during the late eighteenth century was the general merchant community. Of the 120 brewers in the capital valuation survey described here, only nine were merchants in their own right, representing 12 per cent of total valuation. Yet an examination of the business records of many brewery firms in the period 1770 to 1830 shows much more clearly the dominance of this important and influential group. Sequestration processes are particularly useful in identifying the merchant interest, as already indicated by the data in Table 31. Merchant involvement is omnipresent at all levels, from the large, urban brewery partnership to the modest country brewery. The former is well represented by Robert Stein and Company of Canongate, Edinburgh, whose complex business affairs were revealed in bankruptcy proceedings during 1819.[30] Stein and his brother ran a large brewery (valued at over £5000) with a widespread trade, including substantial interests in London (the stock held there was worth £2000). A number of influential Edinburgh, Leith and London merchants had advanced credit to the company, including John Balfour and Company of Leith and William Wilson of London (formerly a Scottish ironmaster). At a humbler level was Thomas Henry of Montrose, who found himself in difficulties some years earlier in 1800, 'owing to various losses and misfortunes in trade.' Three local merchants had invested in his brewery, the sum totalling around £300. Here are only two of the many instances of merchant involvement, either directly or indirectly in brewing. There can be no question that merchants, more than any other group, were aware of the potential of consumer industries like brewing, and their enthusiasm can often be seen as a natural development of existing interests.

Investment in primary processing industries, in mining, quarrying and transport, was seen by most landed gentlemen and superior farmers as a logical extension of agricultural and estate 'improvement.'[31] Many of the more enlightened or astute gentry (and it was generally they who were most interested in economic development) saw in industries like grain milling, tanning and leatherworking, distilling and brewing, the obvious opportunity further to increase profits from the animal and arable products of their estates. Instead of marketing high bulk and relatively low value produce, they could take even greater advantage of fast expanding demand for flour, meal, leather, whisky and beer. Moreover, in the economic environment of late eighteenth century Scotland, where regional, rural-based markets were only just beginning to break down, the average estate with its adjacent agrarian or industrial village had to be relatively self-sufficient. So in a dual sense it was very much in the interest of the gentry to encourage primary processing activities, because the expanding local population (often in planned, estate villages) provided a ready-made market—quite apart from other external areas of demand.

Landowners building or financing breweries in their own planned industrial or agricultural villages often did so in the interests of good order and improved efficiency. There are many examples of gentry encouraging the development of breweries to combat spirit drinking amongst the local working population. James Murray of Broughton and Cally did this in 1784 at the cotton spinning village of Gatehouse-of-Fleet in Galloway, and indeed his interest in brewing and tanning actually encouraged the development of other processing and manufacturing activities. George and Alexander Ross established a large brewery c1790 in the seafaring, fishing and textile centre of Cromarty, Easter Ross 'in order that the inhabitants and manufacturers might be supplied with beer.'[32] Many similar instances elsewhere in Scotland could be cited, particularly the establishment of local country breweries in planned villages.[33] Farmers, especially those near the larger breweries of the Lothians, Fife and Stirlingshire, often had more than a financial interest (either directly or through middlemen grain merchants) in brewing. A significant trade in brewery waste (draff) had existed since the middle of the century and this was starting to develop into a substantial business by the 1780s. The rapid growth of this activity in the closing decades of the eighteenth century was yet another indicator of rising urban demand for foodstuffs: it strengthened still further the already close links between maltster, brewer, land-owner and farmer.

There are numerous examples of landed and farming investment in brewing in the years after 1760. We have seen the example of the North Street Brewery Company of Aberdeen, while a similar, if earlier rural example from Perthshire was Thomas Smyth of Alyth, who found himself 'in distressed circumstances' in 1777, despite cash advances and bills of credit from no fewer than eight local farmers.[34] William Brown, a maltster in the important malting town of Falkirk, who 'failed in his credit and circumstances' during 1822, was also typical. With his two brothers (a surgeon and a lawyer) he had until that time successfully pursued diverse business interests, including grain dealing (a major part of his trade), malting and brewing, as well as running the large farm of Broomage Mains near Falkirk.[35]

Another group closely associated with both the land and primary processing were corn or grain merchants—the intermediaries between farmer and brewer. The trade in grain (and especially oats and barley) was of very great importance in the Scottish economy during the latter half of the eighteenth and early part of the nineteenth centuries, and grain merchants were a highly influential business group. They seem to have invested equally in the land itself and in primary processing industries using grain as their basic raw material, such as milling, malting, distilling or brewing. Although it is often difficult to differentiate grain merchants from other more general merchants, there can be little doubt that many breweries in Scotland were partly financed by this group, particularly those located near the main centres of the grain trade in Edinburgh/Leith, Dunbar, Haddington, Dundee, Montrose, Aberdeen, Glasgow and Kilmarnock.[36] Many brewers were themselves heavily involved in the grain trade: as we saw in Chapter Three, the Letter Books of the leading Glasgow brewer, J. and R. Tennent, are full of correspondence with farmers and grain merchants in Dumfries and Galloway; and a local rival, Robert Cowan and Son, also carried on a considerable grain trade in the west of Scotland. Both no doubt saw their dealings in grain, meal and flour as a logical and profitable extension of their main business of brewing.[37]

The interest of the legal profession in business investment occasions little surprise in the context of late eighteenth century Scotland. The law courts and lawyers played a significant role in the Scottish business world, which had a high respect for the law. Recourse to the courts was very often the traditional solution when a business faced some adversity or perhaps even bankruptcy. Lawyers were therefore well versed in the law as it related to business (in any case very favourable), and the laws of excise (which became an increasing burden to consumer industries before and during the Napoleonic Wars). Many lawyers were thus familiar with aspects of the legal, business, commercial and banking worlds, and had access to clients' funds. Apart from this, successful lawyers often invested in land and agriculture, buying estates and becoming landed proprietors in their own right. They therefore shared with the landed gentry an interest in raising rents and profits and investing surplus funds in potentially attractive industries like brewing.[38]

It was traditional for well-to-do and successful lawyers and accountants to seek the local agency of one of the chartered banks or to become secretary or treasurer of a private or country bank. This gave them positions of unparalleled power in the community, with control over the disbursement of loans and the discounting of bills for local farmers, merchants and businessmen.[39] Obviously, many acted in their own interests: William Wilkie, lawyer and accountant in Haddington, who was local agent for the Bank of Scotland there, had substantial personal investments in the East Lothian brewing and malting trade. He held a one-third share in the Dunbar brewery concern of Henry and William Knox (sequestered 1789) and used his influence to discount bills in its favour through the Bank of Scotland's head office in Edinburgh and the Haddington branch. Similarly, Duncan Grant, writer in Inverness, 'entered into co-partnery of Trade in the Brewery way' with two local merchants and a grain miller from Kingsmills, Inverness, to establish the Inverness Brewery Company in 1771. Grant was no sleeping partner: not only did he supervise the erection of the maltings and a brewhouse, but also undertook active part-time management of the day-to-day business.[40]

If any group of investors were in a position to realise the potential of the drink industries in Scotland during the Industrial Revolution, it was the customs and excise men. Their financial participation in malting and brewing should therefore occasion little surprise, for they had an intimate working knowledge of brewing technology, the business of the brewery, and the levels of taxation on malt, ale and beer, and finally methods of tax evasion! It is naturally very difficult to measure the extent of participation, but it is probably safe to assume that many former excise officials invested in brewing under the guise of innkeeper, merchant or farmer—occupations generally favoured by retired officers. One major Scottish firm at least was founded by a retired exciseman, William Younger, who established his Abbey Brewery just beyond the grounds of Holyrood Abbey in 1749.[41]

Finally, the participation of the chartered banks and later of private (or country) banks in the financing of primary processing industries in Scotland between 1770 and 1830 was simply a natural extension of their interest in agrarian and estate improvement. If the evidence of bankruptcy proceedings in the Court of Session is to be relied upon, banks had a considerable interest in making credit available to breweries. The standard means were the extension of bonds, cash-credits, or the discounting of bills. Table 32 shows a list of banks associated with the breweries during the period 1786-1828 (with amounts advanced on bills, bonds or cash credits where known), derived from business sequestrations and other sources. As the table shows, the major contemporary chartered or commercial banks, including the Royal Bank of Scotland, the British Linen Company and the Commercial Bank of Scotland had made advances to many of the 21 firms surveyed here. The breakdown of loans or discounts between the major and country banks is shown in Table 33.

Of the various forms of bank credit, bill discounts dominate the sample: brewers generally wanted credit, not loan capital. The largest bank debtors here are Robert Stein and Company, a prominent Edinburgh brewer, who owed the Commercial Bank and the British Linen Company a total of £3,750 (mostly advances and accommodation bills) in 1819; and John White and Son (paper makers at Eskmills, Dalkeith and brewers at Haughhead, both in Midlothian), whose creditors included the Royal Bank of Scotland and the Commercial Bank—

Brewer	Town	Type of Credit	Amount Loaned or Discounted (£)	Source
Thomas Low	Auchterarder	Bills	—	CM Seq L 1/14
John Alexander	Aberdour	Bills	200	CD Seq A 1/12
James Scott	Kincardine	CC	150	SP 387/28
Archibald Richardson	Newton Douglas	Bills	900	CD Seq R 1/18
Peter Leslie	Edinburgh	—	500	RH 15/766
William Younger	Edinburgh	Bills	800	Younger Mss
Robert Allan & James Dundas	—	—	—	SP 477/43 & 44
Alexander Cowie	Banff	Bond	300	CM Seq C 1/31
Auchtermuchty Brewing Co.	Auchtermuchty	CC	500	SP 628/26
John Irving	Langholm	Bill	200	RH 15/2048
Archibald Colquhoun	Falkirk/London	—	700	SP 188/22
Edward Robertson	Edinburgh	—	—	SP 262/20
John White & Son	Dalkeith	Bills	3000	RH 15/803
Inverness Brewery Co.	Inverness	—	—	SP 510/46
Robert Stein & Co.	Edinburgh	Bonds/Bills	3750	RH 15/780
J. & R. Tennent	Glasgow	Bills	600	Tennent Mss
Aberdeen Brewery Co.	Aberdeen	Bills	1000	UP ID A 8/7
A. Hedderwick	Glasgow	Bills	500	CM Seq H 2/7
John Kirk	Edinburgh	Bills	700	RH 15//1332
James Eadie				
John Fairweather	Arbroath	—	600	RH 15/355-7

Table 32

Scottish Banks and Breweries 1786-1828

Date	Bank(s)	Brewer	Town
1786	Bank of Scotland (Perth Ag.)	Thomas Low	Auchterarder
1795	British Linen Co/Leith Banking Co	John Alexander	Aberdour
1798	Paisley Banking Co	James Scott	Kincardine
1799	Bank of Scotland (Wigtown Ag.)	Archibald Richardson	Newton Douglas
1802	Bank of Scotland/Sir Wm Forbes & Co	Peter Leslie	Edinburgh
1806	Sir Wm Forbes & Co	William Younger	Edinburgh
1807	Stirling Banking Co	Robert Allan & James Dundas	—
1809	Aberdeen Banking Co	Alexander Cowie	Banff
1809	British Linen Co	Auchtermuchty Brewing Co	Auchtermuchty
1810	Galloway Banking Co	John Irving	Langholm
1811	Bank of Scotland/Cupar Banking Co	Archibald Colquhoun	Falkirk/London
1812	Commercial Bank of Scotland	Edward Robertson	Edinburgh
1814	Royal Bank of Scotland/ Commercial Bank of Scotland	John White & Co	Dalkeith
1818	Bank of Scotland (Inverness Ag.)	Inverness Brewery Co	Inverness
1819	British Linen Co/ Commercial Bank of Scotland	Robert Stein & Co	Edinburgh
1821	Royal Bank/Ship Bank/ Paisley Banking Co	J. & R. Tennent	Glasgow
1822	Bank of Scotland/Commercial Bank/ Aberdeen Banking Co	Aberdeen Brewery Co	Aberdeen
1826	British Linen Co/Royal/ Commercial Bank of Scotland	A. Hedderwick	Glasgow
1826	Fife Banking Co/British Linen Co/ Commercial Bank of Scotland	John Kirk	Edinburgh
1827	Stirling Banking Co	James Eadie	
1826	Dundee Union Bank	John Fairweather	Arbroath

Table 33

Loans or Discounts by Chartered and Private Banks

Bank	No. of Loans etc.	
Bank of Scotland	6	
Commercial Bank of Scotland	6	
British Linen Co	5	
Royal Bank of Scotland	3	(20)
Aberdeen Banking Co	2	
Stirling Banking Co	2	
Sir Wm. Forbes & Co	2	
Paisley Banking Co	2	
Galloway Banking Co	1	
Dundee Union Bank	1	
Colin Dunlop, Houston & Co (A)	1	
Leith Banking Co	1	
Fife Banking Co	1	
Cupar Banking Co	1	(14)
Total	34	

(A) The 'Ship' Bank
Sources: as indicated in Table 32.

both were owed a total of £3,000.[42] Advances by private or country banks were naturally more modest and usually made to local breweries, for example, the Aberdeen Banking Company's £300 advance to Alexander Cowie of Banff, and the £200 credit by the Galloway Banking Company in favour of John Irving, a brewer in the Dumfries woollen textile town of Langholm.[43] What is quite obvious is that chartered and commercial banks in Scotland were just as willing to extend credit or make advances to brewers as their English counterparts, and that private and country banks followed suit with perhaps greater enthusiasm. The evidence presented in Tables 32 and 33 substantially supports this view.[44]

Local loyalties and the encouragement of local enterprise were of paramount consideration, though this was not always true. The Paisley Banking Company, for example, discounted bills for James Scott, farmer, maltster and brewer at Kincardine (Fife). In this particular instance, Scott was singularly unfortunate in his choice of bank—as the bank itself had proved in the selection of its Alloa agent.

The branch there, opened in 1792, had been committed to the care of Alexander Birnie, a local lawyer and 'a man of fair character much employed in the line of his profession,' but who nevertheless 'disappeared suddenly' in 1794 with most of the assets!ced[45] Significantly, the majority of advances or discounts by the larger banks (including firms like Sir William Forbes and Company, Colin Dunlop, Houston and Company and the Dundee Union Bank) would appear to have been facilitated by local agencies—the agent usually being a lawyer or accountant familiar with the commercial and business affairs of town and neighbouring countryside.[46]

Although it is possible to examine in some detail the capital structure of individual firms within the Scottish brewing industry before the mid-nineteenth century, estimates of fixed capital valuation for the industry as a whole in the late eighteenth and early nineteenth centuries must necessarily be speculative. One significant source of information is provided by the diverse and immensely rich legal records of the Court of Session, the majority (but not all) concerned with the affairs of bankrupt firms. There are undoubtedly many pitfalls for the unwary in the use of these sources, for sequestered firms were not necessarily representative of the industry as a whole, despite the fact that the casualty rate (at least in the period 1790-1820) was relatively high. Apart from this obvious bias, litigants were notoriously inarticulate when it came to discussions about capital and management practices, and even where such data are apparently sufficiently detailed to be of value, they must be treated with the usual caution. Nevertheless, the value of legal records in the study of capital formation, entrepreneurship and general commercial affairs must be duly acknowledged. At the very least they provide a useful check on other data sources.[47]

A macro-survey of capital formation in the Scottish brewing trade before 1800 has been made possible by the detailed examination of contemporary insurance policy records. The resulting survey follows closely the methodology described by Dr Stanley Chapman and applied by him to a study of the cotton industry in Britain.[48] As Chapman himself points out, the numerous valuations of firms in the registers of the Sun Fire Office have to be interpreted with some caution, but nevertheless they present a detailed calendar of investment and investors for a limited but critical period at the end of the eighteenth century.[49] The present survey draws on the insurance policy records of 120 Scottish breweries, registered in the Sun Fire Office between 1793 and 1815. The majority of policies are dated 1793-96, and thus provide a significant and detailed profile of at least two-thirds of the Scottish brewing industry during this period. A full tabular statement is provided in Appendix II, giving data on the designation of the insurer (often the principal partner in the case of larger firms or sole proprietor in those of small businesses), fixed capital, stock and total valuation where known.

The total fixed capital valuation (i.e. buildings, equipment and utensils) for 120 firms based on these data is slightly in excess of £50,000 which, as Table 34 shows, results in a 'guesstimate' of £75,000 for the industry as a whole. But if it is assumed that the average brewer undervalued his fixed assets in much the same way as cotton mill masters appear to have done, then this latter figure must be doubled or even trebled to give the gross actual value of fixed capital in Scottish brewing. This results in figures of £150,000 and £225,000 respectively. A sum between £100,000 and £150,000 is as accurate a guess as can be made, given the incomplete nature of the data. An examination of the Sun Fire policies for Scottish cotton mills (a very complete series, as most mills were insured) provided a valuation of around £300,000 (say a total real valuation of £450,000), which affords some measure of comparison with the much less capital-intensive brewing industry.[50]

Table 34

Estimated Valuations of Scottish Brewing Industry c1795

	Fixed Capital (£ 000s)	Total Capital (£ 000s)
A.	50	100
B.	75	150
C.	150	300
D.	225	450

A.	120 firms as per survey
B.	180 firms (i.e. total industry) assuming constant average values.
C.	Value assuming industry half undervalued on policies.
D.	Value assuming industry two-thirds undervalued on policies.

Source: GH, Sun Fire Insurance Office Policies.

Total policy valuation including stock ('that most important variable') for 120 firms based on these data amounts to over £100,000, giving a conservative estimate of £150,000 for the whole industry (180 firms). If we assume, as Butt estimates for the cotton industry, that the insurance policies generally represent half the true value, this results in a fixed value of £150,000 for the industry as a whole, and a corresponding total value of £300,000. Cotton mills, however, were comprehensively insured because of the high fire risk and it bears emphasis that what applied in the cotton industry and in textiles generally was not necessarily true of an industry like brewing, where units were often small and the risk of loss by fire was modest. Although it is necessary in this exercise to gross-up the data in a fairly crude way (as Pollard and Higgins have rightly observed) without much certainty as to how representative the sample is, there can be little doubt that the Sun Fire Office's coverage of Scottish breweries was very impressive.[51] Despite the facts that some lesser Edinburgh and Glasgow breweries are missing, and that the data for some of the major firms (like Tennents and Youngers) are less comprehensive than those of minor firms, taken as a whole the information from the policies is of considerable value. The range and distribution of country breweries, from Thurso in the north to Duns in the south, is certainly the most interesting and remarkable feature.

Data from the insurance valuation survey make possible the construction of a detailed profile of the capital and business structure of the Scottish brewing industry. As Tables 35 and 36 show, the Scottish brewing industry was essentially

Table 35

Grouped Frequency Distribution of Scottish Breweries c1800 by Capital Valuation

Valuation (£)	No. of Breweries	Per Cent
0 - 250	63	52.5
251 - 500	27	22.5
501 - 1000	13	11.0
over 1000	14	11.5
No data	3	2.5
Total	120	100.0

Source: GH, Sun Fire Insurance Office Policies.

Table 36

Grouped Frequency Distribution of Scottish Breweries c1800 by Total Valuation

Valuation (£)	No. of Breweries	Per Cent
up to 999	90	75.0
1000 - 1999	13	11.0
2000 - 2999	6	5.0
3000 - 3999	4	3.3
4000 - 4999	2	1.6
5000 and over	2	1.6
No data	3	2.5
Total	120	100.0

Source: GH, Sun Fire Insurance Office Policies.

characterised by small firms, with fixed capital of less than £250, the majority country breweries in market towns, like Dunkeld, Kilmarnock or Lanark.[52] Moreover, 75 per cent of all businesses had a capital of under £500, while the remainder were almost equally divided between those having a capital of £500 - £1,000 and those exceeding £1,000. The figures for total valuation given in Table 36 also emphasise the number of modest firms whose capital equipment and stock together were worth less than £1,000. The large businesses having a capital exceeding £1,000, fourteen in number, represented together nearly half the total valuation for the 120 firms included in the survey (see Table 37). All but three

Table 37

Scottish Brewers with Capital exceeding £1,000 c1795

Brewer	Town	Fixed Capital (£)	
Addison	Bo'ness	3000	
Ainslie	Duns	1500	
Black	Aberdeen	1700	
Blair	Greenock	1800	
Brown	Haddington	2000	
Colquhoun	Falkirk	2600	
Cowan	Glasgow	1250	
Knox	Greenock	1000	
Murray	Edinburgh	1300	
Ramsay	Perth	1250	
Tennent	Glasgow	2000	(E)
Watt	Greenock	1400	
Younger	Edinburgh	1400	(E)
Young	Aberdeen	2400	
Total		24,600	

(E) estimate: probably higher.
Source: GH, Sun Fire Insurance Office Policies.

(those in Duns, Haddington and Bo'ness) were what could be described as strictly 'urban' breweries, and this directly reflects a long-established structural feature of the Scottish brewing industry: the concentration of larger, more capital intensive plants in the old centres of production. The larger firms often had a capital substantially above that of the average business. The largest here, Charles Addison of Bo'ness, had plant and machinery worth £3,195 and stock on hand valued at over £4,000. Another, James Brown of Haddington, had total insured assets of £3,300, including two malt kilns, a threshing mill and a counting house.[53] The average large firm would be a family business or partnership concern valued at slightly less than £2,000, with stock of roughly equivalent worth (though occasionally more). William Ainslie of Duns had a substantial country brewery serving the surrounding Berwickshire farming community, his insured assets in 1802 being as follows:

	£
Dwelling house	380
Household goods	250
Counting house at Clockmiln with bakehouse adjoining	50
Household goods therein	20

Millhouse, brewhouse and small	
beer cellars	900
Stock & utensils therein	300
Kiln	80
Stock & utensils therein	20
Cellar & malt lofts	400
Stock & utensils in cellars	30
Stock & utensils in malt loft	600
Stable with loft over	80
Stock & utensils therein	20
Cottages	30
3 barns & a byre adjoining	40
	3200

These figures are partly confirmed by a valuation of his stock the following year, 1803, when Ainslie was in temporary difficulties and being harrassed for payment by local farmers, merchants and carriers. The stock on hand at the brewery was valued at £1,400, including 450 bushels of malt worth £700, 3000 lbs of hops worth £150 and ale worth nearly £350.[54] Stockholdings in 1802 were worth only £970, probably some indication of seasonal variations in the trade.

The medium-size firm was of two main categories: the smaller had a fixed capital of between £250 and £500 (27 breweries are in this category), with stock in hand worth twice or perhaps three times that valuation (Table 36), the average being worth in total around £1,500 - £2,500, with a fixed capital of £500 - £1,000 and a circulating capital probably double that. The Port Glasgow brewery of James King, Snr was typical of the first category, his brewery, malt barn, kiln, grain lofts and stock being worth £1,300 in 1794; while John Ramsay & Company of Perth provide a good example of the larger business, with an extensive brewhouse, cellars and housing worth over £2,000, including stock.[55]

More than half the firms in the Scottish brewing industry had been established with initial capital of under £250. The average small firm might be worth about £700 or £800, with a stock of barley, malt and beer in hand. Typical was Henry Abercrombie, whose malt barn and brewery at the foot of Mary's Wynd in Stirling (with stock and utensils) was insured with the Sun Fire Office in 1795 for £600. A number of firms within this category in the mid-1790s had considerable growth potential, including, for example, Robert Meiklejohn of Alloa, whose business was worth something less than £750 in 1795. Significantly, many of these modest businesses survived the troubled times of high grain prices, more burdensome taxation and greater competition from rival drinks, and the majority were still brewing for local customers as late as 1830.[56]

As this survey makes clear, the initial capital required to establish a brewery was modest. Some brewers setting up business would rent the premises, but if they decided to build for themselves, a small plant could be equipped in the 1790s with a kiln, boiler, wooden mash tun, fermenting vat, cooler, hopback, pipes and pumps for less than £300 (about the same as a small grain mill, or a small mill with half a dozen hand spinning jennies). A much greater proportion of expenses was represented by circulating capital, the stocks of barley, malt, hops, beer and empty barrels in store. Yet, as Mathias points out, the small brewer was often in a better position financially than many other businessmen: he usually bought his barley or malt on credit (two or three months was normal), but mainly sold for cash. Good customers would settle weekly or monthly, and if the brewer were fortunate enough to own an inn or public house he would have an even more certain outlet for his product and a quicker return.[57] Integration with farming also probably helped small country breweries more than was likely with urban breweries in general, because intermediate costs could be reduced.

Quick returns typified most successful breweries, large or small, and the Cash and Day books of Patrick Murison, a brewer in Edinburgh's Canongate, show this to advantage.[58] Only if business expanded to include customers buying by the barrel, larger customers at a distance in the country, or agents and merchants in the export trade, would credit start to become a factor of critical importance. For the judicious country brewer with a modest local trade, these circumstances would hardly ever arise; they would be much more likely to affect the town brewer. It comes as no surprise that many of the larger urban breweries which went to the wall in the period 1790-1825 did so in many cases because country customers (usually merchants, farmers and publicans) themselves failed in their credit.[59] As far as the export trade was concerned, the long-term nature of returns was a major disincentive to many Scottish brewers interested in selling abroad, although many ventured into the trade with success.[60]

Undoubtedly, the balancing of short-term working capital with longer-term profits and income was critical to the success of most breweries, especially the larger ones with a country or export trade. Substantial capital was invested in plants and machinery, and anything up to three times fixed capital was tied up in the stock of malt and unsold beer (particularly 'Export' ales or porters, which were longer in maturing). The latter obviously represented the brewer's prime asset, although the stability of his trade was often a determining factor in assessing his credit worthiness. The fact that fixed capital was often only in seasonal use must have made the provision of trading capital more speculative. If the brewer was just setting up in business and did not have enough capital of his own, friends might finance him or provide security to banks, grain merchants and maltsters until he was established. Indeed, the whole credit mechanism depended on security and trust. 'Men beginning business acquire cash credits on giving security,' said Henry Monteith in his evidence to the Select Committee on the Circulation of Promissory Notes in Scotland (1826), adding that 'this affords great security to the accuracy of their conduct, by making the sureties, as well as the banks, spies on their conduct.' If working capital did not derive from personal wealth or brewery profits, then the brewer would resort to the credit facilities open to him to finance malt and hop purchase (especially at harvest time, when he would buy in bulk), to pay wages of clerks and labourers, to repair or extend the plant, or perhaps acquire a public house to widen the market for his product.[61]

The operation of the credit mechanism involved most of the 'external' groups described earlier in this chapter: grain merchants, farmers, accountants, lawyers and banks. A case in point is that of Henry and William Knox, brewers and merchants in Dunbar. The business had been founded c1770 by William Knox, Snr, who built up a prosperous trade and soon after married the sister of a local landowner and wealthy farmer. His two sons, William, Jnr and Henry, were less successful, however, and soon had to resort to seeking credit from sympathetic local sources, including (as we have seen) William Wilkie, the local agent for the Bank of Scotland in Haddington, Charles and John Dudgeon of the Belhaven Brewery in Dunbar, and a cross-section of East Lothian farmers and merchants. Wilkie explained the mechanics of the credit system in a petition to the Court of Session, pointing out there that three main types of bill were involved, mostly redeemable two or three months (though sometimes up to six months) after issue: firstly, bills would be issued to the order of farmers from whom the brewers purchased grain (generally in barley value), which the bank would later discount 'for the accommodation of the farmers who indorsed them'; secondly, there were the bills 'drawn by the company on the purchasers of their malt and ale'; and thirdly, there were accommodation bills ('mostly personal') accepted by friends of individual partners to the order of the company. Simple capital flows to and from the brewers thus linked the fortunes of various vested interests.[62]

The chances of success in brewing depended principally on the price of raw materials and the stability of the brewer's trade. The sensible brewer would realise that although he had little control over prices in the grain market, he could by diligent application build up a substantial outlet for his ales and beers. Before he fell on bad times when grain prices became so inflated during 1799-1800, Patrick Murison, a brewer in North Back of Canongate, Edinburgh had built up a successful business with an annual turnover of nearly £3,000. His brewery produced about 400 barrels of strong ale (worth £5 per barrel) and 200 barrels of table or small beer (worth roughly £4 per barrel), which he sold to the two hundred or so customers on his books, including several innkeepers. He had a small but growing country trade reaching as far as Haddington, Dalkeith and Bo'ness and no doubt hoped to expand further afield. Annual production costs c1795 were £2,500, the main items of expenditure being distributed as follows:

Materials (malt, hops and coal)	49 per cent
Excise (malt and ale)	44 per cent
Wages	7 per cent
	100 per cent

Unit costs were therefore dominated by the price of materials and the level of excise duty, but even in the difficult times of the mid-1790s Murison could reasonably expect between 15 and 20 per cent return on capital.[63] The experience of the Gillies family, country brewers in Brechin, also indicates this sort of rate of return. Colin Gillies, a merchant turned brewer, who started his business in the mid-1780s, had insured assets worth £900 in 1794. Twenty years later the business was worth nearly £5,000 and the founder's son, William, headed a successful partnership brewing porter 'on a great scale' and marketing it in Aberdeen, Edinburgh, and even London.[64] The Ednam brewery of Samuel and Peter Robertson paid similar dividends: the business was worth a mere £600 in 1795, but by 1815 it had grown to rival the breweries of nearby Berwick and would have fetched nearly £4,000 if exposed for sale.[65] All the evidence would seem to indicate that the returns from brewing were considerable, once a business had established a good local trade. High transport costs tended to protect most local monopolies, while demand was more stable and more widespread than for the majority of consumer products. Local loyalties were strong, and an astute brewer could capitalise on this and exert considerable influence over his customers by producing a palatable drink more to their taste than those of his nearest rivals.

NOTES

1 SL, SP 128/17, Pet. of James Yates, 1765; SRO, COS. 1st Div Inglis M 2/27, Maltmen of Glasgow v R.Tennent, 1749.
2 Keir, op.cit. 6-8.
3 SRO, COS, Index to the Testaments of the Commissariat of Edinburgh 1801-29 CC 8/8; Index to the Inventories of Personal Estates of Defuncts in Edinburgh, Haddington and Linlithgow SC 70/1; CC 8/8/8147 f. 47 William Scott; CC 8/8/144 f. 213 Robert Aitken.
4 Mathias, op.cit., 256-7.
5 SL, SP 628/26, Seq. of Auchtermuchty Brewing Co. 1815.
6 Mathias, op.cit. 312-6.
7 SL, SP 273/13, Contract of Copartnership amongst the Anderston Brewery Co. 1763.
8 T.M.Devine, 'Glasgow Colonial merchants and land, 1770-1815', in Ward and Wilson (eds); T.C.Smout (1969), 502-3.
9 SRO, Reg. of Deeds, vol 216, f.802, Anderston Brewery Co. 1774; SP 273 13, Contract of 1774.
10 SL, SP 273/13, Pet. of George Munro, 1812.
11 SRO, COS, ODV Vol 173 f. 360-76, Contract of Copartnery of the Pleasance Brewery Co. Dundee, 4 Feb. 1820.
12 COS, UP, ID A8/7, Aberdeen Brewery Co. v Gray, 1822-3.
13 SRO, GD 23/14/198, Bught Papers, Papers re Brewery Co. of Inverness 1771-84.
14 SL, SP 510/46, Pet. of Alex. Anderson, Banker in Inverness, 1818; *OSA*, 9, 625.
15 SL, SP 628/26, Seq of Auchtermuchty Brewery Co. 1815.
16 G. Robertson, *GVA Kincardine* (1813), 433; SL, SP 283/13, Ans. for Craig & Hunter, Merchants in Leith, 1814.
17 SL, SP 378/88, Pet. of Th. Goldie, Factor to Robert McMurdo & Co. 1797; W. Singer, *GVA Dumfries* (1812), 422-3; Donnachie (1971), 51-2.
18 SRO, RH 15/803, Seq of John White & Son, 1814-17.
19 Jones, 25.
20 Mathias (1959), 255-6; Mathias (1969), 157; Crouzet, 174-5, 177-80.
21 Hamilton, 103-10; Campbell, 68-75.
22 For a discussion of the 'external' and 'internal' sources of capital concept see Crouzet, 164.
23 P.Mathias, 'Agriculture and the brewing and distilling industries in the eighteenth century', *EcHR*. 5 (1952), 249-57.
24 See, for example, *OSA*, 3, 416.
25 SL, SP 128/10, Answers for John Pagan & Co. 1765.
26 Guildhall Library, Sun Fire Insurance Office valuations.
27 SRO, COS, Extracted and Unextracted Processes; those consulted are listed in full in the bibliography.
28 SRO, COS, CM Seq 1/24, T.Monteath, 1801; ibid, CM Seq H 2/7, A.Hedderwick, 1826.
29 GH 11937/44, Sun CD 724928, 14/11/1801.
30 SRO, RH 15/780, Seq R. Stein & Co, 1819.
31 T.C.Smout, 'Scottish landowners and economic growth 1650-1850', *SJPE*, 11 (1964), 218-34.

32 SRO, GD 10/1265, Tack of two fields occupied by the Brewery Co; *OSA*, 12, 255; Sir J.Sinclair, *GVA Northern Counties* (1795), 65.
33 Numerous examples are reported in the *OSA* and *GVAs*.
34 SRO, COS, ID Seq A 8/7, North Street Brewery Co, Aberdeen V Gray, 1822; ibid, ID Seq S 1/5, T.Smyth, 1777.
35 SRO, CD Seq B 1/57, Wm Brown, 1822.
36 *Pigot's Commercial Directory for Scotland, 1825-6.*
37 Tennent Mss. Rough Letter Copy Book 1785-9.
38 R.H.Campbell, 'The law and the joint stock company in Scotland', in Payne (ed).
39 Hamilton, 314-39; A.E.Kerr, *History of banking in Scotland,* 131-3.
40 SL, SP 356/20, Pet. of Wm. Wilkie, 1789; SRO, GD 23/14/198, Papers re Brewery Co. of Inverness.
41 D.Keir, *The Younger centuries* (1951), 9-15.
42 SRO, RH 15/803 Seq of John White & Son, 1814-17; RH 15/780, Seq of R.Stein & Co., 1819.
43 SRO, CM Seq C 1/31, Alex. Cowie, 1809, Pet. of Peter Cameron; RH 15/2048, John Irving, 1809-11.
44 Pressnell, 338-9, 341, 345.
45 SL, SP 387/28, Answers for the Paisley Banking Co. 1798.
46 Younger Mss. provide a good example of credit advances by Sir Wm. Forbes & Co.
47 J. Imrie, 'National archive sources for business history' in Payne (ed), describes the value of such sources in the Scottish context.
48 S.D.Chapman, 'Fixed capital formation in the British cotton industry, 1770-1815,' *EHR,* 23 (1970), 235-66.
49 S.D.Chapman, 'Fixed capital formation in the British cotton manufacturing industry' in Higgins and Pollard (eds), 57.
50 Chapman in Higgins and Pollard (eds), 102-3; see also the discussion following this paper, 115-7.
51 Higgins and Pollard (eds), 9.
52 (a) GH 11937/3 Sun CD 625044, 12/2/1794; (b) GH 11937/4 Sun CD 627369, 28/4/1794; (c) GH 11937/11 Sun CD 648850, 23/11/1794.
53 (a) GH 11937/44 Sun CD 724928, 14/11/1801; (b) GH 11937/8 Sun CD 635505, 26/11/1795.
54 GH 11937/46 Sun CD 729066, 30/1/1802; SRO, RH 15/73/, Seq of Wm Ainslie, 1802, SB, 37.
55 (a) GH 11937/4 Sun CD 623987, 8/2/1794; (b) ibid. Sun CD 613353, 8/2/1793.
56 (a) GH 11973/8 Sun DC 6 38501, 17/2/1795; (b) GH 11937/9 Sun CD 640435, 13/4/1795.
57 Mathias (1959), 253-8.
58 SRO, RH 15/1705 - 23 and 1785, Misc. Cash and Day Books of Patrick Murison, 1786-1800.
59 For example, RH 15/780. Seq. of R.Stein & Co, 1819.
60 Tennent Mss; Younger Mss; SL, SP 128/10, Answers for J.Pagan & Co. 1765.
61 Mathias (1959), 253-8; PP 1826-7 VI Report from SC on Circulation of Promissory Notes in Scotland, 167.
62 SL, SP 356/20, Pet. of Wm Wilkie, 1789.
63 SRO, RH 15/1705-23, Misc. Cash and Day Books of Patrick Murison: 1706, Cash Ledger 1792-5; 1707, Cash Book 1795-7 (with Account of Malt Brewed); 1719, Strong Ale Day Book 1795-6; 1715, Small Beer Day Book 1795.
64 (a) GH 11937/4 Sun CD 625324, 27/2/1794; (b) ibid.11937/111 Sun CD 910016, 22/8/1815.
65 (a) GH 11937/10 Sun CD 644362, 27/7/1795; (b) ibid.11937/111 Sun CD 910449, 21/8/1815.

5

Management and Labour

DESPITE the survival of numerous business records relating to brewing, and voluminous ledgers and letter books giving details of day-to-day transactions, we have very little evidence on management practice and less about conditions and rewards of labour. The business of brewing inevitably involved a combination of skill and muscle, brains and brawn. Yet brewing was fortunate in qualitative terms, for labour requirements divided themselves into two distinct categories: a small number of highly skilled men on the permanent staff, and a body of general labourers. The brewer or his manager would have oversight of operations, while one or more clerks would see to the accounts. Below this level very little evidence has survived about the people employed in breweries, their conditions of work and employment, their pay or their precise functions. Mathias makes the point that 'intermediary grades of semi-skilled men and women, which other industries needed in such a high proportion and amongst whom came the great difficulties of adjustment to factory conditions were conspicuously absent in the breweries,' and, indeed, the majority of unskilled labourers would find themselves undertaking tasks in a brewery akin to those on the farm. So, even at this level, the contact with the countryside was closely — if indirectly — maintained. Relative to other industries, labour costs were low in brewing, and the fewer workers employed needed strength more than skill.[1]

The actual process of brewing itself required great judgement as well as skill, and several related activities around the brewery, like malting, malt grinding, millwrighting and coopering, also called for skilled tradesmen. Different skills were needed by the clerks, for most breweries generated vast and complex accounting procedures.[2] On the other hand, the muscle was provided by general brewery labourers, draymen, hauliers and carters, whose job it was to unload sacks of malt and hops, turn malt in the humid heat of the kiln, load the mash tuns, draw off beer and ale into barrels, and stoke the fires and boilers — in short, all the unskilled work needed to keep a brewery in day-to-day production. The smaller country brewery probably had no more than half a dozen hands: the brewer, his assistant (perhaps his son), a full-time labourer, a drayman, and a couple of men employed only in the brewing season. There are numerous examples of such a structure, and in nearly all cases the brewer would combine his role with that of bookkeeper. If he could produce a palatable ale acceptable to the locality and at the same time keep a careful eye on grain prices, his accounts and his stock, he would undoubtedly prove successful. What held for the modest country enterprise was equally true of the larger urban partnership.

This chapter reviews firstly something of the origins and characteristics of management in the Scottish brewing industry during the pre-1850 period, and the problems of management associated with the running of a brewery in Scotland during the late eighteenth and early nineteenth centuries, when the first consumer revolution presented as many pitfalls as it did possibilities. Secondly, it examines the limited information available on labour in Scottish brewing, the workers' tasks, conditions and rewards. Due to the limitations placed on this enquiry by the lack of relevant source material, the picture which emerges is less full than could have been hoped. Much more information exists on management practice and labour conditions in the other major Scottish drink industry, distilling, primarily because it was much more subject to government scrutiny for revenue purposes. Nevertheless, there is much valuable information in random legal and business records which touches upon management and labour in Scottish brewing before 1850.

Management

General duties of management were common to brewing as to any other industry during the Industrial Revolution: the raising of capital and business; the co-ordination and management of raw materials, labour and transport; the oversight of output and the quality of the product (the latter all-important in the drink industries); and marketing and sales in an increasingly competitive environment, especially where the extension of transport facilities soon broke down old, local monopolies.[3] As in so many other areas of business, these functions of management raised numerous problems for the brewer-entrepreneur. Few of these problems were especially new in an industry which had always maintained close links with its sources of raw materials and its customers, but brewing was certainly among the first to experience the problems created by large-scale production for a mass consumer market. In this regard the English experience described by Mathias had a more modest parallel in the brewing industry north of the Border.[4]

In examining the origins of a managerial class, Pollard wrote that during the Industrial Revolution 'the typical entrepreneur was his own manager.' He was careful to add that the concept of a 'manager' (not very clear even today) had no fixed meaning at the time, nor had a host of related terms such as 'superintendent,' 'overseer' or 'foreman.'[5] Yet in craft industries like brewing things were perhaps more clear-cut, because many brewer-managers would have started out as apprentices in the trade, perhaps accumulating enough capital over the years to start up on their own in later life. The few 'professional' managers in Scottish brewing during the early stages of expansion at the beginning of the Industrial Revolution seem to have been technical men who had risen by their efforts from the 'shop floor.' A few had undoubtedly started out as bookkeepers and clerks, learning enough about the business of brewing to set up their own businesses. In the period before 1850 there is little indication which route to management or ownership was the most important. The technical men tended to dominate in partnership concerns, like those of the Anderston Brewery in Glasgow, the North

Street Brewery in Aberdeen, and the Pleasance Brewery in Dundee—all important urban plants large enough to employ full-time professional brewer-managers.[6] Technical expertise seems to have been of paramount importance in all of the larger family businesses: sons were apprenticed to the business at an early age and often sent south to gain experience of working in an English brewery, generally in Burton-on-Trent or London.

Technical men sometimes came to Scotland from England or Ireland, no doubt attracted by the remuneration offered them by larger Scottish breweries anxious to improve the quality of their product or to produce new drinks like the popular English beverage of porter. The introduction of porter brewing to Scotland was, in fact, a function of migrating skills from the south and of rising incomes amongst the Scottish middle and artisan classes, who were the very mainstay of commercial and business success during the Industrial Revolution years.[7] Perhaps it is no accident that the first major porter brewery in Scotland was established, not in the brewing and financial metropolis of Edinburgh, but in the potentially more dynamic Glasgow. Nathaniel Chivers, a London porter brewer, who had also worked in Dublin (presumably with Guinness), was employed by the large and important Anderston Brewery Company (see Chapter Four for partnership details), to establish porter brewing in 1775. Chivers was engaged on condition that he kept his knowledge to himself, as his agreement shows:

London, September 1775

Messrs Murdoch, Warroch and Company

Gentlemen—Having engaged to impart to you the London method of brewing strong beer, commonly called porter, and in order to give evidence of my knowledge therein, have further engaged to brew such beer at your brewery as shall have the London flavour and keeping qualities, for which purpose you have engaged to pay me £25 st. as my expenses to and from Glasgow, upon condition that I do not impart the art of brewing to any other in your place and neighbourhood, which I have approved; and do hereby covenant and promise, that I will not communicate that art to any but you and your brewing servant, under the penalty of one hundred guineas — N.Chivers.[8]

Chivers ultimately received over £300 from the Anderston Brewery Company and, despite his promise, also taught another Glasgow brewer, John Struthers of Gallowgate, the technique of porter brewing. Later, at the beginning of the nineteenth century, both William Younger of Edinburgh and Robert Meiklejohn of Alloa employed London brewers: about 1806 Younger engaged a porter brewer 'of great ability' who succeeded in producing porter that could reputedly vie with any brought north from the metropolis; while about the same time Robert Ferguson (probably a Scot by origin) was employed at Meiklejohn's Candleriggs Brewery in Alloa and, by introducing London brewing techniques, 'instilled fresh life into the concern.'[9] Judging by the evidence presented in Court of Session cases of the period and from the list of brewers in *Pigot's Commercial Directory of Scotland* for the mid-1820s (see Appendix), many Scottish breweries were either owned or managed by Englishmen. Yet the major breweries which came to dominate the Scottish industry by the middle of the nineteenth century generally remained firmly in the hands of the families that had created and managed them with success over so many years.[10]

During the formative years in the rise of the Scottish brewing industry, non-technical men played a critical role in general entrepreneurship, but there are fewer recorded instances of their rise to management status than among their technical colleagues. Although there is no clearly defined pattern in the host of small, country breweries (where the owner-brewer probably employed a clerk to keep the accounts), the evidence for larger concerns is more positive. Larger, urban breweries (mostly dominated by partnerships) might employ a manager to look to the books and raise business, as well as a full-time brewer-craftsman to supervise the day-to-day operations in the brewhouse. In family firms, whether a large brewery like Tennents' Wellpark plant in Glasgow, or a modest country affair such as Dudgeons' Belhaven brewery at Dunbar, duties of accounting and book-keeping would be shared by the members of the family participating in the business. Often the practical sons became technical brewers, while the more studious looked to the books.[11]

However, most of the recorded examples of clerks or bookkeepers attaining management status occur in country partnerships, such as those of the Dumfries and Auchtermuchty breweries. The Dumfries Brewery of Robert McMurdo and Company provides an early case of the successful bookkeeper rising to management and eventual partnership. John McKinnel of Midglen was employed by the company in 1771 to 'manage their business and keep their cash and books, in the view of his being assumed a partner in the concern.' A year later the partnership structure was revised and McKinnel became a partner in the new concern 'to the extent of/7/20th parts of its stock.' He retained his job as cashier and bookkeeper to the new company and was paid a salary in addition to his share of the profits.[12] The Auchtermuchty Brewing Company, a Fife partnership of local merchants and farmers established in 1809, was managed by one Thomas Adamson. He acted as 'bookkeeper, secretary and cashier,' while David Cation, who apparently could not spell and was a bad writer, superintended the brewing of strong ale and beer for local sale. The difficulties which this company encountered have already been described in Chapter Four, but clearly the problems of coping with high raw material costs and other adverse market factors were not helped by the animosity which so dominated relationships between the bookkeeper turned manager and the technical brewer. After the company ran into difficulties in 1811, apparently through no fault of Adamson, David Cation persuaded the partners to employ him as manager. The result was even more disastrous and within a year the company had fallen on even worse times and despite all efforts eventually succumbed.[13]

Not a few partnership breweries were managed by the members of the copart-nery themselves, a common practice in many Scottish businesses in the late eighteenth and early nineteenth centuries. The Inverness Brewery Company and the North Street Brewery Company of Aberdeen were at first managed by a quorum or committee of partners. They raised any necessary capital, supervised the brewhouse, sought out custom and looked to the books, an arrangement which certainly ensured participation if not efficiency.[14] Most family businesses, like those of the Younger, Tennent and Aitken families, were managed along similar lines, although, as already indicated, the bond of kinship was often a great strength, ensuring continuity of interest in good management and labour relations.

In 1825 about thirty breweries out of a total of 233 in Scotland were family or partnership concerns likely to employ a manager. All but a handful were located in the main brewing centres of Edinburgh, Glasgow, Alloa, Dundee and Aberdeen. For example, of thirteen breweries in Aberdeen, six were probably large enough to boast a professional manager, but only three were so designated in the commercial directory of 1825-26, including the important Gilcomston Brewery where George Emslie was then manager.[15] This situation typified the slow emergence of a distinct managerial class in the Scottish brewing industry, a close parallel to the Irish experience noted by Lynch and Vaizey in their analysis of the Guinness and other breweries in Ireland before 1845.[16] Not until the middle of the nineteenth century were the majority of Scottish breweries large enough to consider departing from the long-established practice of general family or partnership participation in the day-to-day running of the brewery (indeed, William Younger's descendants were until recently very much involved in the management of Scottish and Newcastle Breweries, the well known brewing group, which with Tennent-Caledonian now dominate the Scottish brewing industry). By that time, of course, the long process of business rationalisation in Scottish brewing that was to continue into the twentieth century had already begun, so that the need for professional management in larger, more integrated firms became increasingly more important.

The successful manager in the brewing trade required the same qualities demanded of any businessman active during a consumer revolution, and although he had many advantages over fellow-businessmen in other manufacturing sectors, he was just as exposed to the vagaries of the natural and economic cycle. Firstly, the survival and expansion of his business would depend very much on his ability to gauge the state of the grain market, source of his most vital raw material, barley. Secondly, the success of his product relied heavily on his own judgement of public taste and palate — indifferent or bad beer would clearly command no market. Certainly the majority of brewers who came to financial grief in the period before 1830 were victims of primary product price inflation (especially in the war years 1793-1815) or of associated short-term depressions, such as those in 1810-11, 1816, 1819-20, 1826 and 1829.[17] The brewer buying grain at inflated prices in a year of poor harvest would need plenty of faith in both the quality of his ale and the enthusiasm of his regular customers to drink it at a higher price. If the brewer was unfortunate enough to buy dearer grain than his competitors, he would quickly price himself out of the market unless his product was of a very special character and much in demand.

Many peculiar — but essentially qualitative — problems faced the brewer: he needed a reliable source of top quality raw materials of barley and hops; a good, steady water supply (preferably from a well); clean, well-equipped and well-maintained maltings and a brewhouse; an unskilled but nevertheless reliable labour force; and a steady custom for his product. He could certainly take steps to ensure these, and he had the advantage of being less at the mercy of the market and demand forces than most of his fellows in other manufacturing industries.[18] Yet any close examination of the Scottish brewing industry during the Industrial Revolution period is sufficient to indicate that technical and financial acumen alone did not make a successful brewer: the element of risk and chance was undoubtedly considerable.

Clearly, the brewer's relationship with farmers and grain merchants was of prime importance, and it is no surprise that the interests of all three were, as we have seen, so closely related. The brewer needed to be a good judge of malting barley, and on his judgement alone depended the quality of his products. The farmer or miller turned country brewer, like William Ainslie of Duns, would have many advantages, although he need not necessarily combine technical expertise with financial savoir faire. It is very significant that numerous brewers, both in town and countryside, maintained close connexions with the grain trade, and in many cases ran grain and meal businesses as sidelines to brewing.[19]

Certain managerial functions in Scottish brewing raised (though on a more modest scale) the same complex problems of credit and book-keeping observed by Mathias in the English context, notably the operation of the country trade and the export trade. A closely related problem was that of quality control, for 'keeping beers' had invariably to be better brewed than stuff for immediate and often very local consumption. Other management headaches were heightened if not generated by the distance trade — the maintenance of accounts and the updating of letter and copy books. By its very nature the brewer's trade often involved dealing with numerous customers buying modest quantities of beer or ale, and when clients lived a long way off they were usually more trouble than they were worth. Even if the brewer were fortunate enough to have reliable country customers, there was always the problem of rendering accounts. Like the coastal trade, the country trade was dogged with problems of transport, breakages and spoiled liquor. Good management could only go so far in attempting to lessen the hazards of the country trade.[20]

Some of the hazards of the country trade and the coastwise trade were also common to foreign export. The problems of the foreign-going trade from Scotland in the 1760s were common to most of our period: damage and breakage in shipping, beer and ale spoiled by heat, extended credit to agents and customers at a great distance, and finally having to cope with the mountain of correspondence which all of these potential hazards inevitably presented. Only time and experience could solve these problems, as the following court case so well illustrates.

Two Glasgow merchants, John Pagan and Alexander Wilson, were probably first to enter the ale export trade on any scale during the early 1760s, and in this activity they were associated with William Baird, another merchant and brewer. Before his formal association with Pagan and Wilson, Baird himself had shipped some beer to Boston 'which turned out very well,' and thereafter he joined forces with the others to venture further afield. On 15 March 1762 they shipped 336 gallons of strong ale in 498 dozen bottles packed in 63 casks (valued at £139) for New York, carried in the ship 'Shannon' to Beverley Robertson, a merchant there. But all was not well, for on 21 July Robertson wrote to Pagan with some sad news:

I am sorry to tell you that the ale proves to be in very bad order. Several hogsheads I have sold have been returned, the greater part of the bottles being empty; two or three casks had not a full bottle in them. This I think is owing chiefly to the bad corks, most of the bottles having the corks in them with wax on, and the bottles entirely whole and strong, so that the ale must have worked thro' the corks. A very small proportion of the bottles are broke. For the future I shall only be able to sell by unpacking and delivering the number of dozens out.

Alexander Wilson had a similar experience with Baird's ale in the West Indies. About the same time he shipped 121 dozen bottles in 16 casks to Thomas Baillie, factor in St. Kitts, and 60 dozen bottles in 8 casks to John Hamilton, merchant in Guadeloupe, and much of this turned out badly. 'Many bottles are broken or blown ... and the ale run out,' they wrote in disgust. Apart from loss and damage, there was the problem of credit, always acute in distance trading. Pagan, Wilson and Baird apparently gave an allowance in price to their foreign agents 'in proportion to the quantity of beer spoiled.' The Lord of Session in his judgement gave remarkably sensible advice to exporting brewers, saying, 'ale intended for the American market must be of a particular quality; it is not enough that it is of a quality fit for home use, it must be duly flattened in itself and corked in its package.' He continued in more general terms:

Ale or beer intended for exportation to hotter climates than those of Britain, must be what brewers call *flattened*; it must be kept so long until the seeds of fermentation are dead otherwise it will ferment, and burst the bottles, or make the corks fly, or ooze thro' the corks, if the corks are of a poor substance or carelessly driven in.

His conclusion was that 'an infant branch of business in this country' might well be checked if Scottish brewers and exporting merchants continued to be so careless — even allowing for natural vagaries.[21]

John and Robert Tennent, the Glasgow brewers, shared a similar experience of the export trade even in the 1830s, although they were more persistent and found it to their profit. By that period they had a widespread foreign market with outlets in the United States (mainly New Orleans, the great cotton port of the South), the West Indies, South America and the East Indies. A mass of correspondence in their rough Letter Books shows the considerable hazards of the trade: heavy breakages, shipping difficulties, troublesome agents and problems with payment. During the crisis of 1837 there is a flurry of correspondence with agents in New Orleans and the West Indies; to Holmes and Mills, their agents in New Orleans, they write on 15 April:

Great distress has prevailed in this country in consequence of the great fall in Cotton and other Produce, many American Bills have been returned.

To George Freer in Jamaica, in a letter dated 13 June, they write that 'the banks have become exceedingly stingy in discounting bills ... and have told us we must *diminish* our business to shorten the credits.' Yet despite such problems Tennents built up a substantial foreign trade during the late thirties and forties, and by mid-century were one of the major Scottish export brewers with an Empire-wide market for their 'India' and 'Export' ales.[22]

Accounting procedures in most breweries were complex. They would generally be carried on in the counting house (probably located above the pend or close leading to the brewery forecourt) — the realm of the manager and his clerks. The counting house was the hub of the enterprise, no matter how modest, and here one might find the brewer's clerk and his apprentice hard at work on the massive ledgers and account books, transferring figures and entries from Day Books and Cash Books. The range of account books which even a country brewery might possess was formidable. Here is a list of books presented to the trustees on the sequestered estate of William Ainslie, brewer at Duns, who was declared bankrupt in 1802, a casualty of fluctuating primary product prices during the Napoleonic War:

1 Day Book 1793-95
1 Day Book 1795-97
1 Day Book 1799-1801
1 Day Book 1801-02

1 Petty Ledger for Ale 1797-99
1 Petty Ledger for Ale 1799-1802

1 Large Ledger 1793-95
1 Large Ledger 1795-97
1 Large Ledger 1797-1802

1 Cash Book 1793-97
1 Cash Book for Ale Alone 1797-1802

1 Bread Day Book 1801-02
1 Bread Cash Book 1801-02
1 Bread Ledger 1801-02
1 Private Cash Book 1797-1802
8 Miscellaneous Books and Memoranda[23]

This was not atypical, for in the period 1786 to 1800 Patrick Murison, the Edinburgh brewer, generated no fewer than nineteen massive cash, day and account books, containing a mass of detail about his day-to-day operations. Here there is a vast range of data about malt made, small beer and strong ale brewed, barley purchases, and details of nearly 220 customers in Edinburgh and surrounding districts.[24]

An analysis of the surviving business records of J. and R. Tennent, the foremost Glasgow brewers, provides an insight into the management of a brewery in the period 1780 to 1830. Tennents was an old-established family firm managed by a succession of master-brewers, who, by the closing decades of the eighteenth century, had diversified from brewing and innkeeping into farming, grain dealing and shipping. Even in the air-conditioned atmosphere of the computer and data department of the modern brewery at Wellpark, there is still a heavy odour of domesticity mingled with ledgers and letter books. Here we find all the random evidence of day-to-day activity and decision-making necessary to keep a brewery in business: letters to farmers and grain dealers in Dumfries and Galloway enquiring about the harvest; memoranda about shipping and problems of credit in the export trade; letters about the family farms and other personal business. Numerous random account books show an extensive home market in the west of Scotland, and, by the 1830s, a growing export trade through Glasgow and Liverpool, mainly to North and South America. Above all, there emerges the fact that, like any other older Scottish family firms, Tennents were particularly long-lived and successful.[25] Even in the face of external adversities and internal family disputes, most were fortunate enough to produce able individuals who rescued them from misfortune or even extinction. Family control and continuity in brewing were certainly greatly helped by the specialised craft tradition surrounding their product, which demanded unbroken fidelity to public taste rather than radical change. Even in the mid-nineteenth century the brewers' craft presented a tight-knit and relatively exclusive group.

As evidence in surviving business records testifies, many professional brewers and their managers did well by their efforts. When the Anderston Brewery was established in 1763, John and William Cunningham, brewers in Edinburgh, were appointed joint managers of the concern at a salary of £150 per annum, with a house and 'coal, candle, and strong beer for their families' use.' They had to agree to give up their own business and keep regular books showing the state of the brewery affairs, and in return would receive above their salaries a payment on sales varying from 4 to 6 per cent. Although William later resigned, brother John stayed on as joint manager with James Warroch, and such was the success of the enterprise under their direction that when John sold out his share of the business in 1774 he received £1,700.[26] Similarly successful was Andrew Roy, manager of the Alloa Brewing Company, which developed into a substantial concern in the difficult years after 1811, and by 1825 was a close rival to both the Younger and Meiklejohn breweries in that important centre of the trade. John Gilzean, who became manager of the Inverness Brewery Company about 1780 at the modest salary of £30 per annum, also ended up as a partner in the business. Managing partners sometimes enjoyed substantial incomes — and in the Scottish brewing industry professional management and ownership never really became separated until the latter half of the nineteenth century.[27]

The fruits of successful business management in brewing are just as evident as the failures. Charles Addison of Bo'ness had household goods, furniture, linens, china, glass, prints and pictures worth nearly £1,500 in a fine residence overlooking the River Forth.[28] Henry Bardner, the Alloa lawyer turned brewer and maltster, invested the substantial profits of his business in estates which he acquired in 1805, and it was his enthusiasm for agricultural improvement which brought him to near bankruptcy some years later in 1827. He bought the Saline estate for £9,000 and invested a further £4,000 in enclosures, fences, drains, plantations and the construction of a fine house. His library contained an impressive range of books reflecting interests wider than the law and brewing, although on these and other related subjects the collection was comprehensive, including Reynoldson *On Malting*, Tuck's *Brewers' Guide*, the *Abridged Excise Statutes*, *Pigot's Commercial Directory*, and the *Farmers' Magazine*.[29] Even the country brewer could expect just rewards: William Ainslie of Duns could afford a pleasant dwelling house worth £400, and Thomas Littlejohn of Stirling one valued at £300.[30]

Labour

Quite understandably we know far more about the brewers and even the clerks and bookkeepers than we do about the day-labourers and draymen. The latter lived in a world of sacks, shovels, barrels, carts and horses, and no business archives can convey much about the day-to-day mechanics of brewing or the working conditions of the ordinary labourer. As Mathias has indicated in the context of the English brewing industry, little is known about wage rates (or indeed most running costs) or continuity of employment. A search of the major business records of firms like John and Robert Tennent and William Younger and Company (together with the later Edinburgh firm of William McEwan and Company) has sadly provided little evidence. If wage books were kept by these and other more modest brewers before 1850, they must have been lost or destroyed — a fact which again emphasises Mathias's point about the relative insignificance of labour costs in brewing.[31]

As indicated in Chapter Three, the relationship of the brewing industry to the countryside was always close, and what was true of raw materials, entrepreneurship, capital and management also held for labour. Many brewery labourers (like fellow-workers in other primary processing trades) had probably drifted into the town from the countryside, with which they might retain close contact through relatives or former employers. Brewing being a seasonal activity, labourers might be laid off from the late spring to early autumn and most workers in country breweries at least would take on jobs as farm servants or labourers for the summer. The majority certainly seem to have worked in the fields at harvest time, but this was common in many country trades, especially milling and tanning, which also tended to be seasonal.[32]

Although brewing required essentially unskilled men for tasks involving heavy labour, they would need to have a modest knowledge of the processes involved, especially in a smaller brewery. Brewery labourers would therefore be expected to turn their hand to a wide range of tasks in and around the brewery. A workman at a country brewery in Haddington could find himself driving a cart load of barley from a local East Lothian farm to the brewery one day, spend the next in the humid heat of the maltings or malt kiln, and the day following delivering ale to publicans and private customers in the neighbourhood. Flexibility was therefore required of a labourer who may have lacked skill in a particular trade, but whose ability to turn his hand to most jobs made him a very considerable asset to the brewer. Specialisation of labour was a function of increased unit size and production, and was therefore uncommon in all but the large breweries of Edinburgh, Glasgow, Alloa, Greenock, Dundee and Aberdeen much before the beginning of the nineteenth century. Even in such a brewery the unskilled labourer might find himself undertaking a variety of jobs in different parts of the plant.

Breweries did employ some skilled labour: those allotted specific tasks in and around the brewhouse, and related craftsmen like coopers, smiths and millwright-engineers. The unskilled labourer set to turn grain in the kiln might in time become an expert maltster, or the general labourer in the brewhouse might acquire enough skill to rise to brewer's assistant. Coopers were employed to repair casks as well as make them. In most larger breweries the cooperage and its adjoining smithy must have been kept busy throughout the year. Maintenance work and repairs to the wooden casks were at their peak in the summer before the onset of the brewing season.[33] The construction and upkeep of brewery equipment was done by the millwright, and large firms might employ their own mechanic. Some of the élite craftsmen in and around the brewery would be on the same status level as the clerks — and probably remunerated at the same rate.

For the majority of labourers work in the brewery involved long hours and considerable physical effort. In the season, brewing could be virtually a continuous flow process, especially at a large plant, such as those in Edinburgh, Glasgow or Alloa. However, there is no evidence of shift systems being operated in breweries much before the present day. Nor do we have any indication of the hours labourers were expected to work. Yet labour relations seem to have been good in breweries, and this situation was possibly reflected in the lack of trade union organisation before the end of the nineteenth century. Informal relationships between the brewer and his workforce were probably commonplace in smaller breweries, and lower wage costs would encourage a certain tolerance on the brewer's part: free beer for the workers remains a feature of many breweries to this day.[34]

We do not know if loyalty was well rewarded, for although there is some information about wage rates in distilleries at the close of the eighteenth century, little evidence is available for Scottish breweries. Distillery men in Argyll were paid 9s (45p) a week in 1797, while two maltmen, four distillery men and a carter each got 10s (50p) in Blair and Martins' Greenock Distillery. The expenses of running a distillery at Linlithgow about the same period included £25 per annum for 'drams to servants and others,' and no doubt many breweries also relied on the free perks to smooth labour relation problems.[35] Most breweries at least provided tied housing for some of their workforce — generally near the brewhouse. The clerk at Charles Addison's Bo'ness brewery was provided with a house worth nearly £70 per annum in 1801. John Ramsay of Craigie Brewery, Perth, had two lots of servants' quarters: adjoining his malt barns and kiln was a 'servant's room' (presumably for unmarried draymen and apprentices), while behind the brewery was a row of thatched cottages for his married servants. Likewise, John and Robert Tennent had stables and tenement housing for their labourers near the Wellpark Brewery, valued at over £300 in 1811.[36]

The expansion of the brewing industry in Scotland before and during the Industrial Revolution owed much to the craftsman-brewer turned technical manager, and to his colleague, the clerk or bookkeeper who rose to the status of brewer-manager. These men came to play a vital role as the industry developed on more formal lines in the large-scale production units that were becoming increasingly common by the 1780s. Apart from technical and accounting expertise, few other skills were required to run a brewery. Most of the other tasks could be accomplished by general, unskilled labour, and indeed much of the work in the brewery was akin to that carried out on the farm. Even at this level the links between the trade, land and agriculture were irrevocable. As an essentially primary processing industry, the success or failure of brewing at any point in time was governed as much by the vagaries of the harvest as by fluctuations in demand for beer and ale amongst a growing and more affluent population. Any brewer-manager alive to the possibilities presented by this situation stood to gain. Using his craft skill and resources, he could build up a successful business. Although many entrepreneurs succumbed in the process, the balance undoubtedly lay with the more dynamic survivors.

NOTES

1 Mathias (1959), 35-6.

2 Ibid, 28. The main reason for complex account books was the number of small customers and a multitude of orders.

3 S. Pollard, *The genesis of modern management: a study of the Industrial Revolution in Great Britain* (1968 ed.), 14-16.

4 Mathias (1959), 28-37, 102-109.

5 Pollard (1968), 127.

6 SRO, Reg. of Deeds, ODV Vol 216 f. 802, Contract of Copartnery of Anderston Brewery Co. 1774; SL, SP 273/13, Answers for John Cowan & Son 1818; SRO, COS, ID A8/7, Aberdeen Brewery Co. v Wm Gray 1822-23; SRO, Reg. of Deeds, ODV Vol 173 f. 360, Contract of Copartnery of Pleasance Brewery Co., Dundee, 1820.

7 Mathias (1959), 151.

8 'Senex' (R. Reid), *Glasgow: past and present* (1884) vol II, 176-80.

9 Keir, 29-31; *Report of Meiklejohn's centenary 1874* (1875), 7.

10 *Pigot's commercial directory of Scotland 1825-6* lists brewers by town with addresses and managers' names where appropriate. A. Barnard, *Noted breweries of Great Britain and Ireland* (3 vols 1889), gives family histories of the older Scottish brewers, notably the Edinburgh and Alloa Youngers and the Aitkens of Falkirk.

11 I am grateful to Mr G.Bertram of Scottish & Newcastle Breweries, and Mr C.K.Mills of Tennent Caledonian Breweries for their helpful discussion of past business practice. practice.

12 SL, SP 378/88, Pet. of Th. Goldie, Factor to R.McMurdo & Co., Brewers in Dumfries 1797.

13 SL, SP 628/26, Bill of Suspension for David Cation and Michael Henderson v Th. Adamson 1815.

14 SRO, GD 23/14/198 Bught Papers, Papers re Brewery Co. of Inverness 1771-84, Contract of Copartnership 1771; SRO, COS, ID A8/7, Aberdeen Brewery Co. v Wm Gray 1822-3.

15 *Pigot's commercial directory of Scotland 1825-6*. See Appendix for full list.

16 Lynch and Vaizey, 233-6.

17 A.D.Gayer et al, *The growth and fluctuation of the British Economy 1790-1850* (1953), vol I, 58, 110, 172.

18 Mathias (1959), 253-4.

19 SRO, RH 15/731, Seq of Wm Ainslie, 1802.

20 Mathias (1959), 146-8.

21 SL, SP 128/10 Ans. for J. Pagan & Co., mchts in Glasgow and for A. Wilson to the Pet. of W. Baird, mcht and brewer there 1765.

22 Tennent Mss., Rough Letter Copy Book 1834-7.
23 SRO, RH 15/731, Seq. of Wm. Ainslie, Brewer at Duns, 1802, SB, List of Books at Clockmill.
24 SRO, RH 15/1705-23, Business Books of P. Murison 1786-1800.
25 Tennent Mss. Misc. Letter Books; 'Messrs J. & R. Tennent,' *The Mercantile Age*, 10 July 1883.
26 SL, SP 273/13, Pet. of G. Munro, 1812; Ans. for John Cowan & Co., 1818; Contracts of co-partnership, 1763, 1774, 1800.
27 SRO, COS, UP Currie Mack A 5/5, Alloa Brewery Co. v T.Thomson, 1814; ibid, GD 23/14/198, Papers re Brewery Co. of Inverness.
28 GH 11937/44, Sun CD 724928, 14/11/1801.
29 SRO, RH 15/325, Seq of H.Bardner, 1827.
30 GH 11937/46, Sun CD729066, 30/1/1802; GH 11937/17, Sun C 666100, 29/3/1797.
31 Mathias (1959), 35-7.
32 Ashton (1959), 6-7.
33 K.Kilby, *The Cooper and his trade* (1971), 53-60, 148.
34 I am grateful to Ian McDougall, Secretary of the Scottish Labour History Society, for information on trade union activities of brewery workers in the late nineteenth century.
35 PP 1798-9 XI (1st Series), Two Reports from the SC on Distilleries in Scotland, 497-8, 506.
36 Sun Fire Insurance Policies; Tennent Mss., Inventory and Insurance Policies, 1811. Good examples of nineteenth century workers' housing provided by breweries can still be seen at the former Mains Maltings of Aitken & Co and in Holyrood Road, Edinburgh. The former are cottages, the latter tenement housing.

6

Scottish Ales :
Breweries and Brewing to 1850

JUST as brewing was in the vanguard of commercial organisation, entrepreneurship and marketing during the Industrial Revolution, so it was at the forefront of technological change and mass production. The nature of its product and generally expanding demand created the essential climate for technological development and large-scale production during the latter half of the eighteenth century. In this, Scotland shared some of England's experience. Bearing in mind, as Mathias has shown, that many of the developments which took place in Scottish brewing during the Industrial Revolution were owed to a slow northward migration of English skills, this chapter reviews the nature of the industry in Scotland with particular reference to the brewing process.[1] While agreeing fundamentally with Mathias, we should not overlook the fact that Scotland had, after all, a long and independent brewing tradition which pre-dates whisky distilling by many centuries, and that by the eighteenth century, the trade had already evolved many of its own techniques independent of English influence. We examine the actual process of brewing and malting, the brewery site, brewing equipment, brewing techniques and types of beer, and finally, general developments in the period between 1770 and 1850. Our concern is not to prove any distinctive Scottish characteristics, but merely to describe developments in the Scottish context as they relate to this study as a whole.

Before the widespread introduction of standardised mass produced beers in Scotland during the latter half of the nineteenth and early part of the present century there were many local variations in brewing technique and numerous distinctive local brews. These were no doubt of the kind which are now rapidly disappearing from the scene south of the Border, where the survival of country breweries into the twentieth century has been more in evidence than in Scotland. Technological development as much as changing patterns of demand and business rationalisation contributed to the rise of standardised beer and ales in Scotland, but before examining the impact of such developments it would be best to describe the basic brewing process—both at the present and as practised in Scotland before the middle of the nineteenth century. Brewing in Scotland had its own distinctive features, and some of the practices would have been alien to a contemporary English brewer. Yet the basic process was no different and many innovations were, of course, English in origin.

Brewing produces alcoholic beverages by fermentation, modern beers containing from two to seven per cent alcohol. Brewing is essentially a simple flow process, involving the use of large volumes of liquid (water), which are at various times heated and cooled, and to which various quantities of solids (malt, hops etc) are added from time to time. The length of the process depends on several factors, the most critical being the period of maturing of the beer in store: one beer might take as little as a week from brewing to dispatch, another might take perhaps several months. The modern brewing process is illustrated on the flow-diagram in Fig. 3. Selected barley is brought to the maltings (1), where it is converted into

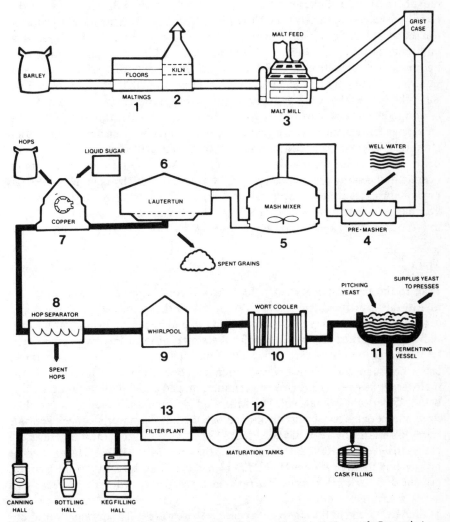

Fig. 3. Flow diagram illustrating modern brewing process. (Scottish & Newcastle Breweries)

malt. The barley is soaked in water, allowed to germinate, at the right time the germination process being stopped by kiln-drying (2). The resulting malt is matured before use in the brewery. There it is milled to crush the grain (3) and then mashed through the pre-masher with well water which has been heated to a pre-determined temperature, usually ranging from 145-155 degrees F. (4). This mash is left to infuse for a period of up to two hours in the mash-mixer (5), after which it is transferred to the lauter tun (6), where the liquid malt extract or 'wort' is washed from the grains by spraying with hot water. The wort is then pumped into coppers (7), where sugar and hops are added and the contents boiled to extract the bitterness and produce the aroma from the specially selected hops. Next, the wort is passed through a hop separator (8), piped to the whirlpools (9) for extraction of excess protein matter, then pumped through a special cooling system (10) into the fermenting vessels (11). Here yeast is added and fermentation starts: in this the yeast acts on the wort and produces alcohol and carbon dioxide. Yeast also multiplies at this stage and shows a large head on top of the fermenting wort. Fermentation is controlled very closely day and night, the yeast head being skimmed off at intervals and passed to yeast presses where it is compressed into a soft cake (after laboratory examination the best yeasts are retained for future brewing, the remainder being sold for commercial use). After three to six days the beer in the fermenting vessels is ready for cask filling or for transfer to maturation tanks (12), where it will condition and mature, then pass through a filter plant (13) before being bottled or canned or filled into kegs. Apart from electronic pumping, heating and cooling and the control of the whole process by computer, modern brewing practice in, for example, the Scottish & Newcastle plant at Holyrood, Edinburgh, differs little from that followed by William Younger when he started his Abbey Brewery on the same spot in 1749.[2]

Malting

Prior to the brewing process, the basic raw material, barley, is converted into malt. Malt is artifically germinated barley, with the germination arrested at a certain point to conserve the saccharine in the budding grain, which, as we have indicated, is turned into alcohol under the action of yeast in fermentation. The type and quality of barley are critical to the maltster: when steeped in water, under controlled conditions, almost every grain must grow. To produce a good malt, the maltster requires 97 - 100 per cent germination, and at the present time anything below 95 per cent is unacceptable. All-round germination is made impossible if the grain is damaged, bruised, skinned or killed in drying or storage. For safe keeping, malting barley is always dried to 12 per cent moisture, the temperature of the grain never exceeding 110 degrees F. or the corns will be killed. The maltster or brewer has to store his barley at 12-13 per cent moisture to ensure uniform growth, and barley in storage is aerated or turned every two or three weeks as a safety measure.[3]

Even by the end of the eighteenth century there were still many local variations in malting technique all over England, and despite the publication of technical manuals and handbooks the process varied very much from maltings to maltings.[4] This was certainly just as true in Scotland, where during the Industrial Revolution period brewers generally made their own malt, either at maltings adjoining the plant or at premises located in the surrounding countryside.[5] Most country breweries, such as those in the Lothians, Fife and Angus, used local barleys and no doubt evolved over the years strictly local practices to produce their own distinctive malts. Only in the large urban breweries of Edinburgh, Glasgow or Alloa using imported English barleys were standard practices likely to develop—and this had almost certainly taken place by the closing decades of the eighteenth century. The four basic stages of the malting process as described by Roberts in *The Scottish Ale Brewer and Practical Maltster* (1837) were, however, common to all localities: namely, steeping, couching, flooring and kiln drying.[6]

Malting, like brewing, was generally practised in the winter months of October to May, because germination, like fermentation, required coolness: the seasonal cycle of the farm was therefore common to both activities.[7] Nor did the similarity with work in the countryside end there, for as W. H. Roberts wrote:

> There is no process in any known manufacture, in which nature so directly operates, as in malting, and the closer we follow her footsteps, the nearer may we hope to arrive at the desired result.[8]

In fact, he says, 'we ought to regard the malt-house as an artificial field.' The first process in malting is steeping, the vessel used being a steep — a square cistern made of wood, and lined with stone or lead. According to excise legislation, it had to be permanently fixed, the sides and ends being straight and at right angles and no deeper than 40 inches. After the barley had been well screened and measured it was either placed in the steep and water run on it, or shot into a water-filled steep. As in brewing, the quality of the water was of critical importance, and in Scottish maltings well water was preferred to any other. The Mains Maltings of James Aitken and Company at Linlithgow were supplied from a well 600 ft. deep, water being pumped to a square iron cistern at the top of the plant.[9] In the steeping process time and temperature were critical variables. The maltster would measure the temperature of both barley and water, so that when they came together in the steep the resulting temperature was between 47 and 50 degrees F. The good, heavy grain would immediately sink to the bottom of the steep, while the refuse and seeds floating to the surface were skimmed off. Otherwise they would add to the volume and consequently increase the duty as well as spoiling the malt. Certain minimum times for steeping were enforced by law (40 hours, see below), but in fact this was usually determined by the type and quality of barley being malted. The average steeping time in Scotland would be about 75 hours with 'good new Scotch barley,' but maltsters using imported English barley could shorten the time to 60 hours. At any rate, the barley was soaked for three to four days, during which time it might be gauged several times by the Excise Officer, as the regulations indicate:

> Every maltster, whether the malting premises be situated in the officers' residence or otherwise, is required by law to give 24 hours' notice in writing, before beginning to wet any corn or grain to be made into malt.
>
> In every such notice must be expressed the day and hour when such grain is intended to be wetted or steeped, under the penalty of £100. But maltsters will not be subject to the last mentioned penalty, for not commencing to set at the hour expressed ... provided the grain be covered before the expiration of three

hours afterwards.

No maltster can legally begin to wet or steep any corn or grain to be made into malt at any other time than between the hours of *eight* in the morning and *two* in the afternoon, under the penalty of £100.

Maltsters are required to keep their corn or grain covered with water for the full space of *forty hours,* under the penalty of £100, and they may keep it covered with water in the cistern so many hours longer as shall be found necessary.[10]

After the required time had elapsed, the water would be drained off and the barley left in the cistern for about half a day to allow the temperature to rise. Then the couching process would begin.

The barley was placed in a large wooden receptacle called a 'couch' or 'couch-frame,' in larger maltings gravity-flow being used to convey the material from one level to the next. Couch-frames had to be constructed in accordance with Excise regulations 'so that the officer may be enabled easily and conveniently to gauge in every part of such couch-frame, the corn or grain contained therein.' Barley might remain in the couch for anything up to a day and a half, at which stage it was gauged by the Exciseman:

All corn or grain emptied into the couch-frame must be laid flat and level by the maltster, and kept and continued so laid for the space of *twenty-six hours* at least. But in cases where the same shall not be gauged, and taken account of by the officer within that time, such corn and grain is to be deemed to be in *couch*, and gauged, and taken account of, *as in couch*, for the space of *thirty hours*...[11]

Very little alteration in appearance would take place in the barley while in the couch, apart from a slight increase in temperature and volume, the real change being brought about in the third process, flooring.

Flooring allows the germination process to proceed at a slower rate by controlling temperature and light, and in this all the skill of the maltster is brought to bear. The heap of barley from the couch-frame was spread over the malting floor (frequently laid with tiles for moisture and cleanliness) to a depth of from 10 to 16 inches, depending on prevailing temperature. After about 24 hours the temperature of the grain began to rise and 'sweating' took place: at this point the maltster would turn the floored grain with wide, wooden shovels. Temperature would be controlled at about 50 degrees F, throughout the duration of the flooring period, which might last anything up to a fortnight, floors being turned as necessary. Great care was clearly necessary and labourers working on the floor would often 'plough' the grain barefoot with their wooden shovels.[12]

So to the final process of kiln-drying the terminated grain. The kiln itself was as distinctive a feature of the maltings as that of the grain mill, with a tapered roof and ventilator (called in Scotland the 'coul') above a kiln floor constructed of perforated tiles or cast iron plates supported on cross-beams of wrought iron. A furnace or fireplace was located in the base, usually fuelled with wood, peat, charcoal or coke, and great care was necessary to avoid too much smoke, which might impair the flavour of the malt:

Malts are dried with several sorts of fuel, as the coke, Welch coal, straw, wood, fern, &c; but the coke is reckoned, by most, to exceed all others for making

Malt of the finest flavour, and of a pale colour, because it sends forth no smoke to affect it ...

There is a difference in what is called coke, the right sort being large pit-coal, charked, or burned, in some measure, to a cinder, till all the sulphur is consumed and evaporated, which is called coke: and this when properly made is the best of all fuels ...[13]

Many Edinburgh maltsters and brewers (and probably their fellows throughout Fife and the Lothians) used coked 'sea-coals' until the end of the eighteenth century. There were four main types of malt: pale, amber, brown, and patent or black, the production of each being regulated again essentially by time and temperature. The following temperatures were used by Scottish maltsters for the various kinds:

	Degrees F
Pale	up to 140
Amber	150-155
Brown	165-170
Patent or Black	about 175

Once the malt had been spread on the kiln floor, drying would begin at a temperature of about 70 degrees F and a kilnman would turn it four or five times a day to ensure even heat. The temperature would then be gradually raised to the required level, the whole process taking up to 90 hours for a pale malt and somewhat longer for the other varieties.[14] Before we follow the malt to the brewery and see its conversion into Scots ale and beer, it would be as well to examine the site, layout and plant of some typical late eighteenth and early nineteenth century breweries.

The Brewery and its Utensils

Given access to adequate supplies of barley and a ready market for beer, the prime requisite in the siting of a brewery was the availability of good water supplies. 'To procure water suitable for brewing,' wrote Roberts, 'is an object of the greatest importance, both with respect to the flavour of the ale, and to the quantity of extract to be obtained from the malt.'[15] This is nowhere better illustrated than in the brewing metropolis of Edinburgh, where all but a handful of breweries at the end of the eighteenth century were located in and around Canongate, Cowgate and Fountainbridge (the name speaks for itself), above a structural trough holding limitless supplies of pure water. The well at Archibald Campbell's Argyll Brewery in the Cowgate was one of the deepest in Edinburgh, stretching down to water at over 750 ft. below ground level.[16] One of the major assets of John and Robert Tennent's Wellpark Brewery in Glasgow was the quality and quantity of its water supply. Within the brewery is a famous well which drives nearly 1,000 ft. into the ground and yields a quality of water remarkable for its purity and its suitability for brewing purposes.[17] Most Scottish brewers used well water, which is generally soft and pure and, therefore, ideal for brewing.

The typical brewery would consist of a series of two-three storey buildings grouped around a courtyard, incorporating the brewhouse, maltings, stores, granary, a cooperage, stables and, if the brewery were large, a counting house or office. An advertisement in the *Edinburgh Evening Courant* of 18 February 1788 provides the following description of a large but compact urban brewery in the Cowgate, Edinburgh:

That large and commodious Brewery and Malting lately belonging to the deceased James Dick, lying at the foot of the College Wynd, fronting the Cowgate and by a large arched entry from the College Wynd; they comprehend a most extensive area of no less than 904 square yards. One of the barns runs from South to North 81 feet by 23 feet broad; and over it there are lofts for Victual of the same dimensions. There is another barn and steep 49 feet by 19 feet. There is also a large Kiln, besides several other buildings of very considerable extent, used as stable and lofts, which might be converted into Malt Barns; and there is also a large area where another steep could be erected if necessary; and the premises are plentifully supplied with water.[18]

At the time there were probably anything up to a dozen similar breweries in Edinburgh, and others on a similar scale elsewhere in Glasgow, Greenock, Alloa, Stirling, Perth and Aberdeen. Such breweries might be valued at anything from £1,000 upwards in the mid-1790s. Most smaller, country breweries would consist of a brewhouse and related offices on a more modest scale, with perhaps a malt barn and kiln adjacent—the whole plant valued at anything from a couple of hundred pounds upwards. Typical of a medium-size country brewery was that of James Hoggart, located in Nungate, Haddington, described as follows in 1801:

	£
His dwelling house	70
Household goods etc.	40
Malt barn and kiln	190
Stock, including grain and utensils	100
Stable	30
Stock and utensils in a loft and	
Brewhouse	200
Brewhouse and cellars	70
	700[19]

Yet no matter the scale of the brewery, the layout of the interior and the plant would be very much the same.

The interior of a small English brewery, from a plate in Alexander Morrice's *A Practical Treatise on Brewing* (1827), is reproduced in Plate 4, and provides a useful starting point for this tour of the brewery.[20] Since brewing is a flow process and gravity an effortless means of conveying liquid or grain from floor to floor, most breweries would be at least two storeys high, and inside, the majority of utensils would be linked one to the other by hoppers and pipes. E.N.Hayman's description of the interior of a brewery is a useful complement to Plate 4:

The liquor back should be placed in a situation sufficiently elevated to command every other part of the brewery. The copper should be next in point of elevation, with the copper back above it, to receive the worts in from the underback ...

The mash tun should be placed at a convenient distance from the copper, in a direction towards the coolers.

The hop back should be placed close to the copper, sufficiently elevated to command the whole of the coolers. Next to the coolers come the working tuns; and these should be placed so elevated that the process of cleansing may be conducted without using a pump.

The coolest part of the premises should be devoted to storehouses. The malt stones should be placed as near the mas tun as possible, so as to obviate the necessity of grinding the malt into sacks; and the malt lofts should closely adjoin the grinding room, as should the hop loft to the copper.[21]

Most of the equipment (like that in most grain mills or tanneries) would therefore be constructed of wood, with copper or lead being used for lining vats or tuns, and for connecting pipes or pumps. Here, as everywhere in the brewery, cleanliness was vital, for as Morrice told his young brewers in the introduction to his *Treatise*, 'if the Fox, or Must get into your Utensils, you will be much troubled to remove the Taint.'[22]

A detailed inventory of the utensils in Robert Stein's Canongate Brewery, Edinburgh, dated 1819, provides some idea of the complexity of plant required to equip and maintain a large brewery, the whole valued at nearly £5,000:

State of Affairs of Robert Stein & Co. Brewers, Edinburgh 1819
Inventory of Brewery Utensils

1 Mash tun
1 Underback with copper pump
3 coppers, 1 of 35 barrels, 1 of 25 barrels, 1 of 13 barrels
1 Cast iron hop back and hair cloth and a spare hair cloth
1 Cast iron cooler, 22 ft. by 18 ft.
1 Wooden cooler, 40 ft. by 13 ft.
6 Fermenting tuns, four of 40 barrels, two of 13 barrels each
2 Stillons, 42 ft. by 2 ft.
1 Stillon, 30 ft. by 2 ft.
22 Stock tuns, one of 70 barrels, two of 70 barrels, nineteen of 13 barrels
Lead pipes communicating with the whole
1 Cast iron metal steep for 24 bolls
1 Wooden steep for 20 bolls
2 Couch-frames
A horse mill for grinding Malt and furnishing Water
2 Horses
2 Drey carts
1 Closed cart
Casks

Adjoining the brewery was a malt barn 'in which there are two cobles (or steeps), one floor and two lofts above the said floor, kiln, haircloth and peathouse ... together with the well, bucket, chain and pulley, and lead pipe from the well to the Brewery.'[23] Pumps were an essential part of brewery equipment, that of Imray, Young and Company at their Inverness plant being of peculiar interest:

The brewery (has) a singular pump, which brings water up from the River Ness to their work, through leaden pipes, over a distance of nearly a quarter of a mile. Pipes run through several of the streets of the town, and the elevation to the loft of the brewery is 28 ft, from whence the pipes take a perpendicular ascent to the top of the brew-house, making the elevation altogether 55 ft. The pump is able to force up 40 hogsheads in a day, when wrought by two men only; but generally, no more than one man is employed.[24]

Given the value of so much of the metalwork in most breweries, it is no surprise to find a coppersmith entering into a brewery partnership, as was the case with Thomas Baird's involvement in the North Street Brewery Company of Aberdeen, founded in 1820. Baird himself actually constructed and installed the plant, carried out the smith work, designed 'an Engine for working the Pumps,' and erected a 'Malt Miln' in the brewery.[25]

The installation of equipment clearly represented a substantial investment on the part of the brewer. In practically all of the Scottish brewery valuations recorded by the Sun Fire Office c1795, fixed capital represented from a third to a half of the total, the remainder being stock (beer, malt, barley etc) on hand.[26] Some of the special machinery required in a medium to large-scale brewery was complex and expensive: Peter Robertson, a brewer at Ednam, near Kelso, had in 1815 a malt mill worth £100 and a threshing machine valued at £90, as well as bottling equipment in his brewhouse; while several of the larger urban breweries were being equipped with steam engines from the beginning of the nineteenth century.[27] Much of the installation seems to have been carried out by millwrights —those versatile craftsmen responsible for so much apparently simple engineering technology during the Industrial Revolution.[28] Yet it is only when one looks at features as simple and straightforward as a country meal mill with its appended kiln, or a farm threshing barn and horsemill, that one can really begin to appreciate the work of these men — and other craftsmen in wood, iron and stone — in the construction of complex plant in cotton spinning mills and integrated mass-production breweries, like that of Robert Stein.

By 1825, when Scotland had a total of 233 breweries, there were perhaps upwards of thirty as big as Stein's in Edinburgh's Canongate, the majority being located in the main brewing centres. By this period, of course, many of the more successful urban brewers had created large businesses and greatly extended their plant. Typical was Archibald Campbell and Company of Argyll Brewery, Cowgate in Edinburgh, whose plant was valued at nearly £6,000 in 1830, and with total assets worth over £10,000. The impressive schedule of the company assets shows the complex range of equipment possessed by a brewery—from the copper worth £90 to the malt shovel valued at a mere 1s 6d.[29] Breweries operated by Youngers, Berwick and Company, the Edinburgh & Leith Brewing Company (who took over Robert Stein's old plant in 1820), Abraham Combe, and Andrew Drybrough (all in Edinburgh), James Aitken and Company (Falkirk), Charles Dudgeon (Dunbar), George Younger and Robert Meiklejohn (both Alloa), and J. and R. Tennent of Glasgow, must all have been on a similar scale—and firms like these had already come to dominate the Scottish brewing industry by the third decade of the nineteenth century.

Scottish Brewing Techniques

W.H.Roberts' *Scottish Ale Brewer and Practical Maltster*, the first edition of which was published in 1837, with subsequent editions in 1846 and 1847, provides the most comprehensive review of Scottish brewing practice before the middle of the nineteenth century. Roberts is at pains to point out in his introduction that techniques of brewing in Scotland had been much influenced by English practice, and points out that he describes the art in Scotland 'more particularly with reference to the system which obtained in former times, when Scotch Ale deservedly held, as it still holds, the first rank amongst fermented liquors of British manufacture.'[30] Having introduced the young brewer to the raw materials of his trade—malts, hops and water—he describes the various brewing processes prevalent in Scotland at the time: grinding or crushing, mashing, sparging, boiling, cooling, fermenting and cleaning. The important differences between English and Scottish practice, he says, are: firstly, in sparging (or sprinkling) instead of mashing a second time, using special equipment fitted to the mash tun; secondly, mashing at a higher temperature; and thirdly, in fermentation at low temperatures rather than high, at least until increased demand for ales forced Scottish brewers to adopt English technique in this regard.[31]

The usual brewhouse was a large three-storey building, entered from the main courtyard. The main processes in brewing began with malt grinding or crushing. The malt mill was usually located near or above the mash tuns: it might be of conventional mill-stones, stone rollers or steel blades, and be driven by horse, water or steam power. Many breweries seem to have had mills driven by horse-power, no doubt because there were always plenty of dray horses around the brewery to harness up to the machine when needed. Grinding with old-fashioned millstones was much favoured by brewers: experience showed that the powdered malt produced by this method resulted in a finer extract from the malt in the mashing process. Rollers, on the other hand, tended merely to crush the malt, producing a flinty rather than a meally texture. Steel mills operated much like a large coffee grinder, and they seem to have been introduced to Scotland about the middle of the eighteenth century, much to the chagrin of millers, who were deprived of considerable business. The steel mill was less efficient but more convenient than either millstones or rollers, and even a small mill could grind six or seven quarters of malt in an hour.[32] In fact, if the malt was coarsely ground, length of time in the masher might well produce as good a result.

The ground malt was then added to water (probably pumped from the brewery well) in a mash tun, and the mashing or infusing process could begin. Temperature here was of critical importance, because, as Roberts observed, 'much of our future success, both in quantity and quality of extraction, depends upon the judicious management of the heat of the liquor for the first mash, as well as our attaining an early and spontaneous fineness in the barrel.'[33] Scottish brewers generally mashed at much higher temperatures than their English counterparts, ranging from 178 - 190 degrees F. With an air temperature of 45 degrees F, the temperature of the liquor in the mash tun would average 180 degrees F. In Scotland the liquor would be run into the mash tun at a higher temperature than required, allowed to cool, and the malt grist added, either run from a hopper above the tun, or simply emptied in from sacks. Mashing would be carried out, as in England, with wooden oars, and the process 'performed with greatest care, until every lump or ball is broken, and the whole uniformly mashed.'[34] When this had been completed (after about 45 minutes to an hour), a bushel or two of grist would be poured on to the liquor, to provide a seal and maintain temperature. Thereafter the tun would be covered up for two or three hours, according to the temperature, and throughout this time (as with so many other processes in the brewery) the use of the thermometer was critical. By the 1830s many of the larger, urban breweries had installed mashing-machines, which reduced labour costs and produced a better extract. After the required time, the brewer would set the tap and allow the wort to run into the under-back, or, in some breweries, the wort copper, considerable skill being required to regulate the flow of liquor from the mash tun. The brewer would naturally watch anxiously the appearance of his wort in the under-back or wort copper, because if his temperature had been right the wort would not only be transparent but also have a fine, light head. Then the next process, sparging, could begin.

Sparging, using specially constructed eqipment, was a process long adopted by Scottish brewers instead of the English technique of second mashing. Sparging would begin almost as soon as the taps were set or 'slacked,' most brewers allowing about a fifth of the wort to run off into the under-back first. The sparger, consisting of a copper tube and receiving cup, is illustrated in Fig. 4. It was simply fitted over the mash tun and used in the following way:

The liquor is run by a shute from the copper (having been pumped up from the under-back) into the receiver, or cup of the sparger, and falls into the cylindrical tube, called the wings or arms, setting it immediately in motion; and, at the same time, flowing through the small holes in a light shower over the mash.

The temperature of the liquor during the sparging process would be maintained at 8 to 12 degrees higher than in mashing, and the machinery could cope with ten to twelve barrels of wort per hour.[35] Roberts indicates that many English brewers adopted the practice of sparging, despite much condemnation by traditional brewers south of the Border. The gravity of the wort, at all stages, would be measured with a saccharometer—that other simple instrument of science used by Scottish brewers in increasing numbers after the beginning of the nineteenth century. When all the wort had been run off into the under-back, pumped up to the copper, sparged and returned to the copper, the brewer might run more pre-heated liquor into the mash tun to brew weak table beer or small beer, a popular drink in Scotland.

Boiling was conducted much as in England, the only major difference being that Scottish brewers tended to boil the worts for a shorter time, ranging from an hour to an hour and a half. Over-boiling could very badly damage the flavour of

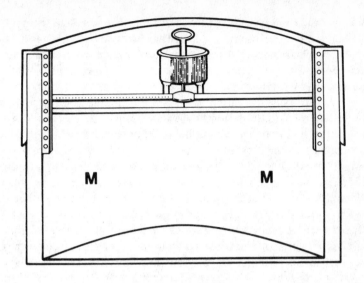

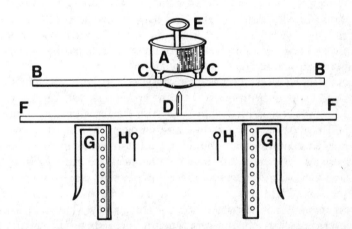

Fig. 4. A. cup or receiver, BB.arms, CC. conduits for supplying the arms, D. pin in the centre of the bar, which runs up the cylinder through the cup to the pivot (a piece of steel placed just below the handle (E), E. handle of sparger, F. bar which is thrown across the mash-turn, GG. grooved iron loops to support the bar, HH. pins which support the bar when in the loops. (Edinburgh University Library)

the ale and ruin the fine aroma imparted by the hops. The most popular hops with brewers in Scotland were from East Kent or Worcestershire, and, with the usual eye for economy, these would be used a second time, like the grist, to flavour small beer. When boiling was completed, the wort would be run from the copper into the hop-back or jack, although breweries in Scotland seldom had a fixed hop-back, preferring to use a moveable wooden receptacle with a temporary bottom of hair-cloth. There was no standard practice in transferring the wort from the copper to the cooler: some brewers would run the worts directly from the copper into the hop-back over the cooler, while others might run them through the back over a tun and then pump them into the cooler. Many Scottish brewers maintained that the impurities which passed through the hop-back or hair-cloth contributed unique properties to Scots ales, acting as a preservative agent in cooling and inducing vigorous fermentation.

The coolers were located at different heights, to allow the worts to flow from one to the other and then to the fermenting vats or tuns. The cooler was a shallow wooden vessel with sides of six to eight inches, there being anything from three to six in a medium-size brewery, placed in the 'most exposed situation' so that the worts 'might have the benefit of a free current of air passing continually over their surface.' In cold weather cooling presented the brewer with few problems and the process could be carried out in six to eight hours. But in hot or muggy weather spontaneous fermentation might occur in the coolers, resulting in what brewers called 'foxed worts,' a reddish mould which would ruin the brew. For this reason strong ale brewers in Scotland confined their operations to the colder months of the year, their coppers being empty from May to October. Artificial cooling devices were being adopted by Scottish brewers after the beginning of the nineteenth century, including coolers made of cast iron and zinc rather than wood, fanners to supply a current of air over the cooling worts, and spirals passed through tanks of cold water, of the kind used by distillers. Robert Stein, the Edinburgh brewer who fell on hard times during 1819, was a pioneer of artifical cooling devices in Scotland, and it is worth noting that his inventory, mentioned earlier, listed a cast iron cooler 22 ft. by 18 ft.[36]

The next stage in production was fermentation, 'a process which is the most difficult of all to conduct properly, the most precarious in its results, but at the same time of the greatest importance.' Scottish fermentation techniques before the 1830s differed quite radically from those employed by English brewers. South of the Border fermentation was generally begun at a high temperature (around 75 degrees F), while brewers in Scotland used temperatures ranging from 44 to 58 degrees, and averaging 50 degrees. These differences in temperature very much affected the time of fermentation: in Scotland it could be anything up to 21 days, the corresponding time in England being five or six days. The quantity of yeast used in a fermentation was also very much influenced by temperature and the season of the year, as well as by the quality of the liquor used for mashing, and the gravity of the worts. With slow fermentation at a temperature of 50 degrees, there would be little motion in the tun for up to twelve hours, and only after forty or fifty hours would the head cover the whole surface. According to Roberts, skimming was rarely carried out in Scotland, except where it was necessary to check a vigorous fermentation. Gravity having been checked throughout fermentation and the process completed, the brewer was in a position to proceed to the last operation in the production of ale or beer, cleaning or clearing.

Here the technique in Scotland again differed substantially from that in England. Instead of being drawn off into casks, the ale would be run off into a vat of similar dimensions to that of the fermenting tun, and it would remain there for anything from 12 to 36 hours before being drawn off. Casks would not be placed in stillions, but merely left upright on the pavement of the brewery cellar or store-room. Scottish brewers rarely made use of isinglass in fining—fining itself being apparently little practised in Scotland.[37] Beers and ales manufactured by the Scottish method could be casked and ready for dispatch from the brewery within forty-eight hours, although strong or export beers would be stored for much longer. Before we examine the varieties of ales and beers made in Scotland before 1850, it may prove worthwhile to finish this tour of the brewery by visiting some of the other departments, notably the cellars, cooperage, and stables.

Most breweries, even modest ones in the country, would require a great deal of storage space for barley, malt, hops, and full and empty barrels. The cellars were certainly an important feature of any brewery producing 'keeping' beers—either strong beer or 'export' beers and porters. Some porter beers manufactured in Scotland might be stored for anything up to six months or a year before sale, although this was perhaps exceptional.[38] It is clear from the insurance policy valuations survey that most breweries held considerable stock, often with the malt or barley stored in the adjacent granary being worth as much as the brewhouse and its utensils. The cellars of Robert Stein's brewery in the Canongate, Edinburgh, for example, held the following impressive range of ales and porters:

Stock of the Beer on Hand 1819

104½ barrels of £5 Ale	£522 10s	
82 barrels of £6 Ale	£492	
		£1014 10s
40½ barrels of 115s Porter	£232 17s 6d	
433¾ barrels of 90s Porter	£1951 17s 6d	
16 barrels of 80s Porter	£64	
4 barrels of 40s Porter	£8	
30 barrels of 30s Porter	£45	
		£2301 15s
		£3316 5s[39]

The cellar, like the stable, was the realm of the drayman—an individual endowed with considerable muscular strength, 'whose dexterity in moving heavy butts, each weighing about 1,800 lbs is surprising,' wrote the artist-engraver, W.H.Pyne.[40]

Near the cellars were the stables for the drays—and these might be kept in con-siderable numbers if the brewery were large, like those of William Younger or John and Robert Tennent by the beginning of the nineteenth century. Almost all of the brewers' cash books contain entries relating to the feeding and care of the horses, such as the charming little entry in Patrick Murison's Cash Book for June 1787, which reads quite simply, 'To Grass For the Horses.'[41] Brewers relied heavily on the horse and cart for both the urban and country trade: William Younger's massive ale carts were trundling far beyond the confines of the city of Edinburgh by the end of the eighteenth century, as far afield as the Lothians and

Berwickshire; while Archibald Campbell sent wagons to Glasgow even earlier, carrying his prime porter to the discerning merchants and businessmen of the west of Scotland.[42]

An important department in any brewery was the cooperage, probably located on the opposite side of the courtyard from the brewhouse. Coopering was an important wood and metalworking industry which grew in the wake of several primary processing activities, notably brewing, distilling and fish curing. *Pigot's Commercial Directory of Scotland* lists nearly 270 coopers in 1825 (see Table 38), there being a notable concentration in the main brewing centres of Edinburgh, Glasgow, Aberdeen and Perth, as well as in ports and harbours associated with the herring fishery.[43] If breweries were not large enough to warrant making their own barrels, they would certainly employ a cooper or two to maintain the stock of barrels in good repair. Coopering was big business, and several firms in Edinburgh, Leith, Aberdeen and Glasgow were substantial concerns. One of the biggest was the Scottish Patent Cooperage Company of Glasgow, established in 1816 by John White, Thomas Leader, James Graham (all Glasgow businessmen) and Bryce McMurdo of Netherton, Dumfries, a shipowner and landed proprietor. The company registered a patent for:

> making casks by Machinery upon geometrical principles, by which the Staves of Barrels, Hogsheads, Puncheons and Butts, or any other description, are cut and moulded by a fixed scale so that a single Stave is a perfect counterpart in form of every other of the class or size to which it belongs, and the Heads and Bottoms being similarly formed and joined, and their grooves cut by Machinery.

The resulting casks, they maintained, would be superior to hand-cut ones, more durable and much more readily repaired. The company did well until the late 1820s, counting J. and R. Tennent as one of its local customers. When it fell on bad times in 1830 it had assets valued at nearly £12,000, including two warehouses in Edinburgh and Leith.[44]

Table 38

Number of Coopers by Centre 1825

Town	No		Town	No
Edinburgh	26		Montrose	9
Leith	26		Dunbar	3
Aberdeen	35		Haddington	2
Ayr	8		Inverness	8
Kilmarnock	5		Glasgow	46
Duns	4		Linlithgow	5
Alloa	5		Perth	14
Dumbarton	3		Greenock	11
Dumfries	5		Paisley	11
Elgin	3		Jedburgh	3
Cupar	2		Kelso	6
Dunfermline	4		Falkirk	5
Kirkcaldy	3		Stirling	4
Arbroath	4		Dundee	10

Source: *Pigot's Commercial Directory of Scotland*, 1825-6.

Products

Even after the introduction of English porter, mainly from the 1780s, the most popular malt liquors drunk in Scotland were small or table beer and strong ale. Small or table beer (usually bottled by the time it reached the consumer) was known in Scotland as 'Twopenny' — a reference no doubt to its original price per quart some time about the middle of the eighteenth century. We have already seen that small beer was often nothing more than a byproduct—brewed with what amounted to spent grains, after strong ale worts had been drawn from the mash tun, and the result must have been a very thin and uninteresting drink, vastly inferior to what we might today call pale ale. Many contemporaries certainly thought little of small beer. Even the minister of Stirling (an important brewing and malting centre), the Rev. James Somerville, said in his report to the *Statistical Account* in the mid-1790s that 'no wholesome beverage' could be obtained by the working classes except 'thin, vapid, sour stuff under the name of small beer.' It was therefore hardly surprising in his view that they were turning to whisky.[45] Yet small or table beers seem to have been remarkably successful at home and abroad and were manufactured in considerable quantities by Scottish brewers. As Table 39 indicates, one Edinburgh brewer, Patrick Murison, produced an average of about 5,000 gallons of small beer per annum in the period between 1796 and 1800, mostly for sale locally. Scottish small beer production consistently represented nearly two-thirds of the total beer charged with duty in the years 1803 to 1830, and production in 1825 was 244,000 barrels.[46]

Strong ale, on the other hand, was the premier Scottish liquor, popular in the domestic market and much sought after in England and further afield (see Chapter Seven). The large Scottish brewers, like Tennents, Youngers, Campbells, Aitkens and Meiklejohns, all built up their reputations on strong ale, which became the main item of export to the Colonies and elsewhere for these and other companies after the 1800s. Even modest country breweries established reputations for their strong beer: that produced at the Banff Brewery had 'long been in high repute' at the end of the 1790s and was 'in great demand, from various and distant parts of the country'; while in Fife, 'a considerable quantity of strong ale' was made by the numerous small-town breweries scattered along the shores of the Firth of Forth, mostly sold to colliers, fishermen, seamen and country folk.[47] Strong ale production remained remarkably constant, averaging 110,000 barrels per annum between 1800 and 1830. The fairly constant demand nationally is supported at local level by evidence from brewers' records. William Murison, probably son and successor to Patrick, produced each year around 15,000 gallons of strong beer for sale during 1800-1805, and there is little sign of fluctuating demand, even in the same month in succeeding years.[48]

The fashion and taste for English-style porter began to be popular in Scotland in the early 1780s, when increasing quantities were shipped coastwise from the great London porter houses (see Chapter Eight). But Scottish brewers soon responded to this new market and began brewing their own porter, some with a considerable measure of success. There were soon notable porter breweries in

Table 39

Patrick Murison's Small Beer Sales 1796-1800

	1796 Gals.	£	1797 Gals.	£	1798 Gals.	£	1799 Gals.	£	1800 Gals.	£
Jan.			700	27	723	32	665	28	519	22
Feb.			629	28	685	31	559	24	451	19
March	n/a		720	32	702	33	674	30	396	17
April			690	31	726	32	639	27	414	17
May			779	33	732	33	641	27		
June	622	26	619	27	527	24	601	25		
July	514	21	689	29	464	23	573	25		
Aug.	444	18	590	26	476	20	560	23	n/a	
Sept.	267	11	590	25	447	19	—	—		
Oct.	347	15	590	26	484	21	475	20		
Nov.	423	18	617	27	489	21	481	20		
Dec.	524	23	684	30	614	27	484	20		
Totals	3141	132	7897	341	7069	316	6351	269	1780	75

Source: SRO, RH 15/1715 Patrick Murison's Small Beer Day Book, 1796-1800.

many places, as far apart as Dumfries and Banff. One Dumfries merchant, a former provost of the town, Gabriel Richardson, started porter brewing in 1783, and his product was soon widely recognised for its quality, being considered 'very superior to what is often made in Scotland under that name.' The Brechin Brewery Company of William Gillies had an even wider reputation because, according to one contemporary, it seemed to have 'hit the taste of the public for this kind of liquor.' Brechin porter commanded a nationwide market in Scotland and even sold in London under its own name. The same was true of the Devanha Brewery of William Black and Company in Aberdeen.[49] Its porter was shipped coastwise to Edinburgh, Glasgow and London. William Younger and Company, like the Anderston Brewery, employed English skill when they came belatedly into the porter brewing trade in 1806, as a newspaper advertisement shows:

TO PORTER DEALERS

Archibald Campbell Younger and William Younger have commenced Brewers of Porter under the firm of A.C. and W.Younger. To enable them to obtain a complete knowledge of the art of making that article, they have engaged a London brewer of great professional ability, and they are happy to say that he has succeeded in producing porter that will vie in every respect with the best that can be imported from London. The following very low prices will justify A.C. and W.Y. in confining their dealings in this concern to ready money only, viz.

Porter of the very best quality,	£3 6s 0d)	
Porter of the second quality,	£2 16s 0d)	Per hogshead
Porter of the third quality,	£2 6s 0d)	

Orders from the country, accompanied with cash, carefully attended to.[50]

The porter trade was probably at its height in the years 1800 to 1820, but thereafter strong ale began to reassert itself as the premier drink for the Scottish domestic market.

The years before the middle of the nineteenth century saw little change in brewing techniques or breweries from the peak of activity recorded towards the end of the classic Industrial Revolution era. Many country breweries succumbed to the competition of larger, urban rivals, and it was in the great brewing centres of Edinburgh, Glasgow and Alloa that the integrated mass-production plants were developed. Much of that expansion and related technical change took part in the latter half of the nineteenth century, and is considered later in this study.

NOTES

1 Mathias (1959), 151.
2 I am most grateful to Mr Balfour Thompson, Chief Brewer, Scottish & Newcastle Breweries, Edinburgh for showing me over the brewery and explaining the various processes.
3 Institute of Brewing, *The production and storage of malting barley* (1973).
4 Mathias (1959), 405.
5 See Chapter Three. Many Edinburgh brewers had maltings in East Lothian, and Glasgow brewers were generally associated with those in Linlithgow, Stirling and Falkirk.
6 W.H.Roberts, *The Scottish ale brewer and practical maltster: a comprehensive digest of the art of brewing ales according to the Scottish system* (1837). The ed. used here is the 3rd of 1847.
7 T.S.Ashton, *Economic fluctuations in England 1700-1800* (1959), 6-7; Mathias (1959), 405-6.
8 Roberts, 181.
9 *Two hundred years of progress: James Aitken & Co Ltd 1740-1940* (1940), 9.
10 Excise Regulations quoted in Roberts, 189-90.
11 Ibid., 192.
12 E.S.White, *The maltster's guide* (1860).
13 A.Morrice, *A practical treatise on brewing the various sorts of malt liquor* (1827), 28-9. Scottish maltings often used peat for kiln-drying.
14 Roberts, 200-04.
15 Ibid, 37.
16 I am grateful to Mr T.C.Ferguson, Joint Managing Director, Whitbread (Scotland) Ltd. for showing me over the Argyll Brewery and providing so much useful information on the history of Archibald Campbell & Co.
17 *J. & R. Tennent's Wellpark Brewery, Glasgow* (1966), 2-3.
18 *Edinburgh Evening Courant*, 18 Feb. 1788, NLS.
19 GH 19937/37, Sun CD Series 714988, 10 Feb. 1801 Policy of James Hoggart.
20 Morrice, frontispiece and legend, also 19-20.
21 E.N.Hayman, *A practical treatise to render the art of brewing more easy* (1823), 1-4.
22 Morrice, 20.
23 SRO, RH 15/780, Seq. of R.Stein & Co., Brewers, Edinburgh, 1819, Sederunt Book, 29-44, 64-5.
24 J.Robertson, *GVA Inverness* (1808).
25 SRO, COS, UP Innes Durie A 8/7 Aberdeen Brewery Co v W.Gray, 1822-3, Ans for W.Gray, advocate in Aberdeen, 7.
26 See Chapter Four.
27 GH 11937/111, Sun CD Series 910449, 21 Sept. 1815, Policy of Peter Robertson.
28 I had the privilege of knowing, until his recent death, James Reid of Alness, Easter Ross, one of the last old country millwrights. I owe much of my knowledge of and enthusiasm for simple machinery in the countryside to him.
29 SRO GD 241/62 Thomson, Dickson & Shaw Mss. Papers of Archibald Campbell, brewers in Edinburgh, Inventory of Utensils etc in Argyll Brewery, 1 Jan. 1830.
30 Roberts, xii.
31 Ibid, xiv, 77-8, 108.
32 Ibid, 49; SL SP 425, John, Earl of Hopetoun, Prop. of the Mill of Bathgate and John and James Bells, Tacksmen v George and James Shaws and James Cuddy, Brewers, 1752.

33 Ibid, 54-5. Much of this account of Scottish brewing technique draws upon Roberts.
34 Ibid, 72.
35 The sparger illustrated here was said by Roberts to be made by a coppersmith in Leith.
36 SRO RH 15/780 Seq. of R. Stein & Co. SB 1819, Inventory.
37 Roberts, 150.
38 D.Souter, *GVA Banff* (1812), 304.
39 SRO RH 15/780, Seq. of R.Stein & Co. SB 1819, 28.
40 W.H.Pyne, *The world in miniature: England, Scotland and Ireland* (1827), vol III, 154-5.
41 SRO RH 15/1705-23 Business Books of P.Murison 1786-1800, Cash Book No 1, 1786-91.
42 Keir, 30; SL SP 128/17 Pet. of James Yates 1765.
43 Data from *Pigot's Commercial Directory of Scotland 1825-6*.
44 SRO RH 15/784 Seq. of Scottish Patent Cooperage Co. 1830.
45 *OSA*, 8, 293-5.
46 RH 15/1715 Small Beer Day Book 1796-1800; Beer Charged With Duty 1787-1830.
47 *OSA*, 20, 357; J.Thomson, *GVA Fife* (1800), 302.
48 SRO RH 15/2029 Business Books of Wm Murison, Strong Ale Day Book 1800-04.
49 W.Singer, *GVA Dumfries* (1812), 422-3; G.Robertson, *GVA Kincardine* (1813), 433. SL SP 28313
Ans. for Craig & Hunter, mchts in Leith, 1814.
50 NLS, *Edinburgh Evening Courant*, 3 Nov. 1806; Keir, 30.

7

The Market for Scottish Ales

THE rise of the Scottish brewing industry in the latter half of the eighteenth century and subsequent developments during the Industrial Revolution were the direct consequence not only of changes in public taste and drinking habits, but also of a whole series of complex market forces. Brewing remained a widespread domestic activity until the late eighteenth century, while innkeepers and publicans brewing their own beer and brewing victuallers were not uncommon even early the following century. Long before the period of expansion following the 1770s, as we have observed, the Scottish brewing industry had to cope with competition from rival drinks: at the upper end of the market there was the challenge of imported wines and spirits, at the lower, cheap—often illicit—Highland whisky. Brewers had therefore to evolve a sophisticated system of distribution to tackle successfully the growing drink market, and in this, as Mathias indicates, the brewing industry was very much in the forefront of the retailing revolution which accompanied industrialisation and the rise of an urban mass-market.[1]

Most brewers started out selling in local markets and many country establishments in Scotland probably never found custom much beyond a twenty or thirty mile radius of the brewery. Distance and transport costs were critically important variables. Yet by the time of the Industrial Revolution some breweries had already expanded sufficiently to tackle the growing urban markets of, for example, Edinburgh and Glasgow, to have distant country customers, and even a modest export trade to England or the Colonies. A great many Scottish brewers in Edinburgh, Glasgow, Alloa and Falkirk thrived on this diverse trade during the period 1770 to 1830, while some in these and other centres increasingly brewed for more specialist or particular geographic markets. Of particular relevance in this connexion were the Scottish porter and strong ale trades (both for export to England and further afield), which expanded considerably during the Napoleonic Wars. Some larger country breweries penetrated urban markets with success, especially in and around Edinburgh and Glasgow. The domestic market was always of overwhelmingly greater importance and was early dominated by the older-established urban brewers like Youngers and Tennents, although even in 1825 there were no fewer than 76 towns or villages in Scotland with one or two country breweries serving the local community and surrounding neighbourhood.[2] As we saw in Chapter Two, this period probably marked the ultimate expansion of country brewing in Scotland during the Industrial Revolution, because concentration in urban mass-production units dominating country as well as town outlets became a major feature of the years after 1830.

The public house or tavern was an established feature of social life in Scotland, as in England, long before the era of rapid population growth during the latter half of the eighteenth century, but undoubtedly the whole process of industrialisation contributed to a substantial expansion in premises selling drink. The drink usages and habits of an essentially rural society were readily translated to and adapted by an industrial workforce, and these, just as much as an expanding economy and population, contributed substantially to the growing demand for both beer and spirits. Scottish élites who dominated both local and national government demanded curbs and controls on drinking, at first for the sake of public order, and, later, in the causes of morality and temperance. Licensing came to have an important influence on drink distribution and retailing, especially after the implementation of national as well as local legislation in the 1790s. It is worth emphasising that in Scotland the concern was with the manufacture and sale of spirits; for, as contemporaries were quick to point out, 'if a house is licensed to sell beer, it will infallibly sell whiskey,' and separating the sale of the two would have been quite impossible, 'according to the habits of the people.'[3] Certainly, consistent reduction in the price of spirits (and fluctuating duties) during and after the Napoleonic Wars generally resulted in a massive increase in the consumption of whisky, and this had a profound influence on the Scottish brewing industry. Production, in fact, remained almost constant between 1800 and 1830. Another major difference from England (or at least from London and the Home Counties) was the limited development in Scotland of the tied house system—brewers owning, leasing or controlling the majority of their sales outlets. It was known, but was never prevalent much before the middle of the nineteenth century.[4]

We have already seen in Chapter One something of the origins of an export market for Scottish ales in the middle of the eighteenth century. Foreign exports of ale tended to follow in the wake of Scottish colonial emigration: there can be little doubt that initial demand for Scots strong beers came largely from Scottish merchants and planters in the North American Colonies and the West Indies. In 1785 these two spheres absorbed between them 80 per cent of Scottish exports—then something less than 4,000 barrels per annum. During the subsequent decade there was a dramatic increase in sales to England (mainly sent coastwise to Liverpool, Tyneside and London), so that by 1800 the market south of the Border was the most important non-domestic outlet for strong ale and beer.[5] Not until the late 1830s did the real assault on foreign markets begin, and even after the middle of the century the English trade remained of much greater significance.[6] There was a reverse flow of porter to Scotland from the great London breweries after 1790, mostly sent coastwise like the fine English barley so much sought after by Scottish brewers, to Leith, Dundee, Aberdeen and lesser ports. Often superior to the home brewed product, it always commanded a good price at the luxury end of the Scottish market.[7]

Local, Regional & National Markets

In 1780 there were perhaps fewer than a hundred public breweries in Scotland producing about 200,000 barrels of beer (see Table 40). It is unlikely that any firm brewed more than 10,000 barrels a year, and the majority brewed far less. Twenty years later the number of breweries had increased to 180 and their total production to 386,000 barrels worth around £1.5 million.[8] The distribution of the 120

Table 40

Estimated Domestic Consumption of Scottish-produced Beer,
1770-1830

Year	000s of barrels
1770	100
1780	200
1790	293
1800	382
1810	338
1820	309
1830	326

breweries included in the survey of insurance policy and capital valuation described in Chapter Four is shown in Map 1, while Table 41 provides a useful statistical guide to the structure of the industry at that time.[9] The number of breweries continued to increase until 1822, when there were 241 individual firms, 97 being located in the Edinburgh, Lothian and Fife excise collections.[10]

Table 41

Frequency Distribution of Scottish Breweries c. 1800 by Number of Breweries

No. of Breweries	No. of Places	Total
1	37	37
2	10	20
3	5	15
4	2	8
5	1	5
6	2	12
7	1	7
16	1	16
Total		120

Source: GH, Sun Fire Office Valuations.

In 1825 there were 233 active breweries in Scotland, scattered from Kirkwall in Orkney to Stranraer in Wigtownshire (see Map 2 and Table 42), and data from *Pigot's Commercial Directory of Scotland* for that year provide us with a useful profile of both the breweries and their spheres of influence. Reference to Table 19 provides a county breakdown by ranked order (which is in itself interesting because it shows Lanark and Angus as second and third brewing counties respectively after Midlothian). But it is probably better for our purposes here to examine the regional distribution of breweries within Scotland and thus gain some insight into the regional markets which had evolved by the time the country brewing trade

BREWERIES 1800

INVERNESS

ABERDEEN

BRECHIN

PERTH

CUPAR

7 STIRLING ALLOA DUNF' KIRKCALDY

14 HADDINGTON

GREENOCK GLASGOW EDINB' DALKEITH

KILMARNOCK KELSO

AYR

DUMFRIES

Map 1.

BREWERIES
1825

ELGIN

INVERNESS

ABERDEEN 13

BRECHIN MONTROSE

FORFAR

ARBROATH

DUNDEE

PERTH

CUPAR

STIRLING 8 ALLOA KIRKCALDY

FALKIRK

DUNBAR

HADDINGTON

GREENOCK 22 GLASGOW 29 EDINB'

DUNS BERWICK

KILMARNOCK

AYR JEDBURGH

DUMFRIES

Map 2.

Table 42

Frequency Distribution of Scottish Breweries 1825
by Number of Breweries

No. of Breweries	No. of Places	Total
1	57	57
2	19	38
3	7	21
4	2	8
5	5	25
6	2	12
7	-	-
8	1	8
13	1	13
22	1	22
29	1	29
Total		233

Source: *Pigot's Commercial Directory of Scotland, 1825-26.*

was at its height and no unified nationwide market had yet emerged.

There were eight clearly identifiable regional markets in 1825 and to some extent these corresponded with the barley districts described in Chapter Three: far in the south-east was Tweeddale and the Borders (including Berwick), then to the north, Edinburgh and the Lothians, Fife, Stirling and Clarkmannan, Perth and Angus, and Aberdeen with Buchan and Moray. There were two clearly distinct regional markets in the west: Glasgow and the industrial districts of central Scotland (including Ayrshire), and in the south-west the geographically isolated district of Dumfries and Galloway. Elsewhere were scattered country breweries serving local communities, mainly in the whisky drinking Highlands and Islands, and particularly in Argyll, Easter Ross, Caithness and Orkney. There were breweries at Inveraray, Inverness, Cromarty, Tain, Wick and Kirkwall.[11]

Perhaps the most isolated of all regional markets within the Scottish brewing trade (excepting Dumfries and Galloway) was Tweeddale and the Borders, where the most important brewing towns were Berwick (actually just across the Border, but still the dominant market centre and port for the Merse and lower Tweed valley), Duns and Jedburgh. There were also important small breweries in Ednam, Kelso and Coldstream.[12] In this prosperous farming district with its compact market towns, country custom would always be important, although the woollen textile centres like Galashiels, Hawick, Selkirk and Jedburgh provided opportunities for assault on more concentrated industrial markets. Edinburgh and Lothian brewers naturally always had an interest in this outlet. William Younger was shipping coastwise to Berwick after 1805 and even country brewers outside Edinburgh thought it worthwhile to develop the overland trade, John White of Haughhead Brewery at Penicuik having customers in Kelso, Ayton and Greenlaw, among other places.[13]

Moving further north, the market of the Lothians, dominated by the great brewing metropolis of Edinburgh, was of very great local and national significance. Edinburgh itself had 29 breweries in 1825, some of considerable size and with a wide trade. The other important brewing towns were Dunbar, Haddington, Musselburgh and Linlithgow, while places like North Berwick and Dalkeith had perhaps one or two more modest enterprises. Apart from William Youngers, there were other important firms in Edinburgh, including Alexander Berwick and Company, the old-established Archibald Campbell of Argyll Brewery, Andrew Drybrough, and the partnership concern of the Edinburgh & Leith Brewery Company, which had acquired Robert Stein's brewery in the Canongate following his bankruptcy in 1820.[14] Elsewhere in the area beyond the city boundaries were Charles Dudgeon and Company of Belhaven Brewery at Dunbar, and another old firm with a maltings and brewery on the shore at Prestonpans, John Fowler. Clearly the Edinburgh market itself was of very great importance to most brewers in and around the city, yet many looked beyond its boundaries for country custom. Patrick Murison certainly did not venture far, but he had a number of regular clients in Bo'ness, Dalkeith, Musselburgh and Haddington, and of his 200-odd customers, perhaps a third were out of town.[15] John Kirk of Drumdryan Brewery was a bit more ambitious—to his cost—because he over-reached himself and fell on hard times following the general crisis of 1825. He had customers in Fife, Angus, Perth and Aberdeen, as well as venturing into the English trade which was his undoing, for his agent there, one John Brown, owed him at least £600 and numerous other defaulting customers nearly £4,000.[16]

The market of Fife presented a remarkably cohesive unit, dominated by the brewing centres of Dunfermline, Kirkcaldy, Cupar and St Andrews, while strung along the Forth coastline in colliery, salt panning and fishing villages were small, more localised breweries serving the local community. Typical of this latter group was the small brewery at Dysart (described in Chapter Three) with an annual output in the mid-1790s of 2,500 barrels.[17] The old ports of St Monance, Anstruther and Crail had similar breweries, the majority of customers being taverns frequented by fisherfolk and seamen. In St Andrews, the Argyll Brewery of Ireland and Halket was more representative of a larger production unit serving the university town and its surrounding farming countryside, while Kirkcaldy had five quite substantial breweries with customers in nearby colliery and linen textile working districts.[18] Fife was a prominent distilling county, and even at the time of the first *Statistical Account* in the 1790s contemporaries were complaining of excessive whisky consumption among the local labouring population, especially in industrial neighbourhoods, like that of Dunfermline.[19]

After Edinburgh and Glasgow, the greatest concentration of production in Scottish brewing during most of the period was in the triangle linking the towns of Falkirk, Stirling and Alloa, all three long-established centres of malting and brewing. Together they had a total of 21 breweries in 1825, the majority dating from the period 1770 to 1800. Several were by that time important and well-established firms, even before the close of the eighteenth century, three particularly significant ones being George Younger and Robert Meiklejohn of Alloa, and James Aitken of Falkirk. Such firms with a substantial brewing capacity increasingly sought outlets in non-local Scottish markets, mainly in Glasgow and

Table 43

Number of Breweries by Excise Collection 1822

Collection	No
Aberdeen	22
Ayr	10
Argyll South	1
Dumfries	18
Elgin	6
Fife	25
Glasgow	27
Haddington	30
Inverness	5
Linlithgow	14
Montrose	16
Paisley	6
Perth	7
Stirling	11
Teviotdale	15
Edinburgh	28
Total	241

Source: PP 1822 XXI Accounts and Papers. Misc. Statistics.

the industrial west of Scotland (reached by the Forth & Clyde Canal), but also in the coastal trade to Edinburgh, Newcastle and London. The English trade in strong beer and porter was of considerable importance to both Youngers and Meiklejohns of Alloa, who, in 1821, were considered to be two of the 'principal brewers for England'—and Meiklejohns' ales were said to have been the first introduced to London from north of the Border.[20] This area, like Fife, was also important for its malting and distilling trades, so that competition with the latter's product must always have been fierce in the textile, mining and ironworking towns and villages of Stirling and Clackmannan.

The brewing district of Perth and Angus was dominated by town breweries in Perth, Forfar and Brechin, and in the east coast ports of Dundee, Arbroath and Montrose. In the whole area (including Kincardineshire further to the north) there were 37 breweries by 1825, Perth, Forfar and Montrose each having five. All these towns had a long reputation for malt and beer and nothing but favourable reports were given by contemporaries: the strong ale of Montrose was 'esteemed by good judges equal to Burton Ale,' and the Brechin breweries supplied the town and neighbourhood in the 1790s with 'excellent liquor' and later with porter tasty enough to rival that of London as far as local palates were concerned.[21] There were numerous small country breweries in this area catering for very limited local markets. A brewery in Crieff (Perthshire), which began business in 1791, then produced less than 300 barrels per annum, when the population of the place was 2,225.[22] The only large, urban market in the area was Dundee (population 26,000 in 1801), which was dominated by one brewery, the Pleasance Brewing Company. The convenient coastal location of many breweries in this area made the exploitation of more distant markets a very real possibility, and brewers in Perth,

Arbroath and Montrose found it profitable to send beer and ale to customers in Fife and Edinburgh. The Brechin Brewery Company of William Gillies and David Dakers (founded c1790) was a leader in the coastal trade, shipping porter and stout from Montrose to the Edinburgh market in increasing quantities after 1810.[23]

The largest concentration of breweries in the north-east was in the city of Aberdeen, which had a population of nearly 28,000 in 1801. About 1795 there were seven breweries, three of which had a considerable trade both in the city itself and in its agricultural hinterland of Deeside and the valley of the Don. The oldest was the Devanha Brewery of William Black and Company, founded in 1768 and by 1802 valued at £6,000. It had a wide custom (including coastwise export) for its table beer, strong ale and porter. Two other major firms before 1800 were George Annand and Company, and Brebner, Gibbon and Company, both of which did 'a great deal of business' and were 'in a thriving way' at the time of the *Statistical Account*.[24] Apart from the town and up country trade (helped by the opening of the Aberdeenshire Canal in 1805), there was a third important outlet in the supply of beer to merchant shipping and fishing fleets: one brewery at Peterhead prospered on this particular custom.[25] By 1825 Aberdeen had 13 breweries, and elsewhere in Buchan and Moray there were country breweries at Inverurie, Peterhead (which had two), Banff, Keith, Elgin and Forres. For the majority, customers were almost entirely local, although the brewery at Banff found more distant markets for its strong beer and porter sent coastwise to ports and harbours on the other side of the Moray Firth and south to Aberdeen and Leith.[26] The College Brewery in Elgin, established by Alexander Young in 1784 and extended by his sons, Alexander Jr. and James, maintained the long brewing and malting tradition of this beautiful old cathedral city. Its beer and porter had a high reputation over the whole of the northern counties (as far as Caithness and Orkney) and a flourishing trade was done.[27]

Potentially the most concentrated and lucrative market for beer and ale lay in the new industrial districts of central Scotland, all mostly within a twenty-five mile radius of Glasgow. By the 1790s transport facilities in and around the city had opened up a significant and growing market for consumer goods of every description in the surrounding colliery, ironworking and textile towns and villages of north Lanarkshire, Renfrewshire and Ayrshire. The construction of turnpike roads and canals and the improvement of navigation on the Clyde all opened the door to more distant markets in industrial Stirlingshire, the east of Scotland, and in the ports and harbours along the lower Firth of Clyde. Beyond these lay the country markets, dominated by essentially local breweries such as those in Clydesdale at Hamilton and Lanark.[28]

Glasgow had always been an important brewing centre, and by 1800 had around a dozen breweries, several quite large. These included John and Robert Tennent of Wellpark Brewery and Robert Cowan and Son of Anderston Brewery, both having a wide business in the west of Scotland and further afield.[29] The first couple of decades of the nineteenth century saw a considerable expansion of brewing within the city, and by 1825 there were no fewer than 22 individual firms, many located in the Anderston and Hutchesontown districts or near the Forth and Clyde Canal at Port Dundas. In Renfrewshire there were breweries at Paisley (serving the textile villages of the Cart valley), Port Glasgow and Greenock supplying shipping as well as local markets). Ayrshire had five breweries, two in Ayr itself (previously there had been five smaller businesses), two in Kilmarnock (an important primary processing and textile centre), and the last at Saltcoats, run by a local corn merchant turned brewer, Hugh Watt. In Ayr, Peter Walker's Citadel Brewery was conveniently located near the harbour, and across the river was Newton Brewery. Both dated from the end of the eighteenth century and relied on country customers in neighbouring Carrick.[30] Despite the expansion of country brewing in the west of Scotland (as elsewhere) between 1780 and 1825, the concentration of large-scale units in and around Glasgow is evident, and it was brewers there who were soon able to dominate this whole area and win an expanding market at the cost of smaller, less efficient breweries in neighbouring country towns and Clyde ports.

The remaining and very distinctive market in the west of Scotland was Dumfries and Galloway, an area less Scottish than its geographical position might in fact suggest, partly isolated from the rest of the country and with a self-contained regional farming economy dependent more on markets in Cumberland and Lancashire than on any reached by land or coastwise to the north. Small country breweries were established in most local market centres or Solway harbour ports of Dumfries and Galloway during the closing decades of the eighteenth century, for there was no long brewing tradition outside the town of Dumfries.[31] According to Singer, writing in 1812 about the effects of licensing legislation passed in 1795 (the Sale of Beer Act) on brewing locally, the industry 'fell into a few hands and public breweries increased in number.'[32] The brewery at Gatehouse-of-Fleet, a planned, industrial village with cotton spinning mills, was established in 1784 and originated as a private enterprise encouraged by James Murray of Cally, the local landowner, partly no doubt to discourage spirit drinking amongst the labouring population on the farms and in the mills.[33] Other planned villages, like Newton Stewart (or Douglas) and Castle Douglas, had breweries serving the local community. Seventeen small breweries were operating in south-west Scotland in 1825, and the dominance of Dumfries and its suburb Maxwelltown, with six breweries, is an indication of its growing significance as a market centre for the whole region. Since the whole area had such close trading links with places like Liverpool and Dublin, it seems likely that the general merchandise in return for the farm products of the region included English and Irish ales and porters.[34]

These, then, were the distinct regional markets which so dominated and influenced the growth of the Scottish brewing industry until the 1820s. Already, however, there were many indicators of a changing structure in brewing, as the larger and more cost-effective units looked further afield for custom and eventually began to put pressure on less efficient country brewers. We can see plenty of evidence of this from the 1780s onwards, especially in Edinburgh and Glasgow, but elsewhere as well. Youngers' main market at the turn of the century was in Edinburgh, Fife and the Lothians, but already they had a foothold in the west of Scotland with some customers in Glasgow, Paisley and Greenock. They had an established coastal trade to the north with Angus (the main outlets there being Dundee, Montrose and Arbroath) and to the south with Berwick and London. By the late 1830s their distribution was much more widespread and included customers in Aberdeen and the north-east, with even more distant sales in Easter Ross, Caithness, Orkney and Shetland. The Borders, especially the textile towns of Galashiels, Selkirk and Hawick, were of growing importance, as was the market for strong ales in Tyneside and Northumberland, which is discussed later in this chapter.[35] Tennents similarly dominated the market in the industrial west of Scotland by the beginning of the nineteenth century, with widespread custom in and around Glasgow and in the growing manufacturing and mining towns of Lanarkshire, Renfrewshire and Ayrshire. By the mid-1820s they had few serious rivals and were pushing further afield into central and south-west Scotland. Their main English market was Lancashire, reached coastwise through the port of Liverpool.[36]

Although there was a decline in country brewing after the 1820s, many small breweries with strictly local markets survived until the middle of the nineteenth century—often remaining as active as their counterparts fifty years before. Indeed, small breweries were not confined to the country districts, for in all the main brewing centres there were numerous modest enterprises with limited trade. This is very clearly illustrated for the period around the turn of the century in the capital valuation survey described in Chapter Four and later, in the survival of many brewing victuallers in the early 1830s.[37] Table 44 shows the numbers of

Table 44

Brewers and Licensed Victuallers by Excise Collection 1832
also showing Bushels of Malt Manufactured into Beer

Collection	Brewers	Licensed Victuallers	Bushels of Malt Used	
			Brewers	Victuallers
Aberdeen	24	14	79323	3162
Ayr	14	25	42740	3948
Argyll	1	—	62	—
Caithness	1	71	993	4963
Dumfries	21	12	26340	4473
Elgin	10	20	12895	970
Fife	28	22	43856	7211
Glasgow	18	8	89473	9468
Haddington	23	2	46871	1135
Inverness	6	15	4814	3575
Linlithgow	16	8	37570	2518
Montrose	5	86	21842	37945
Perth	7	18	14031	7254
Stirling	9	15	42751	9636
Edinburgh	33	2	432160	247
Scotland	216	318	893901	96505
UK	2185	24611	16.3m	8.9m

Source: PP 1833 XXXIII Accounts & Papers: Brewers Licensed to Sell Beer.

breweries and brewing victuallers by excise collection in 1832 and also provides a useful indication of the amount of malt consumed by each sector.[38] It is noticeable that the majority of brewing victuallers were to be found in the country collections (for example the 71 in Caithness and the 86 in Montrose) and most of these would be publicans or innkeepers brewing ales for retail on their own premises. All would no doubt have obtained their malt from local brewers and hops from merchants in Leith, or direct from suppliers in the south of England. The decline in the numbers of licensed brewing victuallers began in the 1830s, being reduced to 190 in 1846.[39] This is certainly indicative of the wider markets created by the larger urban breweries after 1830 and also possibly reflects some extension of the tied house system, as the more powerful brewers acquired public houses and inns owned by the brewing victuallers. In fact, the evidence for the existence of a tied trade in Scotland much before the middle of the nineteenth century is very limited. None of the surviving brewery archives gives any hint of it and there are few other positive indicators elsewhere.[40] H.H.Drummond, in his evidence to a parliamentary select committee on the sale of beer in 1830, said there was never any complaint of monopoly in the Scottish brewing trade and that few public houses were owned by brewers: 'the trade is perfectly free,' he concluded.[41]

Throughout the period to 1850, then, there were four distinct markets for Scottish ales: the urban trade, the country trade, the coastwise trade, and the export trade. For many brewers the first two spheres would constitute 90 per cent of the business. With a few notable exceptions, only the larger breweries would venture into the coastal trade or embark on English or foreign markets. The brewer's sphere of influence and custom were generally functions of size and capital. The small country brewery or even a similar one in town would rarely have the capacity to venture beyond the confines of a fairly limited geographical area, and even larger breweries with potential to exploit non-local markets often faced innumerable hazards. Urban breweries with country customers often found them more trouble than they were worth—and much the same could be said of the coastal trade within Scotland and the export trade in general during the years before 1830. Letter books and accounts of numerous breweries show the extent of the trade with country merchants (probably about fifty per cent of the business, though almost entirely made up of small orders), inns and numerous private individuals (often farmers or lesser gentry). The country connexion which so dominated raw material supply and the investment pattern (described in Chapters Three and Four) was clearly of considerable importance to urban brewers involved in distance trading, and quite likely a personal relationship or friendship lay behind many of these modest transactions.[42] Unfortunately for some brewers, bad debts from country trading led to insolvency, particularly where long-term credit had been advanced, and this was particularly prevalent during the difficult years of the Napoleonic Wars.[43]

The coastwise trade within Scotland was a logical development for those breweries conveniently located to ports, harbours or canals, and became significant after the rise of strong ale and porter brewing in the 1790s. It was essentially confined to the east coast, where there was soon an established two-way flow of porter and strong beer between north and south—remarkably similar in character to the trade between Scotland and England. From the north Banff strong ale and porter found their way south to Aberdeen, Dundee and Leith. In 1798 Banff ale was held in high repute and said to be in great demand 'from various and distant parts of the country,' and by 1812 one observer could write that it was 'generally considered equal to any made in Scotland.' Its porter was so popular locally that 'the importation of that article from London will soon, it is expected, be rendered unnecessary.'[44] William Black's Devanha Brewery was only one of several in Aberdeen engaged in the coastal trade to the markets of central Scotland. The firm's porter had 'acquired a great celebrity' by the second decade of the nineteenth century in Edinburgh and Glasgow, where it was sold under the brand label of 'Aberdeen Porter.' So considerable had Black's import to Edinburgh become by 1817 that the city magistrates raised an action in the Court of Session for non-payment of local duties, but despite this the trade continued 'on a large scale.'[45] The Brechin Brewery had run into similar problems a few years before: the local authority in Edinburgh was then demanding 2d per pint on all imported ales. Brechin exported via Montrose, which itself had a fine reputation for the quality of its ales.[46] Elsewhere, brewers in Fife and Stirling, and in the towns of Dunbar and Berwick, were well located to exploit the coastal trade. Dudgeons' famous old Belhaven Brewery at Dunbar found it just as convenient to ship its products to Leith as send them by much more costly land transport, while Aitkens of Falkirk were able to develop custom in both Edinburgh and Glasgow by shipping their strong ales along the Forth and Clyde and Edinburgh and Union Canals.[47] Finally, the major Edinburgh, Alloa and Glasgow brewers were, as we have seen, very much alive to the possibilities presented by the coastal trade, shipping widely within Scotland on both east and west coasts.

Rising population created increased demand for drink amongst all classes of society, whether urban or rural, so that new drinking houses and taverns were almost invariably established at points likely to attract maximum custom. Naturally, the image of the house reflected the potential clientele—from the low whisky dram house frequented by labourers, to the country town inn, haunt of local merchants and farming élites at weekly markets. In fact, the growth in numbers of retail outlets for both whisky and beer very much reflected the transitional society created by the Industrial Revolution in Scotland, when rural and urban values became increasingly and inevitably mingled one with the other. Perhaps we tend to forget that the dynamics of growth affected countryside as much as town and that in Scotland (as elsewhere) population rose in some rural districts almost as fast as in urban, industrial environments. Licensed public houses and inns grew up everywhere people congregated in any numbers for work or leisure. Much of the growth reflected the new commercial environment of the Industrial Revolution: public houses sprang up in mining and manufacturing districts, in planned villages, at fairs and markets, along turnpike roads and canals, and at ports, harbours or ferries. A few examples will suffice. In Govan, a highly urbanised parish near Glasgow, temperance was not a virtue, there being 22 ale and whisky houses in the mid-1790s; and at St Vigeans, another industrial district adjacent to Arbroath, there were 16 public houses.[48] At Moffat, a small posting and spa town on the Edinburgh to Dumfries turnpike, there was 'a capital inn' for travellers; in the parish of Monzie (Perthshire) there were seven ale houses on the roads; and in Linlithgow one could find 'good entertainment' in the local posthouses.[49] The planned, agrarian village of Kirkpatrick-Durham in the Stewartry of Kirkcudbright, a modest place with a population of just over 1000, sported no fewer than seven inns and alehouses.[50]

Licensing

Licensing had an important influence on the general development of drink retailing, mainly because it resulted in quite strict control by local magistrates over the granting of spirit and beer licences and hence indirectly controlled the number of outlets. Most local authorities in Scotland used the national licensing statutes to control the spirit drinking so frowned upon by the governing élite, and especially by the church and the temperance movement. The clampdown was on small and squalid 'dram' or 'tippling' houses selling spirits exclusively, and not on the more respectable public house.[51] The Sale of Beer legislation produced a veritable flurry of local authority licensing records and these give some indication of varying levels of enforcement and control in many different parts of the country. The first licensing legislation applied on any scale in Scotland was under the act of 1759, which gave local magistrates power 'to license such persons as they should think convenient to keep Ale Houses, Tippling Houses, Victualling Houses, or to sell Ale, Beer, or other Excisable Liquors.'[52] Some burghs were slow to implement the act, but in most cases those that did kept very complete records. One was Stirling, and Table 45 shows both the fluctuating numbers of licences granted and the general upward trend which would be expected between 1759 and 1820.[53] The licensees themselves present an interesting cross-section of society, although the majority had some association with brewing or malting. In 1759 the Stirling magistrates granted licences to the following:

Maltmen and Brewers	24
Brewers	19
Merchants and Brewers ⎫ Merchant Retailers ⎭	15
Brewer + another Occupation	8
Vintners	2
Others	4
	72

Many of those with the designation or part-designation 'brewer' were described as 'maltman brewer in his own house'—the forerunner of the brewing victuallers who still survived in small numbers in the mid-nineteenth century. The picture had changed considerably by 1799, when, of the 80 licences, more than half were held by retailers, vintners or spirit dealers, and the number of brewing victuallers had fallen below a quarter of the total.[54]

Table 45

Stirling Burgh: Licences Issued 1759-1820

Year	No.	Year	No.
1759	72	1790	68
1760	71	1	68
1	68	2	75
2	57	3	74
3	57	4	72
4	63	5	70
5	66	6	76
6	63	7	77
7	61	8	76
8	67	9	80
9	67	1800	79
1770	67	1	75
1	71	2	77
2	72	3	79
3	66	4	76
4	62	5	83
5	67	6	81
6	71	7	88
7	76	8	87
8	78	9	90
9	83	1810	89
1780	86	1	87
1	90	2	88
2	94	3	86
3	90	4	84
4	90	5	83
5	80	6	88
6	75	7	95
7	68	8	101
8	67	9	96
9	68	1820	101

Source: SRO, B66/18/11 Stirling Licensing Book, 1759-1820.

Elsewhere there is similar evidence of growth in numbers of licences granted. Supervision was certainly easier in the smaller burghs, like St Andrews, Dunbar or Ayr. Ayr, for example, granted few licences for spirit shops: the majority seem to have remained in the hands of respectable innkeepers and vintners. Several licences were granted each year to fishermen and coopers, who no doubt had a profitable sideline selling ale and whisky to seamen and fisherfolk at the harbour.[55] Not unnaturally, Glasgow presented a marked contrast: there the number of licences issued at the end of the eighteenth century fluctuated between 450 and 900, and a great many of the establishments must have been squalid spirit shops in the warrens and closes of High Street, Trongate and Salt Market. Table 46 shows how much the numbers of licences fluctuated during the period 1779-

1800, although, apart from a slight upward trend, there is no really discernible pattern.[56] In Edinburgh the picture was similar, although there the control of spirit drinking seems to have been less of a problem before the early 1800s. The reaction against whisky drinking was omnipresent during the Industrial Revolution, although it was not until the early 1830s that the Temperance Movement began to have increasing influence as a pressure group on licensing magistrates, distillers and brewers.[57] It certainly bears emphasis again that the local authorities in Scotland had little interest in controlling beer sales in any way, because brewing and the sale of beer were always regarded as respectable activities, and orderly houses dispensing ale were features to be encouraged.[58]

Table 46

Glasgow Public House Licences 1779-1800

Year	No.	Year	No.
1779	476	1790	762
1780	605	1	796
1	604	2	871
2	612	3	665
3	599	4	560
4	596	5	575
5	606	6	596
6	635	7	674
7	664	8	697
8	704	9	732
9	740	1800	611

Source: GCA B8/4 Public House Licenses 1779-1800.

Distant Markets

The distant markets for Scottish ales lay in two clearly defined spheres. Firstly, there was the English market, almost wholly reached coastwise before 1850; and secondly, there were the foreign markets, mainly in Continental Europe and the Colonies. It is important to emphasise at the outset that the extent of Scottish foreign-going trade (and for our purposes this includes the English market) was never impressive much before the 1840s (less than 0.05 per cent of 357,000 barrels in 1815—a very modest total compared with the trade of one of the leading London porter breweries). Less than 14,000 barrels were exported from Scotland in 1815, and although the trade grew substantially in subsequent years, total exports abroad reached only 21,000 barrels worth £62,000 in 1850.[59] The truth is that the real expansion of the Scottish export trade (mainly in strong beers) lay in the latter half of the nineteenth century. Much the same was true of the growing market south of the Border—especially in London, Liverpool, Bristol and Newcastle—for Scots strong ale. Nevertheless, the period from 1780 onwards represents the formative stage of growth in both the English and foreign-going trades and so it deserves attention here. At the same time, we cannot overlook the reverse flow of porter sent coastwise to Scotland from the south (mainly from London), and it seems appropriate to consider this briefly after our examination of the Scottish trade with England.

The structure of the Scottish export trade as a whole during the period 1785-1815 is shown in Table 47.[60] In 1785 North America and the West Indies absorbed 80 per cent of all Scottish exports, while England and Europe accounted almost equally for the remainder. This very much reflected the structure of Scottish trade in general—a pattern firmly established by the middle of the eighteenth century. Nor should the change which had taken place by 1815 occasion surprise, for by that time the English market had grown considerably, and despite an increased volume of exports to North America and the West Indies (and the appearance of a modest South American trade), it already absorbed over 60 per cent of Scots ale sent overseas. Although we lack figures for the level of exports to England after 1820, it seems likely that the pattern established by 1815 remained constant until the middle of the nineteenth century, by which time English markets probably absorbed about three-quarters of Scottish exports.[61]

Table 47

Destinations of Scottish Beer and Ale Exports 1785-1815

Market	1785		1800		1815	
	Barrels	% Total	Barrels	% Total	Barrels	% Total
England	390	11	2,00	43	8,600	63
Europe	350	9	100	3	500	4
N. America	2,040	53	1,100	24	2,000	14
W. Indies	1,020	27	1,400	30	2,250	16
S. America	—	—	—	—	350	3
Totals	3,800		4,600		13,700	

Source: PRO, CUST 14, Scottish Exports.

The tide of ale and porter from England was matched in the years after 1785 by a small reverse flow from Scotland. As Table 47 indicates, England absorbed a mere 11 per cent of Scottish exports in 1785, but fifteen years later English markets represented 43 per cent of total non-domestic markets. Again it is worth stressing the modest nature of this trade, for in 1800 only 2,000 barrels were shipped south to England, the majority then made up of porter (see Table 48).[62] After 1810 porter exports declined and strong ale became much more important— an early measure of success for this beverage amongst Englishmen with the taste and constitution for a drink of greater potency and vigour than local ales. By 1820 over 10,000 barrels of strong ale were being shipped to England each year. There can be little question that Scottish ales were at a premium in most English markets, comparing favourably with Burton and other fine ales.[63] As the following lists of prices at London and Bristol show, Scots ale was an expensive beverage, mostly drunk by the middle classes.[64] Like Guinness, Scotch Ale at first found a market amongst expatriate gentry and merchants, but with rising incomes it was not long before Scottish and Irish ales and porters were commanding a wider audience. This, together with the recruitment of efficient agents in London,

Bristol, Liverpool and Newcastle, provided the basis for an expanding coastwise trade.[65]

Bristol Ale Prices c1820		*London Ale Prices c1830*	
per dozen quarts			**per bottle**
Scotch Ale	11s	Edinburgh Ale	8½d
Burton Ale	10s	Burton Ale	8½d
Taunton Ale	9s 6d	Guinness's Stout	7d
Bristol Ale	9s	'Ordinary' Ale	6½d
London Porter	7s	London Stout	5d
Bath Porter	7s	London Porter	4½d
Dublin Porter	7s		

The English trade dated essentially from the late 1790s. Mathias records the interest of the Commissioners of Excise in this new development when they noted during 1779 that Scots ale export to the south had 'been lately extended, and is likely to be increased to a very great degree.'[66] Despite its relatively modest extent, once underway it grew rapidly, as Table 48 clearly indicates.

Table 48

Exports from Scotland to England 1785-1820 (Barrels)

Year	Ale	Beer	Porter	Total
1785	108¾	64¼	115½	388½
86	153½	83½	12	249
87	92	133½	321	456½
88	107	52½	403	562½
89	74¾	42¾	283½	401
1790	188¼	131¾	237	557
91	181½	119¼	424½	725½
92	190½	267¾	236½	694¾
93	115¼	57½	203½	376¼
94	266¼	12½	701	979¾
95	153½	27	389½	570
96	478¼	244¾	536	1259
97	523¾	138½	553	1215¼
98	279¼	189	588¼	1056½
99	402½	131	1450½	1984
1800	290¾	51	1668	2009¾
01	453½	1357¼	488½	2317¼
02	363¼	2107½	673½	3144¼
03	563¼	2898¼	284¼	3745¾
04	733½	2580	424¼	3737¾
05	1008¼	2153½	880¼	4042
06	1231	3661	1049¼	5941¼
07	2496¼	3361¼	1496½	7354
08	2943½	3377	1022	7342½
09	2971½	4417	1384	8773
1810	4872¾	4084	2181¾	1138½
11	6616½	1208	3348½	12073
12	5659½	225	1062½	6947

Exports from Scotland to England 1785-1820 (Barrels) (Cont.)

Year	Ale	Beer	Porter	Total
1813	4822¾	170	1496	6488¾
14	5950¾	382	632	6910¾
15	7011	210¾	1366½	8588¼
16	9144¾	65¼	1426	10636
17	11896½	30	844½	12771
18	15984½	44½	803	16832
19	11475	139½	936½	12551
1820	10094¾	63½	1693¾	11851½

Source: PP 1821 VIII Report on ... Malt Duty in Scotland, 87.

At the time of the first *Statistical Account*, brewers in Edinburgh, Alloa, Glasgow and Aberdeen were already involved in the English coastal trade: on the east to Newcastle and London, and on the west to Liverpool and Bristol. Glasgow brewers apparently also exported to Belfast and Dublin, although there are no indicators beyond the general export figures as to the extent of trade in this particular sphere. It was certainly modest—a mere 38 barrels worth £81 in 1800.[67] The leading export brewers were then William Black and Company of Aberdeen, J. and R. Tennent and Robert Cowan and Son (both of Glasgow), William Youngers of Edinburgh, and George Younger and Robert Meiklejohn (both of Alloa). Youngers were fairly representative of Scottish brewers in the English trade. They began selling in the London market seriously after the turn of the century and by 1802 were advertising both cask and bottled ales at the 'Edinburgh Ale Vaults' in the Strand. Youngers' agent in London, Thomas Wilson, proudly announced that a ship had just arrived from Leith with a cargo of

Mr William Younger's much admired ALE, in casks and bottles, which, being carefully selected by himself from the stock of that famous brewer, will be found to surpass in strength and flavour any ever offered to sale in London.[68]

By the 1820s Scots ales had acquired a wide reputation in England, where they were advertised and sold variously as 'Edinburgh Ale,' 'Alloa Ale,' or simply 'Scotch Ale' (as at Bristol in 1820).

William Berwick, a prominent Edinburgh brewer and maltster (who himself had few dealings in the English traffic), told a parliamentary select committee in 1821 that the 'principal brewers for England' were Dudgeons of Dunbar, Youngers of Edinburgh and Meiklejohns of Alloa, while Archibald Campbell and Company of Edinburgh were the leading porter brewer exporting to the south.[69] As we have already noted, Robert Meiklejohn of Alloa was said to have been the first Scottish brewer to ship for London, and this particular firm seems to have maintained considerable momentum in the metropolis throughout most of the nineteenth century.[70]

Breweries in Edinburgh and Berwick (as well as several smaller country breweries on the Scottish side of the Border at Coldstream and Duns) supplied colliery and farming districts in Northumberland, as well as sending coastwise to Newcastle and industrial Tyneside.[71] This particular branch of the English coastwise trade seems to have been well established by the beginning of the nineteenth century, mainly, it would appear, because of the limited development of brewing in and around Newcastle itself at that particular period.[72] Once developed, the connexion between certain Edinburgh brewers (mainly Youngers) and the potentially lucrative market of Tyneside grew in importance. It is indeed interesting that one of the largest Scottish-based brewing enterprises at the present time—Scottish and Newcastle Breweries Limited—had its origins in a modest traffic for Scots strong ale at the beginning of the nineteenth century. William Younger had a growing number of customers all over north-east England by the late 1830s, particularly in Newcastle, Sunderland, Gateshead and Darlington, as well as further afield in Hull and York, and this market expanded considerably before 1850.[73]

Of the Glasgow brewers, only J. and R. Tennent had the capacity and drive to succeed in the English market. Their main outlets were in Liverpool and Bristol, both readily reached coastwise from the Firth of Clyde. An Order Book for 1822 shows numerous customers in and around Liverpool, where Tennents' porter and table beer seem to have been remarkably successful.[74] All the problems of distance trading discussed by Mathias are evident in Tennents' dealings with their English customers: credit problems, damaged stock, bad debts and extensive correspondence. One wonders if such trade was really worth the trouble it clearly caused. Yet the Liverpool connexion was important to Tennents in another sphere, for much of their foreign trade to North and South America was shipped from there after the beginning of the 1830s.[75]

Lynch and Vaizey, in their comprehensive survey of *Guinness's Brewery in the Irish Economy 1758-1876*, described what might well be an intriguing aspect of the Scottish trade to the south. They say that Scots ales may well have been shipped by Guinness from Glasgow and Alloa (by the Forth and Clyde Canal) for sale in Liverpool, Bristol and elsewhere under the label 'Guinness's Alloa Ale,' and that this trade grew substantially throughout the 1830s. Perhaps this development was not so surprising, given the high prices commanded by good Scottish ales and beers in most English markets. Adulteration could generally be detected by anyone with a discerning palate, but downright fraud might well escape notice.[76]

We have already seen something of the origins of porter drinking and brewing in Scotland, and it was this commodity which made up the bulk of English imports to Scotland during the Industrial Revolution. London, the great porter brewing centre, was also the focal point of British coastal shipping, and naturally brewers took advantage of the possibilities presented by distant markets like that north of the Border.[77] Although the trade was not confined to the east coast or the North Sea ports, we know much more about operations and markets there than we do about trade via the Irish Sea to the ports of the Clyde. It is probably fair to say that the majority of outlets for Scottish porter were located in the more affluent east of Scotland (especially in and around the capital) and that the merchants and businessmen of Glasgow received their supplies from that quarter either overland or more likely by canal. Thomas and Robert Allen, the London brewers, claimed in 1798 to be 'the oldest dealers in the Scots trade' from the metropolis, while

George Pearson and John Courage, though having less experience, also 'dealt extensively in sending porter to Scotland.' The porter trade certainly had its origins in the early 1780s: Donald Bain, an Inverness shipmaster, began carrying porter north from London in 1784; while John Machin of Dundee had 'carried down a great deal of porter (to Scotland) ... these many years.'[78] Shipping in the stormy conditions of the North Sea seems always to have been an acute problem, much good porter being spoiled by the motion of the ship or barrels burst if not properly stored and vented. Most of the trade in Scotland was focussed on Edinburgh and Leith, concentrated in the hands of porter dealers or general merchants. One such was Edward Robertson, an Edinburgh merchant who started in the trade about 1800 and proved so successful in this and other business ventures that by 1812 he had risen to become Secretary of the Commercial Banking Company of Scotland. Most of his dealings were with Barclay, Perkins and Company and Meux and Company, and he employed the Edinburgh and Leith Shipping Company (in which he himself and almost certainly the Commercial Bank had shares) to ship the porter north from the Thames. Robertson's agent (described as 'a travelling agent'), George Andrew, apparently made 'regular journeys' throughout Scotland to effect sales of porter.[79] English porter, like Scots ale in England, was an expensive drink, mainly aimed at middle-class consumers. All the evidence would seem to indicate that locally brewed porter was just as drinkable as the imported kind, and, being cheaper, probably ousted English brews in all but the most sophisticated outlets.[80]

Exports to Foreign Parts

As early as 1765, a Scottish Lord of Session giving judgement in a court case between two Glasgow merchants was prompted to observe:

> The exportation of strong beer is of late years become a very material article of commerce for Scotland; perhaps it is next in consequence after the linen, the black cattle and the tobacco trade. It has this advantage, that it rebounds directly to the benefit of the landed interest; both by consuming a vast quantity of barley, and by encouraging in the farmers the culture of barley; a crop for which, when the ground is prepared, it is in the fittest state for any crop whatsoever.[81]

This was said at a time when the commercial brewing industry in Scotland was only just entering a phase of expansion and foreign-going exports were running at the imperceptibly modest level of 40,000 gallons per annum, valued at a mere £2,000.[82] It is just this sort of dimension which dominates the Scottish ale export trade throughout most of this period, for as we have already said, it was not until the middle of the nineteenth century that foreign markets assumed major importance. Yet, despite its modest dimensions before 1840, there is much of interest to say about the scale and organisation of the foreign export trade, the brewers who ventured into this sphere, the hazards they faced, and the destinations of Scottish export ales at various different periods between 1750 and 1850.

Export traffic in Scots ales was a mere incidental in the much more extensive

Colonial trade which developed after the third decade of the eighteenth century, but not until the 1750s do we have any evidence of its existence. One gets the impression that from the outset ale and beer export was simply a consignment trade to make up cargoes. In the ten years after 1755 the beer export trade grew

Table 49

Foreign-Going Exports of Beer 1755-1850

Year	Gallons	Barrels	Value (£)
1755	2074		104
1760	20856		1041
1765	35804		1810
1770	159733		13010
1775	101563		5124
1780	113219		5658
1785	136829		7125
1790		1447	3134
1795		1167	2153
1800		2550	5329
1805		2901	6095
1810		5349	11236
1815		5173	17247
1820		3493	12285
1825		2751	8124
1830		3451	10295
1835		4308	12517
1840		16697	41060
1845		16937	40456
1850		21181	62676

Source: PRO, CUST 8, 9 + 14 Scottish Exports.

Table 50

Destinations of Foreign-Going Exports 1755-1825: Percentage of Total Volume

Year	North America U.S.	Canada	W. Indies/ C. America	S. America	Europe	Ireland/ Isle of Man
1755	-	62	-	-	-	37	-
1760	-	52	-	-	-	48	-
1765	30	- 31	17	-	19	2
1770	-	4 -	2	-	4	90
1775	16	- 3	9	-	6	65
1780	42	- 10	23	-	8	16
1785	45	- 15	32	-	5	1
1790	17	- 13	58	-	15	5
1795	35	- 24	33	-	3	4
1800	25	- 17	55	-	2	1
1805	8	- 14	76	-	2	-
1810	3	- 10	79	1	3	1
1815	3	- 35	44	7	10	1
1820	2	- 21	52	11	7	2
1825	1	- 25	58	1	3	3

Source: Data derived from PRO, CUST 8 + 14.

Plate 1. Nineteenth century print showing Candleriggs Brewery, Alloa (from A. Barnard: *Noted Breweries of Great Britain and Ireland*, 4 vols. (1889–91)).

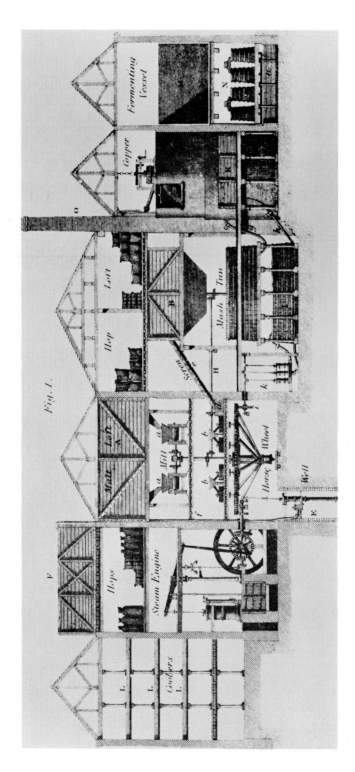

Arrangements of Utensils and Machinery in a Large Brewery c. 1845

Plates 2 and 3. The two plates here are reproduced from T. Thomson's *Brewing and Distillation* (1849), by kind permission of Edinburgh University Library.
Plate 2—A The mill house or malt loft. a Hoppers. B Brewhouse. b Millstones. E Well. F Waterback or reservoir. f Forcing pipe. G Copper. H Horizontal drive for masher. I Underback. K Jackback. L Coolers. M Fermenting tun. N Fermenting casks or cleaning vessels.

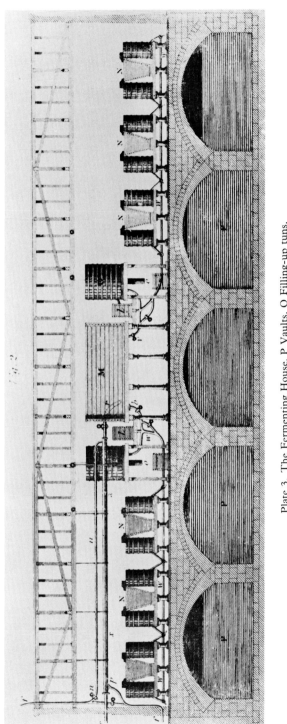

Plate 3. The Fermenting House. P Vaults. O Filling-up tuns.

Plate 4. Interior of a small brewery. LB is part of the LIQUOR BACK. MT is part of the MASH TUN. UB is part of the UNDER BACK. CB is part of the COPPER BACK. C is part of the COPPER. JB is part of the HOP BACK or JACK BACK. B is part of the BACK or COOLER. Sq is part of the SQUARE or WORKING TUN. The COPPER is represented as with a Dome Head or Cover, but without the pan. Every fixed Utensil is required to be marked and numbered in regular progression, and Numbers or Letters are attached to every Cock and Conveying Pipe in the Brewhouse. (*Edinburgh University Library*)

from 2,000 gallons per annum to over 35,000 gallons, and this development was largely the result of brewers and merchants testing sales in Colonial markets. Foreign traders, wrote an observer in the 1760s, 'being sensible of the great consequence of this article to their native country,' were very willing to send 'an assortment of Scots strong beer' with their cargoes, 'in order to spread its character everywhere.' Formerly, he noted, English beer was sent instead.[83] In 1765-6 foreign exports were 35,800 gallons valued at £1,810 (see Tables 49 and 50), the markets being distributed as follows:

	Per Cent of Total Volume
North America:	
Canada/Newfoundland	31
North American Colonies	30
West Indies/Central America	17
Europe	19
Ireland and Isle of Man	2

Prior to that date the market had been concentrated almost wholly in Europe and North America, the former absorbing about one third, the latter two thirds of exports by volume. The market in North America reflected the concentration of Scots émigrés in Maryland, Virginia and the Carolinas, while Jamaica and Granada were the most important outlets in the West Indies. Markets in the Baltic, a traditionally Scottish sphere of influence (particularly Denmark and Norway), were of equal importance with Holland, and together they absorbed about half of European exports.[84]

Looking at the foreign export figures as a whole (Table 49), we can see steady growth until 1815, followed by a slump and slow recovery after 1830. Between 1765 and 1815 there was growth until the late 80s and a slump during the 90s, corresponding with the years of trading difficulty during the Revolutionary and Napoleonic Wars. The year 1770 is typical of several apparently anomalous years when exports surged above 200,000 gallons, mostly directed at Irish markets. It is possible that this was caused by English porter and ale being directed there through Scottish entrepots. To some extent the redirection of exports to Ireland during the mid-1770s reflected the uncertainty of the Colonial markets, especially in the rebellious North American Colonies.[85] Recovery from the low levels of the 1790s had been achieved by 1810, when 5,350 barrels worth over £11,000 were exported.

The year 1815 was the last in which exports topped 5,000 barrels before the late 1830s: Table 51 shows the destinations of Scots ale by volume and value, while comparison with the data in Table 50 provides a useful indication of the market structure. The European market absorbed 10 per cent of exports, with Germany (mainly the Baltic ports) being the most important destination. The market in the United States had by that time virtually disappeared—as much a reflection of a developing brewery industry there as of the general pattern of British trading following the Napoleonic War and the Anglo-American War of 1812.

Table 51

Beer and Ale Exports from Scotland 1815

Destination	Tuns	Value (£)
Russia	11	186
Sweden	4	136
Norway	9	186
Denmark	16	171
Germany	24	523
Holland	3	102
Azores	3	103
Gibraltar	3	118
Ireland	7	240
New York	11	287
Pennsylvania	2	49
S. Carolina	7	224
Newfoundland	89	1844
Canada	88	2014
New Brunswick	6	190
Nova Scotia	78	1545
Antigua	13	380
Barbados	5	121
Dominica	1	23
Granada	21	699
Jamaica	106	2298
St. Kitts	1	32
St. Vincent	10	221
Tobago	8	174
Tortola	4	118
Trinidad	31	837
Bahamas	23	549
Berbice	14	333
Demerara	62	1509
Martinique	12	317
St. Thomas	12	317
Surinam	10	287
Buenos Aires	18	497
Brazil	9	205
Honduras	17	377
TOTALS	739	17247

Notes: (i) all figures rounded
(ii) excludes several hogsheads exported to Prussia and
Portugal
Source: PRO, CUST 8/3, Exports from Scotland 1815.

Further north, Canada, an area of great attraction to Scots settlers, accounted for more than a third of all foreign-going exports, and clearly a great proportion of this was drunk by the fisherfolk and farmers of Newfoundland and Nova Scotia. But the warmer climes of the West Indies, Central and South America represented the largest single market for Scots ales—sold to planters and merchants in

Jamaica, Demerara, Trinidad and elsewhere. In common with the general pattern of British trading during and after the wars, the South American market absorbed a modest seven per cent of exports, the main outlet being in Buenos Aires.[86]

By 1850 the picture had changed quite dramatically, yet still very much reflected the general trend of the mid-Victorian export economy, when Britain was 'workshop of the world.' As the data in Table 52 show, exports had risen to over 21,000 barrels worth £62,000. Nearly half were sent to Asia and Africa and well over half to the Americas. Scots beer exports had followed the flag to India, the East Indies and elsewhere in the Far East, while pioneer settlers in New South Wales, Victoria and South Australia might drink Edinburgh and Alloa ales, if they could afford them.[87] This particular market was to prove of very great importance to Scottish export brewers later in the nineteenth century, and this was especially so for William McEwan of Edinburgh, who built up a considerable trade in Australasia after the beginning of the 1860s.[88]

By the beginning of the nineteenth century, Scottish brewers produced special beers for the export market: before the 1820s many brewers in the general export trade had developed strong 'Export' ales and beers, while 'Imperial' or 'India' ales

Table 52

Beer and Ale Exports from Scotland 1850

Destination	Barrels	Value (£)
Europe		
Germany (A)	592	
Holland	97	
Portugal	72	
Malta	65	
Gibraltar	45	
		3359
Africa		
Mauritius	558	
South Africa	158	
		2265
Asia		
East Indies	3743	
New South Wales	1295	
S. Australia	816	
Victoria	958	
Others	1278	
		23059
America		
Canada	631	
British W. Indies	3876	
Foreign W. Indies	1459	
C. and S. America	2577	
Others	1881	
		34013
Totals	21181	62676

(A) Hanseatic towns
Source: PRO, CUST 9/39, Produce of the UK Exports, 1850.

were also increasingly popular. The major brewers of Edinburgh, Alloa and Glasgow had by this period fairly extensive experience of brewing for the export market—always a risky business because of the uncertainties of shipping, storage and climatic extremes. The problems faced by the adventurous brewers exporting Scots ales to the North American colonies in the 1760s, which we have just seen, were still a major impediment to the ale export trade in the 1840s. 'Good, sound beer always fetches its price in India,' wrote W.H.Roberts in 1847, a sensible observation, bearing in mind that 'a very great proportion' of ale imported to India arrived there in such a bad state. One of Roberts' correspondents in India saw no fewer than 800 hogsheads of beer turned into Bombay harbour in July 1845.[89] The original 'India Pale Ale' was produced by the London brewer Hodgson—a refreshing drink highly impregnated with finest hops. English provincial brewers (especially at Burton) and Scots brewers soon realised that it had as much potential as strong 'Export' ale in the India and other new colonial markets, and before long were brewing their own brands of 'India' pale ales. Clearly, a great deal more care was necessary in the brewing of 'India' pale ale, but the result was a 'strengthening, exhilarating and wholesome beverage,' much sought after at home as well as abroad. General 'Export' ales were much more mixed in quality. Those produced by Scottish brewers in the early part of the nineteenth century were similar in character to 'India' beers, although many later assumed the character of a good heavy beer, which could travel and store well.[90] 'India' and 'Export' ales, specially brewed by the major firms like Tennents, Youngers, and Meiklejohns, almost certainly made up a substantial part of the Scottish export trade by 1850, although these and other lesser Scottish brewers continued to export ordinary table beer and strong ale to other international markets in Central and South America, Africa and Australasia.

NOTES

1 Mathias (1959), 100
2 Pigot's Commercial Directory of Scotland 1825-6.
3 PP 1830 X Report from SC on Sale of Beer by Retail, 129.
4 Mathias (1959), 118.
5 PP 1821 VIII Report from SC on Petitions Complaining of Malt Duty in Scotland, 87; PRO, CUST 14/5 (1785-6); CUST 14/13B (1800-1).
6 Mathias (1959), 151; Keir, 29-32.
7 SL, SP 392/27 Pet. of Th. and Robt. Allen, Brewers in London (1798) provides a valuable history of the English porter trade to Scotland.
8 Sun Fire Insurance Policy Valuations; Beer Charged with Duty: Scotland.
9 Based on Sun Fire Policies.
10 PP 1822 XXI Accounts & Papers. Misc. Statistics.
11 Pigot's Commercial Directory of Scotland, 1825-6.
12 PP 1821 VIII Report ... on Malt in Scotland, evid. of T. Jopland, brewer at Coldstream, 34-5.
13 Younger Mss. Ledger 1805-08; SRO, RH 15/803 Seq. of J. White & Son, 1814-17.
14 SRO, RH 15/780 Seq. of R. Stein & Co. 1819-20.
15 SRO, RH 15/1721 Seq. of P. Murison, Ledger No. 4 1796-8.
16 SRO, RH 15/1332 Seq. of J. Kirk, 1826-7.
17 OSA, 12, 515.
18 J. Butt, IA of Scotland (1967), 259.
19 OSA, 13, 438-9.

20 PP1821 VIII Report ... on Malt in Scotland, 28; *Report of Meiklejohn's centenary 20 Nov. 1874* (1875), 7.
21 *OSA*, 5, 38; ibid, 461; G.Robertson, *GVA Kincardine* (1813), 433.
22 *OSA*, 9, 593.
23 SL, SP 283/13 Ans. for Craig and Hunter, merchants in Leith, 1814.
24 GH 11937/46 Sun Fire Series CD 731254, 6/4/1802; *OSA*, 19, 224-5.
25 J.Lindsay, *The canals of Scotland* (1968), 99-112; *OSA*, 16, 629.
26 *OSA*, 20, 357; D. Souter, *GVA Banff* (1812), 304.
27 Mackintosh (1914), 115.
28 Hamilton (1963), 234-41.
29 Tennent Mss; SL, SP 273/13 Pet. of G.Munro, Ans. for J.Cowan & Co. and Contracts of Co-partnership of Anderston Brewery.
30 *Pigot's Commercial Directory of Scotland, 1825-6;* A.I. Dunlop, *The royal burgh of Ayr* (1953), 179.
31 Donnachie (1971), 51-2, 55.
32 W. Singer, *GVA Dumfries* (1812), 422-3; *OSA*, 1, 195; ibid, 11, 313.
33 SRO, GD 10/1265, Broughton & Cally Mun., Tack of two fields occupied by the Brewery Co 1784; ibid, VR 106/14, Stewartry of Kirkcudbright 1870-1, parish of Girthon.
34 Donnachie (1971), 152-3, 167; I. Donnachie and I.Macleod, *Old Galloway* (1974), 62-5, 86, 91.
35 Younger Mss. Ledger 1805-8; Cash Book 1839-43.
36 Tennent Mss. Order Book 1822; Sales Accounts 1806-10.
37 There is plenty of evidence in *NSA* of brewing victuallers in the late 1830s and early 40s.
38 PP 1833 XXXIII Accounts & Papers: Brewers Licensed to Sell Beer.
39 PP 1846 XLIV A & P: Brewers Licensed to Sell Beer.
40 Mathias (1959), 118. There are some odd refs. in *OSA* and *NSA*, and the major Glasgow and Edinburgh brewers were certainly involved in the tied trade to some extent.
41 PP 1830 X Report from SC on Sale of Beer by Retail, 125.
42 Mathias (1959), 142-3.
43 A great many sequestrations in the period 1780-1830 could be thus attributed.
44 *OSA*, 20, 357; D. Souter, *GVA Banff* (1812), 304; *NSA* 13 Banff, 43.
45 G. Keith, *GVA Aberdeen* (1811), 587; SL SP 502/38 Pet. of the City of Edinburgh 1817; *NSA* 12 Aberdeen, 68.
46 SL SP 283/13 Ans. for Craig & Hunter, mcts. in Leith to the Pet. of the City of Edinburgh 1814.
47 J. Thomson, *GVA Fife* (1800), 302; R.Somerville, *GVA E. Lothian* (1805), 124; SRO RH 15/642 Brewery Cash Book of A.Bruce, Dunbar, 1784-5; *OSA*, 5, 480; *NSA* 2 Haddington, 86; *Two hundred years of progress: James Aitken & Co Ltd. 1740-1940*, 3.
48 *OSA*, 14, 295; ibid, 12, 175.
49 *OSA*, 2, 295; ibid, 15, 252; ibid, 14, 575.
50 *OSA*, 2, 254; Donnachie and Macleod, 67.
51 This is very evident in all contemporary reports, especially in *OSA* and PP.
52 Act quoted in SRO B6/17/1 Lic. Records of the Burgh of Ayr 1785-1829.
53 SRO B 66/18/1 Stirling Lic. Book 1759-1820.
54 Ibid.
55 SRO B 6/17/1, as above.
56 GCA B8/4 Public House Lics. 1179-1800.
57 B.Harrison, *Drink and the Victorians* (1971), 95-6.
58 See, for example, evid. in PP 1834 VIII Report from the SC on Inquiry into Drunkenness, 136-50.
59 PRO CUST 8/3 Exports from Scotland 1815; ibid, CUST 9/39 Prod. & Manuf. of UK Exports 1850.
60 Based on PRO CUST series 14/5, 14/13B and 8/3.
61 Tennent and Younger Mss.
62 PP 1821 VIII Report from the SC on Pets ... on Malt in Scotland, 87.
63 Mathias (1959), 150-1.
64 P.Lynch and J.Vaizey, *Guinness's brewery in the Irish economy 1758-1876* (1960), 132, 140.
65 Ibid, 140; Tennent and Younger Mss.
66 Excise TLB 1356 f. 40, quoted in Mathias (1959), 151.
67 PRO CUST 14/13B.
68 Keir (1951), 29; Younger Mss.
69 PP 1821 VIII Report from SC on Pets ... on Malt in Scotland, 28.
70 See note 20.

71 *OSA*, 3, 416; PP 1821 VIII, evid. of T.Jopland, 10-13.
72 Bt. Assoc. *Handbook of the industries of Newcastle and district* (1889), 229-32.
73 Younger Mss. Cash Book 1839-43; Cash Book 1843-5.
74 Tennent Mss. Order Book 1822.
75 Ibid., Rough Letter Copy Book 1834-7.
76 Lynch and Vaizey, 123, 131-2.
77 Mathias (1959), 148-50.
78 SL SP 392/27 Pet. of T. & R. Allen, Brewers in London 1798.
79 SL SP 262/20 Pet. of G. Andrew 1811; Ans. for E. Robertson, formerly mcht. in Edinburgh 1812.
80 *OSA* has numerous refs. to the quality of locally brewed porter.
81 SL SP 128/10 Ans. for J.Pagan & Co., mchts. in Glasgow and for A.Wilson to the Pet. of W.Baird, mcht. and brewer there 1765.
82 PRO CUST 14/1A, Scotch Exportation 1764-5.
83 As note 81.
84 As note 82.
85 PRO CUST 14/1B and 2, 1770, 1775.
86 PRO CUST 8/3 Exports from Scotland 1815.
87 PRO CUST 9/39 Exports 1850.
88 McEwan Mss. Cash Ledger 1860-64, Journal 1865-6.
89 W.H.Roberts, *The Scottish ale brewer* (1837) 3rd ed. 1847, 156-7; W. Black, *Practical treatise on brewing* (1835), 72.
90 Roberts, 158.

8
Expansion and Change 1850-1914

THE expansion of the brewing industry in Scotland during the latter half of the nineteenth century far outstripped its growth during the Industrial Revolution. Despite the emergence of large and successful firms and considerable concentration in the traditional centres, like Edinburgh, Alloa and Glasgow, the general structure elsewhere in 1850 was still one of fragmentation and localisation. Large numbers of brewers, each supplying a small market area, were scattered throughout the country. In common with other industries, however, brewing benefited from the rapid advances made in science and technology. Production techniques and the processing of raw materials improved, and better transport facilities became available. These advances—in Scotland as elsewhere—could best be exploited on the basis of increased throughput requiring greater capital investment. As a result, the period between 1850 and 1914 was marked by a consistent trend toward the production of an increasing proportion of the beer output in larger production units. In particular, the use of bigger vessels in larger breweries and a greater scientific knowledge and understanding of the brewing process were the main contributing factors. Those firms which harnessed this knowledge effectively and had the financial resources to exploit the new technology took the lead. Improved technology raised the capital threshold of entry to the industry, although for longer established firms the increased volume of profits which typified much of the period allowed for greater reploughing in new plant and technologies.

In all of these developments Scotland came increasingly to share the English experience, which has been succinctly described by Lord Vaizey in his general economic study of the evolution of the modern brewing industry between 1886 and 1951, and more recently by Dr H. Corran of the Guinness Museum, Dublin, in his history of brewing.[1] The present chapter examines the main developments of the period as a whole, with particular reference to a series of growth indicators, other significant changes in science, technology and business organisation, and, finally, the course of events during the 'Brewery Boom' of the late eighties and nineties as they affected Scotland. Subsequent chapters examine the most significant developments in greater detail: capital and companies in the 'Brewing Boom'; innovation and organisation in Scottish brewing; and domestic and overseas markets. The growth in capital which accompanied the brewing boom was a major feature of the expansion. Most concerns of any size which had previously operated as family businesses, partnerships or joint-stock companies, registered as limited liability companies. Some were large enough to go wholly public, though in the majority of instances the original management was retained—a feature common to other businesses of the period, as Professor Payne lately indicated.[2] Certain important modifications in technique during this period contributed to the growth of industrialized brewing. Before 1870 these were essentially concerned with innovation in the engineering sphere. Thereafter progress depended on pure science, which contributed to a greater understanding of the chemistry of brewing. The old ways in management and business organisation were modified to cope with the challenges of the increased scale of operations and of greater competition for custom. There were a number of developments in retailing, particularly the granting of loans to publicans and the extension of the tied-house system, which were used to secure outlets. The market for the output of breweries in Scotland grew considerably, both at home and overseas. Apart from local markets in and around the brewery, most of the major firms found outlets in the urban industrial districts of central Scotland and the north of England. A number of firms established a reputation for the production of pale ales, which became increasingly popular in domestic and foreign markets. Scotland's export record was considerable by the eighties, and she still maintains a significant position in world markets.

Indicators of Growth

One of the most consistent trends in the history of brewing in Scotland during the second half of the nineteenth century was the steady growth in output—from around 500,000 barrels in 1850 to over 2 million barrels in 1900. Table 53 provides detailed output statistics for the period to 1914 and allows comparison of Scotland's performance with that of the United Kingdom as a whole. In the table, column A shows the official production figures derived from parliamentary returns after 1880, when the Beer Duty Act re-introduced taxation on beer after nearly fifty years. Between 1830 and 1880 the tax was on malt, rather than beer, hence no production figures exist for that period. The earlier figures given in column A are derived from trade sources and are therefore somewhat suspect. Column B gives adjusted statistics calculated by George Wilson for his work, *Alcohol and the Nation:* the figures for the years before 1880 he calculated from statistics of malt made into beer, rather than actual output. He also made adjustments to take account of changes in the basis of taxation and in the measurement of units of production, i.e., the standard barrel of 36 gallons. Column C gives United Kingdom output in millions of barrels, while column D indicates Scotland's percentage share of total production.[3]

In 1857, according to official statistics the brewing industry in Scotland produced 588,000 barrels, which represented 3.4 per cent of total United Kingdom output. By 1865 production in Scotland had more than doubled to 1.2 million barrels, or 5.3 per cent of that of Great Britain, an unmistakable measure of growth which continued until the early seventies. Between 1870 and 1886, output from Scotland—like that of Britain as a whole and subject to the influences of the trade cycle—remained fairly constant at a figure of 1.2 million barrels per annum.

Increased production after the late eighties was a reflection of the general boom in the brewing industry which lasted until the turn of the century. Output rose from 1.3 million barrels in 1887 to over 2 million barrels ten years later, and nearly 2¼ million barrels at the peak of the boom in 1899. Until 1902 production topped the 2 million barrel mark, nearly 6 per cent of the U.K. total. Thereafter output fell off and remained at the 1.8 million barrel mark until 1914, just over 5 per cent of the general figure.[4]

Table 53

Beer on which Duty was paid in Scotland 1850-1914

	(000s of barrels) A	B	million barrels C	D
1850		476		
1851		534		
1852		564		
1853		686		
1854		686		
1855		460		
1856		539		
1857	588 (T)	616	17.9 (T)	3.4
1858		673		
1859		774		
1860	810 (T)	816	20.3 (T)	3.9
1861		767		
1862		802		
1863		893		
1864		986		
1865	1207 (T)	1111	22.4 (T)	5.3
1866		1254		
1867		1205		
1868		1171		
1869		1089		
1870		1026		
1871	1227 (T)	1227	26.4 (T)	4.6
1872		1342		
1873		1424		
1874		1403		
1875	1179 (T)	1179	31.0 (T)	3.8
1876		1158		
1877		1127		
1878		1279		
1879		1003		
1880	1143	1143	30.7	3.7
1881	1037	1037	27.3	3.7
1882	1088	1123	27.8	3.9
1883	1122	1151	27.1	4.0
1884	1216	1235	27.7	4.3
1885	1237	1292	27.9	4.4
1886	1236	1338	27.1	4.5
1887	1322	1421	27.9	4.7
1888	1392	1561	28.2	4.9
1889	1485	1654	28.6	5.1
1890	1666	1762	30.8	5.4
1891	1767	1753	31.9	5.5

Beer on which Duty was paid in Scotland 1850-1914 (Cont.)

	(000s of barrels)		million barrels	
	A	B	C	D
1892	1736	1710	32.2	5.3
1893	1700	1717	32.1	5.2
1894	1744	1804	32.1	5.4
1895	1758	1866	31.6	5.5
1896	1970	2024	33.8	5.8
1897	2000	2037	34.2	5.8
1898	2055	2128	35.6	5.7
1899	2179	2205	36.4	5.9
1900	2136	2112	37.0	5.7
1901	2137	2116	36.3	5.8
1902	2075	1965	36.0	5.7
1903	1939	1888	35.9	5.4
1904	1877	1825	35.3	5.3
1905	1813	1771	34.4	5.2
1906	1825	1840	34.1	5.3
1907	1811	1806	34.3	5.2
1908	1811	1752	34.4	5.2
1909	1720	1721	33.3	5.1
1910	1718	1750	32.9	5.2
1911	1769	1858	33.6	5.2
1912	1886	1845	35.0	5.3
1913	1837	1970	34.8	5.2
1914		1858		

Sources: PP, Mis. Accounts and Papers, 1850-1914; *Brewers' Almanack*, 1894, 1904, 1914; Wilson, op.cit., 369-70.
(T) Figure derived from trade source.

In overall terms Scotland's performance more than matched that of the industry as a whole and the production figures show how closely the fortunes of brewing were linked to general economic conditions. The peaks and troughs of production can be identified in Table 54 and show a close relationship to fluctuations in industrial activity over the period as a whole. Peaks in the graph of production coincide with peaks in economic activity and troughs in production with economic depression. Although imports of cheap grain were available, domestic harvests still influenced the general health of the industry. But increasingly more general economic conditions were becoming of greater importance. The consumption of beer was undoubtedly greatly influenced by activity rates and employment. 'The brewery industry,' said the *Brewery Manual* of 1907, 'is one of the first to participate in the benefits attending a trade revival, just as it is the first to feel the brunt of trade depression.' Again, in the issue of 1909 it was noted that 'beer consumption is the readiest index available of the prosperity or penury of the working class.' Earlier the Reports of the Inland Revenue had noted (1860-61) that the bad harvests of the previous year had 'a large share in restricting consumption both immediately and consequentially,' and in 1867-68 they noted that 'the trade of the brewer is much affected by a want of full employment in the working classes, and there can be little doubt it was so affected in 1867.' Depressed industrial conditions and unemployment clearly affected output and sales, as can be seen in the downturns of 1869-70, 1875-83, 1903-05, and after 1907. On the other hand the upturns of the early 1860s, the late eighties and the nineties could be ascribed 'to the healthy state of the general trade of the country, to full employment and higher wages enjoyed by the working classes.'[5]

Comparison of Tables 54 and 55 (which gives annual percentage growth rates from two base years of 1850 and 1880) provides a useful basis for a more detailed

Table 54

Fluctuations in Activity and Production in Scottish Brewing 1853-1913

| | Year | Production (000s Barrels) | |
		Peak	Trough
Peak	1853	686	
Trough	1855		460
Peak	1860	816	
Trough	1861		767
Peak	1866	1254	
Trough	1870		1026
Peak	1873	1424	
Trough	1877		1124
Peak	1878	1279	
Trough	1879		1003
Peak	1880	1143	
Trough	1881		1037
Peak	1890	1762	
Trough	1892		1710
Peak	1899	2205	
Trough	1900		2112
Peak	1901	2116	
Trough	1905		1771
Peak	1911	1858	
Trough	1912		1845
Peak	1913	1970	
Trough	1914		1858

Source: Based on data in Table 53.

overview of the period 1850 to 1914. Steady overall growth occurred between 1850 and 1873, interrupted by two major downturns between 1854-58 and 1866-69, and a minor one during 1860-61. An annual growth rate of nearly 5½ per cent was recorded between 1850 and 1860, although at the same time the halt of the mid-fifties reflected the uncertainty of domestic economic conditions during the financial crisis of 1857 and possibly export difficulties caused by the Crimean War. The trough in production occurred in 1855, and although 1857 and 1858 were also bad years, output was running anticycle, continuing to recover until 1860. In 1861 there was a slight pause. The downturn of the later sixties with an associated trough in 1870 reflected general commercial uncertainty and industrial difficulties, although the upward trend was resumed by 1871, to reach a peak in the boom of 1873. Between 1850 and 1870 the overall growth rate had been around

Table 55

Growth Rates of Output 1850-1914

Terminal Years	Length of Period	Growth Rate % Per Annum
1850-60	10	5.4
1850-70	20	3.9
1850-80	30	2.9
1850-90	40	3.3
1850-1900	50	3.0
1880-90	10	5.0
1880-1900	20	3.1
1880-1910	30	1.4
1880-1914	34	1.4

Source: Based on data in Table 53.

4 per cent. From the peak of 1873-74 output slipped somewhat to a trough in 1877, picking up in 1878, and falling more sharply in 1879. After another minor cycle between 1879-1881, the upward trend was resumed once more. The late eighties brought substantial growth, indeed the period between 1880-1899 in particular saw unprecedented growth in beer output from 1.2 to 2.2 million barrels, interrupted by only one minor setback during the depression of 1892-93. The growth of these years reflected the general experience of the brewing industry in Britain during the boom. The downturn after the peak of 1899 mirrored general difficulties both in brewing and the economy as a whole. After a period of stagnation in 1901 a downward course was resumed until 1905. Thereafter output picked up marginally to 1911, with one final cycle between 1912 and 1914. A further feature of the period was the increased concentration of production on a smaller number of units. The number of breweries (Table 56) in itself provides some indication of the changing structure of the industry between 1850 and 1914. At the beginning of the period there were still many small firms at work: even those

Table 56

Number of Breweries 1860-1910

Year	Common Brewers	Victuallers	Others	Total
1860				220
1870				210
1875	78	120		198
1880	90	45	20	155
1885	101	45		146
1890				153
1895				137
1900				125
1905				103
1910	88		26	114

Sources: PP Accts. & Papers, Returns re Brewers.

brewing fewer than a thousand barrels per annum had to have a licence and were therefore included in the excise returns. Unfortunately the returns do not provide a breakdown by size, although it seems probable that half the firms active in 1850 brewed less than a thousand barrels a year and the remainder accounted for nearly four-fifths of Scottish beers. As Table 57 indicates, victuallers still existed in large numbers and in 1852 used almost 14 per cent of total malt manufactured into beer. The measure of concentration was still greater by 1880, when according to official statistics there were more than a third fewer breweries than there had been in mid-century. On the other hand, the amount of malt used had more than

Table 57

Brewers, Victuallers and Malt used, 1852, 1880 and 1910

	1852	1880	1910
Common Brewers	146	90	88
Victuallers	14,752	45	—
Others	—	20	26
Malt Used (B)	939,000	1,852,000	2,648,000
Malt Used (V)	128,000	104,000	

Malt used is in bushels.
Sources: PP 1852, LI, Accts & Papers, Returns re Brewers; ibid 1881, LXXXIII, Acct. of No. of Brewers; ibid, 1911, LXXXVI, Acct. of No. of Brewers.

doubled and production had almost trebled. There was a slight increase in numbers after the boom of the early nineties, but by 1900 the number had slipped back to 125. In 1910 there were 88 breweries malting over 2.6 million bushels of malt into 2.1 million barrels of beer. No more than a dozen could have been described as 'country' brewers of modest output, for the industry was by then almost wholly dominated by larger firms.[6]

As the number of breweries declined, so the remainder became increasingly concentrated in the major brewing centres, a feature well-established before the middle of the nineteenth century. Although there were a number of minor changes in the boundaries of excise collections, the data in Table 58 indicate the increasing concentration which took place between 1852 and 1910. In 1852 there were 146 breweries, including many small ones probably brewing less than 1,000 barrels per annum, such as those in the country collections of Aberdeen, Dumfries and Haddington. At that particular date the collections in Glasgow and the west of Scotland had 18 breweries, those in central Scotland 23, and those in Edinburgh and the east 50 breweries. By 1880 the total number had been reduced to 90, 37 of which were in Edinburgh and the east of Scotland and 19 in Glasgow and the west. The Aberdeen collection still had 15 breweries, those of Haddington and Dumfries 8 each. New collections included those of Falkirk, Greenock and Dundee, replacing Linlithgow, Montrose and Ayr respectively. Thirty years later there were 88 breweries and the degree of concentration was considerable. The Edinburgh, Falkirk and Glasgow collections had a total of 40 breweries between

Table 58

Numbers of Brewers by Excise Collection 1852, 1880, 1910

Collection	1852	1880	1910
Aberdeen	19	15	14
Ayr	13	—	—
Caithness	1	—	—
Dumfries	12	8	3
Elgin	9	—	1
Glasgow	5	9	6
Haddington	19	8	—
Inverness	4	—	1
Linlithgow	10	—	—
Montrose	10	—	—
Perth	—	5	6
Stirling	23	3	10
Edinburgh	21	28	31
Falkirk	—	1	3
Greenock	—	10	4
Orkney	—	1	—
Dundee	—	2	9
Total	146	90	88

Sources: PP 1852, LI, Accts & Papers, Returns re Brewers; ibid
1881, LXXXIII, Acct. of No. of Brewers; ibid, 1911, LXXXVI,
Acct. of No. of Brewers.

them, while Dundee had another nine. Elsewhere the number of breweries had
been reduced, although the Aberdeen collection still returned 14 active breweries
and Dumfries three. The number of victuallers and others licensed to brew beer
also declined dramatically. Victuallers still existed in very large numbers in the
mid-nineteenth century, practically every innkeeper or publican holding a licence
to brew beer. Those brewing for sale had been reduced to 120 by 1875, 65 by 1880
and 22 by 1910—all essentially private individuals not licensed for public sale.[7]

Other major indicators of expansion and change between 1850 and 1914 are
provided by statistics of capital, labour and exports, each discussed in greater
detail in subsequent chapters. The capital devoted to the brewing industry in
Scotland grew by a factor of ten between 1850 and 1914, the labour force doubled,
and exports increased by a factor of six over the same period. Table 59 summarises
the growth of each of these factors between 1850 and 1900:

Table 59

Capital, Labour, Exports 1850-1900

	1850	1870	1885	1900
Capital (£m)	0.6	2.0	2.5	6.0
Labour (thousands)	1.0	1.3	1.8	2.0
Exports (thousands of barrels)	21.0	52.0	65.0	123.0
Output (thousands of barrels)	476	1026	1292	2112

Capital rose from over £½ million in 1850 to £2.5 million on the eve of the boom in brewing during the mid-1880s, reaching nearly £6.0 million in 1900.[8] During the period there was considerable extension of existing plant and many new breweries incorporating the latest scientific and technical developments were built, mostly in the established centres of Edinburgh, Glasgow and Alloa.[9] Labour remained of minor importance. Nevertheless, the workforce directly employed in breweries increased from about 1,000 in 1850, to 2,000 in 1891, and 2,400 in 1911. Increased use of scientific methods in larger plant undoubtedly required a larger skilled supervisory staff than before but the majority of jobs in the brewhouse still called for muscles rather than technical knowhow.[10] If exports were to be the sole measurement of growth in the Scottish brewing industry during the latter half of the nineteenth century, then by any standards its achievements were considerable. Exports rose steadily from 21,000 barrels in 1850 to 48,000 barrels in 1880. They afterwards surged ahead to reach 167,000 barrels per annum until 1914. During most of the period from 1890 onwards, Scotland accounted for at least 25 per cent of British beer exports, mostly destined for India, Australia, New Zealand and South Africa, where Scottish settlers and regiments provided ready markets. Much of this success was undoubtedly owing to the Scottish brewers' adapting to changing public taste for lighter ales like India Pale Ale—and the advantages they enjoyed through their experience in the manufacture of such products.[11]

Other developments

A whole range of developments in other spheres greatly changed the character of Scottish brewing from what was still essentially a craft in 1850 to a mass production industry by the 1890s. The most significant developments were in the fields of technical and scientific progress, business organisation, transport improvements and marketing. All of these developments were directly or indirectly responses to increased demand for the products of the brewery amongst a growing population, both in domestic and overseas markets. Changing taste was a significant influence on the structure of demand, and many of the scientific and technical developments of the era made possible the production of the types of beer and ale sought by the public at home and abroad. The securing of retail outlets through the Scottish version of the English tied-house system, improved distribution and more systematic marketing, and advertising all became increasingly important in an age of greater competition. The Scottish brewers were generally leaders in the development of new products, and their grasp of the possibilities presented by new technologies and modes of business organisation kept several in the forefront of the trade before 1914.

Technical and scientific developments brought great changes to the scale of production and range of products in the Scottish brewing industry during the latter half of the nineteenth century, and contributed much to the growing efficiency of the larger breweries. Education in brewing was greatly improved, both in the scientific and engineering areas: special courses for brewers were run by Heriot-Watt College in Edinburgh and by other technical institutes from the

1880s onwards. Firms like William Younger, William McEwan, John and Robert Tennent were early amongst those who employed trained scientists in laboratories to examine the product and to analyse any reasons for bad beer or for variations from the normal quality. This not only eliminated waste, but also contributed to the development of a more reliable product which might subsequently become the basis for national sales. Much of this progress depended on pure science: discoveries by Pasteur and others greatly improved the brewer's understanding of the fermentation process, the activity of yeasts, and the chemistry of malt. These developments went hand in hand with the introduction of bigger brewing vessels and more sophisticated machinery which facilitated the movement of grains and liquids from one part of the maltings or brewery to the other. The creation of a more reliable product, together with other innovations like refrigeration and carbonization, helped in the development of bottling, particularly of the increasingly popular pale ales.[12] Bottling was largely a hand process until the 1870s, when bottling machines were becoming increasingly common. Improvements in filling machinery and the invention of more efficient bottle caps greatly reduced the costs of the process. Although bottling was still essentially small-scale before 1914, probably a quarter of the market for bottled beers and ales was in the hands of the Scottish brewers.[13]

Other innovations of the period were to have long-term effects: they included greater use of steam power, electricity and motor transport. Steam power was extensively used in most of the bigger breweries by the mid-nineteenth century, but after 1860 it was increasingly applied to the heating of liquids in mash tuns and coppers. Later, in the eighties and nineties, steam power was applied to electricity generation, mainly for lighting in and around breweries. After 1900 it was increasingly used to power machinery. Motor transport was also appearing in breweries at this time, although horse-drawn drays remained the main means of transport for many years, despite the apparent savings brought about by using motor lorries or steam-powered drays.[14]

In an age of growing competitiveness, good business organisation and effective management became important characteristics of the successful firm. As already noted in the introduction to this chapter, entrepreneurs in the Scottish brewing industry responded quickly to changes in demand. Members of the founding families continued to dominate many firms, even after they became public companies during the brewing boom of the eighties and nineties. Nevertheless— and perhaps because of the close family ties—management became increasingly professional. The latter half of the nineteenth century saw the emergence of two types of specialist in brewery management: the commercial manager and the brewer-chemist. The former concerned himself with brewery administration, finance, staff and sales, the latter with the manufacture of a product of uniform quality acceptable to the customer. No beer could compete successfully with rivals without efficient marketing and this aspect of business organisation became a major concern of brewers during the period under review. In most of the large breweries, therefore, an increased proportion of the staff was devoted to the increase of sales.[15] Brewers sought an increasing degree of control over retail outlets by the extension of loans to publicans, through the Scottish equivalent of the English tied-house system. There is very little evidence of its importance much before the seventies, although it became increasingly common with the onset of greater competition during the brewery boom. The larger brewers in Scotland, such as William Younger, began to seek secured outlets by this means in the nineties, both in Scotland itself and in the north of England. The development of the partial-tied system in Scotland took place against a background of more stringent licensing laws, which brought about a reduction of 20 per cent in the number of licensed premises between 1886 and the beginning of World War I. Despite these difficulties, there is little to indicate a fierce battle for retail outlets in Scotland of the kind that typified the so-called 'Brewers' Wars' south of the Border.[16]

Perhaps the most important element in extending the brewers' markets in the second half of the nineteenth century was improved and cheaper transport. Prior to the development of canals and coastal shipping, which were often useful to brewers in Glasgow, Edinburgh, Falkirk and Alloa, most markets were limited to the distance that could be reached by a brewer's dray. Hence the size of any potential market was initially a function of population in any particular locality. Urban brewers in the traditional centres were doubly advantaged, and several had developed a considerable trade with more distant markets before the mid-nineteenth century. Both steamshipping and railways enabled those larger Scottish brewers to widen their domestic markets in Scotland and south of the Border, as well as greatly increasing their effectiveness in more distant colonial outlets. Several of the firms active in English markets, notably William Younger and Company, continued to ship their products to the south by sea even after the creation of a national railway network. On the evidence of surviving brewers' records, the most important English market was on Tyneside, readily reached both by sea and rail.[17]

Improved transport and communications also made possible the increased use of commercial travellers to raise business on the brewers' behalf. Most of the brewers had travelling salesmen by the 1860s—some based in head offices, others in stores, depots or sub-offices in other towns or cities. The activities of a salesman were much more readily controlled and supervised than those of an agent. The salesman generally had the sole interest of his firm at heart, whereas an agent might also act for other brewers or distillers. A salesman or traveller could be used to keep an eye on public houses where the brewer sold his beer, reporting back on the general management and state of sales. In this connexion—as in many aspects of business activity in brewing and other commercial fields—the telegraph and later the telephone were of enormous value in the development of trade.[18]

In the atmosphere of growing competition after the seventies, marketing began to play an increasingly important role in the sales activities of brewers. More and more brand names and registered trade marks were used to give the products of individual breweries distinctive identities memorable to the consuming public. Among the leaders in the field in Scotland were John and Robert Tennent, William Younger and Company, William McEwan, and Drybrough and Company, whose trade marks had been in regular use for up to twenty years when first registered in the late seventies. Trade marks could be further exploited in labelling and advertising, the former of course an essential in bottled beers, the latter increasingly important in newspapers or public places generally.[19]

The Boom and Aftermath

Scotland shared the experience of the industry as a whole in the 'Brewery Boom' and aftermath of the years 1885 to 1900.[20] During this period output doubled, most of the large firms sought corporate status, and the capital devoted to the industry increased threefold. The course of events and changes brought about during the boom are well documented in the brewing press and elsewhere. Most commentators were agreed that the industry in Scotland enjoyed many advantages over certain sections of the trade south of the Border. Concentration was seen as a prime advantage, although others included the specialist production of such liquors as pale ales and bottled beers, and an outstanding export record. A great deal of the general comment about the industry as a whole at that time, therefore, applies to Scotland with modification. We have to take account not only of the advantages noted by contemporaries, but also of the great differences which existed in Scotland, particularly in the relatively modest scale of operations and in the licensing system and retailing.

Reporting the state of the trade in 1884, the *Brewers' Guardian* said that the decline in production during the late seventies and early eighties had been due to a number of factors, most notably general economic difficulties, poor barley and hop crops, and the introduction of the Beer Duty Act in Gladstone's Budget of 1880. There was no doubt in the trade that the Beer Duty Act had contributed to 'the regular and marked decline' in the number of brewers, 'especially the small ones.' The concentration of the trade had many advantages, however. It brought about a 'general improvement in the quality of beer,' for large breweries 'were able to brew beer of better quality than smaller competitors.'[21] The customer probably thought it reasonable to query the proposition that the large breweries brewed *better* beer, although they did produce *cheaper* beer of standard quality!

In 1885 severe depression in trade was reported, yet many brewers had succeeded in doing reasonably well. Because raw material prices remained low, good profits had been made. British exports in general were said to be falling, largely because of foreign competition, particularly from Germany 'which produces beers suitable to every climate.'[22] This was not the experience of Scottish brewers in the export trade, because of their advantages in the production of light ales of the kind required in colonial markets. In fact, the *Brewers' Guardian* of the following year emphasised both the increased production in Scotland and her success in the export trade. 'In Scotland,' the periodical noted, 'the trade is far more concentrated than in England ... and this gives considerable advantages.'[23]

By 1886 there was still some concern about 'diminished demand and excessive competition,' yet most brewers continued to make good profits because of low primary product prices. 'The success of Guinness Company,' it was noted, 'will no doubt lead to the conversion of many private companies into joint-stock companies.'[24] The leading Scottish firms were the first to go public in the late eighties and early nineties, notably William Younger, William McEwan and John and Robert Tennent. In 1890-91 their shares were said to be 'doing well,' being quoted publicly for the first time in 1891.[25] Numerous other firms followed, so that by 1899 the total authorised capital of 35 registered companies in the brewing industry in Scotland was in the region of £6 million.[26] In the majority of cases the vendors retained a strong hold over their businesses, and this was a continuing characteristic of the industry in Scotland long after 1914.

The general optimism following the short-term depression of the early nineties is mirrored in numerous trade reports of the period. A review of the trade in 1893 said that beer had 'continued to hold its own as the national beverage,' although exports (from England, not Scotland) continued to fall, 'owing no doubt to the establishment of large colonial and foreign breweries.'[27] During the boom which lasted until 1899, Scottish brewers did remarkably well, both in terms of overall output and export performance—as the data in Tables 53 and 59 indicate. The peak of 1899 brought with it an unprecedented output in Scotland of 2,179,000 barrels.

As the industry slid into the depression of the early 1900s, general activity in the trade was reported to be 'limited,' partly due, it was thought, to the prolonging of the Boer War, general increases in taxation, and uncertainties on the overall economic front. The trade complained of all the usual disadvantages, higher prices for raw materials, increased excise duty, and, additionally, of the infamous 'Arsenic Scare' of 1901. This last had arisen from a case in Manchester over adulteration of beer by the introduction of additives found to contain minute quantities of arsenic. Despite the open verdict, numerous other actions were raised—mostly without justification—against other brewers. The incident played right into the hands of the Temperance movement. Yet despite these difficulties many brewers continued to do well. As far as 1901 was concerned, the position was not as gloomy as it seemed, for 'the conclusion of the war and the Coronation' ought to prove 'excellent things for the trade.'[28]

Reports of activities in 1903-04 were less optimistic. Many firms—especially those with capitalisation difficulties—had passed dividends. The Edinburgh United Breweries, a major Scottish amalgamation which had been dogged with financial difficulties since its inception at the beginning of the boom in 1889, paid no dividends in 1904, 'owing to dull times, bad weather, Government duty and other causes.'[29] Stocks and shares were 'very depressed' during the years 1900 to 1905, although many brewers continued to develop a good trade with profits 'well maintained.' By 1905 the situation had started to improve: at least three major Scottish companies reported favourably. Gordon and Blair of Glasgow had sustained their share of losses, although overall they had performed with satisfaction. Tennents had enjoyed a 'steady run of prosperity' and were able to declare profits of nearly £18,000. 'At a critical time for brewery companies over the period since 1897,' the annual general meeting of shareholders was told, 'the average dividend has been 12½ per cent.' Hugh Baird and Sons, also of Glasgow, were reported to be doing well, having made £10,500 profit on the year's trading, and thus were able to declare a dividend of 7 per cent.[30] The Census of Production for 1907 provides an interesting series of figures relating to output in brewing, malting and related trades as a whole, although this is less useful than it might be for brewing in terms of employment and productivity calculations, because no breakdown is provided for individual sectors. In 1907 output was 1,800,000 barrels worth £3,036,000.[31] Thereafter the continuing fall in production was halted until 1908-10, when trade was again caught in economic recession. A measure of recovery took place before 1914 when the onset of the war brought major distortions to the drink industries as a whole.

The many changes which took place in the period between 1850 and 1914 laid the basis for the subsequent evolution of the modern brewing industry in Scotland. By 1914 the bulk of the industry was already highly concentrated in a dozen or so large and profitable firms. Healthy but far from fierce competition existed between the brewers—the real competition for retail outlets was to occur later. The movement for incorporation and the subsequent reconstruction of companies was largely over. The political difficulties of the industry were dormant, largely the result of licensing legislation which had reduced the numbers of public houses. The fluctuations and changes which produced this situation can therefore be set against a background of relative prosperity in the industry, best reflected in the experience of the major and long-established Scottish brewers.

NOTES

1 J.Vaizey, *The Brewing Industry 1886-1951: an economic study* (London, 1960), especially pp. 3-19; H.Corran, *A history of brewing* (Newton Abbot, 1975), particularly good on technical and related developments.

2 P.Payne, *British entrepreneurship in the nineteenth century* (London, 1974), 17-23. On the large-scale companies including breweries see also his 'The Emergence of the Large-scale Company in Great Britain, 1870-1914' *Economic History Review*, 2nd series 20 (1967), 519-542.

3 G.Wilson, *Alcohol and the nation* (London, 1940), 369-70.

4 Up till 1904 Scotland's contribution was 5.4 per cent on average, from 1904-14, 5.2 per cent on average.

5 *Brewery Manual*, 1907; ibid, 1909.

6 *Brewers' Almanack* 1914, 370-71.

7 Ibid.

8 See Table 60.

9 See the section on 'Brewing Technology and New Products' in Chapter Ten.

10 PP 1912-13 CVIII Report on Earnings and Hours of Labour: VIII, Food, Drink and Tobacco Trades in 1906, 204; W. Stanley-Smith, 'Labour in the Brewhouse,' *Brewers' Guardian*, 1902, 72-5.

11 PRO CUST 9/39, 49, 59, 69, 79 United Kingdom Exports (Beer and Ale) 1850-1870; PP Accounts and Papers 1875-1914.

12 For a discussion of patents see Section on 'Brewing Technology and New Products' in Chapter Ten, especially Table 66.

13 A.J.Puddick, 'Changes in British bottling techniques,' *Brewers' Guardian* Centenary Issue, 1971, 117-119; Anon, 'The brewing trade in Edinburgh,' *Brewers' Guardian*, 1903, 112; M.Rankin, 'The brewing industry of Edinburgh,' in M.P.Fogarty (ed.) *Further studies in industrial organisation* (London, 1948), 209,23.

14 Barnard, op.cit., has many references to steam power usage in Scottish breweries; F.G.Ansell, 'Electricity in modern breweries,' *Brewers' Guardian*, 1903, 125-8; F.M.Maynard, 'Motor traction for

brewers.' *Brewers' Guardian*, 1900, 218-21, 230-33, 241-2.

15 J.Baker, *The brewing industry* (London, 1905), 142.

16 Wm. Younger Mss. Travellers' Statistics Book. PP 1899 XXV Report of the Royal Commission on the Liquor Licensing Laws, Final Report, 27; Vaisey, op.cit., 14-16.

17 Many of the new breweries built during the latter half of the nineteenth century incorporated loading bays and railway sidings.

18 Baker, op.cit., 139-40.

19 *Brewers' Guardian*, 1880, 335, 369.

20 P.Payne, 'The Large Scale Company,' op.cit., 530-32.

21 *Brewers' Guardian*, 1885, 15.

22 Ibid. 415.

23 Ibid. 1886, 401-03.

24 Ibid, 357.

25 Ibid, 1891, 10, 14-15.

26 See Table 63.

27 *Brewers' Almanack*, 1894, 88-9.

28 *Brewers' Guardian*, 1902, 13-14, ibid, 1901, 18, 30, 31-8.

29 Ibid., 1904, 287, 337.

30 Ibid., 1905, 102, 183.

31 PP 1910 CIX Census of Production 1907, Part V, Re...Brewing and Malting, 38-39.

9

Capital and Companies in the Brewing Boom

IN the period between 1850 and 1914 the brewing industry in Scotland experienced a dramatic change of structure and organisation. Large commercial breweries gradually displaced small producers, and although the displacement of craftsmen and country brewers was by no means complete by the beginning of the present century, the major companies dominated the industry in Scotland long before the boom of the eighties. The bigger breweries, as we have seen in Chapter Eight, continued to grow faster. As Vaizey has indicated, their growth was accelerated by improvements in transport, the expansion of urban markets and the increasing mechanisation of the brewing process.[1] Brewing, like other trades of the time, was by the 1880s undergoing a process of concentration in larger units, and in this the Scottish industry shared the general experience of breweries throughout the United Kingdom. The capital devoted to brewing in Scotland increased by a factor of ten, the growth being mainly financed by the private resources of the families who owned the firms. The process was a gradual working out of the consequences of the advantages of industrialised brewing over craft techniques and the re-ploughing of profits from successful enterprise. New breweries were founded and several became as important as older companies, but they were exceptions. In the middle of the nineteenth century there were still many small breweries of modest capital which produced only enough beer to satisfy the demands of the immediate locality. Probably three-quarters of the country's 100-odd breweries produced less than a fifth of the total barrelage and represented much the same proportion of the total capital. Therefore about 25 firms accounted for four-fifths of the industry and for capital totalling nearly £500,000. A handful of the leading and older-established firms like William Younger in Edinburgh and John and Robert Tennent in Glasgow dominated the industry. The latter was reported to be worth in the region of £200,000 in 1855 and the former firm must have been at least as valuable.[2]

In the period of growth which preceded the boom of the eighties, the leading group—mainly urban breweries—expanded to meet the demand of growing markets both at home and abroad, at the same time absorbing the trade of the remaining small firms. Several new breweries were established, the leading firm being William McEwan, founded in 1856. By 1870 the capital of the Scottish brewing industry was in excess of £2 million, at least half of this being accounted for by half a dozen leading firms in the traditional brewing centres of Edinburgh, Alloa and Glasgow. The growth of the period 1850 to 1870 was more than matched

160

by subsequent expansion in the brewing boom of the eighties, for by the turn of the century the authorised capital of breweries registered in Scotland had risen to a sum in excess of £6 million. Of the total, almost £4 million was represented by seven leading companies—an indication of the further degree of concentration achieved in Scottish brewing during the boom.[3]

The experience of the Scottish brewing industry in relation to capital during the period under review was a reflection of general developments in the industry as a whole throughout Britain. Before looking at the Scottish situation, it is therefore worth examining the main trends in brewing history as it relates to capital and companies, particularly during the boom of 1886 to 1900. In England the tendency towards concentration had been a feature of the trade for many years and it continued with increased momentum after the middle of the nineteenth century. For reasons which are explained in greater detail in Chapter Eleven, the large and expanding brewers in the south began increasingly to seek greater assurance of sales through the tied-house system. This required capital on a scale commensurate with or greater than that needed to extend the plant which gave such firms their considerable economies of scale. In the sixties and seventies this expansion continued, despite the increasingly hostile views of temperance advocates and some politicians, and by the early eighties the atmosphere in the trade was 'calm and gradualist.'[4]

The most important initial development in the brewery boom came in 1886, when the giant Dublin-based firm of Arthur Guinness and Son was floated as a limited liability company—the first large brewery flotation. The authorised capital of £6 million was subscribed 28 times over. It was not surprising that the success of this issue should attract other breweries to follow Guinness into the market. Substantial capital gains could clearly be made by the vendors from share issues, and there was ample opportunity to find funds on a scale adequate to finance the continued expansion of ambitious brewing firms. Ind Coope and Samuel Allsopp—both of Burton—were next to offer some proportion of their business to the public, and gradually more and more firms came on the market. By 1888 shares to the vaue of £25 million had been issued, and subsequently during the years 1889 to 1903 no less than £106 million was sunk in breweries, mainly in preference shares and debentures. Among the major English breweries, Bass, Courage, Combe, Reid & Company, Watney, Meux, and Whitbread went public. Most offered the public the security of preference shares and debentures, while retaining the ordinary shares and profits of the concerns. Thus the brewing families kept control of their firms. The sums at which breweries were sold were phenomenal: on the sale of 237 businesses, no less than £57 million was paid to the vendors in cash in addition to £30 million in debentures and £60 million in fully paid ordinary shares, the bulk of which the vendors retained, offering to the public only the preference shares and debentures.[5]

The increase of brewery capital coincided with, and was to some extent responsible for, the extension of the tied-house trade. Brewers were increasingly obliged to seek further outlets and such was the degree of competition that prices of public houses were often twice or three times the actual value of the house. Excessive and unwise sums were sunk in the take-over of smaller breweries, the acquisition of tied houses, or in loans to publicans, especially in the decade of the nineties. Even old-established and conservative firms indulged in these purchases—a policy which left most of them with a great burden of fixed-interest charges on debentures raised in order to give them ready cash to buy property quickly. Even in the early stages of the boom many of the major firms had built up such substantial charges that they had become extremely vulnerable in any period of bad trade. The end of the boom at the turn of the century left many companies substantailly over-committed. Even before the depression of 1903-04 it became increasingly difficult to deal in brewery stock. Between 1903 and 1907 the preference shares of 14 leading firms—other than Guinness and Bass—fell from £11.5 million to £5 million. There was little dealing in debenture stock. Inevitably, considerable capital was written down in the aftermath of the slump, many firms being revalued and reconstructed. Ordinary, preference and debenture capital, having a par value of £106 million, stood in 1913 at £88.5, a loss of nearly £20 million, and if the figure for other companies whose capital was never quoted is added, the loss must have been considerably greater. Yet despite these difficulties, as Vaizey has shown, the brewing industry, even in bad patches of trade brought on by depression, showed remarkable staying power. 'The steady above average yield of many brewery companies,' he has written, 'was indicative both of their great profitability before flotation . . . and their conservative administration.'[6]

Capital

The main problem in trying to estimate the total capital of the Scottish brewing industry throughout the period under review is that no data are available for many lesser firms. Even some of the bigger firms active before 1914 remained private companies, and little information is therefore available. However, it is possible to arrive at estimates for the capital of the industry in Scotland, using a variety of sources including the register of companies, parliamentary papers, trade directories and the brewing press. The results are shown in Table 60. As previously

Table 60

General Estimates of Capital 1850-1900

		1850	1870	1885	1895	1900
A	No of Breweries	225	210	146	137	120
B	Output (000s barrels)	500	1,250	1,237	1,758	2,136
C	Capital (£m)	0.6	2.1	2.5	5.0	6.0
D	Fixed Capital (£m)	0.2	0.6	1.0	1.5	2.0
E	Trading Capital (£m)	0.4	1.5	1.5	3.5	4.0
F	Quarters Used (000s)	108	300	288	430	534

Includes brewers producing less than 1,000 barrels per annum.
Sources: PP 1850 LII Accounts and Papers; ibid 1899 XXX Accounts and Papers; H. Stopes, *Brewery Companies* (London 1895), pp. 43-51; *The Brewers' Guardian*, 1871, pp. 60-62; PP 1852 LI Accounts and Papers; ibid, 1872 Accounts and Papers.

indicated, the actual numbers of brewers (A), though interesting in themselves, provide little indication of the scale or capital of the industry: indeed, they are somewhat unreliable because of the different basis of calculation at different points in time. But the same parliamentary accounts include amounts of malt used (F), measured in either bushels or quarters, the returns being by excise collection. Firmly established official returns of output, already described, are shown in line (B) of the table. Total capital is given in line (C), fixed capital in line (D) and trading capital in line (E), further explanation of the basis of calculation being indicated below.

Professor L.Levi, a prolific Victorian economist, published a detailed study of the brewing industry in 1871, entitled 'The Liquor Trades,' in which he provided detailed calculations of the capitals of the various drink industries in Great Britain, based on data for 1870.[7] The total fixed capital of the brewing trade he put at £12.4 million, of which £11.0 million was in England, £0.8 million in Ireland and £0.6 million in Scotland. He arrived at these figures by estimating that £2 of fixed capital was required to brew each quarter of malt. This was a low estimate, especially if land was included. Levi calculated that a small to medium-size brewery with plant to mash ten quarters per day, working six days per week in the six winter months brewing 2,300 quarters producing 9,200 barrels per annum, required a fixed capital in buildings, utensils, machinery, casks, drays etc of £4,500. But, as he pointed out, the fixed capital varied from place to place, especially between town and country, where land values were very different. In addition, some of the smaller breweries (of which there were many in Scotland) had old buildings, plant and machinery and therefore might be worth less than average. On the other hand, in larger breweries as much as £3 per quarter might have been invested in capital equipment, particularly if recent expansion had taken place. Assuming the lower figure of £2, the fixed capital value of the industry in Scotland was £600,000. Levi's figures for the liquid capital in brewing in Great Britain were as follows:

	£ million
6.2 million quarters of barley at £1.8 per quarter	11.2
600,000 cwt of hops at £5 per cwt	3.0
350,000 cwt of sugar at £1.5 per cwt	0.5
Total for Materials	14.7
Production costs	10.8
Duty	6.5
Total	32.0

The above production costs were calculated on an average barley price of 36 shillings per quarter for the decade 1860-70, and the costs of malting at 5 shillings and of brewing at 30 shillings per quarter. These costs included depreciation of plant and casks, coals, wages and interest payments on capital or loans. Scotland's proportionate share was £1.5 million, although as Levi indicated, 'floating capital is constantly in motion ... and probably half the total will fairly represent the amount invested at any one time.'

Estimates of the capital of the drink industries as a whole are also worthy of examination and comment at this point to indicate the relationship with brewing and the extent of other sectors, such as distilling and general retailing. The figures are given in Table 61.

According to these figures, brewing represented about 10 per cent of the total value of the drink industries and their penumbra of service activities. Clearly some proportion of the bottling trade and a significant share of the public houses' capital was owed to brewers, although it is not possible to arrive at any firm figures. Levi thought that 'a considerable proportion of the fixed capital of public-houses' belonged to the brewers, but he was mainly referring to the situation south

Table 61

Total Capital of Scottish Liquor Trades 1870 (£ 000s)

Sector	Fixed Capital	Trading Capital
Brewing	600	1,500
Distilling	2,400	6,900
Glass and Cork manufs.	300	100
Wine and Spirit dealers and Bottlers	500	—
Foreign Spirits and Wines	—	1,700
Wages of Dealers, Workmen and Bottlers	—	1,000
Public Houses	3,600	—
Wages of Public House Servants	—	960
Licence Duties	—	128
Totals	7,200	12,288

Source: L.Levi, 'The Liquor Trades,' *Brewers' Guardian* 1871, 60-62.

of the Border where there were many more tied houses. Scotland had 12,000 public houses in 1870, worth on average £300 per annum each. It is clear that brewing in Scotland occupied a modest place in relation to the drink industries as a whole, for the fixed capital of the distilling industry far exceeded the total for brewing.

The capitals for other years are based on these calculations and on data of raw material inputs and production. The figures for 1850 are perhaps on the low side, though output in that year was only two-fifths that in 1870, using a third of the quantity of malt, barley prices being about 20 per cent lower. Other production costs were lower, but in 1850 there were probably many more older plants with antiquated equipment and therefore unit costs might well have been higher. The 1885 figures could not have differed much from those of 1870, although brewing was severely affected by general depression, and it is likely that the industry was operating at a good deal less than capacity.

After the start of the brewing boom in the late 1880s, an increasing number of Scottish brewing firms registered as limited liability companies and a great deal more information is therefore available on capital in subsequent years. Because of the general interest in brewing, an increased amount of attention was paid to the activities of firms in the trade by the investing public, a great deal being written by way of comment to meet this need. One analyst of the trade at that time was Henry Stopes, a maltster turned author-journalist on trade topics. According to one of Stopes's articles in *The Statist* of 20 October 1894 (later reprinted in his book *Brewery Companies*, published the following year), the total capital invested in 417 limited liability companies in the United Kingdom was £104 million.[8] Scotland at that period accounted for approximately 5.4 per cent of total United Kingdom production, so that proportionately the total capital of breweries in Scotland could have been as high as £5.6 million. The total authorised capital of those companies which had registered by 1895 was over £4 million, the degree of concentration being considerable. Of the £4 million total for 1895, something like £3.2 million was represented by the authorised capital of six major firms, including, as Table 63 shows, the two major Edinburgh firms of William Younger and William McEwan at £1 million each. Edinburgh United Breweries had a capital of £450,000, while John and Robert Tennent had an authorised capital of £260,000, and both Thomas and James Bernard of Edinburgh and Archibald Arrol of Alloa were registered with capitals of £250,000. Four other important firms, Steel Coulson & Company of Glasgow and Edinburgh, Hugh Baird of Glasgow, John Aitchison and Drybrough and Company (both Edinburgh) had capitals of at least £100,000. In 1895 three-quarters of the total brewing capital in Scotland was represented by twenty-odd major firms in Edinburgh, Glasgow and Alloa. The remainder were relatively small breweries with a total capital between them of about £1 million.[9]

Following the wave of registrations and public issues in the latter half of the nineties, there were 34 limited liability brewery companies in Scotland with a total authorised capital of £5,841,000. Half a dozen medium-size firms, including John Jeffrey of Edinburgh and G & J MacLachlan of Glasgow, had not bothered to register, but the total value of such businesses is unlikely to have been in excess of £500,000.[10] The situation in 1905 is indicated in Table 62, by which time one additional firm had registered. The concentration of capital in large businesses was greater than before. Of the 35 limited liability companies, 15 firms with individual capitals in excess of £100,000 represented no less than 83 per cent of the total authorised capital. The remaining 20 firms with capital of less than £100,000 represented only 16.5 per cent of the total. Only a handful of small firms had registered, so we in fact know very little about the remainder.[11]

The fixed capital of the brewing industry in Scotland (Table 60, line D) grew from around £250,000 in 1850 to £1 million on the eve of the company boom in 1885. Much of the growth in this period was accounted for by investment on the part of major brewers in plant and machinery. Alfred Barnard's tour of Scottish breweries about this time gives a fair indication of the amount of rebuilding and extension which had taken place prior to his visits.[12] Between 1885 and 1895 the fixed capital rose to around £1.5 million, although it was probably nearer £2 million if companies which had not registered are included. At the end of the boom

Table 62

*Grouped Frequency Distribution of 35 Brewery Companies
by Authorised Capital 1905*

Valuation £	No.	Total Capital £000s	Percentage of Total Capital
Up to £10,000	4	31	0.5
£10 - 50,000	7	205	3.5
£50 - 100,000	9	750	12.5
£100 - 500,000	12	2,185	37.5
Over £500,000	3	2,750	46.0
	35	5,921	100.0

Sources: SRO, Register of Dissolved Companies; *Brewers' Guardian; Manual of British and Foreign Brewing Companies* (various dates).

in 1900 the fixed assets of the Scottish brewing trade were between £2.5 and £3 million, most being concentrated in 20 or so major plants in Edinburgh, Glasgow and Alloa, with more modest breweries in Falkirk, Dundee and Aberdeen. The calculation of trading capital, including loans to public houses, is indicated in line E of Table 60. These estimates are essentially based on production data and on the calculations of Professor Levi for 1870 and Henry Stopes for 1895. Trading capital rose from less than £500,000 in 1850 to £1.5 million in 1870. It remained relatively static throughout the years before 1885, but grew rapidly[13] during the boom to reach between £3.5 and £4 million by the turn of the century.

A more detailed picture of capitals can be derived from Table 63. The data broadly confirm the view that the expansion of the brewing trade in Scotland was well regulated and less traumatic than south of the Border. This was in part due to close family connexions and conservative management, and in part to the relatively modest capital involved. Although some substantial capital gains were made by brewers, the majority maintained their close connexions with the new

Table 63

Authorised Capital of Brewery Companies Registered in Scotland 1884-1905

No.	Date	Company	Auth. Capital	Ord. Shares	Pref. Shares	Debentures	
1	1884	Sharp	25,000	25,000	—	—	(A)
2	1887	W. Younger	1,000,000	500,000	500,000	—	
3	1888	Steel Coulson	140,000	100,000	—	40,000	
4	1889	McEwan	1,000,000	500,000	500,000	—	
5	1889	Edinburgh United	450,000	125,000	125,000	200,000	
6	1890	Tennent	260,000	200,000	—	60,000	(B)
7	1890	Meiklejohn	50,000	30,000	10,000	10,000	
8	1890	Thomson Marshall	65,000	23,000	22,000	20,000	
9	1891	Young	30,000	16,800	2,000	11,200	
10	1892	Ireland	25,000	—	—	—	
11	1892	Wellshot	20,000	16,000	4,000	—	
12	1894	Baird	160,000	80,000	80,000	—	(C)
13	1895	Arrol	250,000	235,000	15,000	—	
14	1895	Bernard	250,000	75,000	175,000	—	

Authorised Capital of Brewery Companies Registered in Scotland 1884-1905 (Cont.)

No.	Date	Company	Auth. Capital	Ord. Shares	Pref. Shares	Debentures	
15	1895	Craigellachie	10,000	10,000	—	—	
16	1895	Usher	70,000	70,000	—	—	
17	1895	Aitchison	110,000	50,000	60,000	—	
18	1895	Drybrough	100,000	50,000	50,000	—	
19	1896	Haddington	20,000	10,000	10,000	—	
20	1896	R. Younger	180,000	80,000	100,000	—	
21	1896	Campbell Hope & King	220,000	60,000	70,000	90,000	(D)
22	1896	Maclay	75,000	75,000	—	—	
23	1897	G. Younger	500,000	250,000	250,000	—	(E)
24	1897	Ballingall	100,000	50,000	50,000	—	
25	1897	Murray	75,000	75,000	—	—	
26	1897	Carmichael	3,000	3,000	—	—	
27	1898	Turners Ayr	80,000	40,000	40,000	—	
28	1898	Gordon & Blair	150,000	75,000	75,000	—	
29	1898	Thompson	120,000	60,000	60,000	—	
30	1898	South-Western	35,000	17,500	17,500	—	
31	1898	Lynch	8,000	8,000	—	—	
32	1899	Paterson	100,000	50,000	50,000	—	
33	1899	Neave	10,000	10,000	—	—	
34	1900	Aitken	150,000	75,000	75,000	—	
35	1905	Calder	80,000	40,000	40,000	—	
Totals			5,921,000	3,109,000	2,381,000	431,000	

Notes to Table 63
(A) Raised to £45,000 in 1899
(B) Tennent Bros. reconstructed in 1901 with an authorised capital of £275,000.
(C) Company included maltings and hop brokerage
(D) Company included wine and spirit merchants
(E) Capital raised to £750,000 in 1898
Sources: SRO, Dissolved Companies Registers; *Brewers' Guardian; Manual of British and Foreign Brewing Companies.*

companies. The data in Table 64 show that in four out of five instances the price paid to the vendors for properties, stock and goodwill were sums equivalent to at least 60 per cent of the authorised capitals and that in all but a few instances the

Table 64

Capital and Purchase Price of Ten Brewery Companies

Company	Auth. Capital	Purchase Price
Haddington	20,000	7,750
Meiklejohn	50,000	17,500
Ireland	25,000	16,000
Thomson Marshall	65,000	50,000
Aitchison	110,000	60,000
Steel Coulson	140,000	130,000
Campbell Hope & King	220,000	214,000
Bernard	250,000	175,000
G. Younger	500,000	500,000

Source: data derived from Table 63.

financial arrangements of companies were not only realistic but also based on sound assets. Few brewers in Scotland were unwise enough to commit themselves to massive interest payments on loan stock: debentures, including those indicated in Table 63, and William Younger's issue of 1898 shown in Table 65, came to a total of £731,000. The ordinary share capital in 1905 was £3,109,000 and, taking into account increases brought about by extended borrowing powers and reduction of capital indicated in Table 65, had by 1910 risen to £3,334,000. If the sample of 35 firms examined here is typical, the great majority of ordinary shares were retained in the hands of the brewing families, their friends, managements and associates. Preference shares totalled £2,381,000 in 1905: in only two of the 35 firms listed in Table 63 did they exceed the ordinary share capital.

Table 65

Extensions and Reductions of Capital 1896-1910

(A) EXTENSIONS			
G Younger	1898	250,000	
W Younger	1898	300,000	(D)
Sharp	1899	20,000	
Arrol	1899	150,000	
Meiklejohn	1899	15,000	
Tennent	1901	15,000	(R)
(B) REDUCTIONS			
Ireland	1896	5,000	(R)
Arrol	1909	95,000	
Edinburgh United	1910	110,000	

(D)   Debentures
(R)   Involved reconstruction
Meiklejohn's borrowing powers extended in 1899 following reduction of similar sum in 1893.
Source: data derived from Table 63.

Companies

Many problems stand in the way of a detailed analysis of company growth in the Scottish brewing industry during the period 1850-1914. Surviving business records relate almost exclusively to the large companies and by their very nature are fragmentary. They tend almost always to reveal day-to-day activities at several disparate points in time, making it extremely difficult to paint any sort of overall picture of long-term developments. Legal records, where accessible, are less useful than for the earlier history of brewery companies in Scotland: the majority also relate to the major concerns. Inevitably it is difficult to gain much of an insight into the activities of lesser companies, the only really helpful sources being the Register of Companies and a variety of brewery trade journals and almanacs. Nevertheless, we know a great deal about many of the companies listed earlier in Table 63, and the following section is devoted to an examination of company formation in the latter half of the nineteenth century, with particular reference to developments during the brewery boom.[14]

Irrespective of size or capital, four main types of enterprise could be identified by 1900. Firstly, there were the old-established family firms that had been converted by their owners into public companies. Most were still controlled by members of the founding family, who continued to play an active role in management. Secondly, there were a number of firms that had been formed by the amalgamation of two or more smaller businesses. These enterprises were often controlled by the owners of one or other of the incorporated firms. Thirdly, there were the new firms, public companies launched during the brewery boom, either to take over existing plant or build new ones. Fourthly and finally, there was a group of private companies, mainly old family firms, still owned and managed exclusively by individuals or partners. Inevitably we know least about this last group, particularly the small enterprises still operating in country towns beyond the main centres of the industry.[15] In a sense this is a somewhat artificial typology because the main determinants of company formation were common to all four groups of enterprise. However, it will be valuable now to examine each group in turn and look at a few examples of each type in some detail. The family-dominated companies were by far the largest group, accounting for at least 25 of those listed in Table 63, and for a total authorised capital of £4,731,000. Some of the firms had eighteenth-century origins, and the majority could trace their foundation back at least two or three generations. The remainder had been established in the mid-nineteenth century, mainly during the forties and fifties. They had in common family interest and participation, which generally led to conservative but not necessarily over-cautious management. Over the years some of the larger firms in this group had grown from modest enterprises with a small turnover in local outlets to become major brewers of considerable capital serving international markets. It will be useful to look in turn at some examples of small, medium and large firms in this category, and compare their experiences of formation and growth. As it happened, the first firm to register as a limited liability public company was the modest family enterprise of R. & D. Sharp, Blackford Brewery, Perthshire, which had an authorised capital of only £25,000. The firm had been established in 1830 by two brothers, Robert and David Sharp, and in the interim had both built up a good local trade in and around Perth and something of a reputation in the east of Scotland for the excellence of its mild and pale ales. The Memorandum of Association establishing the new company was signed by John Stewart, brewer at Blackford, and Alexander Ferguson, a wine merchant and spirit broker, surviving partners of the old firm, both brothers having died. But the family connexion was still strong; according to the Summary of Capital and Shares in 1884, there were 14 shareholders, the leading being Robert Sharp's widow, James Sharp, her son, John Stewart, Alexander Ferguson, and John Lawson, a local banker. Towards the close of the brewing boom the borrowing powers were twice extended: firstly, in 1898 to £33,000 with additional debentures of £5,000; secondly, in 1899 to £45,000 by the issue of further preference shares. The two largest blocks of shares were then held by the Sharp family and by John Stewart, who by then had become general manager of the company. Stewart had obviously developed the business with considerable success, the extensions of capital being applied to the purchase of a number of public houses both in the locality and in the north of England. The balance sheet of 1912 showed assets of £41,800 made up as follows:

	(£)	%
Brewery and Goodwill	7,472	18
Properties in Scotland	10,465	25
Properties in England (including licence values)	13,297	32
Plant, Utensils, Casks	2,746	6
Stocks	983	2
Debts owed Company	4,429	10
Trade Loans	2,486	6
	41,878	99

The properties in the north of England were all on Tyneside, while the trade loans were to local publicans. Clearly a substantial element of the firm's local trade was through tied houses, a notable feature of retailing in the Perth district.[16]

Several other small but old-established Scottish family firms went public in the initial stages of the brewery boom before 1892. The first and largest was Robert Meiklejohn & Sons of Alloa, registered in 1890 with a capital of £50,000. Meiklejohn's Bass Crest Brewery had been established by Robert Meiklejohn in 1774, and although remaining fairly small, by the early part of the nineteenth century it had built up a solid reputation both for strong and pale ales. After 1840 the firm passed into the hands of the Maitland family, although the Meiklejohn connexion was maintained through marriage. The Memorandum of the Articles of Association of the company was subscribed to by Charles Maitland, brewer, Charles Pearson, a cooper there, and various other local brewers, innkeepers or hoteliers. The former firm of Robert Meiklejohn & Sons were to be paid £35,000 for the brewery, assets and goodwill, £17,500 being paid in cash and the remainder in ordinary shares in the new company. The assets were said to include public house property in North Shields valued at £1,000. For the first year or so after registration Meiklejohn's business prospered, 'but subsequently sustained serious losses through the brewing of bad ales and mismanagement of its commercial department.' Most likely the depression of 1893 did not help the firm in these difficulties, for in that year it obtained a certificate for the reduction of capital to £35,000. Charles Maitland, the principal partner and chairman of the company, surrendered a proportion of his ordinary shares, hence bearing most of the loss. Four years later, however, the company had regained its former position, the nominal capital being increased in 1897 by £15,000. Like the other Alloa brewers, Meiklejohn's main trade by this time was India Pale Ale, mainly it seems sold through agents in the north of England, Merseyside, London and Ireland.[17]

Much more in the tradition of country brewers were the two smaller firms of D.S.Ireland of St. Andrews and John Young of Musselburgh. The latter had established his Ladywell Brewery in the old harbour village of Fisherrow about

1830 and gradually built up a successful local business. The new company was registered in 1891 with an authorised capital of £30,000 in ordinary shares, held by fifty shareholders. Young's brewery, like most of the small firms, remained essentially local with a general trade throughout the district.[18] D.S.Ireland's Argyll Brewery in St. Andrews had been established at the beginning of the nineteenth century and was built up into a prosperous local business by Baillie Ireland, who died in 1890. The family thereafter decided to maintain an interest in the firm but put day-to-day management in the hands of a small public company. This was registered in 1892 with a capital of £25,000 divided into 5,000 shares of £5 each. By a Memorandum of Agreement, £16,000 was to be paid for the brewery property, its assets and goodwill. The directors of the new company included Baillie John Macgregor of St. Andrews and C.A.Scroggie, a Dundee hop merchant who was to act as managing director. According to the summary of capital and shares of 1893, 3,330 shares had been taken up by about a hundred shareholders. The biggest block of shares was held by the family and a number of local merchants and publicans. Ireland must have run into some difficulties, for, like Meiklejohn, it applied for reduction of capital in 1896 to a figure of £15,000.[19]

Three good examples of medium-size firms in this category are Usher of Edinburgh, Ballingall of Dundee and Aitken of Falkirk. The firm of James and Thomas Usher had been established by James Usher in 1831, the original brewery being located near Archibald Campbell's Argyll Brewery in Chambers Street. The business soon grew beyond the capacity of the original plant and Usher moved to the new and much larger Park Brewery in St. Leonard's Street in 1860. The family firm continued successfully to develop a general brewing trade, although by the late eighties it was apparent that further extension of business was becoming increasingly dependent on the advancing of loans to publicans or on the direct acquisition of tied houses. This situation led to a major family quarrel: Thomas Usher, one of the original co-founders, favoured the policy of making advances to expand the trade, while his nephews, Andrew and Harry, opposed it. Thomas ultimately bought out his nephews and shortly afterwards in 1895 became chairman and managing director of the new company, Thomas Usher & Son. The authorised capital was £70,000, most of the shares being held by the family and friends. Usher continued to expand its trade, mainly in Edinburgh and Glasgow, but with limited activity elsewhere, mainly in the north-east of Scotland around Aberdeen. Despite the enthusiasm of Thomas Usher for the development of a tied trade, most of the firm's business, at least before 1914, seems to have been on the open market.[20]

The Dundee firm of Hugh Ballingall had similar origins, the Pleasance Brewery having been founded by William Ballingall in 1844. The founder was succeeded by his son, Hugh, in 1856, and it was he who built the firm into one of the largest and most successful outwith the main centres of brewing in Edinburgh, Glasgow and Alloa. Like other major Scottish firms, Ballingall became specialist brewers of pale ale, which was sold widely in Scotland and the north of England. The firm also had a substantial local trade in traditional beers, mainly sold through tied-houses in and around Dundee. On his visit to the firm's brewery, Alfred Barnard noted that production had increased twelvefold between 1856 and 1890.[21] The old Pleasance Brewery had been enlarged and rebuilt, while an entirely new plant, complete with maltings, the Park Brewery, had been opened in 1881. Hugh Ballingall & Son was registered in 1897 with a capital of £100,000 in £10 shares, 5,000 of them being preference shares. A large proportion of the ordinary shares were retained by the family, five of whom were directors of the new company.[22]

James Aitken of Falkirk was one of the oldest Scottish firms in continuous existence, having been established in 1740. Until the beginning of the nineteenth century its trade was mainly local, but thereafter it began to specialise in the brewing of pale ales for more general sale. The company expanded its business considerably in the sixties and seventies: the brewery was extended in 1866 and again in 1878, while Mains Maltings at Linlithgow were greatly enlarged in 1875. By the eighties a large proportion of sales were for export, although the firm still maintained a place in the home market. Aitkens' share capital in 1900 was £150,000—all held by members of the family and their friends—the managing director being James H. Aitken, senior partner of the former firm.[23]

Finally, in the category of old-established family firms were those of large capital exceeding £250,000. The six considered here, William Younger, William McEwan, John and Robert Tennent, Archibald Arrol, Thomas and James Bernard, and George Younger, together represented a total authorised capital of more than £3.5 million by the end of the brewery boom. The first large firm to go public in Scotland was one of the oldest and most important, William Younger & Company, which was floated in 1887 during the first year of the general boom in brewery issues. Even before the middle of the nineteenth century this progressive family enterprise was the leading brewer in Scotland, with a major share of trade in English and overseas markets. The firm expanded considerably in the seventies and early eighties and by 1885 its home sales alone were worth more than £400,000 per annum. At the time of registration the company's authorised capital was £1 million, divided equally into ordinary and preference shares. However, very few shares seem to have been offered to the public at the outset, for the existing partners, Harry Younger, Alexander Bruce and Andrew Smith, took the whole of the ordinary shares, and together with other staff and friends they seem also to have held the majority of preference shares. Only after 1890 did an appreciable number of Younger shares appear on the market, especially after 1898 when debenture stock with a total value of £300,000 was issued. The growth in business around this time, particularly in the acquisition of tied houses and the extension of trade loans to other publicans, was ample justification for this issue. It made William Younger the largest brewer in Scotland.[24] Of later origin was the other major Edinburgh firm of William McEwan and Company, which was registered in 1889 and had a nominal capital of £1 million divided into 50,000 ordinary shares and 50,000 five per cent cumulative preferential shares of £10 each. Only a proportion of the preference shares seem to have been put on the market at the outset, William McEwan retaining most of the ordinary shares for himself and family. The company had been formed to take over the Fountain Brewery in Edinburgh, established by McEwan in 1856. The average profit over the period since 1885 was calculated at £92,500. The ordinary shares were to be taken by McEwan in part-payment of the purchase price of the brewery and plant, which, together with stock and customers' outstanding balances, was valued at nearly £408,000. Payment of dividends on the preference shares would cost £25,000 per annum and it was thought that the balance of profits of more than £60,000 would leave ample margin for security. McEwan, elected an M.P. for the Edinburgh Central division in the General Election of 1886, had decided to convert his very successful business into a limited liability company because of the increasing pressures of public life. The business had grown so large, in terms both of trade and capital, that it made sense to convert it into a public company, McEwan passing day-to-day management to a new managing director, William Younger, previously manager of the old company, following the founder's election to Parliament. All of the ordinary shares continued to be held by the family, who in common with other brewing families maintained an on-going interest in the business.[25] The largest and by far the most important firm in the west of Scotland was that of John and Robert Tennent, Wellpark Brewery, Glasgow, which by the mid-nineteenth century had built up a large business in general brewing and a specialist trade in pale ale and stout. In 1855 the value of the business was put at £220,000 and was said in the fifties and sixties to have made 'large and increasing profits.' By 1870 it was worth £300,000 and thereafter expanded considerably under family management. The firm seems to have had a widespread reputation, both for the excellence of its pale ale and for its other products. It was also a leader in brewing technology, being amongst the first to brew lager beers in Britain on a large scale after 1888. When first registered in 1890, the firm had an authorised capital of £260,000, but this was probably not a fair reflection of its actual value. When the company was reconstructed in 1901, it had a capital of £275,000, practically all held by family and staff.[26]

Several major firms went public in 1894-5, following the downturn in economic activity in 1893. Among their number were two major firms registered in 1895, Archibald Arrol & Sons of Alloa and Thomas and James Bernard of Edinburgh, both having nominal capitals of £250,000. The new Arrol company acquired the property and goodwill of the Alloa Brewery and took over two Tyneside breweries, Meikles and Turnbulls, both of Newcastle-upon-Tyne. The Arrol family retained the whole of the ordinary share capital, but two-thirds of the preference capital was publicly subscribed. In 1899 the authorised capital was increased to £400,000 (see Table 65) by the creation of 15,000 preference shares of £10 each, to rank *pari passu* with the existing preference shares. Half were issued that year and the remainder in 1900, with 2,500 being offered to existing shareholders. In 1901, in an effort to acquire more tied houses, another brewery was taken over in Newcastle-upon-Tyne, that of Dover, Newsome Baxter Limited. In 1909, on a revaluation of the properties, the capital was reduced to £305,000 by cancelling 7,900 ordinary shares and 1,600 preference shares of £10 each. Arrols had clearly run into trading difficulties, although their position might have been worse had they been committed to a burden of fixed-interest charges on debentures.[27] The firm of Thomas and James Bernard had been brewing in Edinburgh's Canongate since 1840, but like Ushers rapidly outgrew a cramped site with little room for expansion. A new brewery was built at Slateford on the western edge of the city in 1890, by which time the firm had a considerable reputation for its Edinburgh Ale. The new firm was formed to take over the brewery, goodwill and assets, the nominal capital being divided into 17,500 preference shares and 7,500 ordinary shares of £10 each. John Mackay Bernard, chairman and managing director, retained most of the ordinary shares, only a proportion of the preference shares passing from the family for public issue. Bernard seems to have managed the business with considerable flair and success. The ordinary shares paid 15 per cent, even in the difficult years of the 1900s, and a strong reserve fund was reported even in 1904, when many other brewers were in trouble.[28]

The largest firm outside Edinburgh was the old-established family concern of George Younger of Alloa, no relation to either of the Edinburgh Youngers. The business expanded considerably after 1850, with a great deal of attention being devoted to the production of pale ales for domestic and colonial markets. The premises were greatly extended to include two breweries, two large maltings and a bottling store. When the new company was formed in 1897, the properties included the Candleriggs and Meadow Breweries, the Craigward and Station Maltings, Kelliebank export bottling stores, Eglinton home bottling stores and the Craigward cooperage. The purchase price was £500,000, payable by the issue to the vendors of the whole of the ordinary and deferred share capital, with the balance in cash. George Younger (by then an M.P.) and other members of the family were the leading directors. In 1898 the ordinary capital was increased by 12,500 shares of £10 each and the deferred by 12,500 shares of £10 each to enable the company to acquire two breweries in County Durham, the Sunderland Brewery of R. Fenwick and Company and the Chester Brewery, maltings and public houses of Chester-le-Street.[29]

In the atmosphere of expansion and increased competition which typifies most of the period under review here, it was natural that amalgamations should occur and it is to these that consideration will now be given. Six of the companies registered in Scotland during the period 1884-1905 were amalgamations of smaller concerns, and together they had a total authorised capital of £1,105,000. The six firms involved were Steel-Coulson; Edinburgh United Breweries; Thomson Marshall; Archibald Campbell, Hope & King; Turner's Ayr and Newton Breweries; and Gordon and Blair. Only one firm, Edinburgh United Breweries, was promoted on the English model by a finance house; the remaining companies were chiefly amalgamations of small local firms.

The largest firm in this category was Edinburgh United Breweries, which on registration in 1889 had an authorised capital of £450,000. The company was an amalgamation of the Edinburgh and Leith Brewery of Robert Disher & Company, Ritchie & Sons' Brewery, Robin Macmillan & Company's Summerhall Brewery, and David Nicholson's Palace Brewery. Ordinary shares to the value of £125,000 were retained by owners and managers of the four companies, while another £125,000 in preference shares and £200,000 in debentures was put on the market. A board of directors including William Stewart, former manager of the

Edinburgh and Leith Brewery and Archibald Smith, a former partner of Robin Macmillan and Company, was established with Sir W. Hamilton Dalrymple as chairman. Edinburgh United Breweries, partly through mismanagement and partly through over-capitalisation, ran into trouble from the outset. The annual report of 1890 indicated that the capital was fully paid up 'despite rumours to the contrary.' But the brewery had an initially bad reputation both in the management of its agencies and the quality of its beers. Undoubtedly the interest payments on debentures—the largest issue of any company in Scotland before 1898—caused difficulties. In 1910, as Table 65 indicates, the capital was reduced by £110,000 to a more realistic figure of £340,000.[30]

Although the opportunities undoubtedly existed for successful mergers within the drink industries as a whole, only a few were attempted. Among such amalgamations was one which brought into being the firm of Archibald Campbell, Hope and King in 1896. The company was established to bring about a merger of Archibald Campbell's Argyll Brewery in Edinburgh, and the wine and spirit merchant's trade of Hope and King of Glasgow. Campbell's Argyll Brewery dated from the early eighteenth century and had a well-established reputation both for its pale ales and its general products. With expansion to some extent constrained by its site in the Cowgate, the Argyll Brewery maintained and extended its custom by the quality rather than the quantity of its products. The authorised capital of the new company was £220,000, the purchase price of both businesses being £214,000. All of the ordinary shares were held by the directors, customers and the trade, only the preference and debenture stock being offered to the public. Campbell, Hope and King continued to develop the brewing side of its trade with success, concentrating on outlets throughout central Scotland, especially in Edinburgh and Glasgow.[31]

The remaining amalgamations brought into existence four medium-size companies with capitals ranging from £65,000 to £150,000. The largest, Gordon and Blair, with a capital of £150,000, united various drink interests in both Edinburgh and Glasgow. The new company was to acquire the businesses of James Gordon, brewer, spirit broker and distiller's agent in Glasgow, Charles Blair's Craigwell Brewery, Edinburgh, and Gordon and Blair's Home Brewery, Parkhead, Glasgow, then trading under the name of George Dalrymple and Company. Dalrymple had been established in 1860 and had rapidly built up an 'extensive' business in general brewing, including taditional beers and pale ales. The signatories to the Memorandum of Agreement were James Gordon, Charles Blair, Alexander Walker of Kilmarnock, J.B.Gibb of Glasgow, Alexander Gordon, James Russell and David Robertson. With interests in both brewing and distilling, Gordon and Blair, like Campbell, Hope and King, had advantages over some other firms of similar size, mainly in retailing. Even in difficult times Gordon and Blair continued to develop its business and undoubtedly this was owing to experienced and judicious management.[32]

Steel, Coulson & Company was another Edinburgh-Glasgow amalgamation, which went public in 1888, the second year of the brewery boom. The firms involved were both old-established, the breweries having been in existence since at least 1825. The authorised capital of the new company was £140,000, £40,000 of which was debenture stock. Only 5,500 shares of £10 each were to be issued to the public at first, the majority being debenture stock. According to the prospectus, the company was likely to pay ten per cent on ordinary share capital after providing for the dividend on preference shares and interest on debenture stock. The sum of £130,000 was to be paid to the former companies for breweries, plant and goodwill, £38,000 being payable in shares. The directors of the new company were J.L.Coulson, Frank Coulson, and J.T.Inglis (all of Edinburgh) and Baillie Alexander McLaren and James Bell of Glasgow. Production was gradually rationalised: the firm's Greenhead Brewery in Glasgow produced porter and stout, while the sizeable Croft-an-Righ Brewery behind Holyrood Palace in Edinburgh specialised in pale and mild ales. Steel, Coulson at first sold direct to the trade but later acquired tied houses, both in Scotland and the north of England.[33]

The two provincial amalgamations, Thomson, Marshall & Company of Aberdeen, and Turner's Ayr and Newton Breweries, were both relatively modest concerns uniting smaller local firms. The larger, Thomson, Marshall, brought about the amalgamation of several firms, the oldest being the Aulton Brewery. The properties were to cost £50,000, £30,000 being paid in cash and £20,000 in debentures. The total authorised capital in 1890 was £65,000.[34] The second company registered in 1898 was an amalgamation of two breweries in Ayr, Turner's Brewery owned by A.M.Turner and the Ayr Brewery, Mill Street, of James Watson and Company. The new company, with Turner and a Glasgow accountant, David Rattray, as directors, had a nominal capital of £80,000 in £10 shares, half being 5 per cent preference. It took over both breweries and a number of local public houses in Ayr, Tarbolton, Symington and Ballantrae as going concerns. Like Thomson, Marshall, Turner's Ayr and Newton Breweries was able, through amalgamation, to develop its local trade and scale its operation accordingly.[35]

The third category of company under consideration was the essentially new firm established either to take over and develop existing plant or build a new brewery. Four companies of this type were registered in the period under review, all of modest capital and little more than 'country' breweries. We know little about the first of them, the Wellshot Brewery Company of Cambuslang, Lanarkshire, except that it was registered in 1892 with a capital of £20,000, £16,000 of which was in ordinary shares and the rest in preference shares. At the time of registration, 73 shareholders were reported. Until that time no brewery existed in Cambuslang, so Wellshot Brewery must have built one.[36]

The Craigellachie Brewery Company was established in 1895. Its initial capital was £10,000, divided into £1 ordinary shares, but by Special Resolution of 26 February 1898 the capital of the company was increased to £15,000, again in single £1 shares. The whole of the shares were taken up immediately. The company proceeded to erect a brewery at Craigellachie in Speyside, the cost of the machinery and plant amounting in all to £8,287. This firm was apparently in difficulty from the outset: the brewery was erected at a time of 'abnormally high costs,' and 'extreme keenness of competition' during the trade depression after the turn of the century exacerbated the company's problems. In 1905 the capital was reduced by £4,500 to £10,500. Craigellachie was badly sited from every point of view: it had only a modest local market and stood in the middle of the finest distilling country in the north-east.[37]

Further south in East Lothian, the Haddington Brewery Company was established a year later in 1896. The company's Articles of Association stated that the directors were J.M.Montgomery, brewer in Haddington, D.Sanderson, a spirit merchant there, C.J.Mackness, solicitor in Dundee, and a number of Lothian hoteliers and publicans. The new company acquired the Sidegate Brewery, together with stables, housing and goodwill, at a cost of £7,750. Montgomery was to be paid £5,550 in cash and the rest of the sum outstanding in ordinary shares. The nominal capital of the new company was £20,000 in 1000 ordinary and 1000 cumulative preference shares. Montgomery remained as managing director of the new company, combining this function with other business interests, including the operation of brewers' agencies in East Lothian and also a bottling plant in Dalkeith. Like Craigellachie, the Haddington company was soon in difficulties and went into voluntary liquidation in 1899. The business was sold as a going concern and a new firm with the same name registered a year later in 1900. The company and assets were acquired for £5,750, the directors being W.G.Sinclair and James Thomson, both of Edinburgh. But these efforts to save the company were also short-lived, and it was finally wound up in 1904.[38]

The South-Western Brewery Company was established in 1898 with a capital of £35,000, divided into an equal number of ordinary and preference shares. The new company acquired the brewing business of W.T.Soloman of Queen Street, Newton Stewart, Wigtownshire at a cost of £10,800, and a local hotel and public house at a total cost of £3,000. The directors of the company were Soloman, Joseph Milligan, wine and spirit merchant, Peter Dalrymple of Kirkcowan, Wigtownshire, and J.M.Campbell, a Glasgow lawyer. The South-Western Company seems to have been more successful than the other products of this period and remained active until after the First World War, when it was acquired by Campbell, Hope & King of Edinburgh.[39]

Fourthly and lastly, there was a group of private companies, about which we know a good deal less than the public companies so far described. Firms in this category included several substantial firms, such as William Black of the Devanha Brewery in Aberdeen, John Fowler of Prestonpans, John Jeffrey of Heriot & Roseburn Breweries in Edinburgh, and Lorimer & Clark of the Caledonian Brewery, also in Edinburgh. John Jeffrey was by far the most extensive, the firm having built up a considerable reputation both in bottled ales and in general brewing. As early as 1868, when David Bremner visited the Heriot Brewery in the Old Town of Edinburgh, the firm had outgrown its restricted site and to his eye was 'not arranged according to modern ideas of such establishments.' Jeffrey subsequently expanded at Roseburn near Murrayfield, first of all in the development of ale stores and a bottling department, and later with the addition of a new brewery.[40] John Fowler, on the other hand, provides a good example of the smaller out-of-town company which maintained its independence by successfully specialising in the production of pale ale, the celebrated 'Prestonpans Ale.' The firm also had a good local trade in fishing and colliery villages, though the favourite drink, a more traditional beer known as 'Wee Heavy,' was widely famed and much sought after throughout Scotland.[41] Both William Black of Aberdeen (an old-established firm dating back to the end of the eighteenth century) and Lorimer and Clark of Edinburgh were essentially local brewers who maintained their independence until they succumbed to competition or takeover in the inter-war years.[42]

NOTES

1 Vaizey, op.cit., 3.

2 SRO, COS, Tennent v Tennent, Summons of G.Tennent, 1864, 18.

3 See data in Table 63.

4 Vaizey, op.cit., 7.

5 H.Stopes, *Brewery Companies* (London, 1895), 41, 43-8.

6 Vaizey, op.cit., 10.

7 L.Levi, 'The Liquor Trades,' *Brewers' Guardian* 1871, 60-62.

8 Stopes, op.cit., 41.

9 PP 1896 LXVI A & P Return re Joint Stock Companies 1895, 226-41.

10 *Brewers' Almanack* 1895, 287-8; ibid, 1904, 310-11.

11 Nearly all of the remaining 'country' breweries were private companies.

12 A. Barnard, *Noted breweries of Great Britain and Ireland* (London 1889-91), 4 vols.

13 Levi, op.cit., 61; Stopes, op.cit., 45, 48.

14 The Register of Defunct Companies, now housed in the Scottish Record Office (West Register House) is potentially an extremely rich source of information on business activity in Scotland during the period under review here.

15 A few, but not all, are listed in the *Brewers' Almanacks*.

16 SRO, Dissolved Companies Register, BT 2/1361, R & D. Sharp Ltd. The firm was ultimately wound up in 1927.

17 Ibid, BT 2/1981, Meiklejohn's Brewery Ltd; Anon, *Report of Meiklejohn's centenary, 1874* (Newcastle-upon-Tyne, 1875).

18 PP 1892 LXXII, A & P Return re Joint Stock Companies 1891, 174-85.

19 SRO, Dissolved Companies Register, BT 2/2399, 1892 and BT 2/3123, D.S. Ireland Ltd.

20 PP 1896 LXXVI A & P Return re Joint Stock Companies 1895, 226-41; C.M.Usher, *A history of the Usher Family in Scotland* (Edinburgh, 1956), 69-71; Anon, *Thomas Usher and Son Ltd., History of the company* (Edinburgh, n.d.). I am most grateful to Mr W.Chamberlain, Head Brewer, for much useful information on the company.

21 Barnard, op.cit., Vol. III, 147.

22 PP 1898 LXXXIV A & P Return re Joint Sock Companies 1897, 313; *Brewers' Guardian* 1897, 264.

23 Anon, *Two hundred years of progress: James Aitken & Co. Ltd. 1740-1940*, (Falkirk, 1940); PP 1901 A & P Return re Joint Stock Companies 1900, 286.

24 *The Manual of British and Foreign Brewery Companies* (London 1921), 363, Keir, op.cit., 72; Records of William Younger & Co., Summaries of Capital and Shares to 1912 and Loan Ledgers to 1914.

25 *Brewers' Guardian* 1889, 244-45.

26 SRO, COS, Summons of Gilbert Tennent, Tennent v. Tennent 1864, 18, 23; *Brewers' Guardian*, 1901, 236.

27 *Brewers' Guardian*, 1895, 145; *Brewery Manual*, 78.

28 PP 1896 LXXVI A & P Return re Joint Stock Companies 1895, 226-41; *Brewers' Guardian*, 1904, 471; SRO, Dissolved Companies Register, BT 2/2860, 1895.

29 Anon, *A short history of George Yunger & Son Ltd., Alloa, 1762-1925* (Alloa, 1925); Brewery Manual, 139.

30 SRO, COS, UP, 1st Div. E 7/1 Edinburgh United Breweries v. James A.Mollison, Proof for

Edinburgh United Breweries Ltd. 1892; *Brewers' Guardian,* 1890, 90; ibid, 1904, 287; *Brewery Manual.*

31 PP 1897 LXX A & P Return re Joint Stock Companies 1896, 286; *Brewery Manual,* 108; information from Mr T.C.Ferguson, Joint Managing Director, Whitbread (Scotland) Ltd.

32 *Brewers' Guardian,* 1898, 129; ibid., 1905, 102; Anon, *Glasgow of today: business men and mercantile interests* (Glasgow, 1888), 126.

33 *Brewers' Guardian,* 1888, 156; ibid., 1889, 152; *Brewery Manual,* 254.

34 PP 1890-91 LXXVII A & P Return re Joint Stock Companies 1890, 182-93; *Brewers' Guardian,* 1890, 56.

35 *Brewers' Guardian,* 1898, 69-70. Ultimately merged with Tennent Bros. in 1963.

36 PP 1893 LXXXII A & P Return re Joint Stock Companies 1892, 166.

37 SRO, COS, UP, 1st Div. C 29/7 Pet. of the Craigellachie Brewery Co. 1905.

38 SRO, Dissolved Companies Register, BT 2·259 and 4490, Haddington Brewery Company 1896-1904.

39 PP 1899 LXXXIX A & P Register of Joint Stock Companies, 1898, 314; SRO, Records of the County of Wigtown, B 72/2/11, Reg. of Sasines, F13, 60, 62, 67 1899; ibid, B 72/2/12, F8, 1902. The brewery still survives, used as a store.

40 Bremner, op.cit., 439-43; Barnard, op.cit. vol. IV, 371-4.

41 Barnard, op.cit., vol. IV, 355-66.

42 Ultimately acquired by the Usher-Vaux Group.

10

Innovation and Organisation
in Scottish Brewing
1850 - 1914

THERE were major developments in brewing technology and business organisation during the period 1850 to 1914 and in both of these areas Scotland shared the experience of the brewing industry in Britain as a whole. Innovations in each of these spheres were closely inter-related, for the increasing scale and complexity of brewing in the later Victorian age called for greater professionalism on the part of a new breed of brewer-managers. Innovation, however, had a far greater effect on the technology and science of brewing than on modes of business administration within companies. Major developments took place first in brewery engineering. Iron was substituted for wood in the construction of machinery and greater attention was paid to the layout and design of plant. Vastly increased production after the mid-eighties brought greater mechanisation in all of the brewing processes, but particularly in the manufacture of the increasingly fashionable bottled beers and ales. The scientific discoveries of the age were readily understood by many brewers, and although some continued to practise age-old techniques, the majority of brewers in Scotland seem to have been in the forefront of experiment in the new principles. One explanation of the Scottish brewers' readiness to grasp innovation may lie in the fact that many had come to specialise in the production of pale and light ales for bottling. Much of the experimentation in the brewery science of the day was concerned with low temperature fermentation and cooling, in both of which brewers in Scotland had considerable experience. In line with the contemporary technical and scientific changes, many new breweries were constructed in Scotland, particularly during the boom of the decade 1885 to 1895.

Although public companies dominated the Scottish brewing industry by the early nineties, management was generally retained in the hands of the families who had earlier established and developed the original firms. Whereas in an earlier period the manager or owner-proprietor might combine technical and commercial duties, these functions became separated. Even in the family-dominated business, a pronounced hierarchical structure emerged with the skilled brewer—who might well be a member of the family—at the top, and commercial management beneath. As Vaizey has observed, 'a surprising number of commercial considerations are subordinated to technical points' in breweries, and although this was perhaps less true at the end of the nineteenth century than when he wrote (1960), it was becoming more important after the realisation that science played such an important role in the craft of brewing.[1] Yet in the atmosphere of increasing competition which typified most of the period under review here, commercial aspects of management were of great consequence. Management's prime concern was the development of business through an efficient sales organisation of agents, travellers and public houses. For historical reasons the English-style tied house system was slow to develop in Scotland, so that brewers tended to build up the retail trade by lending money to publicans. This resulted in a partial tie because although the publican could pay the loan off in time, the system secured business for the brewer as long as the debt was outstanding.[2] Many of the larger brewers in Scotland were active in the export trade, both in bulk and bottle, and the development and exploitation of these markets posed many problems akin to those of the latter half of the eighteenth and earlier part of the nineteenth centuries.

The enormous growth in plant and production, involving large-scale capital investment, was hardly matched by a corresponding increase in the labour force. A comparatively small workforce—2000 odd in 1900—was divided into two main groups, the skilled artisans and the manual workers. About two-thirds of the employees were made up of men whose work lay, as it had always done, in their physical strength, concerned as they were with cleaning out vessels, shovelling waste, rolling barrels, loading drays and carrying out other routine tasks. The rest of the workforce comprised mechanics, coopers, foremen and, at a similar (or slightly higher) level in the brewery office, clerks, secretaries and cashiers.[3]

Brewing Technology and New Products

Scotland shared in the general advance of brewing technology during the latter half of the nineteenth century and in several instances pioneered innovations in brewery engineering, techniques and products. Major discoveries in biochemistry contributed to the solution of many scientific problems in brewing and made a major impact on the industry in the closing decades of the century. Up to the 1870s, however, progress was mostly in the engineering sphere, associated with developments in the processes of mashing, sparging, boiling and refrigeration.[4] As the figures in Table 66 show, the number of registered patents relating to the industry greatly increased after 1870, although the emphasis was still essentially on engineering problems. The major innovations in mashing, apart from the increasing use of the thermometer and the saccharometer, were the introduction of cast-iron mash tuns and a variety of mechanical devices for mixing the mash. The transition to metal vessels was slow: when Barnard surveyed the leading breweries in Scotland between 1889 and 1891, some still had wooden mash tuns.[5] A major development in mashing was brought about by an invention of James Steel, a Scottish brewery engineer. His device—largely unchanged—is still used at the present time. Steel's masher, patented in 1853, was a simple device consisting of a cylinder with rotating vanes inside. Hot water and ground malt were mixed together in the cylinder and then allowed to flow into the mash tun. Steel's

Table 66

Patents Relating To Malting and Brewing
(A) Numbers Registered 1851 - 1885

Year	No.	Year	No.	Year	No.	Year	No.
1851	2	1861	24	1871	30	1881	62
1852	15	1862	23	1872	58	1882	65
1853	12	1863	32	1873	53	1883	67
1854	17	1864	34	1874	50	1884	104
1855	14	1865	22	1875	64	1885	108
1856	25	1866	25	1876	48		
1857	25	1867	34	1877	59		
1858	22	1868	33	1878	29		
1859	32	1869	46	1879	56		
1860	26	1870	52	1880	60		

(B) Classified by Type 1850 - 1880

Type	No.	Per Cent
1 Attemperators and Refrigerators	178	41
2 Malt Mashing and Mixing	70	16
3 Brewing	67	15
4 Boiling	52	12
5 Fermenting	43	10
6 Malt Milling	24	6
Total	434	100

Sources: G. Scamell, *Breweries and Maltings*, 2nd. ed. (London, 1880), 137-78; H. Stopes, *Malt and Malting*, (London, 1885), 571-607.

invention made mashing simple and easy, saving time, labour and raw materials.[6] As a result it was widely adopted by brewers. Scottish brewers had also pioneered developments in sparging (see Chapter Six), which by the 1850s were widely used in all but the smallest breweries. Further innovation was concerned with improving the efficiency of these machines. Sparging was also being widely adopted by brewers in England at that time.[7]

Steam power was widely used in most of the larger Scottish breweries by the middle of the nineteenth century, being applied to a variety of mechanical processes in and around the plant. Apart from its obvious mechanical applications, it was widely used in the brewhouse itself. Steam heating became common, both in open and closed coppers. It was more efficient and gave more even temperatures than previously.[8] At the lower end of the thermometer scale, temperature control was also of great importance to the brewer, and it became increasingly critical in the production of light beers and lagers towards the close of the century. In general, artificial refrigeration freed the brewer from his inability to brew at the same volume throughout the year and from a dependence on deep wells for chilling. Refrigeration was introduced in two main stages: the first was the use of air and water cooling on a larger scale than previously; the second, the invention of ice machines and the increased cold storage of beer in special cellars. Water-cooled vertical or horizontal refrigerators remained in common use in Scottish breweries throughout the period to 1914, while ice machines using a variety of coolants—such as ether, hydro-carbons, or carbon dioxide—were being introduced in increasing numbers after 1875.[9]

Undoubtedly, however, the major developments in brewing during the latter half of the nineteenth century were on the scientific side. A great deal of the pioneer work had been done in the early part of the century when German scientists worked on yeast properties and fermentation. But it was Louis Pasteur who, from 1857 onwards, made major discoveries in biochemistry which were to have far-reaching effects on brewing science. Pasteur's *Etudes sur la Bière*, published in 1876, synthesised much of the work accomplished until that time, particularly on yeast culture, fermentation, and what was later to become known as pasteurisation.[10]

By the eighties most of the larger Scottish brewers employed a trained chemist or analyst, whose main occupation was essentially that of quality controller. A capable chemist could save his firm considerable sums annually by the systematic analysis of barley, malt, hops and sugar, for uniformity in the materials meant uniformity in the resulting beers—a matter of great importance for the reputation of a brewery. The chemist would also analyse the beers at all stages of production to test for quality. Beer returned to the brewery would be examined by the chemist to find out why it had deteriorated after dispatch. In many instances a head or under brewer with chemical training might assume this function, and might legitimately describe himself as a brewer-chemist.[11] Many breweries had a suitably equipped laboratory. At Ballingall's Park Brewery in Dundee, the head brewer's room doubled as a laboratory to cope with the new scientific brewing. Alfred Barnard described it as follows:

> On one side of the apartment there is a library of brewing books, a microscope, and a set of scientific apparatus; on the other side are sampling and testing vessels, also a lead-lined sink, together with a counter for working experiments. This room, which is well ventilated and neatly furnished, is fitted up with desks and contains the usual instruments etc.[12]

These arrangements seem to have been typical of most sizeable breweries in Edinburgh, Glasgow and Alloa.

A further burst of innovation was essentially concerned with the production of bottled ales and lagers. Although primarily concerned with engineering design, these developments would not have been possible without prior understanding of chilling, carbonation, and pasteurisation. Prior to the eighties most breweries, while equipped with simple bottling machines, relied considerably on manual labour in this department. Gradually many of the operations were mechanised, including at first bottle washing, filling and sealing. At John and Robert Tennent's Wellpark Brewery, for example, bottles were filled, corked and wired 'by most ingenious machinery' which could cope with up to 5,000 dozen bottles daily in 1883.[13]

Subsequently rotary washing and filling machines were developed, less dependent on manual controls and hand transfer of bottles, the design being altered to incorporate bottle conveyors. Pasteurisation could also be carried out on a conveyor belt principle. The plant was simple in design and consisted originally of shallow wooden tanks containing a series of perforated steam pipes beneath a false bottom, bottle trays being lowered into the water by a system of overhead conveyors. Quick chilling using ice machines further improved the bottling process, and the product could also be carbonated under pressure to give it greater liveliness in the bottle. In general, the period after 1885 saw many significant developments in the treatment of bottled beers, and to keep abreast of these involved substantial capital investment on the part of Scottish brewers specialising in the bottled trade.[14]

These technical and scientific innovations, coupled with the need to increase output, led to considerable developments in many Scottish breweries. Existing plant was greatly extended and many new breweries and maltings incorporating the latest equipment were built. Although these developments took place throughout most of the period, the peak of activity coincided with the Brewery Boom in the eighties and nineties. Practically every brewery in Scotland visited by the indefatigable Alfred Barnard between 1889 and 1891 had at that time recently undergone substantial expansion, including those of George Younger, John Jeffrey, and Hugh Ballingall.

George Younger first leased the Candleriggs Brewery in Alloa from another old-established firm, Robert Meiklejohn, in 1852. Soon afterwards it was purchased for the sum of £1,500, and thereafter Younger pursued a policy which gradually extended the area covered by the brewery. By the eighties the brewery covered an area ten times that of the original plant. The Craigward Maltings were built in 1868, capable of malting 300 quarters per week, while much of the brewery was completely rebuilt in 1889-90. In 1895 pneumatic maltings were installed in the Candleriggs Brewery, and two years later a third large maltings, Ward Street Maltings, was started, being completed in 1899. Such was the expansion of the bottling trade by the mid-eighties that Younger built an enlarged bottling plant, the Kelliebank Bottling Department, in 1889. These buildings were enlarged on two subsequent occasions, in 1895 and 1900, to provide additional cellar accommodation in which to mature the export ale and stout. The bottling department was fitted out with the most up-to-date bottle washing, carbonating and filling plant, capable of turning out 1,000 dozen bottles per hour. Later, in 1912, another bottling department, the Eglinton plant, was added, mainly to cope with additional bottling for the home market.[15]

The Edinburgh brewer, John Jeffrey, undertook a similar programme of expansion. Developments were at first concentrated on the old Heriot Brewery in the Grassmarket, but eventually the company, constrained by the city-centre site, were forced to look elsewhere.[16] The Roseburn Brewery at Murrayfield was, therefore, built by Jeffrey in 1880 'under the superintendence of the firm's engineer.' When Barnard visited it in 1889, he was 'struck with surprise at the numerous handsome buildings exposed to view,' all laid out around a courtyard 'on the most up-to-date principles':

On our right there appeared a long range of maltings and beer stores; on the left, fronted by the magnificent offices another range of maltings and a steam cooperage; and, at the bottom of the yard, the new brewhouse in one detached block four storeys high.[17]

The brewery and related plant were designed on gravitational principles and equipped with the latest innovations. The brewhouse was arranged as follows. On the ground floor were the engine-room, boiler house, malt mill, four large settling squares and extensive cellarage. On the first floor there were a 64-quarter mash tun, several hot and cold liquor tanks and the malt hoppers, as well as a tun room containing two fermenting vessels fitted with attemperators and capable of fermenting 85 barrels each. On the second floor the hop room and two large horizontal refrigerators were located. The third floor housed a hop press driven by steam power and two large open coolers with fans. On the fourth floor were two wort coppers, each having a capacity of 130 barrels as well as various smaller vessels. A nearby cooperage was fully equipped with the latest steam-driven saw mill: it employed 30 coopers. The maltings were also four storeys high and contained seven malting floors and a barley store for 10,000 quarters of grain. There were four large kilns linked to the maltings. The left-hand range of buildings housed bottling stores and beer cellars, and above them more malt stores. Near the gateway were the offices, and on the other side of the courtyard 'a fine range of stables, coach houses and dray sheds.'[18]

Barnard also visited the Dundee firm of Hugh Ballingall, where he was able to see one of the finest modern breweries which had been built in Scotland up to that time. Ballingall, like Jeffrey, had greatly extended his original plant at the old Pleasance Brewery. Before 1880 this brewery had been further enlarged but still did not have the capacity the firm required, particularly for the production of its increasingly popular pale ales. In 1881, therefore, a new brewery was commenced on an adjacent site, 'the new and handsome Park Brewery.' The plant comprised a large four-storey brewhouse with appended maltings, fermenting house, ice machine house, ale stores and other subsidiary buildings. The gravitation brewery was capable of brewing 50 quarters at a time and was 'equipped and appointed with every novelty in machinery and appliances' 'and with iron and copper plant 'of the most modern construction.' The brewery had many of the innovations already described, including steam-heated coppers, Steel's mashers, horizontal refrigerators and ice machines for fast cooling, as well as making extensive use of steam power throughout.[19]

Improved technology in such breweries and the increased understanding of the science of brewing made possible greater use of substitutes for barley-malt in the manufacture of beers. Down to 1847 barley-malt was the sole legal constituent of beer, but in that year the use of sugar became permissible. Substitutes in the form of molasses or sugar had long been used illegally, but with little understanding of the chemistry involved. Research showed that they could be used to advantage in the production of most beers and might be considered suitable for brewing lightly hopped ales of the kind much brewed for bottling in Scotland after the middle of the nineteenth century. A more fundamental explanation for the increased use of substitutes lay in comparative costs relative to barley. Until the early seventies the quantity of sugar used by brewers in Britain was inconsiderable, but it increased rapidly owing to rises in the price of malt, making sugar an economical substitute. By 1880 it had reached 1.3 million cwt. in Britain as a whole, perhaps less than 5 per cent of this being used in Scotland.

A further incentive to use substitutes for barley-malt was occasioned by the repeal of the Malt Duty and the transfer of duty to beer itself in 1880. Until that time the regulation of malting and brewing by the excise authorities had been extremely strict, but after the introduction of the new Beer Duty brewers were given much greater freedom. In his Budget Speech of 1880 Gladstone pointed the way ahead:

> (The effect would be) to give the brewer the right to brew from whatever he pleases, and he will have a perfect choice both of his materials and his methods. I am of opinion that it is of enormous advantage to the community to liberate an industry so large as this with regard to the choice of those materials. Our intention is to admit all materials whatever to perfectly free and open competition.[20]

The importance of substitutes was quickly grasped by brewers, as Dr Shidrovitch, a leading brewers' chemist explained in the eleventh edition of *Encyclopaedia Britannica* (1910-11):

> Substitutes enable the brewer appreciably to increase his turnover: he can make more beer in a given time from the same plant. The brewer has found that brewery operations are simplified and accelerated by the use of a certain proportion of substitutes. Certain classes of substitutes too are somewhat cheaper than malt, and in view of the keenness of modern competition, it is not to be wondered at that the brewer should resort to every legitimate means at his disposal to keep down costs ... The light beers in vogue today (1910) are less alcoholic, more lightly hopped and more quickly brewed than beers of the last generation, and in this respect are somewhat less stable and more liable to deteriorate than the latter were.

The main substitutes used by brewers after the 1870s could be divided into two main groups: first, there were sugar and kindred materials, of which the most important were invert sugar (cane sugar treated by a process which makes it readily fermentable) and glucose (sugar prepared from starch by boiling it with acids, and mainly derived from sago and maize). Secondly, there were corn and similar materials like unmalted barley, rice or maize, adapted for brewing by various mechanical or chemical processes.[21]

By 1886 Scottish brewers already used 80,000 bushel equivalents of sugar, or about 4 per cent of total materials used in brewing. But ten years later the figure had risen to nearly 230,000 bushel equivalents of sugar. As Table 67 indicates, this figure represented an average of something over 6 per cent of brewing materials used in Scotland, although its use varied widely from district to district. Although the 31 brewers in the Edinburgh collection used by far the largest amount of sugar, it represented only 5.5 per cent of total materials used in brewing. On the other hand, brewers in other collections, particularly Glasgow, Falkirk and

Dundee, relied for up to 10.5 per cent of materials on sugar substitutes. This might indicate, on the part of the Edinburgh brewers, a reliance on traditional materials for the brewing of traditional beers, coupled with a concern for quality. It almost certainly indicates the increased use of sugar-substitutes in the production of cheaper beers for bottling by firms like John and Robert Tennent of Glasgow, George Younger of Alloa and Hugh Ballingall of Dundee.[22]

Table 67

Amounts of Malt and Sugar used by Scottish Brewers 1896

Excise Collection	No. of Brewers	Malt (Bushels)	Sugar (Bushel Equiv.)	Malt %	Sugar %
Edinburgh	31	2,809,999	162,924	94.5	5.5
Glasgow	10	237,417	28,336	89.3	10.7
Stirling	4	108,765	6,900	94.0	6.0
Dundee	14	96,662	9,312	91.2	8.8
Falkirk	1	69,286	6,228	91.7	8.3
Greenock	9	65,726	6,256	91.3	8.7
Aberdeen	12	44,229	4,508	90.7	9.3
Dumfries	11	19,380	2,628	88.1	11.9
Elgin	7	16,060	1,680	90.5	9.5
Scotland	99	3,467,574	229,832	93.8	6.2

Source: PP 1899 XXX Report of the Departmental Committee on Beer Materials, 299, Brewers Using Sugar (Scotland).

The Scottish brewing industry produced a great variety of products, for every brewery of any size continued to brew a range of beers, including at least one porter or stout and a pale ale. Practically all the major brewers in Edinburgh, Glasgow, Alloa, Falkirk and Dundee dealt in both bulk and bottled beer for domestic and overseas markets. Gradually, however, some Scottish brewers, whilst not totally disregarding the general market, came to specialise in the production of one particular type of beer, the increasingly popular pale ale. For reasons already explained above, Scottish brewers had some advantages over many of their southern counterparts in the production of light beers. These were to become the mainstay of many breweries in Scotland during and after the brewing boom of the late eighties and nineties. It is easy to see the advantages enjoyed by many breweries in Scotland which were devoted to brewing this specialist product in a number of different strengths, and it is perhaps not surprising that the market-conscious Scots were in general much less affected by the recession of the early 1900s than some English firms. Pale ales were brewed in increasing quantities by Scottish brewers after the middle of the nineteenth century, and many built their reputations on the excellence of their products. One of the largest brewers of pale ale in Scotland was William Younger. The famous India Pale Ale was brewed in the Holyrood Brewery, the plant there being described by Barnard in 1889 as 'an establishment as extensive as the Trentside breweries.'[23] Robert Meiklejohn of Alloa, in common with other brewers in the town, was by the 1870s mainly concerned with the production of pale ale for both the home and export markets. 'These liquors,' wrote a contemporary, 'are exceedingly pure in colour, agreeable in flavour, preserve their briskness, and keep well, an important quality in ale, as everybody knows.' The firm bottled extensively for the export trade, and for 'such customers at home as relish a glass of the 'Scotch Burgundy'.'[24] George Younger of Alloa shared the same success in the brewing of pale ale and was supposedly the first brewer to introduce the drink for 'house consumption' as opposed to general sale. According to Barnard, the firm astutely gauged the shift of popular taste away from strong ale to pale varieties and were therefore able to anticipate demand 'in an incredibly short time.' Other brewers gained an international reputation for their pale ale: Hugh Ballingall of Dundee, who sold their 'superior quality' Scotch Pale Ale throughout Scotland and the north of England, and won numerous medals at Paris and London exhibitions from the sixties onwards, while James Aitken of Falkirk won acclaim for their 'high class' ale at international exhibitions in Sydney (1879), Melbourne (1880) and Calcutta (1884).[25]

After 1870 there was a rapid increase in demand for light, bright beers of low gravity. According to Alfred Chapman, writing in 1896, the change in public taste was partly due to the 'altered conditions under which we are compelled to live and transact our business in large towns,' and partly to the introduction and growing popularity of light German beers. Because of improved railway and steamship services, he argued, many more people had visited the Continent, especially Germany and Belgium and also the United States, and thus had acquired a taste for thirst-quenching beers.[26] The amount of light beer imported, mainly from Germany and of the Bohemian Pilsener type, grew steadily after the seventies and between 1880 and 1895 it increased five times over. These 'lager' type beers were not nearly as strong as traditional ales and were mostly milder than light ales. For these reasons they also became increasingly popular in the colonies, with the result that British brewers found themselves losing business to German, Austrian, American and Danish enterprise.[27]

Lager brewing and storage, like the specialist production of pale ale, presented the brewer with many problems, and this goes some way to explaining why they were never taken up on any scale before 1914. The brewing of lager-type beers required constantly low temperatures throughout, and until the development of more sophisticated water-cooled refrigerators and chemical ice-making machines, it was hardly practicable on any scale.[28] From the beginning of the eighties, many attempts were made to brew lagers but few were successful, and in the words of the *Brewers' Guardian*, 'enterprise in this direction was discouraged.' But despite the problems, lager brewing was taken up successfully at an early date by at least two Scottish brewers, John and Robert Tennent of Glasgow, and John Jeffrey of Edinburgh. Tennents were certainly pioneers, for the Wellpark Brewery began to produce lager beers as early as 1888. Extensive alterations were made to part of the brewery, the plant and equipment being based on those of a German lager brewery. German techniques were applied, the whole of the development stage being supervised by 'an eminent scientific brewer,' probably a German himself.

The beer was so successful that it would 'defy the most delicate palate to detect any difference between it and the best foreign article.' Once bottled, the lager proved so sound that even when shaken 'furiously,' no sediment could be detected. Tennents' product was also said to be cheaper than German beers. By 1906 a new brewery 'complete in all details' had been built in the north-east part of the brewery site at Wellpark, 'devoted to the manufacture of lager, Munich and Pilsener beers.' The firm must have been one of the major producers of lager beers in Britain at that time and probably had a virtual monopoly of the market for this particular product throughout Scotland. Unfortunately no information is available on Jeffrey's lager.[29]

Although bottling of beer was by no means an innovation to Scottish brewing even by the mid-nineteenth century, the period under review saw an enormous rise in the output of bottled beers, largely made possible by the engineering and scientific developments we have already noted above. By 1905 Julian Baker was able to identify three main systems of bottling:

(i)   the old-fashioned system of brewing a special bottling beer, allowing it to mature and then bottling;

(ii)   recently brewed beers, clarified by finings and after bottling rapidly conditioned by storage at relatively high temperatures;

(iii) beer chilled, filtered and then bottled under artificial pressure of carbonic acid gas, known as carbonated beer.

The first method produced the high-class product typical of many Scottish brewers in the bottling trade, particularly those selling in overseas markets. But the major disadvantage was the considerable time-lag between brewing and sale: light beers could take up to a month to come into condition, while heavier beers might take between six and nine months. The second method also had disadvantages because beers brewed and bottled this way did not keep well and after a certain time would rapidly deteriorate. They were susceptible to sudden rises in temperature, which frequently caused the bottles to burst. Assuming the beers were consumed soon after leaving the brewery, this system of bottling was considered simple and useful. The third system was becoming increasingly more important because 'such beers are now greatly in demand by the public.' Although carbonic acid gave a different flavour to the gas formed during any secondary fermentation in the bottle, it did keep the product in good condition, maintaining (some would say wrongly) a lively taste and appearance.[30]

The margin of profit on bottled beer was smaller (at least for the home market) than on draught beer, so that bottling had to be organised in the most efficient and economical way. Increased mechanisation of the kind we have seen did not necessarily mean a decline in quality. As most brewers still maintain, mass-produced beer is probably of higher and more consistent quality than that produced by old-fashioned methods. A great deal of attention was devoted to quality control in the production of beers for bottling, and indeed most of the pioneer work on low temperature fermentation and on pasteurisation was carried out on such products. Chilling, filtering and carbonating of bottled beers also greatly improved their appeal to the palate. Several Scottish brewers were extremely successful in the production of such beers, notably William Younger, George Younger, and John and Robert Tennent. The major revolution in the packaging of beer, however, lay in the early part of this century when taste swung much more dramatically towards bottled beer.[31]

Management and Sales Organisation

'Bad management as much as bad water can ruin a brewery,' said George Mackay of Saint Leonard's Brewery in evidence to a Court of Session case involving the Edinburgh United Brewery Company in 1891-92.[32] He naturally added that the success of a brewery would depend a good deal on its management. Although this had been so at all stages in the development of the brewing industry in Scotland, it became even more critical during the expansion of the years 1850 to 1914. Perhaps because family tradition and participation were so dominant in most of the larger firms, the general level of managerial skill seems to have been high, although somewhat conservative. The latter trait may certainly explain both why there were relatively few business failures in this later period, and why brewers in Scotland seem to have weathered difficult times in the post-boom years with greater facility than some counterparts south of the Border.[33]

The kind of developments in brewing technology and the science of brewing which we have already looked at briefly led to increased specialisation in managerial functions and brought about the emergence of a new breed of management. In 1905 Julian Baker wrote:

A brewer has to be a man of many parts. A knowledge of engineering, chemistry and biology is essential to one who takes an intelligent interest in his work and who wishes to be well provided for in the keen competitive struggle of the present times ... and most important of all, he must be a judge and manager of men, for untold damage may be done by a discontented and malicious workman.[34]

Management tended to develop along twin paths—firstly that of the skilled brewer, secondly that of the clerk-cum-accountant. In many family businesses these functions were often shared between brothers or sons, although increasingly brewery management became more professional, particularly after the boom in public companies when many of the founding families opted out of day-to-day concern with business.[35] Skilled management was certainly a prerequisite for profit-making in what had become by the eighties a very capital-intensive and highly competitive industry.

The skilled brewer concerned himself with the technical operations of the brewery. He might start out as an apprentice and, if he was not of the family or the son of a leading partner, would pay anything up to £250 before the turn of the century in order to learn his trade. After two or three years he might obtain an appointment as an under-brewer with a salary ranging from £50 - £150 per annum.[36] Many time-served apprentices sought further experience at reduced salaries in order to further their theoretical knowledge of chemistry, perhaps at a technical institute, like Heriot-Watt College in Edinburgh, where courses suitable for brewers were offered as early as the eighties.[37] Thereafter, with knowledge and experience a brewer might be promoted to the position of head brewer, his salary being proportionate to the size and importance of the brewery, but probably in excess of £500 about 1900. Cuthbert Day, a brewing scientist employed by William Younger at the Abbey and Holyrood Breweries, was a successful example of technical management. He had risen to a senior position in the firm through his scientific skill, having established within the trade a reputation second-to-none as an expert on barleys and fermentation techniques.[38]

A brewery of any size would also employ commercial management, often designated managing director, secretary or accountant. Whatever his title, the commercial manager concerned himself with the administrative and financial side of the business, buying materials, making contracts and generally controlling sales. In some instances the manager had been a brewer himself and was therefore familiar with most aspects of the production process. He would have responsibility for the general supervision of the brewery, particularly capital, material and labour costs. He and his associates would manage the office of counting house, supervising a body of clerks if the brewery were large enough to employ them, and possibly also some cashiers. Other departments of the brewery, such as the maltings, bottling plant, cooperage and stables came under his general control. In addition, he was responsible for the work of any travellers, making sure that they were successfully selling the beers and generally expanding the firm's trade. Finally, any tied or managed houses would have to be supervised and some degree of control exercised over publicans to whom the firm had extended loans or credit.[39] Managerial specialists were clearly needed in the larger Scottish companies such as William McEwan and William Younger, but in many others responsibility for sales, accounting, transport, labour, and the purchase and grading of raw materials remained in the hands of a modest managerial unit composed of family relatives or partners. Many examples of this last situation could be cited, but good examples are provided by the firms of Thomas Usher & Sons of Edinburgh, James Aitken of Falkirk, and Hugh Ballingall of Dundee.[40]

Two interesting examples of individuals with no apparent prior connexions in the trade provide illustrations of similar routes to professional management in brewing: Alexander Bruce and Thomas Gray. The former was typical of the new breed of management in the Victorian era, for he eventually became deputy chairman of William Younger & Company in 1885. Bruce was born in Edinburgh in 1839 and educated at the High School there. He joined Youngers as a clerk while still in his teens. Within a year he transferred to the London office, where he gradually rose to become manager. He returned to Edinburgh in 1875, and, no doubt equipped with suitable capital provided by his family, became a managing partner in the firm. Bruce had meantime married a daughter of David Livingstone, the explorer, and this connexion was clearly of great help in his business career. He afterwards became a director of the Edinburgh and Leith Shipping Company (which shipped a considerable proportion of Youngers' beer to London) and of the Scottish Widows' Insurance Company. He also had an interest in the African Lakes Trading Corporation. He left an estate of £177,000 on his death in 1893, including a holding of no less than £125,000 worth of shares in William Younger & Company.[41]

Thomas Gray provides another example from the clerical and accounting side of the trade. He was born in 1840 and began his career as a clerk and later became cashier in William Hay & Company's Little Mill Distillery at Bowling. In 1872, using his business experience to advantage, he entered into partnership with James Gillespie to run the Crown Point Brewery (afterwards the Crown Brewery) of Gillespie, Gray and Company. The partnership was dissolved in 1888, but with his accumulated capital Gray built his own brewery, the Anchor Brewery in Glasgow, which he afterwards managed with his sons, William and James. When he died in 1890 his obituary indicated that he had been 'greatly esteemed by the trade in Glasgow.'[42]

Undoubtedly the greatest concerns of management related to the development and retention of custom for the products of the brewery. With the increasing competition which so characterised much of the period between 1850 and 1914, it is hardly surprising that surviving business records are overtly concerned with sales—both domestic and foreign. The records provide something of an insight into three particular functions of management: firstly, the establishment of agencies and teams of travellers; secondly, the development of the Scottish version of the tied house system and the vetting of loans to publicans in order to secure business; and thirdly, the development of overseas markets, which became of greater importance to Scottish brewers after 1875.

From the beginning of the nineteenth century many of the larger brewers with an eye on more than local outlets began to acquire selling agents resident in the town or district where they wished to raise sales. It was a useful way of 'proving' a market before undertaking direct marketing, which could add greatly to costs. The agent usually acted as a wholesaler for several breweries, although it might be that he represented only one firm if it were large enough and did considerable business in the locality. A good agent, like an able traveller, could do much to promote custom. A bad one, on the other hand, might well lose business despite the merits of the product over those of rivals. The agency system was developed first in Glasgow—mostly by the Edinburgh and Alloa brewers—and later extended to many other towns and cities in Britain, notably Newcastle, Liverpool, London and Dublin.[43] By 1850, for example, George Younger of Alloa had agencies in London, Stockton, Manchester and Newcastle, with commission agents—probably also acting for other brewers—in Hull, Liverpool, Glasgow, Dublin, Cork, Sligo, Limerick and Londonderry.[44] William Younger also had agencies in the principal cities and towns, including Newcastle, Leeds, Liverpool and Dublin. The firm's largest agencies and stores were in London and Glasgow, where there were major sales offices by the sixties.[45] Often one brewer acted as selling agent for another producing popular products which would not necessarily compete with his own. Many English brewers acted as agents for Scottish pale ale brewers, as the Newcastle-upon-Tyne Brewery, Longton Brewery, Usher and Company of Bristol, and Reed Brothers of Plymouth did for William Younger by the eighties.[46] Other Scottish brewers preferred to use wholesalers as agents or to establish their own depots: Hugh Ballingall of Dundee had their own depots in Newcastle and Liverpool by 1890, mainly for the sale of pale ales.[47]

The somewhat unfortunate experience of the Edinburgh brewer, Archibald Campbell and Company, over the choice of a London agent provides some insight into the mechanics of the agency system about the middle of the century. Alexander Campbell, then sole partner of the firm, appointed James Galbraith as 'agent for the sale of ales' in London and elsewhere in England in 1843. The contract between the firm and Galbraith indicated that he would receive an assured commission of £200 per annum, the rate of 5 per cent being payable on all sales. Galbraith was to supervise a team of nine salesmen, a clerk and cellerman, all of whom would be based in the firm's London office and store. An account was to be opened for each salesman, and weekly, monthly and quarterly balances submitted to Edinburgh, where duplicate ledgers would be maintained. The agent was to devote his whole energy to Campbell's business, and the firm for its part bound itself not to sell any of its products to other agents, bottlers or publicans. Galbraith's security was a bond for £1,000 in favour of Archibald Campbell & Company to ensure 'his good conduct of the agency.' Subsequently, in 1849, Galbraith's terms and conditions of service were revised to give him 6 per cent commission on all sales and a guaranteed minimum annual salary of £300. But it was not long before his misdemeanours were revealed, for a year later it was discovered that Galbraith had not entered sales of £3,000 in the books and by a series of deceptions had managed to evade the scrutiny of head office over a number of years.[48] Apart from embezzlement, illustrated here, bad debts were an ever-present risk, although this was generally offset by a greater volume of sales and fewer administrative costs than a team of travellers might incur. Other brewers in Scotland were luckier than Campbell, and the agency system continued to be of great importance to the major firms active in English outlets.

Brewery travellers became increasingly important with the improved mobility brought by the railways. Most breweries of any size employed travellers to raise custom for the firm, to market new products, and to keep a watchful eye on all retail outlets, including any public houses tied in whole or part to the brewery. The larger firms started to employ travellers in the fifties, and most brewers—save the most modest—had travellers by the eighties. A few examples will serve to illustrate the extension of the system. George Younger, for example, appointed his first traveller, J.B.Richardson, in 1859 and later others operated from the firm's various agencies. By 1880 there were four full-time travellers, mainly working in Scotland itself. Thereafter Younger increased the sales staff working from the Glasgow and Newcastle agencies—some indication of the importance of these markets can be gained from the fact that by 1895 a dozen travellers operated from both centres—in addition to those employed from the firm's headquarters in Alloa.[49] Even the smaller firm with few tied houses and selling on the open market would require an adequate sales force: John Fowler & Company of Prestonpans employed twelve travellers in 1891, while George Dalrymple & Company of Home Brewery, Parkhead in Glasgow had built up a good general business since the firm's foundation in 1860, using 'a team of energetic travellers' that covered the whole of Scotland.[50] William Younger, probably the largest brewer in Scotland, had a well-established sales force by the eighties. The extensive London office and stores were the base for ten salesmen working the Home Counties, while the Liverpool area was covered by three travellers. Five travellers worked from the Edinburgh head office, four to cover town sales, the other country sales, mainly in the south and north of Scotland. The Glasgow office was similar in scale to that in London. In 1888, Alexander Brown, the Glasgow and west of Scotland manager, headed a large staff including 12 clerks, 10 commercial travellers and 'a large force of draymen and storemen.'[51] By the turn of the century the traveller had become of great importance to the extension of trade—and he remains of considerable value to present-day Scottish brewers—because of his knowledge of local retailers and customers in the district he served.

During the brewing boom Scottish firms began increasingly to make use of the Scottish equivalent of the tied-house system in England to control retail outlets. The loan system could use capital very economically in order to extend markets: tied houses probably consumed more capital per unit of sale. Partially tied houses to which loans had been extended represented secure foundations for penetrating new markets on a permanent basis. The fiscal background against which this development must be seen is described in some detail in Chapter Eleven, particularly as it related to the expansion of the home market. Our concern here is to describe the mechanics involved, with particular reference to the financial and organisational arrangements of one of the major Scottish brewers, William Younger & Company, whose records provide some insight into the system. Although the evidence presented to the Scottish sittings of the Royal Commission on the Liquor Licensing Laws between 1896 and 1899 seemed in general to indicate that the tied-house system as such did not 'generally prevail,' there were many indications that it was becoming increasingly common in certain districts of Scotland. Of much greater consequence, however, was the extension of loans to publicans on security. As the Commission heard, 'brewers and companies advance money to persons to start in business, and where brewers or distillers advance money, the publican is often compelled to take liquor from the firm until the loan is paid off.'[52]

Brewery managements clearly played a critical role in the development of retailing through the partial-tie system. Judicious loans to enterprising publicans with well-managed houses could secure and extend sales, and therefore careful selection and supervision were essential. Sensible brewers attached great importance to the conduct of public houses with which agreements had been made, for if the publican lost his licence, loss of valuable capital and business would inevitably result. Hence management, agents and travellers had an important joint supervisory function to ensure the good conduct of the firm's houses, particularly in those districts where licensing authorities or public opinion generally were known to be especially hostile to the trade. The fourth clause of the agreement between a brewer and a publican placed great emphasis on good conduct.

Loans were either arranged directly by the brewers or by their agents, probably on the advice of one of the firm's travellers familiar with the licensee and the potential of the public house in question. Publicans might also approach the firm directly for loans. Most loans were granted on the security of the property, of the licence (for which insurance would be obtained) and of the goodwill of the house. Loans might be repaid over varying periods of time and further loans[53] granted at a later date should the publican require them and should the brewery be satisfied both as to the conduct of the premises and the repayment of outstanding advances.

The most detailed record of the period relating to the management of loans is preserved in the records of William Younger & Company, summarised here in Table 68. It seems unlikely that the details given in this table represent anything like a complete picture, because many of the relevant records have disappeared without trace. In common with other firms of any size in Scotland, Younger appears to have initiated loans to publicans about 1890, although the number of loans on record amounted to half a dozen worth a total of £5,000 before 1895. The two major loans were to public houses in Stockton-on-Tees and Ayr (respectively arranged by the firm's agencies and offices in Stockton and Glasgow), while the remainder were for smaller sums to pubs in the Edinburgh locality, arranged directly by the company from head office. One of the first loans on record was of £1,000 to Thomas Fraser, landlord of the Cross Keys in Ayr, the security in this instance being an assignation of the property and its goodwill. Fraser was given further loans in 1896 of £700 and in 1899 of £300, making a total of £2,000. In all 48 loans were granted—with additional extensions—between 1895 and 1904, averaging around £1,400. As can be seen from the figures given in Table 68, the largest sums were granted in 1899 and 1903, between which dates nearly £48,000

Table 68

William Younger's Loans to Public Houses 1895-1904

Year		Accumulated Loans Outstanding £
1895	1,500	5,000
1896	—	6,500
1897	2,000	8,500
1898	5,500	14,000
1899	12,850	26,850
1900	1,750	28,600
1901	10,000	38,600
1902	11,000	49,6900
1903	12,850	62,450
1904	4,300	66,750

Source: Records of William Younger & Company, Loan Ledger 1891 - 1907.

was loaned by the firm. Apart from the half dozen north of England houses, the bulk of those in Scotland were divided roughly equally between the Edinburgh head office and the Glasgow and west of Scotland office. The former was responsible for loans to and supervision of pubs in the Lothians and Borders, the latter for those in Lanarkshire, Ayrshire, Argyll and the south-west. Most of the ties with houses in the north of Scotland had been made by head office. It is clear that this particular set of records gives only a partial picture, because Younger's certainly had the largest tied trade of any Scottish brewer—including houses in the north of England—before 1914. The firm does not seem to have begun any serious assault on retail outlets in the north of England until 1910. At that date Younger had fourteen pubs there, including seven in Sunderland, two in Stockton and two in West Hartlepool.[54]

The records of the more modest firm of Robert Younger of the nearby St Ann's Brewery at Holyrood confirm the relatively cautious start made by most Scottish brewers in the development of tied outlets. Robert Younger began to grant loans to publicans about the turn of the century, and by 1907-08 these were of the order of £10,000 per annum loaned to a dozen or so publicans. In the two years mentioned, a total of 24 loans were extended on the usual security of property and licences, the average amount being around £1,000. The geographical coverage was extensive, although at least half were to publicans in Fife and the Lothians. With the exception of a few in the west of Scotland and on Tyneside, the remainder were to houses in Dundee and Aberdeen. The largest loans were invariably to publicans in the locality, presumably because supervision was easier than at a distance from the brewery.[55]

The development of overseas trade, essentially to colonial markets, has been the subject of detailed discussion in Chapter Seven. In the period before 1850, described in that chapter, the export of beer from Scotland was very modest. Volume grew considerably during the latter half of the nineteenth century, especially after 1875. The actual expansion of trade in new colonial spheres is the subject of more detailed comment in Chapter Eleven, but our concern here is with a few of the management and organisational problems experienced by brewers selling abroad during the period between 1850 and 1914.

The raising of foreign business was largely a matter of trial and error, as those brewers already active in the overseas trade before 1850 had experienced. For example, the records of John and Robert Tennent illustrate some of the problems of shipping relatively modest volumes of beer and ale to distant markets, with all the difficulties and potential losses associated with shipping, breakages and failure of credit. Nevertheless, this firm, at least from the evidence of one year's shipping between 1859 and 1860, found that persistence paid off, with growing and remunerative shipments to the West Indies, South America and Australia, either directy from Glasgow or via Liverpool. Other brewers who took similar risks found that the effort required to break into overseas trade paid off in the long run, particularly when colonial markets opened up on a larger scale after the seventies.[56]

William McEwan, a newly established brewer with a keen eye on potentially lucrative outlets, was already turning his attention to the colonial opportunities by the mid-sixties. He faced the usual problems of high shipping and related charges, delays and difficulties in the transfer of credit, breakages, heavy insurance charges, and general problems of communication with agents and customers. The charges on a typical shipment of 60 casks of No. 1 'Virginia' to Port Louis, Guadeloupe, in the West Indies, amounted to more than a third of the value of the beer:

60 Casks No. 1 'Virginia'	636 dollars
Discount, Breakages, General Duty, Quay Duty	131
Lighterage, Cartage, Store Rent	16
Coolie Hire, Watching, Freight	53
Insurance, Commission	47
Total	dollars 247

McEwan built up his overseas trade through resident agents in the colonies who probably acted as general shippers to brewers and distillers. The bulk of his exports, as shown in Table 81 of Chapter Eleven, were to Australia and New Zealand, where agents used by the firm had familiar Scottish names like Alexander McFarlane & Company of Melbourne, McPherson & Company of Hobart, Robert Symington of Sydney, W. & S. Turnbull of Wellington, John Barr & Company of Dunedin, and Gillfillan & Company of Auckland. There were many problems in selling to customers on the other side of the world, but, once established, reliable agents could be of inestimable value. They could report on the state of the market and of the demand for various different beers or ales—as they invariably did in their own interests. Once safely arrived in the colonies, there seems to have been little complaint about the quality of McEwan's export: many of the shipments to New Zealand in the sixties were sold by auction immediately on arrival at their destinations. Credit facilities—usually in the form of 60-day bills—were by this period readily extended by a variety of commercial and colonial banks. McEwan used the English, Scottish and Australian Bank, the Colonial Bank, the Union Bank of Australia, the Bank of New South Wales, the South Australian Banking Company, the Oriental Bank, and the Chartered Mercantile Bank. A typical transaction was paid by a 60-day bill in favour of McEwan issued by McIndoe, Rogers & Company of Bombay through the Chartered Mercantile Bank. Safe arrival of the cargo in India without damage through heat or breakages meant payment without deductions—probably more usual in 1866 than it had been for the pioneer exporters at the end of the eighteenth century.[57]

The experiences and problems of Tennent and McEwan were shared with other Scottish brewers in the export trade, notably George Younger of Alloa, James Aitken of Falkirk, and William Younger. These five leading firms had amassed a great deal of experience in overseas markets and were able to capitalise on this during the export boom of the seventies and eighties. They were particularly alive to the shift in taste away from heavy beers towards lighter products for consumption in the hot climates of Egypt, India, Australia and New Zealand. Considerable expertise in the bottling of ales for export had also been gained and the firms were, therefore, in the forefront of the bottling revolution brought about by increased mechanisation. They were, therefore, well placed to meet the demand for light bottled beers in the colonies. Such was their success that by 1890 brewers in Scotland accounted for a third of British exports, a position they maintained almost unchallenged until the outbreak of World War I.[58]

Labour

Discounting 'allied trades,' the numbers actually employed in brewing, although doubling in the period under review, remained extremely modest. There was a steady rise in numbers employed after 1850, as the figures in Table 69 indicate. Between 1861 and 1881, when large-scale expansion was beginning to get under-

Table 69

Numbers Employed in Breweries 1861-1911

Year	No.
1861	1,146
1871	1,330
1881	1,674
1891	2,084
1901	2,052
1911	2,405

Sources: Occupational Census Abstracts for years indicated.

way, numbers employed in breweries and others engaged in brewing rose from 1,146 to 1,674. The growth of the labour force was most marked in the inter-censal decade 1881-91, which coincided with the brewery boom. By 1891 the labour force exceeded 2,000 workers. In 1901 the labour force was only slightly lower than it had been ten years before, but this downward trend clearly reflected the uncertainties of the industry at that time. There was probably a continued decline until 1905, but thereafter recovery in brewing and related trades took the figure to the 1911 level of 2,405.[59]

The increasing concentration on traditional brewing centres was also clearly reflected in labour statistics. In 1861 the brewing trade in Edinburgh employed 22 per cent of the total labour force, Glasgow 15 per cent, and Alloa, Falkirk, Dundee and Aberdeen another 15 per cent between them. By 1881, as the figures in Table 70 show, Edinburgh employed nearly a third, while there had been little

Table 70

Numbers Employed By Centre 1861-1911

Centre	1861	1871	1881	1891	1901	1911
Edinburgh	249	387	603	949	928	1013
Glasgow	172	250	226	327	399	564
Alloa	39	82	65	103	190	186
Falkirk	20	25	27	31	45	45
Dundee	60	45	39	56	55	42
Aberdeen	61	50	35	47	25	11

Sources: Occupational Census Abstracts for years indicated.

growth elsewhere. Breweries in both Edinburgh and Glasgow—where developments were most marked—expanded their labour force considerably between 1881 and 1891. By this last date labour in Edinburgh represented 45 per cent of the total employed in all Scottish breweries, that in Glasgow still being around 15 per cent. By 1911 the city of Edinburgh employed 1,013 brewery workers, roughly 45 per cent of the total labour force, Glasgow's share then being somewhat less than 25 per cent and the remaining centres shown in Table 70 accounting for around 10 per cent.[60]

Yet, despite this high degree of concentration, the figures of labour employed in breweries throughout Scotland shown in Table 71 give some indication of the persistence of small breweries beyond the main centres, even as late as 1911. Discounting the leading counties of Edinburgh and Lanark, a ranking of the next eight in terms of numbers employed in 1871 and 1911 produces some interesting points:

	1871	1911
1	Edinburgh	Edinburgh
2	Lanark	Lanark
3	Aberdeen	Clackmannan
4	Forfar	Forfar
5	Clackmannan	Stirling
6	Fife	Aberdeen
7	Perth	Perth
8	Ayr	Elgin
9	Stirling	Fife
10	Renfrew	Haddington

Table 71

Numbers Employed By Counties 1871 and 1911

County	1871	1911
Aberdeen	92	41
Argyll	11	21
Ayr	32	19
Banff	23	25
Berwick	12	4
Bute	1	1
Caithness	3	3
Clackmannan	82	186
Dumbarton	4	12
Edinburgh	387	1143
Elgin	25	32
Fife	74	30
Forfar	92	66
Haddington	27	30
Inverness	15	10
Kincardine	11	12
Kinross	1	—
Kirkcudbright	11	1
Lanark	255	478

Numbers Employed By Counties 1871 and 1911 (Cont.)

County	1871	1911
Linlithgow	6	7
Nairn	1	1
Orkney	1	6
Peebles	2	—
Perth	46	37
Renfrew	30	19
Ross & Cromarty	7	3
Roxburgh	20	3
Stirling	31	47
Sutherland	1	2
Wigtown	9	7
Dumfries	12	6

Sources: PP 1873 LXXIII and PP 1913 LXXX, Occupational Abstracts.

In 1871 the third and fourth most important counties in terms of employment were Aberdeen and Forfar. Although there were three medium-sized breweries in the city of Aberdeen itself, a number of country breweries were apparently still active. In 1850 the county had the largest number of brewers of any in Scotland, and all must have been run by a man and a boy. In Forfar, Dundee brewers were the largest employers, but there were still breweries in towns like Montrose, Arbroath, Brechin and Forfar. Clackmannan, dominated by the old brewing town of Alloa, came fifth and Fife was not far behind in sixth place. By 1911 the dominance of the brewing centres of Alloa, Dundee and Falkirk was greater, while Aberdeen had slipped to sixth place. Perth maintained its former position in terms of labour employed, while Fife had slipped to ninth place. Ayr and Renfrew had dropped out of the first ten altogether, to be replaced by Haddington and, rather surprisingly, Elgin (where there was a flourishing old-established brewery with a good local trade).[61]

Further information on labour and wage rates in brewing is provided by evidence presented in parliamentary papers of the early nineties. The first, of 1890, indicates that in a typical firm salaries and wages accounted for 9.4 per cent of outlays:

Outlays	Per Cent
Material	46.4
Beer Duty	16.2
Salaries & Wages	9.4
Discounts, allowances, commissions	5.1
Repairs	4.4
Carriage, Cartage, Freight	3.0
Horse Keep	2.5
Rates and Taxes	2.2
Expenses of Stores	2.2
Coal	2.1
Others	6.5
	100.0[62]

The second, of 1893-94, provides details of employment and wage rates based on a survey of 19 companies in Edinburgh, Glasgow and other parts of Scotland shown in Table 72. Wage rates in Scotland, as indicated in Table 72(A), were substantially lower than those paid in the south, particularly those of London. Rates in Edinburgh and Burton were more directly comparable, while Glasgow's average was less than that elsewhere in Scotland. The occupational breakdown for Edinburgh, shown in Table 72(B), indicates that coopers were the highest paid group, while maltmen and draymen were paid roughly comparable rates.

Table 72

(A) *Wages and Employment in Breweries 1885-86*

District	No. of Returns	No. of employed Men	No. of employed Lads	Total Wage Bill	Total Annual Wage	Average Annual Wage	Average Weekly Wage
London	6	1557	22	1579	122717	£77 14s	29s 11d
Burton	9	2657	263	2920	161797	£55 3s	21s 2d
Edinburgh	11	762	88	850	44749	£52 13s	20s 2d
Glasgow	2	60	21	81	3984	£49 4s	19s 0d
Other Parts of Scotland	6	80	10	90	4608	£51 4s	19s 8d

(B) *Average Weekly Wage Rates in Edinburgh 1885-86*

Occupation	No. Employed	Average Wage
Maltmen	150	22s 3d
Cellarmen	95	20s 2d
Coopers	113	27s 1d
Draymen	51	22s 0d
Labourers	59	17s 7d

Source: PP 1893-94 LXXXIII General Report on the Wages of the Manual Labour Classes in the U.K. 1886 and 1891, 107-108.

A more detailed picture of employment in Scottish breweries at the turn of the century is provided in Table 73, which indicates the numbers employed and the average weekly wage of the various occupations. The total includes only those directly employed in brewing and does not take account of management, technical staff or those employed in retailing, such as travellers or publicans. It is probable that the 'Others' category includes clerical and related staff, although the figure seems somewhat low. Of the total of 2,393 workers, 1,690 could be classed as semi- or unskilled, earning less than 25s per week. Those in the unskilled category included rackers, cask washers, bottlers and general labourers, while the semi-skilled group was composed of mashroom men, maltmen, storemen and draymen. The essentially skilled workers were the foremen, coopers, mechanics and engine-men, mostly earning in excess of 30s per week. Finally, there was the lowest paid group earning 10s per week or less, composed largely of apprentices, but including

Table 73

Labour Employed and Wage Rates 1906

Occupation	No.	Average Weekly Wage
Foremen	153	33s 3d
Maltmen	364	23s 7d
Mash Room & Fermenting Men	208	23s 0d
Rackers	144	22s 0d
Coopers	300	30s 1d
Cask Washers (A)	154	21s 2d
Bottlers	56	21s 9d
Storemen	39	22s 6d
Draymen	157	23s 2d
Mechanics	59	30s 10d
Mechanics' Labourers	50	22s 10d
Enginemen & Stokers	56	26s 11d
General Labourers	75	20s 11d
Others (B)	135	25s 5d
Apprentices	421	10s 5d
Women	21	9s 9d
Girls	1	7s 6d
Total	2393	

(A) Includes 33 washers on piece rates, who earned 4s 9d
    more per week.
(B) Probably includes clerical and related staff.
Source: PP 1912-13 XVIII, Report on Earnings and Hours
of Labour: VIII Food, Drink and Tobacco Trades in 1906,
204.

women—the latter probably employed in bottling. In 1906 the average in breweries throughout Britain as a whole was 26s 3d for men and 10s 5d for apprentices. The average for maltmen was 22s 4d and for mash room men, 23s 6d, although these figures did not include the traditional beer allowance.[63]

Increased mechanisation and the growth of more scientific approaches to brewing necessarily involved the need to employ more skilled labour for certain tasks in and around the brew-house. Quality control—the prime concern in every brewery—had become the responsibility of the head brewer, the brewer's chemist and perhaps the foreman, but skilled tradesmen were required to maintain the equipment which made possible the enormous increase in output between 1885 and 1900. After the foremen, the mechanics and the coopers were of vital importance to the efficient running of the brewery. Skilled engineers, required to build and maintain new plant and machinery, could often be hired in the first instance from specialist firms in Glasgow or Leith. George Scamell's work on *Breweries and Maltings*, first published in 1871, shows the degree of sophistication which had already been reached in the design and construction of plant for breweries by that date. The brewery's reputation often depended on the condition of its casks and the cooper was, therefore, one of the highest paid manual workers.[64] Scottish brewers tended to remain very self-sufficient in these and other ancillary trades.

Apart from apprentices, malting employed the largest number of workers in Scottish breweries, the majority of men being semi-skilled. The success of the malting depended to a great degree on the foreman in charge. He had to see that the deliveries of barley from the farmer were up to the standard of the sale sample and he would be answerable for all the men employed in the maltings. He would be responsible for the different malting operations and had to see that the floors were turned at the right times, that the temperature on the floor was not allowed to rise unduly and that the sprinkling was properly done. He would have to supervise the loading and unloading of the kiln. A good foreman maltster would usually be paid between £100 and £120 per annum. The maltmen, whose job involved back breaking work turning malt in the heat of a kiln, were paid between 20s and 25s per week in 1905-06.[65]

Other semi-skilled groups in and around the brewhouse included the mash room men, fermenting men and draymen. Those employed in the mash and fermenting rooms had to tackle a wide variety of jobs which required mainly physical effort, though also some knowledge of brewing skills. Larger numbers of draymen were required to deliver the increased output of breweries to customers. Though generally labouring beyond the brewery gate, the reliable drayman was a great asset. He had not only to lift heavy casks of beer, but also to tend the dray and costly horses. The honour of the firm, to some extent, lay in his hands.[66]

The essentially unskilled and the apprentices made up the bulk of the remaining categories still to be considered, and included rackers, cask washers, storemen, general labourers and females. It seems likely that the figures for these groups given in Table 71 are somewhat low. Women and boys were certainly employed in increasing numbers to tackle jobs like bottle-washing, bottling and packing, though perhaps on a part-time basis. All of these tasks, although requiring little skill, were extremely important in that they were concerned with the storage and dispatch of the brewery's products.

There was undoubtedly a considerable increase in ancillary staff, particularly after the boom of the eighties, although how far this is reflected in the available labour statistics is impossible to verify. The growth in business experience by the majority of firms must have necessitated the employment of more clerks, book-keepers and cashiers. Accounting procedures changed little and remained essentially dependent on the transfer of sets of figures from one enormous ledger to another. There was certainly a great increase in sales staff, with growing numbers of travellers employed to sell competing products. The increased mobility of the travellers gave them considerable advantages both over their mid-Victorian predecessors and the once popular resident agents. It was also to the firm's advantage to employ travellers who were directly under its own control and could be deployed wherever there was an opportunity to extend business. As regards 'allied trades,' it is clearly difficult to know where to draw the line. The retail side of brewing, like that of distilling, employed many times more people than the industry itself. Publicans and others were of great importance to the trade, but could not be considered part of the brewery labour force.

NOTES

1 Vaizey, op.cit., 92.
2 See section on 'Licensing Laws and Retailing' in Chapter Eleven for a discussion of the historical background to the development of the Scottish system.
3 PP 1912-13 CVIII, Report on Earnings and Hours of Labour: VIII Food, Drink and Tobacco Trades in 1906, 204.
4 Corran, op.cit., 183-211.
5 Barnard, op.cit., vol. II, 194, 434-5; vol. III, 157-66; vol. IV, 371.
6 *Brewers' Guardian*, 1891, 373; Barnard, op.cit., vol. IV, 371. British Patent No. 2614, 1853; Scamell, op.cit., 146.
7 Baker, op.cit., 81.
8 Ibid., 88; Barnard, op.cit., gives an impressive list of steam engines used in the breweries he visited.
9 Corran, op.cit., 198-201; J. O Harris, 'Changes in British Brewing Techniques,' *Brewers' Guardian Centenary Issue*, 1971, 105-108; Barnard, op.cit., vol. III, 157-66.
10 E.C.Stevenson, 'Pasteurisation Progress,' *Brewers' Guardian Centenary Issue*, 1971, 121-4.
11 Baker, op.cit., 141-42.
12 Barnard, op.cit., vol. III, 160.
13 *The Mercantile Age*, 10 July 1883, 538-9, 'Messrs. J. & R. Tennent, Wellpark Brewery, Glasgow.'
14 Corran, op.cit., 236-7; A.J.Puddick, 'Changes in British Bottling Techniques,' *Brewers' Guardian Centenary Issue*, 1971, 117-119.
15 Anon, *A short history of George Younger & Son Ltd, Alloa, 1762-1925* (Alloa, 1925), 8-16; Barnard, op.cit., vol. II, 434-5.
16 Bremner, op.cit., 439-43; Barnard, op.cit., vol. IV, 371.
17 Barnard, op.cit., vol. IV, 373.
18 Ibid., 374.
19 Ibid., vol. III, 157-66.
20 Full text of the speech in Hansard's Parliamentary Debates, 3rd Series, vol. 252 (1880), cols. 1622-57.
21 Wilson, op.cit., 51-53.
22 PP 1899 XXX, Report of the Departmental Committee on Beer Materials, 299, 303.
23 Barnard, op.cit., vol. II.
24 Anon, *Report of Meiklejohn's Centenary 1874* (Newcastle-upon-Tyne, 1875), 22.
25 Barnard, op.cit., vol. II, 431; vol. III, 165; vol. II, 190.
26 A.Chapman, 'The Production of Bottled Light Beer,' *Brewers' Guardian*, 1896, 148-50.
27 For further comment on foreign competition see section on 'Overseas Markets' in Chapter Eleven.
28 Corran, op.cit., 225-28; more than a dozen papers on lager brewing and the production of light or sparkling ales appeared in the *Journal of the Institute of Brewing* between 1899 and 1910.
29 *Brewers' Guardian* 1889, 162.
30 Baker, op.cit., 124.
31 Ibid., 125.
32 COS, UP 1st Div. E 7/1, Edinburgh United Breweries Ltd v James Molleson, 1891-2, Proof for the EUB Ltd., 149-52.
33 Vaizey, op.cit., 10-11.
34 Baker, op.cit., 139-140.
35 Two major brewers, as we have seen in Chapter Eight, entered politics and left their businesses to professional management, George Younger and William McEwan.
36 Baker, op.cit., 141.
37 I am grateful to Professor Anna Macleod for information on the history of her department at Heriot-Watt University.
38 *Brewers' Guardian*, 1892, 20.
39 Baker, op.cit., 142.
40 Keir, op.cit., 72, 76; C.M.Usher, *A History of the Usher Family in Scotland* (Edinburgh, 1956), 70-71; Anon, *Two Hundred Years of Progress: James Aitken & Co. Ltd., 1740-1940* (Falkirk 1940), 3-4; Barnard, op.cit., vol. III, 147. Other examples are discussed in section on 'Companies' in Chapter Nine.
41 *Brewers' Guardian*, 1893, 339; ibid, 1894, 81.
42 *Brewers' Guardian*, 1890, 60.
43 *Glasgow Post Office Annual Directory 1850-51* (Glasgow, 1850), 433.
44 *A Short History of George Younger*, op.cit., 26.

45 Barnard, op.cit., vol. II, 36.
46 Records of Wm. Younger & Co., Travellers' Statistics Book, 1881-1912.
47 Barnard, op.cit., vol. III, 164.
48 SRO, COS, Currie Dal C 18/2 A. Campbell & Co. v. J.S.Galbraith, 1851, Print of Documents and other papers.
49 *A Short History of George Younger*, op.cit., 26-28.
50 Barnard, op.cit., vol. IV, 366; Anon, *Glasgow of Today: Business Men and Mercantile Interests* (Glasgow, 1888), 126.
51 Ibid., 229.
52 PP 1899 XXV, Report of the Royal Commission on the Liquor Licensing Laws, Final Report, 182.
53 PP 1898 XXXVIII, Report of Royal Comm. on Liquor Licensing Laws, 4th Report, 55-56.
54 Records of Wm. Younger & Co. Loan Ledger 1891-1907; Ledger of North of England Public Houses 1910-13.
55 Records of Robert Younger, Loan Ledger No. 2, 1907-08.
56 Tennent Mss, Shipping Book, 1859-60.
57 Wm. McEwan Archives, Journals 1865-70.
58 See Table 77.
59 Occupational Census Abstracts 1861-1911.
60 Ibid.
61 PP 1873 LXXIII and PP 1913 LXXX, Occupational Census Abstracts.
62 PP 1890-91, LXXVIII, Report on relation of Wages in certain Industries to cost of production, 43.
63 PP 1912-13 CVIII, Report on Earnings and Hours of Labour: VIII Food, Drink and Tobacco Trades in 1906, xxvii — xxxi, 204.
64 In 1886 the average weekly wage for a cooper in Edinburgh was 27s 1d, compared with 22s 3d for a maltman (PP 1893-94 LLXXXIII, General Report on the Wages of the Manual Labour Classes in the U.K. 1886-1891, 108).
65 Baker, op.cit., 38.
66 W.Stanley-Smith, 'Labour in the Brewhouse,' *Brewers' Guardian* 1902, 72-5.

11
Markets—Home and Foreign
1850-1914

THE development of markets in the latter half of the nineteenth century was to some extent a reflection of long-established practice coupled with the new opportunities created by large-scale production and lower unit costs. Before 1850 Scottish brewers had successfully developed both domestic and overseas markets and in the face of many difficulties had sought new outlets for their products. The growth in demand for beer associated with the rise in population and general increase in real incomes, particularly amongst the working class, continued unabated until the close of the century. At the same time public taste began to swing away from heavier beers towards lighter ales. The latter could be produced by most brewers in Scotland because they had the advantage of suitable water, which was not generally available in some of the established brewing centres of southern England. Light beers were also in increasing demand in foreign markets. In the hot climates of the British colonies and India, the demand for such beverages was so great that it could not readily be satisfied. Scottish brewers also had considerable experience of bottling beers and ales, and this stood them in good stead both in domestic and overseas outlets.

The optimism of growth built on experience and the challenge of new techniques throughout most of the period between 1850 and 1914 was tempered to some extent by the very considerable political difficulties which faced the drink industries as a whole. The period after 1870 was marked by a rising tide of temperance at both national and local level. The brewers conducted their businesses and the publicans their houses in an increasingly hostile environment. As more and more control was exerted by national and local government over brewing and retail licensing, and an increasing burden of taxation placed upon brewers, so the trade found it necessary to extend its political influence in order to survive. The licensing system in Scotland had a profound impact on the development of retailing, creating a pattern which differed radically from that south of the Border. Retail licences had always been issued annually to individuals (i.e. to publicans, grocers, victuallers etc.) rather than to public houses or shops, as was the case in England. Local licensing authorities in Scotland could therefore always exercise a greater degree of control over retail outlets for drink than was possible in England, where licences could be and were traded freely. As curbs on licensing were increasingly exerted by authorities, so the actual licences and hence the retail outlets became more valuable. In England this produced the battle for tied houses involving almost all of the major brewers, while in Scotland it led to the development of a system whereby brewers made loans or extended credit to licensees who would sell their products. The tied-house system of brewers owning retail outlets on the English model made little headway because of the considerable differences in the licensing system between the two countries.

In the middle of the nineteenth century local markets remained of vital importance to the majority of brewers and this was as true of the large urban breweries in Edinburgh and Glasgow as of their more modest country cousins. Brewers had not been slow to appreciate the advantages of water-borne canal transport, and likewise they were ready to use steamships and railways. These revolutionary improvements in transport enabled the larger firms to develop more distant outlets and greatly to increase their share of the domestic market, particularly in the urban, industrial districts of central Scotland. It is difficult to estimate how much rivalry and open competition existed between the major Scottish firms, although there is little hint in either individual company or more general Scottish trade sources of the kinds of battles in the 1880s in England which earned the label of 'Brewers' Wars.' Most of the evidence would seem to indicate that the majority of Scottish brewers quietly extended their influence in traditional markets, and that the real pressure to seek 'tied' outlets did not come in Scotland until the nineties. This was perhaps the result of Scottish success in English and colonial markets, which may to some extent have relieved the pressure to compete with any real degree of ferocity at home.

Licensing Laws and Retailing

It is impossible in the period under review to escape the political difficulties faced by the drink industries in general, but it is more our concern here to concentrate on a detailed examination of the changing liquor licensing system in Scotland and its influence on beer retailing. No complete history of this important issue has yet been written, although the pioneer study of George Wilson contains much interesting material relevant to Scotland.[1] The cause of temperance was particularly strong in Scotland and, as elsewhere, came to be associated with Liberalism in national politics. But long before the temperance lobby gained national strength and influence in Parliament in the eighties and nineties, it had been able to make a substantial impact locally by exerting its influence on licensing authorities. The main aims of the temperance movements were to reduce the number of licences to retail outlets, and limit public house opening hours and hours of sale in licensed grocers' premises. Many abuses of the licensing system arose from the sale and consumption of spirits out of hours, although it is naturally very difficult to estimate how much the undoubted problem of drunkenness throughout many parts of Scotland could be ascribed to spirits rather than beer.

Some indication has already been given in Chapter Seven of the important effects of licensing legislation on the sale of beer during the late eighteenth and early nineteenth centuries. The 'licence' itself was an old-established means of controlling the numbers of premises selling alcoholic liquors. Under a special act for Scotland of 1801 no licence could be issued to any person who did not produce a justice's 'certificate' (in essence an attestation of character) and it was limited to 'common inns, alehouses or victualling houses.' The basis of nineteenth-century practice in Scotland was laid in the licensing act of 1828, the so-called Home-Drummond Act. The existing law was revised, with justices of the peace in counties and magistrates in burghs confirmed as the authorities for granting certificates, without which excise licences for inns, alehouses and victualling houses could not be issued. The necessary machinery for licensing was established and a form of certificate set out with various conditions attaching to the grant, including one stipulating that the licensee 'do not keep open house or permit or suffer any drinking or tippling during the hours of Divine Service on Sundays, or other Appointed Days, or keep the same open at unreasonable hours'—the first formal intimation of opening hours for inns and taverns in Scotland.[2] The increased activities of the temperance reformers after the 1830s led ultimately to the appointment in 1846 of a Select Committee of the House of Commons, under the chairmanship of Forbes-Mackenzie, to enquire into the system of granting certificates. Among numerous abuses the committee found:

> That the number of houses in which spirits are sold for consumption on the premises is excessive, and ought to be restricted; and in particular, that the number of houses of such inferior class is excessive and productive of evil, and that it would be expedient to repress the evil arising therefrom.

One outstanding abuse (still common in villages and small towns!) was that of drinking in grocers' shops. Grocers used to obtain certificates, despite the fact that their premises did not strictly come within the definition of an inn or tavern. The customer went into the shop and had a snack of bread and cheese with his beer or whisky, and grocers' premises became natural social rendezvous.

As a result of the committee's report the Licensing (Scotland) Act of 1853, better known as the Forbes-Mackenzie Act, was passed.[3] It clearly separated retail liquor licences into two main types—'on' licences (for sale of liquors for consumption on the premises) and 'off' licences (for sale of liquors to be consumed outwith the retail premises), and provided that publicans should not sell groceries and that grocers should not sell liquor for consumption on the premises. Three forms of certificate were substituted for the then existing form, for hotel keepers, publicans and grocers. Numerous restrictive regulations were imposed, two of which touched very much on the social life of many Scottish rural communities: no blacksmith might obtain a licence for his smithy or a house near it, nor might a toll-house keeper maintain licensed premises. General power of entry to licensed premises was given to the police—a power more exercised then than now. The conditions of the certificate contained one important addition, that the publican must 'not open his house for the sale of any liquors, or sell or give out the same, *on Sunday*, except for the accommodation of lodgers and bona fide travellers.' This restriction was not, in theory, a new regulation in Scotland. By the common law of Scotland traders had not been permitted to carry on their ordinary business on Sunday. There was probably always some relaxation of the rules in cases of necessity, such as inns or hotels, but dealing in liquor was always prohibited in other cases on Sunday. The Act of 1828 did, however, in express terms prohibit holders of certificates from carrying on business 'during the hours of Divine Service on Sundays and other days,' and it was held that these words implied permission to grocers and liquor dealers to sell liquor at any other hour on Sundays or other days. But almost complete Sunday-closing of public houses resulted from the 1853 Act. As an incidental, the act also made it illegal to sell or consume liquors between 11 p.m. and 8 a.m.—except in the case of grocers, who might open at 6 a.m.

Six years after the Forbes-Mackenzie legislation a Royal Commission was appointed in 1859 'to enquire into the laws regulating the sale and consumption of excisable liquors in Scotland' and the general operation of the licensing system. 769 witnesses were called, and a very detailed report resulted, a number of provisions being incorporated in later public house legislation. The commission reported favourably on Sunday closing, while other measures sought to regularise several malpractices. The right of local objection to applications for new certificates was extended; power was given to the police to enter unlicensed premises suspected of illicit trading; laws against shebeens and drinking dens were extended; and the illicit hawking of liquor, disorderly conduct and drunkenness made punishable offences.[4] Subsequent legislation sought to curb abuses and in particular to restrict hours of sale. One particularly interesting example was the Passenger Vessels Licences Amendment (Scotland) Act of 1882, which dealt with 'the great evils arisen from the sale of intoxicating liquors on a Sunday on board passenger vessels plying on rivers and estuaries in Scotland,' and empowered excise authorities to impose a condition on the licence prohibiting the sale of liquor during any voyage commenced and terminated on the same Sunday. In 1887 the Public Houses' Hours of Closing (Scotland) Act empowered the licensing authorities to close licensed premises one hour earlier than the statutory hour of 11 p.m.—except in burghs of 50,000 population and over. This provision was extended to all areas by the Licensing (Scotland) Act of 1903 and soon afterwards 10 o'clock became the universal closing hour in Scotland.[5]

During the years 1896-99 the Royal Commission on the Liquor Licensing Laws, presided over by Lord Peel, examined very fully the Scottish position (analysed in detail throughout, but mainly in the Minutes of Evidence in its Fourth Report of 1898).[6] As a result of its majority and minority reports (the latter signed by its chairman), a consolidating act was passed—the Licensing (Scotland) Act of 1903, which gave effect wholly or partly to many of the recommendations. This act still forms the basis of the Scottish licensing code. The act repealed all former statutes but re-enacted with variations their leading provisions. The constitution and duties of licensing courts were re-defined and the districts re-arranged. The power of local licensing authorities was greatly extended, especially as regards the framing of bye-laws, the latter accounting to some extent for the great local variations which existed until recently in many parts of Scotland. The old law that certificates were granted for a year and no longer was re-affirmed, and penalties against illicit drinking and drunkenness were revised.[7]

One final piece of legislation remains to be considered, although its importance to both publican and brewer lay in the future, especially the 1920s and 1930s. In 1913, as a result of long and vigorous political controversy, the Temperance (Scotland) Act became law. This gave localities the power of 'local option' in respect of the issue of certificates or licences for the sale of liquor. After the expiry of eight years from the end of 1912, areas could hold a vote or poll (renewable thereafter every three years if desired), the options being no change, limitation, or no licence.[8]

Licensing laws and the system briefly described had a major impact on the nature of liquor retailing and, although they affected all sections of the trade, it is our purpose here to give some indication of their impact on brewers and the retailing of their products in the domestic market. Some attention has already been given to the business and financial arrangements contracted between brewers and publicans. Therefore this analysis is more concerned with assessing the general climate in which the Scottish retailing system developed, particularly with reference to the impact of changes in licensing arrangements and to comparisons with English experience. Licensing legislation undoubtedly had a major impact in restricting the number of retail outlets and contributed substantially to what one witness before the Royal Commission on the Liquor Licensing Laws of 1896-99 described rather neatly as 'practically the tied house system.'[9]

In general terms the Scottish licensing laws were the means of bringing about a considerable reduction in the numbers of public houses and other retail outlets for beer, wine and spirits. According to evidence laid before the Royal Commission in 1899, there had been about 18,000 licences in 1830, but by 1850 the number had fallen to 14,500. Population during the same period had increased by over half a million. Licences were, in fact, broadly distributed according to population. In 1851, for example, more than 60 per cent of licence holders resided in the excise collections of Glasgow, Ayr, Linlithgow, Edinburgh and Stirling—the most populous districts of the industrial lowlands. After 1850 the reductions in licences proceeded apace, so that by 1886 the number was down to 12,000 (see Table 74) and finally reached around 10,000 in 1914. The complexity of the overall licensing position in Scotland is well illustrated in Table 75, which shows the wide range of overlapping and duplicate licences which existed. Many retailers apparently held one or more licences, as was the case with grocers who sold beer and wine as well as spirits. In 1893, the figures worked out at 3.5 licences per 1,000 of the population in Scotland. The figures for other parts of the United Kingdom were: 4 per 1,000 in Ireland, and 4.5 per 1,000 in England, the average being 4 per 1,000.

It is difficult to say how far reductions or increases in licences were due to adjustments in population in a locality. It seems more likely that pressure from the temperance and anti-drink lobby on the one hand and trade and popular demand on the other played a part. The data in Table 74 support the view that local licensing authorities sought to reduce licences whenever possible, although they were also obliged to respond to community needs or demands. This was clearly so in the populous city of Glasgow, where the total number of licences was relatively stable (but the numbers of public houses dropped, while licensed grocers increased). The position varied greatly from district to district (as it still does),

Table 74

(A) *Licensed Premises in Scotland, 1886, 1906, 1916*

Type	1886	1906	1916
Hotels & Inns	1,742	1,650	1,533
Public Houses	5,920	5,442	5,024
Licensed Grocers	4,515	3,903	3,301
Total	12,177	10,995	9,858

(B) *Licensed Premises In Four Sample Districts, 1886-1916*

District	Hotels and Inns			Public Houses			Licensed Grocers			Total		
	1886	1906	1916	1886	1906	1916	1886	1906	1916	1886	1906	1916
Aberdeen	29	17	15	101	113	113	249	200	173	379	330	301
Edinburgh	44	30	23	327	310	292	451	414	332	822	754	647
Dundee	8	6	6	229	212	212	221	198	186	458	416	404
Glasgow	20	17	15	1465	1330	1359	261	304	321	1746	1651	1695

Sources: PP, Accounts and Papers, 1887, 1907, 1916-17, Returns of the Number of Persons Licensed for the Sale of Beer and Spirits.

depending on the attitude of local licensing authorities. In the county of Aberdeen the number of public house licences declined markedly from 96 in 1886 to 30 in 1916, whereas the figures in Table 74 show that in the city of Aberdeen the number remained fairly static at around 110. The number of licences elsewhere in Scotland was markedly reduced over time. This cannot always be explained by a decline in rural areas, or by falling population densities, or the actions of temperance-minded justices. In the county of Renfrew, for example, the number of licences was reduced from 244 in 1886 to 86 in 1906 and 66 in 1916, whereas in Paisley the cut-back was less severe—from 161 in 1886 to 127 in 1916. Almost everywhere, however, the reduction in numbers greatly enhanced the value of individual licences and therefore greatly increased the desire of brewers to gain some control over them.[10]

Before examining the development of the Scottish brewers' relationship with their retail outlets, it is worth looking briefly by way of contrast at the English experience during the nineteenth century, when the classic tied-house system was becoming increasingly prevalent. Some questions of definition apply in part to both countries: the free house, the tied house, and the managed house. A free house, as the name suggests, is a public house owned by the occupant, or rented from someone other than a brewer, the publican being completely at liberty to obtain his liquor wherever he thinks fit. A tied tenant is one who rents a public house from a brewery firm and is bound to purchase his beer and possibly other commodities (like spirits from an associated distiller) from that brewery. Similarly a partially tied-house is one where the licence holder has obtained a mortgage on his property from a brewer (a familiar feature in Scotland). The managed house is one that is under the charge of a salaried manager, usually run on behalf of a brewery, private individual or company.[11] The tie or partial tie developed initially as a means of entering the publican's trade, the retailer obtaining a loan from a brewer and undertaking to purchase supplies from him. Brewers began to develop the tied-house system in an atmosphere of increasing competition during the first half of the nineteenth century. Even before 1850 the majority of retail outlets in England were tied houses, while in Scotland the system was known but not common.[12] Because licences would be obtained by anyone who could fulfil certain easy conditions, they had comparatively little value. But in England, as in Scotland, legislation after 1850 sought to control the issue of licences, and so a steadily decreasing number assumed substantially greater value.

Table 75

No. of Licences Issued in Scotland 1893

Type	No.
Publicans	7,268
Beerhouses	461
Grocers retailing spirits	3,858
Dealers in Beer	191
Dealers in Spirits	618
Dealers in Wine	188
Retailers of Beer & Wine	
'On'	141
'Off'	3,485
Dealers & Retailers of Sweets	106
Passenger Boats	158
Distillers and Rectifiers	152
Total	15,463

Source: *Brewers' Almanack 1895*, 108, Table XVII.

Brewers, therefore, began to invest in retail outlets and enforce the tied-house system. Similar restrictions of the kind already noted in Scotland were also enforced south of the Border, particularly with regard to the conduct of licensed premises. The general risks and responsibilities of running licensed premises increased enormously and many publicans could safeguard their interests only by selling out to a brewery, which, having greater capital and more public houses, could better afford to take risks on any particular property. When the eighties brought the so-called 'Brewers' Wars' there was still greater competition, so that the sensible publican with a well regarded pub and valuable licence could do very well out of a mutual agreement with a brewer.

Licence reformers and temperance advocates were highly critical of the tied-house system and variants that developed during the latter half of the nineteenth century. The Chief Constable of Greenock, in evidence to the Royal Commission on the Liquor Licensing Laws, described the tied-house publican as 'a well-conducted slave' forced to push drink down the throats of his customers.[13] This well-worn argument was constantly reiterated in the temperance press. One of the leading temperance journals, *Truth*, in its issue of 9 May 1906 published an article under the heading 'Beerlord and Tenant,' in which the tied-house system was described as 'mischievous and intolerable.' The only interest of the landlord or publican, it maintained, was 'to induce every man or woman who enter his house to swallow the greatest possible quantity of the landlord's brew, good, bad or indifferent.' The writer added that if the tenant 'fails to push down his customer's throat a sufficient quantity . . . woe betide him,' for 'in nine cases out of ten he is in the hands of a corporation which has neither soul to be damned nor body to be kicked.'[14]

Scotland's experience of beer retailing was very different, although it did have parallels with that of England. The final report of the Royal Commission on the Liquor Licensing Laws reported that 'with respect . . . to tied-houses, the case of Scotland differs considerably from that of England.' The tied-house system did not 'generally prevail' and it was considered exceptional for a public house to be owned by wholesale traders, because 'the houses are almost invariably the property either of the licensees themselves or of private owners.'[15] Plenty of the evidence to the Royal Commission substantiated this view: the Chief Constable of Glasgow did not know of any public house 'tied down absolutely to any particular firm' in the city; in Edinburgh there were few tied houses; while in Aberdeen and the north of Scotland generally 'very few' pubs were tied to either brewers or distillers. The reality of the position was different, for according to the Solicitor General for Scotland, C.S. Dickson, the tied-house system 'existed to some extent,' although he was forced to admit it was obvious only 'in those cases where one sees 'So & Sos beer only sold on these premises'.'[16] It was difficult to know if these were 'tied' in the English sense or were simply public houses whose licensees had been lent money by brewers. For some years, many witnesses reported, brewers had been advancing money to start publicans out in business, licensees being compelled to take beer from the firm until the loan was paid off. Although the situation varied greatly from district to district, there was considerable evidence of brewers extending credit or giving loans to publicans throughout Scotland. In Dundee, according to the Chief Constable, 'many young men started out in business as publicans aided by brewers and wholesale houses, the arrangement being that they are bound to take their liquor from the party advancing the money to start the business.' A number of public houses in Dundee were actually owned by brewers. In both Perth and Greenock the system was well established. In the former, nearly every licensed house which had changed hands had been bought by a brewer or, more exceptionally, a distiller, often at inflated prices. In the latter town new firms in the brewing trade had bought out several publicans to secure outlets for their beers, in all cases paying large sums for the goodwill of the premises.[17] Although the evidence to the Royal Commission of 1896-99 indicated the presence of the tied-house system on the English model, the most common practice on the part of Scottish brewers was the partial tie brought about by the extension of credit or the making of loans to publicans. During the brewing boom of the nineties the partial tie gained considerable ground in the home market and was also extended to outlets in England if houses were not already tied. Most of the major Scottish brewers granted loans or gave credit to licensees on security— usually the public house mortgage, or insurance policies (including the licence insurance, which became very important as licences rose in value). The system became commonplace after 1900, by which time even small breweries of modest capital had secured retail outlets by extending credit or giving loans. By 1914 a large proportion of retail outlets in Scotland—perhaps 60 per cent—were tied financially to brewers.[18]

The brewer's interest in controlling his retail outlets might have been widely condemned by advocates of temperance, but it brought obvious advantages to both the trade and customer. Brewer and publican benefited, the brewer by obtaining an assured outlet for his beers, the publican by a loan or credit to develop his business. The brewer had an interest in the good management of the house and encouragement of custom. In turn patrons would find a well-conducted house, serving well-kept beers. On the other hand, the ill-run establishment was unlikely to attract custom and would almost certainly attract the attention of both the law and licensing authorities, becoming a liability rather than asset if the licence were lost for some offence. The partial tie as it developed in Scotland after 1890 was, therefore, a logical response both to changes in the licensing laws and to the environment of increasing competition in domestic markets.

Home Markets

By the middle of the nineteenth century the larger Scottish breweries of Edinburgh, Alloa, Glasgow and other centres had developed widespread markets throughout Scotland. The major Scottish brewers, as we have seen, also shipped their products south of the Border, mainly to Tyneside, Merseyside and London. After 1850 the railways both opened new markets and facilitated development of existing outlets. The growth in population and a general rise in real incomes, particularly amongst the working class, created an expanding domestic market for many consumer products including those of the drink industries. The most important markets therefore lay in the urban, industrial districts and it was undoubtedly there that the greatest competition existed, particularly in the boom years after 1890. Scottish brewers had also to compete to a limited extent with English brewers, although losses sustained at their hands were recouped in the markets of northern England and London. Several Irish brewers sold in the Scottish market. The largest was Arthur Guinness, but the special character of that firm's product posed little threat to the general trade of most brewers.[19]

There was a marked change in public taste during the period under review, which resulted in a switch from heavy beer to light ale. Of course this move created problems for some brewers, because they could not stop producing traditional brews like heavy beer, porter and stout, which still commanded a substantial segment of their market. The production of light and pale ales for bottling also necessitated expenditure on new plant, particularly refrigerators and bottling equipment, the latter requiring much more labour than was needed in the dispatch of draught beers. However, many Scottish brewers had considerable experience in the production of light beers for both domestic and overseas markets, and were therefore able to exploit the demand for this particular product to their advantage. Several of the major firms, like William Younger, John and Robert Tennent, and George Younger established themselves as specialist brewers of pale ales, rivalling the Burton brewers in markets at home and abroad.

As indicated in Chapter Ten, the Scottish brewers exploited the domestic market by four main methods: direct sales to customers, who might be private individuals or public houses; through a system of agents, acting as wholesalers to the trade; by travelling salesmen, representing their product; and, through retail outlets, either directly or indirectly tied to the firm. Direct sales to customers accounted for a considerable proportion of brewery trade in the middle of the nineteenth century, and with improved communications the brewer was able to extend his business much further afield. Throughout the sixties, for example, William McEwan pushed his trade over an increasingly wider market that ultimately encompassed customers from Stockton-on-Tees to Wick.[20] The agency system was widely adopted by Scottish brewers, practically all of the larger firms having agents in the main cities and towns of England and Ireland. Travelling salesmen became increasingly more important when competition grew fiercer, though to some extent they tended to replace agents in English markets. Finally, markets could be secured by tying retail outlets, and many brewers sought to make such arrangements with publicans in many parts of Scotland and the north of England.

The first concern of the majority of brewers throughout most of the period was the market on their own doorsteps which could readily be serviced by drays and carts. This was usually described by the urban brewers of Edinburgh and Glasgow as the 'Town Trade,' even though it invariably extended beyond the immediate city boundaries. In many cases the local trade might represent a large proportion of total business. Certainly some small breweries continued to serve traditional markets in the neighbourhood, although they dwindled in number rapidly after the 1880s. Yet even as late as 1900 there were upwards of a dozen such firms in towns like Inverness, Elgin, Banff, Montrose, St. Andrews, Perth, Kilmarnock, Dunbar and Jedburgh, selling their beer to local customers or through a few public houses in the district.[21] However, the survivors from an earlier era in the development of brewing in Scotland were atypical, for the majority of small businesses had been absorbed by larger breweries before the turn of the century. Urban brewers were, therefore, able to extend their 'Country Trade' at the expense of small brewers, whose former advantage of proximity to customers had been progressively eroded by cheaper transport costs.

In the period from 1850 to 1880 the typical medium-to-large brewery in Glasgow or Edinburgh relied on local markets to dispose of up to 50 per cent of output, while the country trade might account for another 25 per cent, and markets south of the Border or in Ireland for 15 per cent. The balance was exported, probably to India or the Colonies. Brewers of any magnitude elsewhere, such as those in Alloa, Falkirk or Dundee, had more disparate markets, with the additional expense of transport to any outlet of consequence. In most cases Scottish markets probably absorbed less than half the production of these provincial brewers, who by the 1870s, as we have seen, had already begun to specialise in light ales for the general market. The country trade therefore fell increasingly into the hands of Edinburgh brewers, while those in Glasgow made little effort beyond the west of Scotland. The latter group did, however, have substantial interests in the north-west of England, which in Tennents' case accounted for anything up to 25 per cent of sales before 1870.[22]

William McEwan, the Edinburgh brewer, provides a good illustration of the general pattern indicated here. With a turnover of around £40,000 in 1860 (only a few years after the founding of the business), McEwan already did more than half his trade with Glasgow and the west of Scotland. Most of the business lay beyond Glasgow itself in the colliery and iron districts of Lanarkshire, in the Renfrewshire textile towns, and in the colliery towns of Ayrshire. McEwan's strictly 'country' trade was mainly in the north of Scotland and in Perth, Angus and Fife, while ventures on Tyneside accounted for something in excess of ten per cent.[23] The firm's foreign trade, described in the following section, was of little significance before 1865. By way of contrast, a somewhat more modest Edinburgh firm, Thomas Usher & Son, contented itself with essentially local outlets, venturing only as far as Glasgow on any scale before it became a limited liability company in 1895.[24]

The relative importance of markets changed considerably after 1880, particularly during the brewing boom of the nineties. Some indication of the nature of the changes can be gained from the records of William Younger & Company for the years 1880 to 1914. Youngers were the leading Scottish brewers by the early seventies, when the firm had an annual turnover in excess of £250,000. By 1880 annual sales were worth in the region of £350,000. Scottish markets absorbed just over half the sales: Edinburgh accounted for 25 per cent, Glasgow for 15 per cent and 'country' outlets the remainder. London was the largest single market with 35 per cent, but a high proportion of this must have been destined for export abroad. Yorkshire and Liverpool each absorbed 5 per cent, while Dublin and Manchester, with other modest outlets, accounted for the remainder. Unfortunately, no figures are available for Newcastle for 1880, but the following year that district absorbed around 20 per cent of sales, so the previous year's figures would require some adjustment in that light. More complete figures become available after 1885 and are given in the Statistic Book. Table 76 summarises the percentage distribution of Younger's main markets for the period 1885 to 1900. In 1885 the domestic market in Scotland absorbed over a third of sales, while Newcastle accounted for more than a quarter. London outlets took over 20 per cent and other places in England a total of 10 per cent. Ireland took just under 4 per cent. The corresponding figures for 1890 indicate the growing importance to Youngers of the Tyneside market, taking more than a third of sales, and of outlets in the west of Scotland based on Glasgow. Apart from Newcastle, most of the English outlets (while taking roughly the same amount of sales) were

Table 76

Market Distribution of William Younger & Company 1885-1900
Percentage Sales by Value

Market	1885	1890	1895	1900
Edinburgh	23.1	18.5	20.4	20.6
London	22.2	19.5	19.5	15.7
Liverpool	3.7	1.3	—	—
Glasgow	12.8	17.1	18.3	22.5
Yorkshire	4.0	3.5	3.6	2.1
Manchester	1.7	2.3	2.8	1.8
Dublin	3.9	3.3	0.2	2.2
Newcastle	26.9	33.7	32.2	34.5
	98.3	99.2	97.0	99.4
GROSS SALES £000s	407	631	769	896

Source: William Younger Mss., Travellers' Statistic Book 1881-1912.

beginning to show problems. The Liverpool connexion was severed after 1890 because the growing number of tied houses on Merseyside closed the market to outsiders like Youngers. Data for later years show a similar problem in other English outlets, especially in London. As the figures for 1895 and 1900 indicate, the Scottish outlets assumed their former importance to the firm, accounting for over 40 per cent of sales in 1900. The Tyneside market was one in which Youngers had an established reputation and a firm foothold, through its association with the Newcastle-upon-Tyne Brewery, a number of tied or partially tied houses, and a team of active travellers.[25]

The somewhat different experience of George Younger, the Alloa brewer, indicates the problems faced by Scottish brewers in the English and Irish markets when the extension of the tied-house system restricted sales. In the 1860s the firm had established agencies in Newcastle, Stockton, Manchester and London, and had commission agents in Hull, Liverpool, Dublin, Cork, Sligo, Limerick and Londonderry. By 1875, however, the English outlets were presenting problems, and the agencies in London, Manchester and Stockton were closed. Hull was given up in 1891, and Liverpool shortly after. The Irish agencies had all been closed down by 1897, business there no longer being profitable. Only the Newcastle connexion was developed successfully, the solution to the problem of tied houses being overcome by the purchase of two breweries in Sunderland and Chester-le-Street. Apart from the export trade, which probably accounted for about a quarter of the firm's business, Younger enjoyed a large trade throughout Scotland based on a long-established reputation.[26]

Having examined the general character of the domestic market and the relative importance of different districts at various times, it will be valuable to look in greater detail at developments in (i) Glasgow and neighbourhood, (ii) the Scottish 'country' districts, and (iii) England and Ireland.

Glasgow and the industrial west of Scotland provided the most ready market and many brewers—including English and Irish firms—had a major interest there. By the middle of the nineteenth century the district had a number of well-established firms, mainly city-based, although more substantial firms were active in places like Paisley, Greenock, Kilmarnock and Ayr. The most successful brewers locally were John and Robert Tennent of Wellpark Brewery and Hugh Baird of Canal Brewery. Together they must have commanded a substantial share of custom in and around the city, although they faced considerable outside competition. Brewers from Edinburgh, Alloa, Falkirk and elsewhere had long been successfully developing their trade with the west of Scotland, mainly through local agents. As early as 1850, no fewer than eight Edinburgh brewers had agencies in Glasgow, while James Aitken of Falkirk had an ale store in the city. Three notable English firms—Allsopp, Bass and Meux—already had agencies for their products.[27] Subsequently there was a considerable extension of the agency system in Glasgow to serve the city and surrounding outlets. By 1870 there were no fewer than 48 agencies representing brewers from many parts of the United Kingdom:

Edinburgh	19
Dublin	10
London	7
Alloa	5
Burton	4
Cork	2
Bristol	1

All the major brewers in Scotland had stores or agents in Glasgow, including Aitken, Bernard, Campbell, the Edinburgh and Leith Breweries, Jeffrey, McEwan, Meiklejohn, Usher, Robert Younger, George Younger and William Younger.[28] William Younger probably did the largest trade, although the Alloa brewers were extremely active in Glasgow. Archibald Arrol had a large bottling vault at 119 East Milton Street, and Robert Meiklejohn did a considerable trade in their Export Ale, both in the wood and bottled. Of the English brewers, the most successful seem to have been the Burton firms: Henry Allsopp told the Select Committee on the Malt Tax in 1867 that his firm's trade with Scotland was 'enormously increasing,' while C.P.Matthews of Ind, Coope indicated that there was a growing market for pale ale in the industrial towns of the west of Scotland.[29]

The growth in importance of outlets in the west of Scotland—despite the problem created by licence restriction—is clearly reflected in the expansion of the brewing industry in Glasgow during the boom of the eighties and nineties. Four firms which underwent expansion and had substantial interests in the local market were Steel, Coulson of Greenhead Brewery, Gordon and Blair of Home Brewery, Parkhead, T.Y.Paterson of Petershill Brewery, Springburn, and G.&T. Maclachlan of Castle Brewery, Maryhill. Competition between these and other firms must have been considerable, but unfortunately there is no record of the rate at which tied or partially tied outlets developed. Licence restriction was undoubtedly more vigorously pursued in some of the industrial towns and districts than in other parts of Scotland, and this must have forced brewers to contract arrangements with licensees in order to maintain their share of the market, particularly after 1890. Beyond Glasgow itself the only major brewer of any consequence, Turner's Ayr and Newton Breweries, provides a good example of an essentially local firm that had taken steps to secure its custom. It catered for several surrounding towns and villages, a high proportion of its trade being through tied houses.[30]

Although the 'Country Trade' was important though troublesome to the large urban brewers, it was the lifeblood of a number of firms located beyond the industrial heartland. Most were old-established brewers who had ventured into nearby markets and had gradually absorbed smaller, less ambitious firms once common all over the country. In Aberdeen there were two such firms, the Devanha Brewery of William Black & Company and the Aulton Brewery of Thomson, Marshall & Company. With outlets in the Granite City itself, in the fishing towns of Peterhead and Fraserburgh, and in smaller market centres, the two firms had a substantial share of the market in the north-east of Scotland. Four smaller breweries were still active in the north: Graham & Company in Banff, the old firm of A.&J.Young in Elgin, and two firms in Inverness, Guild & Wylie of Thornbush Brewery, and Buchanan & Company of Haugh Brewery. All four had an essentially local trade, although they probably sold further afield in places like Easter Ross and Caithness, until they closed in the early 1900s.[31] Further south, Dundee was served by two breweries, the larger being Hugh Ballingall & Son of the Park and Pleasance Breweries, and the more modest Victoria Brewery of John Neave. Ballingall had developed a large business more in keeping with the brewers of Alloa and Falkirk, for the firm did a nationwide trade in its Pale and Export Ales.[32] About half the local trade in the eighties was in heavy beer, porter and stout, which the firm marketed through tied and partially tied houses. Only one country brewery survived elsewhere in Angus, Davidson & Company of Montrose, but this had given up business by 1900.[33] In Perth R. & D. Sharp of Blackford Brewery built up a successful trade based on local markets, mostly secured through tied houses in and around Perth.[34] The only brewery of importance left in Fife was D.S.Ireland's Argyll Brewery in St. Andrews, which had an essentially local trade in the East Neuk and some outlets in the coastal fishing and colliery villages as far as Kirkcaldy.[35] The Alloa brewers Maclay & Company of Thistle Brewery had (and still have to the present time) an essentially local trade, although by the nineties the firm had extended northward and eastward by the acquisition of public houses in Perth and Kinross. Finally, James Aitken of Falkirk, whose main concern was production of ales for nationwide distribution and export, also served local markets in the colliery and ironworking districts of east Stirlingshire.[36]

In southern Scotland most of the country breweries had closed down by the 1880s, although several small breweries were still active in the Border towns and in Dumfries on the eve of the First World War. Typical was the South-Western Brewery Company of Newton Stewart, already noted in Chapter Nine. It served the town and district and also owned a hotel and public house.[37] Dudgeon & Company of Belhaven Brewery, Dunbar was a larger country concern with a well-established trade in East Lothian and Berwickshire, mainly through its own tied outlets.[38] Most of southern Scotland attracted the attention of Edinburgh brewers, with the firms of William Younger and William McEwan most active in the field. The former had a number of secured outlets there by the turn of the century.[39]

South of the Border the main attention of Scottish brewers was directed in order of importance to Tyneside, London, and Merseyside. Other markets were found in the West Riding of Yorkshire and in the south-west, in Bristol. Significantly, all were markets where Scottish beers and ales had enjoyed something of a reputation and to which increasing quantities had been shipped coastwise since the beginning of the nineteenth century. A combination of competition from local breweries, from the English brewery giants, and the inevitable extension of the tied-house system made things increasingly difficult for many Scottish brewers; eventually only those with sufficient capital to build up their own tied trade were able to compete successfully with English rivals.

The nearest of the English markets, particularly convenient for the east coast brewers in Edinburgh and Alloa, was Tyneside, an area of expanding working class population and apparently insatiable appetite for both traditional heavy beers and light ales from the barrel or bottled. Many Scottish brewers found a ready market for their products on Tyneside and before 1870 had well-established agencies in Newcastle-upon-Tyne. Among the most active in the district were William Younger, William McEwan and Robert Younger of Edinburgh, George Younger, Robert Meiklejohn, James Calder and Archibald Arrol of Alloa, and Hugh Ballingall of Dundee. During the brewery boom and after, most acquired tied houses or gave loans to contract a partial tie in the Scottish manner. Both George Younger and Archibald Arrol acquired local breweries when competition began to increase in the later nineties and thus gained their own tied houses by these means.[40] William Younger's experience may have been exceptional, in that a third of the firm's sales by value were destined for Tyneside during most of the period before 1914, and yet there seems little doubt that something like a quarter of the output from a half dozen leading firms in Scotland found its way to the pubs and clubs of the district.[41] The switch in public taste to lighter ales was certainly less obvious in the north-east of England than elsewhere. Like the industrial districts of central Scotland, it was an area with a taste for traditional beer, although, as everywhere, increased sales of bottled beers and light ales were made.

London was another market in which the leading Scottish firms had much experience, dating back, as Chapter Seven indicates, to the closing decades of the eighteenth century. The London market grew in importance between 1850 and 1890, and Scottish brewers, while dealing generally in a whole range of products, were able to exploit a demand for light ales which developed there and elsewhere in southern England. Throughout most of the period the bulk of shipments were sent coastwise, there being no particular cost advantage by rail. The leading brewers in the metropolitan trade were William Younger, William McEwan, Robert Meiklejohn and James Aitken. William Younger dominated the London market for Scotch Ales. The firm made regular and growing shipments to its store on the Thames, which serviced outlets in the city and home counties. No fewer than ten salesmen were employed by 1881.[42] Meiklejohn of Alloa had been in the London market since the beginning of the nineteenth century, and at the time of the firm's centenary in 1874 their product was reported to be 'yearly increasing in public favour.'[43] Much of the ale shipped south from Scotland to London was for onward export to the colonies. It seems likely that some proportion of exports said to be of English origin had actually been imported from north of the Border, though it is impossible to say how much. Beer shipped for the London market or for export probably accounted for up to 15 per cent of total production during the years 1880-1914 and perhaps as much as 20 per cent around 1890.

Merseyside had provided several brewers with a useful outlet since the beginning of the nineteenth century. It was obviously a fairly convenient market for the Glasgow brewers, though as far as can be gathered, the only firm active there was John and Robert Tennent. Their agent, James Marshall, successfully developed the business in Liverpool and Manchester, and as early as the sixties the sales were worth at least £50,000 per annum.[44] When the railways made transport easier, other brewers from elsewhere in Scotland developed Merseyside outlets. The leaders in the field were William Younger, William McEwan, George Younger and Hugh Ballingall. In 1880 William Younger had three salesmen based there doing business to the value of £12,000 per annum.[45] Eventually, however, Scottish brewers were largely forced out of the area, both by the tied-house system and by competition from the local and Burton Brewers.

Foreign Markets

Although exports never absorbed more than 10 per cent of Scottish production in the period 1850 to 1914, they were nevertheless of great importance to most of the larger firms. What started out as little more than an 'adventure' in the fifties or sixties might be built up into a highly remunerative trade, despite omnipresent problems of shipping, breakages, and extensions of credit to somewhat suspect colonialists on the other side of the globe. Long before mid-century, as we have seen, the major Scottish brewers had developed a modest trade in traditional British spheres, such as the West Indies, the United States, Canada and South America. By 1850, however, these markets absorbed only slightly more than half the total, the remainder being accounted for by newer outlets in Africa, Asia and Australasia (see Table 52). That this was perhaps still little more than a carrying trade is reflected in the fact that the total was just over 21,000 barrels worth £62,000.[46] Yet Scottish brewers persisted in the trade with considerable success, raising exports at one time during the boom of the nineties to over 167,000 barrels worth nearly £600,000.[47]

The general level of United Kingdom exports between 1860 and 1910 is indicated in Table 77, which also shows the volume and value of Scottish exports together with Scotland's percentage share in the same period. United Kingdom exports averaged 540,000 barrels per annum, fluctuating between 410,000 and 670,000 barrels, while those of Scotland averaged around 120,000 barrels,

Table 77

United Kingdom Exports 1860-1910

Year	Barrels (000s)	Scotland's % Share
1860	534	7.5
1865	530	10.5
1870	471	11.0
1875	503	12.0
1880	412	12.0
1885	436	15.0
1890	503	33.0
1895	432	31.0
1900	487	25.0
1905	521	24.0
1910	570	24.5

Sources: PP, Accounts and Papers, 1861-1911; *Brewers Almanack*, 1914, 154.

fluctuating between 40,000 and 168,000 barrels. An immediate problem in interpreting these figures is the fact that large quantities of Scottish beer were exported from English ports after initial transport or shipment from Scotland. Therefore Scotland's percentage share, which on the official figures had grown from over 10 per cent in 1865 to nearly a third in 1890, must have been considerably greater. Figures and commentary derived from trade sources suggest that as much as half of United Kingdom exports were Scottish in origin by 1890 and that they remained at slightly below this level until World War I.[48] With this in mind, the figures themselves are worth further analysis.

Annual exports from Scotland grew steadily in the 1850s and by 1860 were just under 40,000 barrels per annum, worth around £145,000. Throughout most of the

Table 78

Scottish Overseas Trade 1850-1913

Year	Barrels (Official Returns)	Value (£)	Barrels (Trade Returns)
1850	21,181	62,676	—
1855	32,269	114,249	—
1860	39,916	145,320	—
1865	56,146	233,824	—
1870	52,103	231,092	—
1875	56,818	262,087	—
1880	58,341	186,898	—
1885	65,714	269,649	152,212
1890	167,979	597,969	—
1895	133,084	429,927	232,673
1900	123,100	423,348	238,000
1905	137,662	389,794	213,500
1910	123,214	276,659	—
1913	140,379	483,222	—

Sources: PRO, CUST 9/39, 59, 69, 79 UK Exports (Beer and Ale); PP, Accounts and Papers, 1875-1914; *Brewers' Guardian*, 1886-1906.

sixties and seventies exports were generally static at around 55,000 barrels. It was not until the 1880s that the Scottish export boom got underway, particularly after 1885 when the barrelage surged beyond the 150,000 mark, worth over £½ million per annum. As the official figures indicate in Table 78, Scottish exports throughout most of the nineties accounted for nearly a third of British overseas beer trade. After 1900 Scottish exports averaged 130,000 barrels per annum, roughly a quarter of the British total.

With the growth in importance of overseas trade and the increasing volume of beer exported, there also came a series of changes in the relative significance of different markets. A comparison of Tables 79 and 80 will indicate that, in some

Table 79

Scottish Exports by Destination (as % of total)

Sphere	1850	1865	1870	1880	1890	1900	1910
Europe	4.0	4.5	2.0	5.0	4.0	10.0	10.5
Africa	4.0	3.0	2.0	10.0	9.0	5.0	2.0
Asia	23.0	18.0	14.0	22.0	40.0	51.0	68.0
W. Indies	25.0	25.0	29.0	14.0	11.5	9.5	8.5
S. America	23.0	22.0	25.0	11.0	3.0	3.0	2.0
United States	4.0	4.0	13.0	4.0	1.5	5.0	—
Canada	3.0	3.0	3.0	1.0	—	—	—
Australia	15.0	14.5	12.0	33.0	31.0	17.0	8.0

Sources: PRO, CUST 9/39, 69, 79, UK Exports (Beer and Ale); PP, Accounts and Papers, 1881, LXXXIII, 1890-91 LXXVII, 1901 LXIX, 1911, LXXXVI.

Table 80

United Kingdom Exports by Destination 1872-1912

	1872	%	1882	%	1892	%	1902	%	1912	%
United States	44,360	8.5	30,881	7.0	44,432	10.0	42,940	8.0	71,247	10.5
Egypt	—	—	—	—	7,585	2.0	19,814	4.0	19,665	3.0
South Africa	—	—	38,790	9.0	19,209	4.0	35,440	7.0	5,757	—
West Indies	27,199	5.0	21,871	5.0	20,630	4.5	19,550	4.0	23,882	3.5
Australia & New Zealand	88,184	17.0	101,641	23.0	118,885	26.0	75,002	14.0	123,226	18.0
India	167,597	32.0	87,412	20.0	94,695	21.0	120,977	23.0	100,193	15.0
Others	194,616	37.0	156,959	35.0	146,555	32.0	212,223	40.0	327,984	49.0
Total	521,956		437,554		451,991		525,316		671,954	

Sources: PP, Accounts and Papers, 1873-1913; *Brewers' Almanack*, 1914.

respects, Scotland differed from the United Kingdom as a whole. This may be explained by the fact that in some instances Scotland was the main supplier to a particular market, as she had become in the case of Indian troop provision by the early 1890s. In the table of Scottish exports for 1870, the traditional markets of the West Indies and South America together account for more than half, while the United Kingdom picture for 1872 shows the dominance of the new colonial outlets in India, Australia and New Zealand.[49] By 1880 the leading market for Scottish exports was Australia, taking a third of total shipments, while Asia was rapidly approaching another quarter. The markets of South Africa, particularly the Cape, absorbed 10 per cent. The West Indies and South America had slipped back, although the former continued to take about 10 per cent of Scottish exports until 1914.[50] Thereafter Asia became Scotland's most important customer, taking 40 per cent in 1890 and no less than 68 per cent by 1910.[51] Colonial breweries elsewhere, especially in Australia (whose states also imposed tariffs on selected imports including beer), were established in increasing numbers, with the result that by 1910 the South African and Australasian markets jointly absorbed only 10 per cent of the total. The North American markets had also virtually disappeared —to be replaced by European outlets which absorbed over 10 per cent of exports after the turn of the century. The overall United Kingdom picture for 1912 broadly reflected these trends, but the largest single market in this instance remained, as before, in Australia and New Zealand. The changing picture is indicated in somewhat more statistical detail as follows. In 1875 the traditional pattern of trade which had obtained at mid-century was still very much evident, the largest single market being the West Indies, taking about 11,000 barrels, with nearby British Guiana accounting for another 6,000 barrels. South America took 10,000 barrels, the largest outlet there being the Argentine. Canada and the United States (probably abnormally high in the late sixties and seventies because of destruction of native breweries during the Civil War) together absorbed 9,000 barrels, while Australia and New Zealand took another 9,000 barrels. Asia (meaning essentially India) accounted for a total of 7,000 barrels worth £35,000. Thereafter the picture began to change considerably, with the result that the old spheres in the West Indies and in North and South America dropped off, and the new colonial markets in South Africa, India and Australasia became of greater significance. For example, in 1885, when total exports were 65,000 barrels worth £270,000, Australia and New Zealand together took 28,000 barrels' worth and India over 12,000 barrels worth £50,000. By 1900 Scottish exports to India had more than quadrupled to a figure of 59,000 barrels worth £174,000, while those to Australasia had slipped back to 21,000 barrels worth £82,000. The West Indies, as previously indicated, was still a steady market, absorbing in that year 12,000 barrels worth £45,000. A decade later exports of beer from Scotland were dominated by shipments to India: of the 123,000 barrels consigned in 1910, 78,000 barrels worth £250,000 went to Asia. The West Indies and Australasia absorbed roughly the same volume, around 10,000 barrels.[52]

A great deal of fragmentary detail has survived in brewery records regarding the development of the export trade, mostly relating to either the early or later part of the period before 1914. In the four instances examined here, the essentially superficial view of activities before 1880 is probably a good indication of the foreign trade in general. The surviving records of John and Robert Tennent and of William McEwan provide some indication of 'adventures' in the fifties and sixties, while those of William Younger provide an overview of that firm's exports between 1880 and 1914. George Younger's experience between 1850 and 1914 seems to mirror exactly the general trend away from the traditional outlets in North America towards the Indian and Colonial markets.

Some indication has already been given of John and Robert Tennent's ventures in the overseas trade. The firm continued to develop its exports in traditional markets where Scottish beer and ales sold well, and by the mid-1850s the firm had connexions with nearly a hundred different markets in the West Indies, United States, India and Australasia. Tennent's ales had special advantages for shipment to distant markets in hot climates:

> The peculiar excellence of the ales of the Messrs Tennent, like those of Burton, is their remarkable keeping quality, and their retention of that delicate flavour of the hops, so often lost by the pale ale brewer, notwithstanding his utmost efforts to secure it.

Other testimony to this effect came from no less than *The Times* correspondent in far away San Francisco:

> California, San Francisco, 12th October 1854.
>
> For malt liquors the demand is not so active as it was a month ago, although it is at all times considerable, and on the increase. Large sales of J.&R. Tennent's bottled ale have been made, during the last fortnight, at 3 dols. 62½ cents to 3 dols. 75 cents per dozen, and a sale of about 300 hhds. of the same brand in wood to arrive at 60 dols per hhd. This brand has a larger sale and is more sought after than any other in the market, from its being peculiarly adapted to the warm climate of the interior, and is much used in San Francisco also.

California became for a time one of the firm's leading and most profitable markets. In the three years 1858-60, beer to the value of nearly £20,000 was dispatched for San Francisco, either by way of Glasgow or Liverpool. New York and Baltimore also took consignments. All of the shipments were made up of Double Strong Ale, India Pale Ale and Brown Stout, roughly a third in bulk and the rest bottled. These Tennent products were particularly well-regarded in India. A report in the *Glasgow Herald* of 6 August 1858 said that the Tennents' Strong Ale had been 'declared second to none for hospital purposes—a proof of its increasing reputation among commissariat officers. It is a pity that our soldiers should not be supplied with such strengthening and nourishing liquor, instead of the acidulated trash which is too frequently contracted for.' Tennents subsequently became specialists in all kinds of bottled ale for export, concentrating on the popular pale ales and stouts, in which they built up a substantial international trade both in the colonies and elsewhere. By the eighties they were amongst the leading Scottish brewers in the overseas trade.[53] One of the important Edinburgh brewers, William McEwan, began his 'adventures' in the export trade in 1863, seven years after the establishment of the Fountainbridge Brewery. In December of 1863, the first shipment from the brewery, 36 hogsheads of No. Three Ale at 80 shillings each, was exported from Leith to Sydney on the vessel *Locheil*. The following year, 1864, more serious efforts were made to develop the Australasian market, with shipments to both Australia and New Zealand. The most important destinations, as we might expect, were the rapidly expanding cities of Sydney in New South Wales, Melbourne in Victoria, Hobart in Tasmania, and Wellington, Auckland, Dunedin, and Invercargill in New Zealand.

McEwan faced the usual difficulties in the subsequent expansion of overseas outlets: high shipping costs, losses through breakage, insurance charges, and the problem of extending credit to distant customers. Nevertheless, other markets were tried with success additional to those already opened up in Australia and New Zealand. The results of these efforts are tabulated in Table 81 covering the period

Table 81

William McEwan's Export Adventures 1865-68 (£ value)

Sphere	1865[1]	%	1866	%	1867[2]	%	1868	%
Australia	3,161	43	5,789	38	547	12	6,231	19
New Zealand	2,083	28	3,659	24	2,009	45	3,375	10
U.S./Canada	654	9	2,128	14	550	12	6,019	17
West Indies	908	12	1,111	7	519	12	3,077	9
Asia (3)	350	5	1,899	12	182	4	5,369	16
S. America	60	—	258	2	400	9	7,350	21
Africa (4)	52	—	257	2	80	2	1,797	5
Others	65	—	172	1	—	—	—	—
Total	7,333		15,273		4,441		33,660	

Notes: (1) July-December only
    (2) January-March only
    (3) Mainly India
    (4) South Africa, Cape Colony and Mauritius
    Source: McEwans Archives, Journals 1865-68

1865-68. The figures for 1865 are unfortunately incomplete, only the half year from July to December being available, but they indicate a moderate expansion into other well-tried markets in the West Indies, United States and Canada. But the leading sphere is Australasia, taking over 70 per cent by value of six months' total overseas sales.

Although only two years of complete figures can be collated from the brewery Journals, these indicate a growing confidence on McEwan's part once the initial difficulties of breaking into the foreign trade had been partly solved. The picture for 1868 is most complete: 250 shipments were made that year with a total value of £33,660. Australasia was still the single most important sphere, although South America took over 20 per cent, with Rio de Janeiro, Buenos Aires and Montevideo the leading buyers. Asian shipments were mainly destined for Calcutta, Madras and Bombay in India, Colombo in Ceylon, and Singapore in Straits Settlement.[54]

William Younger had the advantage over William McEwan of experience, although before the eighties the firm's export trade was also very much at the level of 'adventures' in foreign climes. Younger exported worldwide, concentrating during the sixties and seventies on the United States, and thereafter in the general colonial markets. Table 82 gives Younger's sales by quantity and value for the years 1882 to 1912. The general pattern corresponds closely with the Scottish

Table 82

Wm. Younger & Co. Ltd. Exports 1882-1912 by volume and value

Year	Barrels	Value (£)
1882	14,358	50,402
83	18,001	62,064
84	20,479	72,176
85	23,587	79,077
86	27,310	97,751
87	25,163	99,025
88	31,107	121,717
89	40,758	160,383
1890	35,544	138,406
91	34,257	137,571
92	39,790	137,817
93	35,750	140,201
94	34,997	138,150
95	31,709	106,734
96	33,761	115,211
97	33,644	113,686
98	39,923	136,545
99	42,276	140,682
1900	43,777	128,248
01	42,947	125,408
02	42,483	124,052
03	40,197	117,376
04	39,856	116,380
05	37,170	92,927
06	37,800	89,268
07	38,103	86,114
08	35,474	80,172
09	34,345	77,620
1910	36,902	83,726
11	36,709	83,480
12	38,238	88,697

Source: Wm. Younger Mss. Misc. Export Ledgers.

figures given in Table 78. There was a period of rapid growth in the eighties when the firm's exports more than doubled. At that time Younger's sales accounted for a quarter of total Scottish overseas trade. After 1889 there was a slide to a low point in 1895, then recovery to a peak in 1900, when the firm sold over a third of all beer exported from Scotland. After remaining at much the same level until 1903, the export trade declined, but nevertheless averaged around 36,000 barrels until 1912.[55]

Like other major Scottish brewers, George Younger & Son of Alloa had a considerable foreign trade by 1850. The firm's chief market in the middle of the nineteenth century was Demerara. The beer—a very strong ale—was matured in the barrel, bottled in stone bottles, and shipped in vessels which had a regular coal-carrying trade between Alloa and the West Indies. Although this particular brand had a very high gravity, it was rumoured that the consumers in the West Indies did not consider it strong enough, and that a glass of neat rum was often mixed with every bottle of ale to obtain a drink of sufficient strength.

By the 1860s Younger of Alloa were venturing further afield into colonial and other markets. The main markets included the Australian ports of Melbourne, Sydney, Fremantle and Brisbane, with an occasional shipment to Auckland, New Zealand. There were steady shipments to various ports in the West Indies, including Demerara, Barbados, and Jamaica, which appear very frequently. Youngers had a considerable business in Canada and the United States, shipments being made to Montreal, St Johns, Halifax, New Orleans, New York, Boston, and San Francisco. The Indian and East Indian spheres do not seem to have been of much importance; although beer was exported regularly to Colombo between 1860 and 1875, India as such took only one shipment. Rangoon, a most important outlet after the early 1900s, accounted for modest and infrequent exports. A small but growing trade was developing for Youngers' products in South Africa and South America.

Between 1875 and the outbreak of World War I, George Younger steadily developed an increasing export trade in bulk and bottled ales and stout, the nature of their market broadly reflecting that of Scottish exports as a whole. The firm dropped out of the American and Canadian markets altogether after 1875, and, contrary to the Scottish trend, had little success in Australia and New Zealand. The South African connexion was more profitable, with regular shipments to Cape Town, Port Elizabeth and Durban. Traditional outlets in the West Indies continued successfully, especially Demerara, Barbados, and Trinidad. In the seventies India became more important; there were regular shipments to Madras, with an occasional shipment to Bombay and more frequently to Calcutta. Singapore, Rangoon, and Penang were becoming significant outlets for more than the occasional shipment, although Colombo, which had been a good market before 1875, dropped out completely.

Export sales during the period 1895 to 1907 both in bulk and bottle remained fairly stationary, with a slight fall in the former and a correspondingly modest increase in the latter. The general position of Younger's various export outlets did not change much before 1914. New markets were developed in supplying troops in Egypt, the Sudan and South Africa—the last, like that of Australia, being virtually abandoned after 1908. A final effort was made to keep some of the former trade in Australia by establishing a chilling and bottling plant in Sydney, but it did not meet with any success. The West Indian sphere continued to take supplies steadily, Trinidad in particular being the best and largest market, while Demerara and Barbados continued to be good customers. Exports to India grew steadily down to 1914, and India was the main market for bulk beer after the Australian outlets had ceased after 1908. There were regular shipments to India until 1914; Colombo was added to the list again in 1900. Hong Kong and Shanghai were steady markets until 1907, but were gradually dropping off from that time onwards and had ceased taking supplies by 1914.

One of George Younger's most interesting markets was that of Straits Settlements, which steadily improved throughout the closing decades of the nineteenth century through the ports of Rangoon, Singapore, and Penang. The rubber boom, which started in 1911, brought with it such a sudden and unexpected demand for bottled stout that it was impossible to ship sufficient supplies to meet it. A representative of Younger's agents in Straits Settlements actually came to Alloa with a very large sum of money, as he thought the firm was holding back supplies owing to lack of confidence in their financial standing. He had not realised that stout for export bottling had to mature in cask for a year before bottling and that the shortage of stock could not be remedied overnight.[56]

Broadly speaking, the foregoing description of the export trade in beer from Scotland reflects both Britain's trading progress and contemporary international and colonial economic developments during the period to 1914. The scale of the Scottish export trade was always modest, although, as we have seen, brewers north of the Border eventually accounted for between a third and a half of total British consignments. Trade certainly followed the flag, as the growing imperial markets clearly demonstrate, especially Scotland's trade with India. On the other hand, the traditional market in the West Indies was replaced and surpassed by those in Australia and New Zealand, which in turn fell away in the face of foreign competition and the development of native breweries. Foreign competition in the colonial markets was a force to be reckoned with by the 1880s, especially from Germany and America. Partly this reflected a change of taste to lighter beers more suited to the hotter climates of the colonies. The development of domestic breweries in the colonies was widespread after the 1870s, but native brews seem to have posed less of a threat to Scottish beers than those from European and American sources.

NOTES

1 Wilson, op.cit., 116-120. The best account of the law in the nineteenth century is given in the Final Report of the Royal Commission on the Liquor Licensing Laws (Scotland), 177-79 contained in PP 1899 XXXV. The following account is partly based on this.

2 9 George IV c. 58.

3 16 and 17 Victoria c 67.

4 Most of the relevant evidence is contained in PP 1860 XXXIII Report from the Royal Commission on the Licensing System in Scotland, Vol. II.

5 The respective acts were 45 and 46 Victoria c 66 (Passenger Vessels) and 50 and 51 Victoria c 38 (Hours of Closing).

6 PP 1898 XXXVIII Report from the Royal Commission on the Liquor Licensing Laws, 4th Report.

7 3 Edward VII c 25. E.A.Pratt, *The licensed trade* (London, 1907), 143.

8 Wilson, op.cit., 173 discusses subsequent developments in detail. The relevant act was 3 and 4 George V c 33.

9 Evidence of Dr A.Walker in PP 1898 XXXVIII Liquor Licensing 4th Report, 285.

10 PP 1887, 1907, 1916-17 A&P, Returns of the Number of Persons Licensed for the Sale of Beer and Spirits.

11 Pratt, op.cit., 92-3.

12 E.A.Pratt, *The 'Tied-house' system, origin, operation and economic aspects*, (London, 1910), 3-4; Vaizey, op.cit., 6-7.

13 Evidence of Mr J.W.Angus in PP 1898 XXXVIII Liquor Licensing 4th Report, 55.

14 Quoted in Pratt, *The licensed trade*, op.cit., 92.

15 PP 1899 XXV Report of the Royal Commission on the Liquor Licensing Laws, Final Report, 27.

16 PP 1898 XXXVIII Liquor Licensing, 4th Report, 19.

17 Ibid., 291-2.

18 PP 1916 XII Report of the Advisory Committee on Proposals for the State Purchase of the Licensed Liquor Trade, 536-7.

19 PP 1867-68 IX Report of the Select Committee on the Malt Tax, 98, 113, 118; Lynch and Vaizey, op.cit.
20 Records of William McEwan, Journal 1860-62.
21 Brewers' Almanack, 1895, 287-8; ibid, 1904, 310-11.
22 Records of William Younger, Country Sales Ledgers 1871-85; SRO, COS, Tennent v Tennent, Summons of Gilbert Tennent and others 1864, 17.
23 Records of William McEwan, Journals 1860-75.
24 C.M.Usher, op.cit., 70-71; information from Mr W. Chamberlain, Head Brewer, Ushers Ltd.
25 Records of William Younger, Travellers' Statistic Book 1881-1912.
26 Anon, A short history of George Younger & Son Ltd, op.cit., 26-30.
27 Glasgow P.O. Annual Directory 1850-51, 433; PP 1867-68 IX, Report of the Select Committee on the Malt Tax presents a great deal of evidence given by English brewers about the growing trade in the west of Scotland.
28 Glasgow P.O. Annual Directory 1870-71 (Glasgow, 1870), 563-4.
29 As note 27.
30 Brewers' Guardian, 1898, 69-70.
31 Brewers' Almanack, 1895, 287-8.
32 Barnard, op.cit., vol. III, 147, 164.
33 Brewers' Almanack, 1904, 310-11.
34 SRO, Dissolved Companies Register, BT 2/1361, R & D Sharp Ltd. 1884-1927.
35 Ibid., BT 2/2399, D.S.Ireland, Ltd., 1892-96.
36 Anon, Two hundred years of progress, op.cit., 3-7; Barnard, op.cit., vol. II, 190.
37 SRO, Register of Sasines, County of Wigtown, B 72/2/11 and 12, various legal documents relating to purchase of brewery and public houses.
38 Information from Mr Sandy Hunter, Managing Director, Belhaven Brewery Ltd.
39 Records of William Younger, Loan Ledgers 1891-1914.
40 Anon, A short history of George Younger, op.cit., 28-9; Brewery Manual, 78.
41 Records of William Younger, Travellers' Statistic Book 1881-1912.
42 Ibid., 1881; Keir, op.cit., 75; Bernard, op.cit., vol. II, 36-8.
43 Anon, Report of Meiklejohn's centenary, op.cit., 22.
44 SRO, COS, Tennent v Tennent, 1864, Summons of G.Tennent, 17.
45 Records of Wm. McEwan, Cash Ledger 1860-64, Journal 1865-66; Records of Wm. Younger, Travellers' Statistic Book 1881.
46 PRO, CUST 9/39, Produce of the United Kingdom Exports (Scotland, Beer and Ale), 1850.
47 PP 1890-91 LXXVII Account of Beer Exported, Accounts and Papers.
48 The Brewers' Almanack of this period has a very complete series of statistics relating to the industry, including exports.
49 PRO, CUST 9/79 Produce of the United Kingdom Exports (Scotland, Beer and Ale), 1870.
50 PP 1881 LXXXIII Accounts and Papers, Account of Beer Exported from the U.K. 1880.
51 PP 1890-91 LXXVII Accounts and Papers, Account of Beer Exported from the U.K. 1890.
52 PP 1884-85 LXXI, 1875 LXXI, 1901 LXIX, 1911 LXXXVI, Accounts and Papers etc.
53 Records of J.&R.Tennent, Shipping Book 1859-60; Anon, 'Messrs. J.&R. Tennent, Wellpark Brewery, Glasgow,' The Mercantile Age, 538-9; The Commercial Aspect of Glasgow (Glasgow n.d.), 318-21.
54 Records of Wm. McEwan, Journals and Cash Ledgers 1860-75.
55 Records of Wm. Younger, Export Statistics 1881-1912.
56 Anon, A short history of George Younger, op.cit., 18-25.

12

From 1914 to the Present

FROM the modest beginnings of the eighteenth century, the brewing industry in Scotland had grown and changed immeasurably by the turn of the present century. The Industrial Revolution and later Victorian era had both brought important developments. Yet it would be wrong to suppose that brewing did not retain some of the characteristics of an age-old craft with established modes and traditions. The same pride was still taken in the product, the same attention paid to the likes and dislikes of customers—at the end as at the beginning of our period. The same family-dominated entrepreneurship, interest, capital and control were also maintained throughout among the firms that had pioneered the industry in the latter half of the eighteenth century. During the 'Brewery Boom' of the later Victorian years the majority of firms retained the same impetus and enthusiasm for innovation which had put them at the forefront of mass-production brewing in Scotland by the early part of the nineteenth century. So growth and concentration were not achieved wholly at the expense of tradition and continuity. Naturally there were many casualties, particularly, as we have seen, during the turmoil of the Industrial Revolution. But a great many of the older breweries were still active at the turn of the present century, although their numbers had declined considerably in the face of increasing competition from urban, mass-production brewers.

Against this background, the developments which took place after 1914 were even more dramatic and ultimately altered the character of the trade to the extent that a vastly increased output was concentrated in the hands of a few brewery giants. We have already seen signs of some of these changes in earlier chapters, most notably, (i) the emergence of larger, capital-intensive firms, (ii) the relative decline of smaller firms, (iii) increased rationalisation and amalgamation, which contributed to the growth of larger businesses, and, (iv) the swing in public taste away from 'traditional' beers toward lighter and bottled beers. These and other features were common to the brewing industry elsewhere in Britain, but the trade in Scotland still maintained its own distinct characteristics, particularly in some of its products, and on the retail side, where only a modest proportion of the trade was tied. Although the latter aspect has altered a great deal since 1945, Scottish brewers still do not control as large a percentage of the trade as their colleagues south of the Border. Much of the story is best examined chronologically in three main periods: World War I and its aftermath; the inter-war years and, particularly, the years since 1945.

World War I and Aftermath

Political and strategic requirements of war had considerable effects on the brewing industry, both in terms of production and organisation. Many aspects of the trade—from the volume of raw materials used, to controlling the specific gravity of beer—were subject to government regulation on a national basis. Most notably, the government took a major role in the control of drink retailing, through emergency legislation designed to restrict licensing hours and curb drunkenness. Some of the emergency powers incorporated in the Defence of the Realm Act had previously formed part of the temperance platform—which had received considerable support from Liberal administrations prior to the outbreak of hostilities.[1] Scotland was broadly subject to national legislation, although the usual allowances were made for differing conditions north of the Border. Among other measures was the nationalisation of the liquor trade in areas where munitions factories had been built or around military or naval bases—including the two Scottish districts of Gretna and Cromarty. The emergency measures which created the State Management Districts also engendered an interesting experiment in social control, and strange though it may seem, the government stake in the liquor trade of the two main areas affected—Carlisle-Gretna and Cromarty-Invergordon—was only disposed of in 1971.

Production was very greatly affected from the outset, falling rapidly in the first months of the war due to uncertainties over the supply of raw materials. In the longer term output slumped to almost a third of its pre-war level, falling according to Wilson's estimate to 717,000 standard barrels in the trough of 1918 (see Table 83). More significant perhaps was the reduction in the gravity of beers by dilution, particularly after 1916, and for the first time there began to be a significant divergence between bulk and standard barrelage as beer became weaker. In general, prices rose, partly the result of greatly increased liquor duties, and partly because of higher raw material costs. This had the effect of limiting the brewing of strong ales—and particularly so in the smaller breweries, which were badly hit by the wartime conditions. As in so many other instances, it was the large firms, with all their economies of scale, which were best able to weather the storm, and indeed some made better profits because of increased prices.[2] The concentration of the industry continued: of the 59 companies listed in the *Brewers' Almanack* of 1915, no fewer than 23 were located in Edinburgh, while Alloa had seven, and Glasgow five. Many breweries elsewhere were beginning to experience difficulties and did not survive long after the end of the war.[3]

Government intervention in the brewing industry increased greatly during World War I, particularly after July 1915 when the Central Control Board was created under the Defence of the Realm Act. This body immediately imposed restrictive orders on licensing hours in certain strategic and industrial districts, where drunkenness and disorder had been on the increase. Four areas were designated in Scotland between July and December 1915 — West Central, East Central, Northern (which included Invergordon-Cromarty), and the Western Border (which extended as far south as Barrow-in-Furness). Ultimately restrictive orders covered most of the country, except the eastern Border counties and Wigtownshire. Generally licensing hours were restricted to five a day, two hours at midday, and three in the evening, from 6pm to 9pm.[4] Lloyd George's infamous remark to the effect that 'The drink traffic is a greater danger even than Germany' (otherwise 'Drink is doing us more damage than all the German submarines put together') undoubtedly exaggerated the extent of drunkenness, but there is no question that the problem existed on some scale in and around munitions factories, where workers were highly paid for skilled and often dangerous jobs.[5] The same sort of problem existed in military and naval bases, where, in addition to troops or seamen, there were also large numbers of civilian labourers. In several instances the scale of the problem—caused mainly by a large influx of labour—was too great for the local authorities concerned, and it was there that the Central Control Board resorted to state purchase or direct control.

The largest area affected by state purchase was on the Western Border between Carlisle and Gretna. Nationalisation and direct control arose from the problem created by a massive influx of labour (many Irish navvies included) employed in building a huge National Munitions Factory in and around the village of Gretna. The normal restrictive orders were of little effect, so the Central Control Board began to acquire pubs in the locality, starting in January 1916 with those around Annan, Gretna and Longtown. Restrictions there simply created problems elsewhere, above all in Carlisle, which was besieged by thousands of drouthy labourers who caused a great deal of disquiet and considerable disorder. 'Scenes of the most nauseating and degrading character became a common occurrence,' wrote one observer, for 'men fought like beasts, fierce fights raged round the doors of the public houses ... and almost every alley was littered with prostrate drunken men.' So the area of nationalisation was progressively extended, both north and south of Gretna, and by the end of 1916 it included five breweries in Carlisle and Maryport with all of the licensed premises on either side of the Solway Firth—a district of 500 square miles. The Board suppressed licences and undertook a programme of public house improvement, which included the provision of social and eating facilities. Many of the older houses were closed and replaced with new 'taverns' incorporating 'foodhalls,' and reading, billiard, and smoking rooms, as well as the usual beer halls.[6]

Before the war Invergordon and Cromarty were quiet fishing villages on the Cromarty Firth, which was used by the naval fleet for summer manoeuvres and firing practice. But on the outbreak of the war, the Cromarty Firth was selected as a major naval base for the Home Fleet, a dockyard was established, and repair shops were erected. Invergordon, and to a lesser extent Cromarty and Dingwall, soon experienced the same influx of labourers and sailors that posed major problems in and around the munitions works at Gretna. As a result a scheme of direct control was put into operation in April 1916, which involved the acquisition of thirteen licensed premises in the two towns. Adjoining districts were afterwards added, including Alness and Dingwall. Management policy was framed to suit naval requirements, especially the licensing hours (4½ per day!) and severe restrictions on off-sales.[7]

State purchase in these districts (and several in England), with the associated control of hours of sale and the suppression of licences, was widely praised by temperance reformers, but apart from restrictive orders few other areas were directly affected. The Central Control Board, however, had a major role in the production and quality of beer under a series of acts and orders, like the Output of Beer (Restriction) Act, and the Compulsory Dilution Order.[8] As we have seen, these measures had a profound effect on production during the war years, and despite a marked post-war boom, output never regained its 1913 level. This—and much else that was born of wartime emergency—set new tendencies for the inter-war years, which saw the brewing industry in a generally static environment.

The Inter-War Years

In terms of production (see Table 83), the industry nationally was essentially moribund. Statistics of output for Scotland in the period 1920-39 broadly mirrored the index of industrial production over the same period. Indeed, it would

Table 83

Output and Brewers 1910-1936

Year	Output 000s barrels	Number of Brewers
1910	1,750	92
1911	1,858	88
1912	1,845	81
1913	1,970	79
1914	1,858	75
1915	1,549	71
1916	1,484	70
1917	894	67
1918	717	66
1919	1,360	64
1920	1,652	63
1921	1,438	60
1922	1,203	59
1923	1,294	58
1924	1,431	57
1925	1,425	56
1926	1,300	54
1927	1,365	51
1928	1,365	49
1929	1,419	49
1930	1,346	46
1931	1,121	45
1932	918	45
1933	1,002	43
1934	1,089	44
1935	1,179	42
1936	1,236	43

Source: Wilson, 370, 388-89.

be difficult to find a better barometer of economic conditions. After a good post-war recovery, seen in the figures for 1919-20, output fell to a low point in 1922 of 1.2 million standard barrels (1.5 million bulk barrels). Thereafter an annual average output of around 1.4 million standard barrels (1.8 million bulk barrels) was maintained until the slump of the early thirties. Recovery after the depression of 1932 was slow, with output maintained at a level of around 1.2 million standard barrels until the outbreak of World War II.[9]

The number of breweries continued its steady downward decline, as Wilson's figures in Table 83 show. More than twenty brewers went out of business in the period, many no doubt small and struggling enterprises. In the *Brewers' Almanack* for 1925, 45 companies are listed as brewers with an output exceeding 1,000 barrels a year. The list includes most of the major firms active in 1915.[10] By 1935, the list had shrunk to 39—among the casualties being the long-established Devanha Brewery Company of Aberdeen, William Brown of Craigie Brewery, Dundee, Robert Henderson & Company of the Mills Brewery in Alloa, and Somerville & Company of the North British Brewery in Edinburgh. Other plants had closed in Montrose, Peterhead and Dumbarton. More significant perhaps was the modest trend to amalgamation, best seen in the examples of Lorimer & Clark, whose Caledonian Brewery attracted the interest of Vaux of Sunderland (though still trading under the old firm's name, a common feature), and Turner's Ayr and Newton Breweries, a logical acquisition for the Glasgow giant, J. & R. Tennent.[11]

If the apparent lethargy of the trade in terms of production tended to mirror general economic depression, certain sections of the trade, on the other hand, were far from moribund. Bottling, for example, was a major development of the period, for previously the great bulk of beer had been supplied in the cask. Many of the bigger firms installed modern plants, including George Younger of Alloa, William Younger of Edinburgh, and James Aitken of Falkirk. Younger of Alloa had a large bottled trade, and also showed considerable enterprise in the development and extension of their bottle works at Kelliebank, latterly known as the Scottish Central Glass Works. William Younger led the Edinburgh brewers in the bottled trade by the installation at Holyrood in 1920 of their first plant for bottling chilled and carbonated beer. The first quality to be bottled—at the rate of 100 dozen screw-top pints an hour—was the 90s. Sparkling Ale. Later a new lighter ale, 'Holyrood,' was bottled in half pints. Another famous ale brewer, James Aitken, greatly extended his business in the inter-war years, including the installation about 1930 of new bottling plant at the Falkirk Brewery.[12]

Such developments reflected new demands for different varieties of beer, notably pale ale and lager. The latter became increasingly popular in the twenties and thirties, Scottish brewers like Tennent, Graham and Jeffrey being leaders in the field. Tennent was already established as one of the major British lager brewers, and the firm continued to invest heavily in modern plant in order to maintain its position. Graham of Alloa also specialised in the production of 'Golden Lager,' which apparently grew enormously in popularity in the thirties, and was said in 1937 to be amongst the most widely distributed beer brewed in

Scotland. Lager—like other light beers and ales—was mainly bottled, so that the plant and equipment had to be kept constantly up-to-date. Tennent—and probably others—attempted canning in the thirties. But the tins, with their cone-shaped tops, did not meet with complete approval. Some connoisseurs spoke disparagingly of 'Brasso' tins, and complained that the can imparted a taste to the beer.[13]

In the sphere of business organisation, the most dramatic development was the formal link established in 1931 between William Younger and William McEwan, the two leading Scottish firms. Both were flourishing companies, their authorised capital was the same at £1 million, and the dividends had been uniformly high despite economic difficulties. Against this background the two firms announced that they had

negotiated a combination of certain of their financial and technical resources with the view of further developing the efficiency of the production and distribution of their ales. Each company will continue to be carried on as a separate business, with its present organisation, and it is not intended to alter the individual characteristics of the ales marketed by the respective companies, but by making available to each the technical and other resources of both it is hoped that the already high reputation of both companies in respect of quality and good service will be enhanced.

The arrangement in question will be a private one between the shareholders concerned. There is no present intention of making any public issue of shares. The new combine, known as Scottish Brewers Ltd, came into official being in January 1931. Later the same year, McEwan-Younger Ltd was formed to handle the joint export, naval, and military trade of both firms. Younger's own military business was still flourishing both at home and in many British garrisons overseas.[14]

Temperance and prohibition were, of course, topical questions of the inter-war years, reflected in some instances in the Local Option provisions of the Temperance (Scotland) Act. In a typical year, 1929, sixteen local veto polls took place mainly in industrial districts of central Scotland, including Bathgate, Coat-bridge, Motherwell, Wishaw, Kilmarnock, Clydebank, Kirkintilloch and Glasgow. Polls were also held in three other districts of Ayrshire—the textile towns of Darvel, Newmilns and Stewarton—as well as at Cullen (Banffshire), and Kirkwall, Orkney. A total of 40,000 votes were cast in the sixteen polls, with a turnout of 63 per cent. Fifty-five per cent voted for no change, repeal or limitation, or repeal of no-licence. Three no-licence areas were maintained as a result, Stewarton, Cullen, and Kirkintilloch—the last a well-known 'dry' district until recently. In twelve of the districts the 'No Licence' Party were said to be responsible for the polls. Much the same pattern was repeated throughout the thirties: although Local Option was less and less resorted to with the passing years.[15]

The outbreak of World War II found the Scottish brewing industry in a state of equilibrium. The period between 1919 and 1939 had seen many adjustments to new circumstances, such as the lower production of weaker beer, higher excise duties and prices, an increasing popularity of bottled beers, and demands for improved public houses. Rivalries between companies were never much in evidence, but on the other hand many small firms had gone to the wall and their business had been amalgamated with that of larger breweries. Edinburgh was the second largest brewing centre in Britain, with 23 breweries, representing a capital of between £5 and £6 million. The war of 1939-45 was not to have the dramatic consequences of World War I, with its great increase in government control at all levels, but it intensified many of the processes at work in the industry.

Since 1945

The years since the end of World War II have seen truly dramatic changes and growth in the Scottish brewing industry—characterised particularly by a process of continuous amalgamation and rationalisation, and by an enormous increase in output, mainly in the sixties. In a sense the thirty years 1945-75 are best examined by dividing the period at 1960, a real turning point for the Scottish industry. Until that time production was fairly static: output fluctuated around the 2 million barrel level for most of the period between 1945-60, and the proportion of U.K. production represented by Scotland was also relatively stable at about 12 or 13 per cent (see Table 84). Only after 1960 did the industry begin to feel the impact of

Table 84
Scottish Brewing Statistics 1951-75

Year	Production 000s barrels	% U.K.	£m. Value Net Output	Employees 000s
1951	2,000	11.9		8.3
1952	2,019	11.8		8.3
1953	2,106	12.6		8.3
1954	1,981	11.9		7.9
1955	2,068	12.8		7.9
1956	2,086	12.6		7.9
1957	2,156	12.9		7.9
1958	2,111	12.6		7.8
1959	2,226	13.6		8.9
1960	2,347	13.4		9.6
1961	2,507	13.8		9.6
1962	2,501	13.1		9.7
1963	2,611	13.7		9.5
1964	2,707	13.7		8.9
1965	2,742	13.6		9.3
1966	2,800	13.7		8.8
1967	2,933			9.1
1968	3,096			8.4
1969	3,353			9.5
1970	3,855		64.0	9.1
1971	4,306			
1972	4,474			
1973	4,835			
1974	5,046			
1975	5,413			

Source: *Digest of Scottish Statistics* 1953 onwards; *Scottish Abstract of Statistics* 1973 onwards; *Census of Production* 1970.

large-scale amalgamations which so characterised British brewing as a whole throughout the sixties and early seventies. Increased business size brought greatly increased production. This progress is again clearly indicated in Table 84, where production is seen to rise from 2.5 million barrels in 1961 to 3.8 million barrels in 1970 and no fewer than 5.4 million barrels in 1975.[16]

The array of companies actively brewing in 1950 remained impressive: no fewer than nineteen were of sufficient size to be entered in the pages of the *Stock Exchange Year Book* (see Table 85), while there were upwards of a dozen smaller breweries. The total capital of quoted companies in 1950 was £8.2 million, a figure which probably represented about 90 per cent of the whole industry north of the Border. The only major firm not quoted on the Stock Exchange list was Tennents, which still maintained its private status. Apart from this company, the leaders were the Scottish Brewers combination, William Younger, William McEwan, and George Younger of Alloa. In the second league were Arrol, Murray, and McLachlans—each with capital in excess of £300,000. Smaller companies included many well-known names like Aitken, Campbell Hope and King, Jeffrey, and Usher. Purely in terms of capital, more than two-thirds of the industry was concentrated in Edinburgh, the remainder being in Alloa, Glasgow and Falkirk. Scottish Brewers, with its two associated companies, William Younger and William McEwan, accounted for more than half the total quoted capital, a figure amounting to at least £4.5 million.[17]

Table 85

Scottish Brewery Companies and Capital 1950

Company	Capital (£)
Aitchison	200,000
Aitken	150,000
Arrol	344,000
Bernard	250,000
Blair	150,000
Calder	250,000
Campbell, Hope & King	130,000
Drybrough	100,000
Jeffrey	200,000
McEwan	1,000,000
McLachlans	300,000
Maclay	150,000
Murray	318,000
Scottish Brewers	2,520,000
Steel Coulson	140,000
Usher	140,000
G. Younger	750,000
R. Younger	180,000
W. Younger	1,000,000
	8,272,000

Source: *Stock Exchange Year Book*, 1950.

The picture in 1960, indicated in Table 86, already showed the impact of amalgamation on lesser firms. The *Brewery Manual* of that year gives the capital position of twenty firms, excluding the Scottish & Newcastle group and Ind Coope's Scottish connexions. At least half a dozen companies, like Bernard of Edinburgh, had only just been taken over in the rush of amalgamations which occurred in 1959-60. Some of these firms had ceased to brew immediately on take-over, while others had already closed or were in the process of closure. Scottish & Newcastle had a total capital of £30.5 million, of which approximately half was represented by breweries, trade and other assets in Scotland itself, while the remainder lay elsewhere—mainly in breweries, tied houses and hotels south of the Border. Ind Coope had a well-established Alloa connexion in their lager brewery, which probably represented less than a fifth of their total assets of £17.8 million. Apart from these giants, the leading firms of the late 1950s can be readily identified, notably Tennent (£2.2 million), Bernard (£1.0 million), and Aitken (£0.9 million). The second rank included well-respected brewers like George Younger, Calder of Alloa, and Robert Younger of Edinburgh; while in third rank were such firms as Drybrough, Fowler, Jeffrey, Murray, and Usher. Including the proportions of capital represented by Scottish & Newcastle and Ind Coope, the assets of the brewing industry in Scotland were probably in the region of £30 million.[18]

English brewers always had a substantial interest in Scottish markets and this factor played a prominent part in the pattern of amalgamations during the fifties and sixties. As we have already seen, some of the North of England brewers were pioneers in the takeover of Scottish firms, for Vaux of Sunderland had an interest in Lorimer & Clark before 1935. Another English giant, Allsops of Burton-on-Trent, had acquired an important foothold in Alloa, where lager was brewed by both Archibald Arrol and a subsidiary, Graham. These two examples, typical of their period, did not involve brewery closure, more a rationalisation of production and techniques—the same goals sought by the Edinburgh giants who had brought Scottish Brewers Ltd into being in 1930.

Yet since the late 1950s the pattern of amalgamations has brought about the gradual disappearance of the independent brewer, and his replacement by regional and national brewers. Rationalisation had gone so far in brewing that by 1975 a large share of the market throughout the United Kingdom and Ireland was concentrated in the hands of six brewing giants, the so-called 'Big Six,' Bass Charrington, Allied Brewers, Watneys, Samuel Whitbread, John Courage, and Scottish & Newcastle. Apart from the last mentioned, three of the 'Big Six' (Bass Charrington, Allied and Whitbread) had varying degrees of interest in the Scottish trade—and varying degrees of responsibility for the process of rationalisation which had swept away the majority of smaller firms by the early sixties.[19]

Such are the economics of large-scale production in modern brewing that few companies, even the largest, own more than two or possibly three breweries. When more than one is owned (as is the case with Scottish & Newcastle), it is usually because the costs of supplying a particular area from the main brewery are greater than the savings to be obtained from operating it on a larger scale. So it has been a frequent practice when a larger firm absorbs a smaller for it to close down the newly acquired brewery and concentrate output on the parent brewery, which is either extended or operated at fuller capacity. A brewery might well be saved because of its specialist product, good examples being the lager breweries of Glasgow and Alloa, owned by two of the 'Big Six.' One example from the mid-fifties will suffice—again the result of northern English interests. In 1956 the Newcastle Brewery acquired the ordinary share capital of James Deuchar of Montrose, and the chairman then reported that 'we were able to close down their brewery at Montrose, and concentrate the brewing of the group's requirements at Newcastle and Duddingston. This should result in considerable economies in both production and transport expenses.' The Duddingston brewery had itself been acquired as a result of the purchase of Robert Deuchar in 1953.

Table 86

Companies, Capital and Takeovers, 1960

Company	Brewery/Town	Total Capital £	Takeover Company	Date of Takeover
Aitchison	Edinburgh	400,000	Hammonds UBs.	1959
Aitken	Falkirk	927,000	United Bs.	1960
Ballingall	Park, Pleasance/Dundee	75,000	(Closed 1964)	—
Bernard	Abbey/Edinburgh	1,075,000	Scottish Bs.	1960
Blair	Townhead/Alloa	200,000	G. Younger	1959
Calder	Alloa	525,000	United Bs.	1960
Campbell, Hope & King	Argyle/Edinburgh	250,000	Whitbread	1967
Drybrough	Edinburgh	300,000	Watney Mann	1965
Dudgeon	Belhaven/Dunbar	—	—	—
Fowler	Prestonpans	300,000	United Bs.	1960
Jeffrey	Heriot/Edinburgh	280,000	United Bs.	1960
Lorimer & Clark	Caledonian/Edinburgh	100,000	Vaux	1947
Mackay	Edinburgh	—	Drybrough	1958
Maclay	Thistle/Alloa	150,000	—	—
Maclachlan	Castle/Edinburgh	600,000	Tennent	1960
Maclennan & Urquhart	Dalkeith	—	Aitchison	1955
Morison	Edinburgh	—	Scottish Bs.	1960
Murray	Craigmillar/Edinburgh	375,000	United Bs.	1960
Steel, Coulson	Croft-an-Righ/Edinburgh	140,000	Vaux	1959
Tennent	Wellpark/Glasgow	2,250,000	Charrington	1963
Wright	Perth	—	Vaux	1961
Young	Ladywell/Musselburgh	30,000	Whitbread	1968
G. Younger	Candleriggs/Alloa	750,000	United Bs.	1960
R. Younger	Abbey/Edinburgh	580,000	Scottish Bs.	1960
Usher	Park/Edinburgh	403,000	Vaux	1960

Source: *Brewery Manual*, 1955, 1960, 1965.

Further examination of Table 86 provides an opportunity to elaborate on the pattern of amalgamations experienced by the breweries in the late fifties and early sixties. The first major English brewer, Vaux, had, as we have noted, considerable connexions north of the Border through the Edinburgh firm of Lorimer & Clark. In 1959 Vaux acquired Steel, Coulson, a notable and old-established firm, later adding the larger and more important Usher's Park Brewery of Edinburgh, which in 1960 had a capital of £403,000. A small local firm, John Wright of Perth, was bought over in 1961, completing the Vaux empire in Scotland. Production was soon concentrated on the two main Edinburgh plants, the Caledonian Brewery at Slateford, and the Park Brewery in St. Leonard's Street. Steel, Coulson ceased to brew, and the Croft-an-Righ plant closed. Subsequently there was considerable expansion of the Usher plant, much of the output being marketed through Scottish outlets. A recent development has been the revival in Scotland of the Lorimer & Clark label. Previously a trading arrangement between Vaux and Usher prevented Lorimer's beers being sold north of the Border.[20]

United Breweries (themselves merged with Charrington in 1962) had a major role in the elimination of an important group of independent Scottish companies during the years 1959-61. Under its former name of Northern Breweries the group acquired John Jeffrey of Edinburgh (well-known for their lager and other beers) in 1960—a merger which also involved Hammonds United Breweries (of Bradford, Huddersfield and Tadcaster, among other places), and Hope & Anchor Breweries of Sheffield. Hammonds United had already taken over John Aitchison of Edinburgh in 1959. Aitchison was typical of smaller Scottish companies which attempted to expand their business in the face of growing competition from the major firms in the mid-1950s. An old Dalkeith firm, Maclennan & Urquhart, was bought over in 1955, when the share capital was increased by £200,000. Northern Breweries then acquired the issued share capitals of George Younger of Alloa, John Fowler of Prestonpans and William Murray of Edinburgh, followed rapidly by James Aitken of Falkirk and James Calder of Alloa. In October 1960 the name was changed to United Breweries, and the following year the activities of John Aitchison and John Jeffrey were merged under the new name of Aitchison Jeffrey. Most of the breweries closed within a few years. By 1962 the United Group had merged with Charrington to form Charrington United Breweries Ltd. United Caledonian Breweries (originally Caledonian Breweries) was created as a wholly-owned subsidiary to coordinate the Scottish operations of the new group.

Meanwhile the major Glasgow firm of Tennents had not been idle, having acquired Maclachlans, the well-known brewers and distillers, whose Castle Brewery at Duddingston had been built in 1901. They later added another old west-coast firm, Turner's of Ayr in 1963—by which time the scene was set for the largest ever merger in Scotland (discounting the formation of Scottish & Newcastle Breweries). In that year Tennents joined the Charrington United Brewers Group. By 1966 United Caledonian Breweries was formally merged with Tennents to form Tennent Caledonian Brewers Ltd—within the giant Bass Charrington Group.[21]

Undoubtedly the most impressive amalgamation arose from the long-established links between William Younger and William McEwan, which had traded as Scottish Brewers since 1931. Three important and much respected Edinburgh firms were acquired in 1960, T. & J. Bernard, J & J. Morison, and Robert Younger, which soon ceased to trade independently. Also during 1960 a merger was effected with Newcastle Breweries, by an exchange of shares, Scottish Brewers being used as the vehicle for the merger. The name was then changed to

Scottish & Newcastle Breweries, the company having an authorised capital of £30.5 million. A formal link had at last been forged between two closely associated markets in Scotland and the north of England.

Whitbread & Company arrived rather late on the Scottish scene. By 1968 they had acquired the long-established firm of Archibald Campbell, Hope & King, as well as the smaller Musselburgh brewery of John Young & Company. Campbell, Hope & King had an extensive trade throughout Scotland, and a big interest in whisky blending—the latter undoubtedly another important attraction for Whitbread. The Edinburgh firm had previously acquired the only surviving brewery in the south-west of Scotland, the South-Western Brewery at Newton Stewart, in 1925—which they continued to use as a store. Within a few years brewing ceased at the eighteenth-century plant in Edinburgh's Cowgate, and Whitbread afterwards concentrated its distribution to Scottish outlets on a depot at Rutherglen near Glasgow.[22]

Finally, Watney Mann Ltd obtained an important foothold north of the Border with their takeover of Drybrough in 1965. Drybrough was another old firm with an excellent reputation for its products, which, like both Ushers and Campbell, Hope & King, had built up a widespread Scottish trade. A new, modern brewery was developed at Craigmillar and a vigorous programme of expansion undertaken.

Other external connexions are still maintained in the Allied Breweries lager plant in Alloa (Ind Coope Scotland Ltd), and the Harp lager brewery at the Scottish & Newcastle complex in Edinburgh. The latter group have also developed a large modern lager plant for the production of McEwan's lager—a response to the enormously increased demand for this particular product.

Only two small firms ultimately escaped the trawl net of the brewery giants, the famed Belhaven Brewery at Dunbar, and the equally well-respected Maclay's Thistle Brewery in Alloa. Both are essentially local brewers in the old tradition producing a range of superior ales and beers. They survived the attentions of the major brewers and prospered on the quality rather than the quantity of their products—even a decade ago there was a substantial demand for old-style beers. Indeed such has been the success of these two modest enterprises that they have recently found themselves in the vanguard of the 'real ale' movement, which reached north of the Border in the early 1970s.[23]

The period since 1960 has seen truly remarkable developments in marketing, distribution, and products—all of which must be seen against a major social revolution in attitudes towards drink and drinking. There can be little doubt that the brewing industry—in Scotland as elsewhere—has been able to respond with considerable efficiency to changes in demand. On the other hand, many important developments have been the result of the new technology and clever marketing to which the larger and more influential firms have ready access. But before looking at some of these changes—and the public response to them—it will be worth while examining developments in the licensed trade and social scene generally since the early 1960s.

The relaxation in attitudes to drinking has been accompanied by somewhat slower liberalisation of the licensing laws. The number of licences has tended to increase: between 1969 and 1972, for example, there was a ten per cent increase. Numbers continue to rise, with an associated change in types of licence becoming more obvious. The overall structure of the Scottish licensed trade in 1972 is shown in Table 87, where the diversity can be clearly seen. Licensed restaurants have become increasingly important, although a large number of restaurants in Scotland operate under a public house licence, and hotel restaurants are also significant. Restricted hotels are a relatively new category introduced in 1962—they have no bar and non-residents cannot buy a drink without taking a meal. But the obvious fiction of the bona fide traveller journeying more than three miles to get a drink on a Sunday is long dead.

Table 87

Licences for Sale of Excisable Liquor
(By Type of Premises), 1972

Hotels	2,609
Restricted Hotels	250
Public Houses	4,176
Restaurants	406
Off-Sales	3,819
Clubs	2,125
Total	13,385

Scottish licensing hours have recently undergone dramatic relaxation—essentially the outcome of the Clayson Committee's recommendations following an extensive review of the licensing system.[24] There are still many anomalies, however, and it seems likely that extended hours and Sunday opening (for example) will not be as quickly widespread as many imagined. Temperance, to which we have already made a number of references in the period before 1945, is still something of a force to be reckoned with. In parts of the north, for instance, opposition to Sunday opening is well entrenched, mainly on religious grounds.[25]

Yet in some respects the Scottish licensing system has already provided pointers for changes in England. In Scotland the licence continues to be held by the publican personally, rather than by the brewer and publican jointly. So the historical tradition is still of great importance, for the publican has always been a good deal freer than his English counterpart. The tied-house system is less widespread in Scotland, and the free trade correspondingly more important. Essentially this arises from the old custom of brewers granting loans to publicans for purchase or improvement of premises, without exacting a formal tie in return.

Rationalisation on the scale experienced in the late 1950s and early 60s has brought many new developments, and the old ways are gradually changing. Managed houses—where the licensee is employed by the brewery—have become increasingly common, especially on new housing estates and in New Towns. A tenancy system resembling the English one is taking shape in the previously 'free' area of the trade. Partly in consequence of the brewer's direct involvement in such matters—though probably as much due to wider social change and higher living standards—extensive changes have taken place in Scottish pubs since the sixties. Food and comfortable eating facilities became widely available and the surroundings generally more congenial. Down-at-heel properties have been renovated in great numbers by the brewers—though not always with much sympathy for the original decor and occasionally in questionable taste. The go-go dancers featured in some pubs represent the last vestiges of male chauvinism, for the Scottish pub—and beer drinking for that matter—long ago ceased to be the preserve of the male. All this—although opposed by some, including a few 'real ale' enthusiasts—adds up to a social revolution which is all the more remarkable for its suddenness.

If 1960 was the real turning point for the Scottish brewing industry in terms of the pattern of amalgamations which have subsequently taken place, it also provides a useful opportunity to examine the mouth-watering range of products then available. Table 88 presents a range of established brand names with their brewers, including some evocative products which once quenched the thirst of Scotsmen at home and abroad.[26] Many of the trade names, in fact, date back to the Victorian era. Several, like 'Burns,' brewed by Drybrough, have recently been revived—a phenomenon which is certainly a partial response to the customer's desire for 'authentic' beers. Clearly customer demand is a factor which the brewer ignores at his peril, and this, just as much as improved distribution and marketing, has led to the development of new or better products, prominently keg beers and lagers. A related revolution has taken place in packaging, notably in take-home products in cans.

The development of keg beers—as opposed to those conditioned in wooden casks—sprang from new and improved technology in the early 1950s when the aluminium alloy keg was produced. Stainless steel kegs were also developed alongside aluminium and both are now widely used. Carbon dioxide under pressure is used to raise the beer to the tap, the CO_2 being contained in another compartment in the keg or in a separate cylinder. Where an electric pump is used, CO_2 is generally added to pressurise the cask, although not in the same quantities as through a pressure tap. A very large proportion of output from the major brewers is keg beer—including lagers.[27]

There have been significant developments in the lager brewing sector in recent years, and Scotland holds an important place in the manufacture of this product. Scotland has always led Britain in lager consumption, and such is its popularity that in 1977 it accounted for about 40 per cent of beer sales north of the Border. Tennent-Caledonian Breweries, Scotland's largest lager brewers, have undertaken major expansion at the Wellpark Brewery in Glasgow, while Scottish & Newcastle Breweries began production of McEwan's lager at the New Fountain Brewery in 1976. Ind Coope (Scotland) Ltd continue to brew Skol lager at their Alloa plant. There has been considerable growth in demand for specialist lagers, and Tennent-Caledonian remain leaders in this field, with products like 'Special Lager' and the recently introduced 'Breaker' malt liquor. Continental-type lagers have also been of importance in the Scottish market, and this has led to an extension of franchises with continental brewers.[28]

Table 88

Scottish Brand Names and Brewers 1960

Name	Type	Brewers
Amber Ale	Draught	Usher
Angus	Ales; Stout	Ballingall
Belhaven	Ales; Stout	Dudgeon
Best Cellar	Bitter, bott.	Aitchison
Blue Label	Ale	Scottish Brewers
Brewers Best	Export Ale	Fowler
Burns	Strong Ale	Drybrough
Cameron's Ale	Beer	McLennan & Urquart
Castle	All	Maclachlan
Crown Ale	Strong Ale	Fowler
Dalkeith	Ales; Stouts	Maclennan & Urquart
Dishers	Extra Strong Ale	Jeffrey
Double Century	High Quality Ale	Scottish Brewers
Double Maxim	High Quality Ale	Vaux
Duddingston	Sweet Stout	R. Deuchar
Edinburgh	Brown Ale	Scottish Brewers
Edinburgh	Sweet Stout	R. Deuchar
Elephant	Ale; Stout	Steel, Coulson
Export	Ale	Mackay
Export	Ale	Deuchar
Export	Ale	Tennent
Export	Ale	Usher
Four Guinea Ale	Beer	Maclennan & Urquart
Globe Brand	Various	Scottish Brewers
Gold Label Ale	Heavy Grav. P.A.	Scottish Brewers
Gold Label Export	Extra Strong P.A.	Drybrough
Golden Rule	Ale	Usher
Grouse Brand	Export	Bernard
Highland	Pale Ale	G. Younger
Holyrood	Light Sparkling; Pale Ale	Scottish Brewers
Husky	Export Ale, canned, bottled	G. Younger
King of Ales	Strong Ale	Scottish Brewers
Lochside	Ale	R. Deuchar
Monk	Export, bottled	Scottish Brewers
Oat Creme	Stout	R. Younger
Old Edinburgh	Heavy Ale	R. Younger
Red Star	Export Ale, bottled	Usher
Special Export	Ale	Vaux
Stag Brand	Ale	R. Younger
Starbright	Pale Ale	Drybrough
Sweetheart	Sweet Stout	G. Younger
Treble Top	Pale Ale, canned	G. Younger
Wee Murray	Light Ale	Murray
Wee Samson	Dark Heavy Ale	Murray
Wee Willie	Light P.A.	Scottish Brewers
Witches Brew	High Quality Ale	Ballingall
60s. Pale Ale	Draught	Usher
80s. Pale Ale	Draught	Usher
90s. India Pale Ale	Light Ale	Bernard
90s. Ale	Sparkling Ale	Scottish Brewers
90s. Pale Ale	Pale Ale	Mackay

Finally, no history of the brewing industry in Scotland would be complete without reference to the revived interest in 'real beer.' It may seem somewhat surprising that there has been a resurgence in demand for cask-conditioned beers in recent years when statistics show that the overall ale market has declined as lager has advanced. Kegged or bright beers, as we have seen, are conditioned in brewery tanks and then go through a series of chilling, carbonation, filtration, and pasterurisation processes before being dispatched in kegs, bottles or cans. 'Real' beer, on the other hand, is produced in the more-or-less traditional manner, each cask being filled direct from the fermenting vessel and left to condition naturally. Advocates of cask-conditioned beers argue that the various processes involved in the manufacture of kegged beers impair the flavour and body of the end product, which is overgassed and, to them, unpalatable. Naturally conditioned beers retain the true flavour of malt and hops, found in 'old-fashioned' brews. In 1974 only the two small independent breweries, Belhaven of Dunbar and Maclays of Alloa, were actively marketing 'real' beer, but by 1977 Scottish & Newcastle Breweries, Tennent-Caledonian Breweries, and Lorimers had also developed traditional ales for this sector of the trade.[29] Between 1974 and 1977 the number of retail outlets offering cask beers as an alternative to keg increased more than threefold—and seems likely to rise still further in the future. By accident rather than design, the story of the brewing industry in Scotland has moved almost full circle in the two and a half centuries or so which have been described in the pages of this book.

NOTES

1 Vaizey, op.cit., 20.
2 Ibid, 24.
3 *Brewers' Almanack*, 370-71.
4 H.Carter, *The Control of the Drink Trade: A Contribution to National Efficiency 1915-1917* (London, 1918), provides details of the areas covered.
5 Vaizey, op.cit., 20.
6 Carter, op.cit., 197-214.
7 Ibid, 174-6.
8 Vaizey, op.cit., 22.
9 *Brewers' Almanack*, 1925, 109.
10 Ibid, 291-92.
11 *BA*, 1935, 337.
12 *A Short History of George Younger & Son Ltd, Alloa* (1925), 17; Keir, op.cit., 87; *Two Hundred Years of Progress: James Aitken & Company Limited 1740-1940* (1940).
13 C.A.Oakley, *Scottish Industry Today* (Edinburgh 1937), 92.
14 Keir, op.cit., 90-91.
15 *Brewers' Almanack*, 1930, 276.
16 On general developments see B.Tew and R.F.Henderson (eds.), *Studies in Company Finance* (Cambridge, 1959), esp. Ch. 10 on brewing; G.Turner, *Business in Britain* (London, 1969), esp. Ch. 10 on brewers and builders.
17 *Stock Exchange Year Book*, 1950; *Brewers' Almanack*, 1950, 1955.
18 *Brewery Manual*, 1961-62.
19 Turner, op.cit., 269-70, 282.
20 Information from Ushers Brewery Ltd.
21 *Brewery Manual*, 1961-62, 183, 188, 211.

22 Information from Whitbread Scotland Ltd; *Brewery Manual*, 1970, 190.

23 *Brewery Manual*, 1970, 106, 175.

24 *Report of the Departmental Committee on Scottish Licensing Law*, 1973 (Cmnd. 5354).

25 G.Murray, *Scotland: the New Future*, (Glasgow, 1973), 192-96.

26 *Brewery Manual*, 1961-62, 343-68.

27 R.O. Darling, 'From Barrels to Bulk Tanks,' *Brewers' Guardian Centenary Issue 1971*, 127-132.

28 'Distillers and Brewing,' *The Scotsman*, 20 September 1977.

29 Ibid; Campaign for Real Ale (Scotland), *Scottish Real Beer Guide* (Edinburgh 1975), 19-20.

Bibliographical Note

DAVID Loch, in his *Essays on the Trade, Commerce, Manufactures and Fisheries of Scotland* (1776), was perhaps the first to note the growing national importance of brewing, while contributors to the *Statistical Account* of the mid-1790s provided pointers to the rise of urban and country breweries alike. Sir John Sinclair's *Analysis of the Statistical Account of Scotland* (1825) drew on many of the local references contained in his earlier edited work and on material from the many useful volumes on agricultural conditions in Scotland. Not until later in the nineteenth century were more analytical statements made on the development of the brewing industry. A detailed and thoroughly researched essay on the history of brewing in Scotland was prepared in 1868 by *The Scotsman's* industrial correspondent, David Bremner. This he afterwards revised for publication in his *Industries of Scotland, Their Rise, Progress and Present Condition* (1869). Bremner was a man ahead of his time, making extensive use of statistical and other data from the Blue Books. Like much else that he wrote, his essay on brewing has hardly been surpassed. Another Victorian journalist, Alfred Barnard, visited and wrote about several of the more important Scottish firms in his *Noted Breweries of Great Britain and Ireland* (1889-91). The larger firms were later described by Henry Stopes in a financial work entitled *Brewery Companies* (1895). Several other general works on the development of the brewing industry contain references to Scotland. There are also a number of short business histories of Scottish firms, the best being David Keir's *The Younger Centuries: The Story of William Younger & Co. Ltd. 1749-1949* (1951).

The brewing industries of both England and Ireland have been examined in some detail by modern historians, and this present work owes much to three in particular. Professor Peter Mathias's *The Brewing Industry in England* (1959) is an outstandingly interesting monograph. It is much more than a history of brewing because of its insights into the whole pattern of change in the economic and social condition during the period with which it is concerned. The less ambitious study by Professor John Vaizey and Patrick Lynch of *Guinness's Brewery and the Irish Economy* (1960) provides a parallel with the Scottish experience described here. Professor Vaizey's *The Brewing Industry 1886-1951: An Economic Study* (1960) is also useful.

Writers on the economic and social history of modern Scotland have so far been less conscious of the importance of the brewing industry than their English or Irish counterparts. Both the late Professor Henry Hamilton and Professor Roy Campbell devote some space to distilling, but have little to say in their respective studies about brewing, which was certainly as important in certain areas of the

Lowlands as whisky manufacture in the Highlands.[1] Mr W.H.Marwick, one of the pioneers of industrial history in Scotland, mentions brewing in his *Scotland in Modern Times* (1964). He indicates its important relationship with agriculture through the trade in barley and waste products. Although labour costs were low in brewing, he writes, the industry was greatly handicapped by taxation.[2] Professor John Butt, in *The Industrial Archaeology of Scotland* (1967), also devotes some space to the history of brewing, although his concern is essentially with the industrial archaeology created by more recent rationalisation.[3]

The range of sources open to those working in the fields of business and industrial history in Scotland has grown considerably in recent years.[4] This study draws heavily on legal records held in the Court of Session in Edinburgh, the majority of cases being concerned with business disputes and sequestrations. A proven bankruptcy can sometimes lead to a veritable treasure chest of business records, although inevitably more often to a disappointingly uninformative minute book of the defunct individual's or firm's trustees. Legal records held in both the Scottish Record Office and the Signet Library have proved invaluable in building up a picture of the nature and structure of smaller firms, the origins of entrepreneurship and capital, and the character of markets served, as well as indicating why some firms failed while others survived.

Business records held by surviving brewery firms have been extremely useful as far as they go: perhaps the most disappointing feature of the present study is the fact that it has not been possible to investigate in greater detail the early history of some of the major firms, because, sadly, their records have been lost. However, the archives of both William Younger and Company, one of the oldest Edinburgh firms, and those of their important Glasgow rival, John and Robert Tennent, have been invaluable.

Another series of records has helped to supplement more 'conventional' sources on business history and organisation. The insurance records of the Sun Fire Office of London (used by Dr Stanley Chapman for the cotton industry) provide an interesting source for analysing the capital structure of the Scottish brewery industry. My survey examines the policies of 120 Scottish breweries on a similar basis to that adopted by Chapman for cotton textiles in Britain as a whole during the Industrial Revolution.[5] With regard to the later period under review here, the Register of Dissolved Companies in the Scottish Record Office, as well as brewing trade journals, have proved of considerable value.

Excise duties often represented a high proportion of brewers' costs, and it is therefore hardly surprising that excise records provide an important source of data on the growth and fluctuations of the Scottish brewing industry during the period 1707 to 1830. The excise records present considerable problems of interpretation, more particularly because of periodic changes in the rates of duty throughout much of the latter half of the eighteenth and early part of the nineteenth centuries. Customs records, especially ledgers of exports, have provided a detailed picture of distant markets for beer between 1755 and 1850.

NOTES

1 H.Hamilton, *An economic history of Scotland in the 18th century*, (Oxford, 1963); R.H.Campbell, *Scotland since 1707*, (Oxford, 1965), 169-70.

2 W.H.Marwick, *Scotland in modern times*, (London, 1964), 21-2; 101.

3 J.Butt, *The industrial archaeology of Scotland*, (Newton Abbot, 1967), 44-53.

4 P.L.Payne (ed.), *Studies in Scottish business history*, (London, 1967), shows the scope; see also J.Butt's interesting review of Payne's symposium, 'The role of Scottish business history', *The Journal of Economic Studies* (1967).

5 S.D.Chapman 'Fixed capital formation in the British cotton industry, 1770-1815,' *EcHR*, 23, (1970).

List of Abbreviations

ALP	Advocates Library Pamphlet, National Library of Scotland
Ans.	Answers for ...
BCP	Bill Chamber Process, Court of Session
COS	Court of Session
CUST	Customs Records, Public Record Office
E	Excise/Exchequer Records, Scottish Record Office
EcHR	Economic History Review
EP	Extracted Process, Court of Session
GD	General Deposition, Scottish Record Office
GH	Guildhall Library, London
GVA	General View of the Agriculture of ...
NLS	National Library of Scotland
NSA	(New) Statistical Account of Scotland
OSA	(Old) Statistical Account of Scotland
Pet.	Petition, Court of Session
PP	Parliamentary Papers
PRO	Public Record Office
RPCS	Register of the Privy Council of Scotland
RH	Register House
SB	Sederunt Book
SC	Select Committee
SJPE	Scottish Journal of Political Economy
SL	Signet Library
SP	Session Papers
SRO	Scottish Record Office
T	Treasury Records, Public Record Office
UP	Unextracted Process, Court of Session
VR	Valuation Roll

Bibliography

A) MANUSCRIPT AND RELATED SOURCES
B) PARLIAMENTARY PAPERS
C) BOOKS AND PAMPHLETS
D) ARTICLES

A) MANUSCRIPT AND RELATED SOURCES

i) Signet Library, Edinburgh

Session Papers of the Court of Session, Edinburgh (Class. no. SP)

40/9   Information for Alexander Clunie and others, merchants in Perth v. Walter Millar, 1751.

42/5   George and James Shawes, Brewers v. John, Earl of Hopetoun, 1752.

109/25   Petition of John Straton, Brewer in Portsburgh, 1760.

128/10   Answers for John Pagan & Co., merchants in Glasgow, and for Alexander Wilson of Glanderston, merchants there, to the Petition of William Baird, merchant and brewers there, 1765.

128/17   Petition of James Yates, farmer in Barrowfield, 1765.

176/4   Petition of James Rigg, Brewer in Aberdeen, 1776.

176/18   Petition of James Craig and others, retailers of Ale and Beer in the Burgh of Aberdeen, 1781.

188/22   Barclay, Perkins and Co. v. Archibald Colquhoun, 1811.

262/20   Answers for Edward Robertson, Secretary of the Commercial Banking Co. of Scotland, 1812.

271/5   The Magistrates of Dunbar v. Lorimer and others, 1811.

273/13   Petition of George Munro, Merchant in Glasgow, 1812.

Answers for John Cowan and Co., Brewers at Anderston, 1818. Contracts of Copartnership of the Anderston Brewery Co., 1763, 1774, and 1800.

283/13   Craig and Hunter, Merchants in Leith v. Alexander Ponton, Procurator Fiscal for the City of Edinburgh, 1814.

293/14   Petition of the Alloa Brewing Co. and Andrew Roy, Manager, 1815.

356/20   Petition of William Wilkie, Accountant in Haddington, Trustee of Henry and William Knox, Brewers and Merchants in Dunbar, 1789.

378/88   Petition of Thomas Goldie, Factor to Robert McMurdo and Co., Brewers in Dumfries, 1797.

387/28   Answers for the Paisley Banking Co. and their Cashier to the Petition of James Scott, Farmer and Maltster, 1798.

392/27   Petition of Thomas and Robert Allen, Brewers in London, 1798.

446/20   Petition of Thomas Mollinson, Provost of Brechin and of David Shepherd and Alexander Moug, Manufacturers in Brechin, 1802.

477/43 and 44   Sequestration of the Stirling Merchant Banking Co., 1807.

502/38   Petition of the City of Edinburgh v. William Black and Co., Brewers in Aberdeen, 1817.

510/46   Petition of Alexander Anderson, Banker in Inverness, 1818.

532/36   Answers for John Matheson of Attadale and of William Reid of Muirtown, 1818.

626/21   Petition and Complaint of James Connell, Merchant in Leith, 1812.

628/26   Auchtermuchty Brewing Co. v. Thomas Adamson, 1815.

ii) Scottish Record Office, Edinburgh

Register of Deeds.
Minute Books of the Court of Session.
Index to Testaments, Court of Session.
Index to Inventories of Personal Estates of Defuncts, Court of Session.

Court of Session Extracted and Unextracted Processes (Class. no. COS, followed by the Division of Court and serial no.)

CD A1/12   John Alexander, Aberdour v. William Hog, British Linen Co., 1795.

CD C18/2   Archibald Campbell and Co. v. McLaren and Shields, 1851.

CD E2/1   Brewers of Edinburgh v. Cleghorn, 1784.

CD H1/35   Sequestration of John Hooper and Co., Brewers, Glasgow, 1819.

CD P1/24   Sequestration of James Pinkerton Jnr., Brewer, Glasgow, 1819.

CD R1/18   Sequestration of Archibald Richardson, Brewer, Newton Douglas, 1799.

CD W1/2   John Watson, Brewer in Aberdeen, Sequestration.

CM A5/5   The Alloa Brewing Co. v. Thomas Thomson, 1814.

CM B1/39   Sequestration of A. Broomfield, Farmer and Brewer, Melrose, 1810.

CM B1/40   Sequestration of R. Bowman and Co., Brewers, 1811.

CM C1/42   Sequestration of David Gellatly, Brewer and Innkeepers, Perth, 1823.

CM H1/11   Sequestration of Thomas Henry, Brewer, Montrose, 1800.

CM H2/7   Sequestration of A. Hedderwick, Vendor of Porter, Gorbals, 1826.

CM L1/4   Sequestration of Thomas Low, Brewer, Auchterarder, 1786.

CM M1/24   Sequestration of Thomas Monteath, Brewer, Stenhousemuir, 1801.

CM M2/12   Sequestration of Adam Murray, Brewer, Kincardine, 1822.

CM Mc1/8   Sequestration of James McNee, Brewer in Alloa, 1781.

1st Div. I M2/27   Maltmen of Glasgow v. Robert Tennent, 1749.

ID A8/7   North Street Brewery Co. of Aberdeen v. Gray, 1822.

ID S1/5   Sequestration of Thomas Smyth, Brewer in Alyth, 1777.

McNeill A1/19   Auchmouty and Veitch v. the Brewers of Fife, 1700.

Treasury and Exchequer Records (Class no. E)

207/3   Accounts of the Commissioners of Excise for Duties on Malt, Cider and Perry, 1707 onwards.

207/4   Cash Accounts of the Commissioners of Excise for the Duties on Malt etc., 1707 onwards.

904/3   Account of the Gross and Nett Produce of the Excise for Scotland, 1707 - 1807.

904/4   General Account of All Duties under the Management of the Commissioners of Excise, 1808 - 1832.

Customs Records (Class. no. RH)

20   Customs Records Relating to Scotland: Mis. Accounts, 1762-1807.

General Deposits (Class. no. GD)

10   Broughton and Cally Muniments/1265 Papers re the Brewery Co. at Gatehouse.

23   Bught Papers/14/198 Papers re the Brewery Co. of Inverness.

110   Hamilton-Dalrymple of North Berwick Muniments/1147 Papers re the Brewers of Edinburgh; 615 Papers re Glasgow Brewers, 1742-44.

241   Thomson, Dickson and Shaw Mss. Papers of Archibald Campbell and Co., Brewers in Edinburgh.

Business Records from Court of Session Cases (Class. no. RH 15)

1/113   Ane List of Brewers . . . in Aberdeen, 1693-96.

233   SB of James Graham, Maltster, Alloa, 1826.

253   Cash Book of William Murray and Co., Porter Dealers, Edinburgh, 1793 - 1800.

325   SB of Henry Bardner, Brewer in Dunfermline, 1827-28.

355-57   SB of John Fairweather, Innkeeper, Arbroath, 1826-28.

642   Cash Book of a Dunbar Brewery, 1780-85.

731   SB of William Ainslie, Brewer, Duns, 1802.

766   SB of Peter Leslie, Vintner, Edinburgh, 1802-3.

780   SB of Robert Stein and Co., Brewers in Edinburgh, 1819-32.

784   Sequestration of the Scottish Patent Cooperage Co., 1816-30.

803   SB of John White and Son, Paper Manufacturers and Brewers, Haughhead, near Edinburgh, 1814-17.

1059   SB of Thomas Young, Vintner in Irvine, 1812.

1232   Ledger of an unknown brewer, Aberdeen, 1779-85.

1332   SB of John Kirk, brewer in Edinburgh, 1826-27.

1705-23   Cash and Day Books of Patrick Murison, Brewer, Edinburgh, 1786-1800.

1785   Account Book of Patrick Murison, 1793.

2018   Malt Crop Book of John McKnellan, Maltster, Cambusbarron, 1751-53.

2048   SB of John Irving, Brewer in Langholm, 1809-11.

2213-19   Cash, Day and Account Books of John Wilson and Co., Brewers and Distillers, Stirling, 1740-57.

2261   Brewer's Cash Ledger, 1800-01.

Burgh Records (Class. no. B)
6   Ayr: Licensing Records
18   Dunbar: Misc. Licensing Records.
41   Kirkcaldy: Licensing Records; Register of Sasines.
65   St. Andrews: Licensing Records.
66   Stirling: Licensing Records.

Misc. Papers (Class. no. RH 9/18)
26/30   Papers of John Gordon, Collector of Excise, 1711-27.
27/52   Papers of James Elder, Merchant in Aberdeen. An Account of Hops, 1750-61.
70   Papers of Andrew Downie, Maltman in Burntisland, 1607-26.
279   Papers of Sir James Stansfield re Newmilns Cloth Factory, Wanlockhead Mines, Leith Glassworks and Leith Brewery.

iii) National Library of Scotland, Edinburgh

MS14   Letters etc. on the Excise in Scotland, 1790-94.
MS62   Report to the Treasury by the Barons of the Scottish Exchequer ... on the Public Revenue of Scotland, 1792.
MS 640   Letters and papers re Taxation, 1786-1820.
MS 1058   Papers on Revenue, Customs, Excise and other Taxation, 1792-1829.
MS 2620   Letter Book of an Excise Officer in Glasgow, 1792-97.
MS 2797   Journal of an Inspector of Excise in the South of Scotland, 1710.

iv)   Glasgow City Archives, City Chambers

B8/4   Public House Certificates: Ale, 1779-1824, 3 vols.
TH6   Records of the Incorporation of Maltmen, 1605 onwards.
B8/6   Public House Certificates: Ale and Spirits, 1824-98, 18 vols.
Memorandum of Recommendations made by the Magistrates with ref. to Licensed Premises (nd).
Return by the Superintendent of Police, showing the number of licences granted for the years 1849-1857.

v) Public Record Office, London

T64/241   Accounts of Exports of British Manufactures from Scotland, 1732-72.
T64/257   An Account of Spirits made from Corn and Molasses and the Quantity of Foreign Brandy Imported, 1738-45.
The Excise Distribution for the Year 1793.
An Account of the Gross and Nett Produce of the Duties of Malt etc. in that part of Great Britain called Scotland, 1727-28.
CUST 2/1-10   Inspector General's Accounts of Imports and Exports, 1696-1702.
CUST 3/1-10   Ledgers of Imports and Exports, 1697-1707.

CUST 8/1-110 Ledgers of Exports of British Manufactures, under Countries, 1812-70.
CUST 9/35-80 Ledgers of Exports of British Manufactures, under Articles, 1848-70.
CUST 14/1-23 Ledgers of Imports and Exports, 1755-1811.

vi) Business Archives Held in Private Hands

William Younger & Co. Ltd. (Scottish & Newcastle Brewers)
Ledger 1805-08.
Cash Book 1839-43.
Cash Book 1843-45.
Cash Book 1848-50.
Travellers' Statistics Book 1881-1912.

William McEwan & Co. Ltd. (Scottish & Newcastle Brewers)
Journal 1860-62.
Journal 1865-66.
Journal 1866-67.
Journal 1868-69.
Cash Ledger 1860-64.
Cash Ledger 1867-69.

J. & R. Tennent Ltd. (Bass Charringtons)
Rough Book 1776-1837.
Misc. Cash Accounts 1776-1806.
Rough Letter Copy Book 1785-89.
Inventory of Property 1821.
Insurance Valuation and Policies 1811.
Order Book 1822.
Rough Letter Copy book 1834-37.
Export Ledgers 1830-42.
Misc. Contracts and Deeds 1799-1831.
Shipping Book 1859-60.

Both the Scottish & Newcastle and Tennent archives have been surveyed on behalf of the National Register of Archives (Scotland), the respective surveys being numbered 0274 and 0306.

B) PARLIAMENTARY PAPERS

General Index to the Accounts and Papers 1801-1852.
1798-9 XI (1st Series) Second Report from the SC on illicit practices used in defrauding the revenue, 1784.
Two Reports from the SC on distilleries in Scotland.
1803-04 IV   Report from the SC on the rate of Malt duty.

Report from the SC on Scotch barley and malt.
Report from the SC on the corn trade.
1806 II Papers re experiments relative to qualities of malt from barley and Scotch bigg.
1817 XIV A&P Strong beer, chargeable to excise, brewed in and exported from Scotland, in three years.
1818 III Report from the SC on public breweries.
1819 V Minutes respecting the price and quality of beer.
1821 VIII Report on petitions complaining of the additional malt duty in Scotland.
1821 XXVII A&P Ale etc, Account of the number of barrels on which duty has been paid.
1822 XXI A&P Account of the number of brewers.
Excise, Scotland: Instructions to officers etc. (1821).
1826-7 VI Report from the SC on the circulation of promissory notes in Scotland and Ireland.
1826-7 XVII Account of the quantity of the different sorts of beer made in each kingdom, 1786-1826.
1828 XVIII A&P Number of barrels of beer exported from England to Ireland and Scotland etc. 1808-1828.
1830 X Report from the SC on the sale of beer.
1831 VII Report from the SC on the use of molasses in breweries and distilleries.
Report from the SC on malt drawback on spirits.
1833 V Report from the SC on agriculture.
1833 XXXIII A&P Number of barrels of beer exported; Brewers licensed to sell beer.
1834 VIII Report from the SC of inquiry into drunkenness.
1835 XLIX A&P Account of the quantities of the several articles charged with duties of excise.
1839 XLVI A&P Returns re breweries etc.
1841 XXVI A&P Returns re breweries etc.
1850 LII A&P Licensed brewers; Account of malt made, etc.
1854-5 X Report from the SC on the sale of beer act.
1860 XXXIII Report from the Royal Commission on the licensing system.
1867 XI Report from the SC on the malt tax.
1872 LXIV A&P Articles charged with duty of excise: licensed brewers.
1890-91 LXXVIII Report on the relation of wages in certain industries to cost of production.
1893-94 LXXXIII Report on wages of manual labour classes in the United Kingdom . . . in 1886 and 1891. Part II.
1898 XXXVIII Report of the RC on the liquor licensing laws (Scotland). Fourth Report.
1899 XXXV ibid. Final Report.
1910 CIX Census of production. Part V: Re . . . brewing and malting. 1907.
1912-13 CVIII Report on earnings and hours of labour: VIII. Food, drink and

tobacco trades in 1906.

1916 XII　Report of the advisory committee on proposals for the state purchase of the licensed liquor trade.

1930-31 XV　Report from the SC on licensing (Scotland).

C) BOOKS AND PAMPHLETS

i) Published before 1850

Accum, F.A. (1820), *Treatise on the art of brewing.*

Anon (nd) *Memorial concerning the malt tax.*

(1710), *The brewer's farewell to the magistrates, etc. of the city of Edinburg*

(1713), *Scotland's complaint against the malt tax.*

(1713), *A letter from a brewer . . . concerning the malt tax.*

(1713), *A dialogue between a brewer and a gager re the malt tax.*

(1724), *The act of parliament upon the malt tax.*

(1786), *Resolutions of the landed interest respecting the distillery.*

(1797), *Distilleries . . . in their connection with the agriculture, commerce an revenue of Great Britain.*

Bald, A. (1807), *The farmer and corn dealer's assistant.*

Barclay, J. (1820), *Art of brewing and distillation.*

Baverstock, J.H. (1811), *Practical observations on the prejudices against the brewery.*

(1813), *State of the brewery.*

Bell, A. (1808), *Use of grain in distilleries.*

Black, W. (1835), *A practical treatise on brewing and on storing of beer.*

Brande, W. (1829), *Town and country brewery book.*

Combrune, M. (1762), *Theory and practice of brewing.*

Dunlop, J. (1836),, *The artificial drink usages of North Britain* (4th ed.).

(1839), *The philosophy of artificial and compulsory drinking usages in Great Britain and Ireland* (6th ed.)

Ford, W. (1849), *An historical account of the malt trade and laws.*

Harris, W. (1793), *The brewer, victualler and gauger's assistant.*

Hayman, E.N. (1823), *A practical treatise to render the art of brewing more easy (2nd ed.).*

Keith, G. (1811), *GVA Aberdeenshire.*

Loch, D. (1778), *Essays on the trade, commerce, manufactures and fisheries of Scotland.*

Logan, W. (1849), *The moral statistics of Glasgow.*

Lowe, A. (1826), *A summary of the duties, drawbacks and bounties of excise in Great Britain.*

Morrice, A. (1827), *Practical treatise on brewing.*

Pigot's commercial directory of Scotland 1825-26.

Pyne, W.H. (1827), *The world in miniature; England, Scotland and Ireland* (3 vols.)

Poole, T. (1782), *Treatise on strong beer, ale etc.*

Roberts, W.H. (1837), *The Scottish ale brewer and practical maltster.*
(later eds. 1846 and 1847.)
Robertson, G. (1813), *GVA Kincardine.*
Robertson, J. (1808), *GVA Inverness.*
Ross, W. (1786), *Present state of the distillery in Scotland.*
Sinclair, J. (1793 etc) *The statistical account of Scotland (OSA),* (1795), *GVA Northern counties.*
       (1825), *Analysis of the statistical account of Scotland.*
Singer, W. (1812), *GVA Dumfries.*
Somerville, G. (1805), *GVA East Lothian.*
Souter, D. (1812), *GVA Banff.*
Thomson, J. (1800), *GVA Fife.*
Thomson, T. (1849), *Brewing and distillation.*
Trotter, J. (1811), *GVA West Lothian.*

ii) Published since 1850

Anon (1888), *Glasgow of today: businessmen and mercantile interests.*
       (1900) (and subsequent dates), *Manual of British and foreign brewery companies.*
       (1925), *A short history of George Younger & Son Ltd, Alloa, 1762-1925.*
       (1940), *Two hundred years of progress: James Aitken and Co. Ltd. 1740-1940.*
       (1966), *J. & R. Tennent's Wellpark Brewery, Glasgow.*
Ashton, T.S. (1959), *Economic fluctuations in England 1700-1900.*
Baker, J. (1905), *The brewing industry.*
Barnard, A. (1889-91), *Noted breweries of Great Britain and Ireland* (in 4 vols.).
Boswell, J. (1973), *The rise and decline of small firms.*
Bremner, D. (1869), *The industries of Scotland: their rise, progress and present condition.*
Brewers' Almanack.
Brewers' Guardian.
Brewery Manual.
Brewing Trade Rview.
Brown P.H. (1891), *Early travellers in Scotland.*
Burns J.D. (1881), *A consecutive narrative of the rise, development and extension of temperance reform.*
Butt, J. (1967), *The industrial archaeology of Scotland.*
       (ed.) (1971), *Robert Owen: prince of cotton spinners.*
Butt, J., Donnachie, I. and Hume, J. (1968), *Industrial history: Scotland.*
Campbell, R.H. (1965), *Scotland since 1707: the rise of an industrial society.*
Clark, G.N. (1938), *Guide to English commercial statistics 1696-1782.*
Clarkson, L.A. (1971), *The pre-industrial economy in England, 1500-1750.*
Corran H. (1975), *A history of brewing.*
Crouzet, F. (1972), *Capital formation in the industrial revolution.*
Cullen, L.M. (1968), *Anglo-Irish trade 1660-1800.*
Dickson P.G.M. (1960), *The Sun Insurance Office 1710-1960.*

Dickinson, W.C. (1961), *Scotland from earliest times to 1603.*
Donnachie, I. (1971), *Industrial archaeology of Galloway.*
          (1973), *War and economic growth in Britain 1793-1815.*
Donnachie, I. and Macleod, I. (1974), *Old Galloway.*
Duckham, B.F. (1970), *A history of the Scottish coal industry 1700-1815.*
French, R.W. (1884), *Nineteen centuries of drink in England.*
Gayer, A.D. et al (1953), *The growth and fluctuation of the British economy 1790-1850.*
Graham, H.G. (1901), *The social life of Scotland in the eighteenth century.*
Hamilton, H. (1963), *An economic history of Scotland in the eighteenth century.*
Hamilton, T.W. (1929), *The temperance reformation in Scotland.*
Handley, J. (1953), *Scottish farming in the eighteenth century.*
Harrison, B. (1971), *Drink and the Victorians.*
Higgins, J. and Pollard, S. (eds.) (1971), *Aspects of capital investment in Great Britain 1750-1850.*
Hoon, E.E. (1968), *The organisation of the English customs system, 1696-1786* (new ed.).
Jones, E.L. and Mingay, G.E. (1967), *Land, labour and population in the industrial revolution.*
Keir, D. (1951), *The Younger centuries.*
Keith, A. (1936), *The North of Scotland Bank Ltd.*
Kerr, A.W. (1926), *History of banking in Scotland* (4th ed.)
Kilby, K. (1971), *The cooper and his trade.*
Kyd, J.G. (1952), Scottish population statistics (with Webster's census, 1755).
Lindsay, J. (1968), *The canals of Scotland.*
Loftus, W.R. (1867), *The brewer.*
Logan, W. (1873), *The early heroes of the temperance reformation.*
Longmate, N. (1968), *The Waterdrinkers: a history of temperance.*
Lynch, P. and Vaizey, J. (1960), *Guinness's brewery in the Irish economy, 1758-1876.*
Lythe, S.G.E. (1960), *The economy of Scotland 1550-1625.*
McNeill, F.M. (1956), *The Scots cellar.*
Malcolm, C.A. (1948), *The bank of Scotland, 1695-1945.*
          (1950), *The history of the British Linen bank.*
Marwick, W.H. (1964), *Scotland in modern times.*
Mathias, P. (1959), *The brewing industry in England, 1700-1830.*
          (1969), *The first industrial nation.*
Maxwell, W. (1910), *History of cooperation in Scotland.*
Minchinton, W.E. (ed.) (1969), *The growth of English overseas trade in the 17th and 18th centuries.*
Mitchell, B.R. and Deane, P. (1962), *Abstract of British historical statistics.*
Monckton, H.A. (1966), *A history of English ale and beer.*
Munro, N. (1928), *The history of the Royal Bank of Scotland.*
Payne, P. (ed.) (1967), *Studies in Scottish business history.*
          (1974), *British entrepreneurship in the nineteenth century.*

Pollard, S. (1968), *The genesis of modern management: a study of the Industrial Revolution in Great Britain.*
Pratt, E.A. (1907), *The licensed trade.*
Presnell, L.S. (1956), *Country banking in the Industrial Revolution.*
Reid, R. (pseud. 'Senex') (1884), *Glasgow: past and present* (3 vols.).
Riley, P.W.J. (1964), *The English ministers and Scotland.*
Scamell, G. (1880), *Breweries and maltings: their arrangement, construction, machinery and plant.* 2nd ed. revised and enlarged. 1st ed. pub. 1871.
Scott, W.R. (ed.) (1905), *The records of a Scottish cloth manufactory.*
          (1912), *The constitution and finance of English, Scottish and Irish joint stock companies to 1720.*
Shapiro, S. (1967), *Capital and cotton industry in the Industrial Revolution.*
Smout, T.C. (1963), *Scottish trade on the eve of Union 1660-1707.*
          (1969), *A history of the Scottish people 1560-1830.*
Stopes, H. (1885), *Malt and malting.*
          (1895), *Brewery companies.*
Supple, B. (1970), *The Royal Exchange Assurance 1720-1970, a history of British insurance.*
Vaizey, J. (1960), *The brewing industry 1886-1951: an economic study.*
Ward J.T. and Wilson, R. (1971), *Land and industry.*
White, E.S. (1860), *The maltster's guide.*
Williams, J.B. (1972), *British commercial policy and trade expansion, 1750-1850.*
Wilson, G. (1940), *Alcohol and the nation.*

D) ARTICLES

Chapman, S.D. (1970), 'Fixed capital formation in the British cotton industry, 1770-1815', *EcHR*, 23.
Cole, W.A. (1958), 'Trends in eighteenth century smuggling', *EcHR*, 10.
Collins, E.J.T. (1969), 'Harvest technology and labour supply in Britain, 1790-1870', *EcHR*, 22.
Davis, R. (1962), 'English foreign trade, 1700-1774', *EcHR*, 15.
Donnachie, I. (1977), 'Sources of capital and capitalization in the Scottish brewing industry c.1750-1830,' *EcHR*, 30.
Donnachie, I. and Butt, J. 1967), 'The Wilsons of Wilson town ironworks (1779-1813): a study in entrepreneurial failure,' *Explorations in Entrepreneurial History*, vol. 4.
Glen, I.A. (1970), 'A maker of illicit stills' *Scottish Studies*, 14.
Gould, J.D. (1962), *Agricultural fluctuations and the English economy in the eighteenth century'*, *J. of Economic History*, 22.
Harrison, B. (1967), 'Drink and sobriety in England, 1815-1872', *Inter. Review of Social History*, vol. II.
Harrison, B. (1970), 'The British prohibitionists 1853-1872: a biographical analysis,' *Inter. Review of Social History*, vol. 15.
John, A.H. (1965), 'Agricultural productivity and economic growth in England

1700-1760,' *J. of Economic History*, 25.

Lee, J. (1966), 'Money and beer in Ireland, 1790-1875, I', *EcHR*, 19.

Logan, J.C. (1972), 'The Dumbarton Glass Works Company: a study in entrepreneurship', *Business History*, 14.

Lynch, P. and Vaizey, J. (1966), 'Money and beer in Ireland, 1790-1875, I', *EcHR*, 19.

MacDonagh, O. (1963), 'The origins of porter,' *EcHR*, 16.

McKendrick, N. (1959), 'Josiah Wedgwood: an 18th century entrepreneur in salesmanship and marketing techniques,' *EcHR*, 12.

McKendrick, N. (1970), 'Josiah Wedgwood and cost accounting in the Industrial Revolution,' *EcHR*, 1970.

Mathias, P. (1952), 'Agriculture and the brewing and distilling industries in the eighteenth century,' *EcHR*, 5.

Mathias, P. (1957), 'The entrepreneur in brewing,' *Explorations in Entrepreneurial History*, 1st ser., vol. 10.

Mitchison, R. (1965), 'The movement of Scottish corn prices in the seventeenth and eighteenth centuries,' *EcHR*, 18.

Payne, P. (1967), 'The emergence of the large-scale company in Great Britain 1870-1914', *EcHR*, 20.

Pollard, S. (1958), 'Investment, consumption and the Industrial Revolution', *EcHR*, 11.

Robinson, E. (1963), 'Eighteenth century commerce and fashion: Matthew Boulton's marketing techniques,' *EcHR*, 16.

Sigsworth, E.M. (1965), 'Science and the brewing industry, 1850-1900', *EcHR*, 17.

Smout, T.C. (1961), 'The early Scottish sugar houses 1660-1720', *EcHR*, 14.

Smout, T.C. (1964), 'Scottish landowners and economic growth, 1650-1850,' *Scottish J. of Political Economy*, 11.

Appendix I

List of Scottish Brewers, 1825

ABERDEEN

Aberdeen
The Aberdeen Brewery, 9 Meal Market Lane, Wm McBean
Devanha Brewery, Wm Black & Co.
New Bridge Brewery, Cadenhead, Barron & Co., George Reid, manager
Alex Cowie, 5 Virginia Street
Wm Duthie, Holburn Street
Gilcomston Brewery Co., George Emslie, manager
Ferryhill Brewery, George Gordon & Co., Henry Hogg, manager
John Mowat, Bursar's Court, 61 Castle Street
Seaton Brewery, Peter Nicol
James Sim, Hardgate
Th. Sim & Son, 22 Loch Street
Smith, Irvine & Co., Old Aberdeen
Patrick Still, South Bridge

Inverurie
Peter Anderson & Co.

Peterhead
John Merns, Queen Street
John Paton & Co., School Brae

ARGYLL

Inveraray
Archibald Wright, brewer and baker

AYR

Ayr
John Ramsay, John Street, Wallacetown
Peter Walker, The Fort

Kilmarnock
Th. Greenshields, Grange Street
George Paxton, Richardland

Saltcoats
Hugh Watt, Corn merchant and brewer

BANFF
  Banff
  Wm Bartlett, Seatown

  Keith
  James Gall, Union Street

BERWICK
  Berwick
  Berwick Brewery, Chartres, Elliott & Co.
  Sibbit, Dickson & Thompson, Tweedmouth

  Coldingham
  James Greenfield

  Coldstream
  Thomas Joppling

  Duns
  John Ramsay
  George & Robert White
  James Whitelaw

  Swinton
  Wm Scott, brewer and baker

CAITHNESS
  Wick
  Alex. Millar, Grant Street, Pulteney Town

CLACKMANNAN
  Alloa
  John McNellan, Shore
  Robert Meiklejohn & Son, Candlerigg
  Wm Mitchell, High Street
  Andrew Roy, Alloa Brewery
  John Syme
  Thomson, McDermid & Co., Mills Brewery

DUMBARTON
  Dumbarton
  Dumbarton Glass Work & Brewing Co., Jacob Dixon & Co., High Street

DUMFRIES
  Dumfries
  James Corson, 28 Irish Street
  Samuel Grierson, 18 English Street

Wm Lammie, Whitesands
Wm Richardson, St Michael Street
Jas. Shortridge, Maxwelltown
Robert Shortridge, Maxwelltown

Langholm
Irving & Scott, Drove Street

Sanquhar
Broom & Co.
Dawson & Co.

Thornhill
Wm Jackson, Nith Bridge

EDINBURGH/MIDLOTHIAN

Dalkeith
Th. Archibald

Edinburgh
David Aikman, Campbell's Close
Jas. Anderson, Borough Loch
Bartram's Ale, Pleasance
Bell, Keir & Co., Pleasance
Alex. Berwick & Co., Gentles Close, Canongate
George Bell Brown, N. Back of Canongate
John Blair, N. Back of Canongate
Brunton & Anderson, N. Back of Canongate
Wm Buchan & Co., Grassmarket
Archibald Campbell, Cowgate
James Carr, East Causewayside
Abraham Combe & Co., Livingston Yard, Westport
Combe, Delafield & Co., Old Physic Gardens
Peter Dick, Robertson's Close, Cowgate
Andrew Drybrough, N.Back of Canongate
Edinburgh & Leith Brewing Co., Canongate, Andrew Craig, agent
Robert Fleming, Summerhall
John Glasgow, Cowgate
James Kerr, Newington Brewery, East Sciennes Street
Robert Keir, Pleasance
John Kirk, Drumdryan
Peter Lamond & Sons, Grassmarket
John Miller, Potterrow
James Mitchell, Main Point
John Muir & Sons, N. Back of Canongate
Neal, Ryrie & Co., Croftangry Lane
Jas. Young, Riego Street

Richard Young, S. Back of Canongate
William Younger & Co., Abbey Hill

Midcalder
Alex. Gillies, West & East Mills, corn miller and brewer

Musselburgh
John Handyside, Fisherrow
Howden & Thomson, Fisherrow
Wm Whitelaw, Fisherrow

ELGIN (MORAY)
Elgin
Alex & James Young, College

Forres
John Davidson, Casieford

FIFE

Anstruther
David Rodger, East Anstruther

Crail
James Key, High Street

Cupar
John Inglis, Bonnygate
Robert Philip, Crossgate
Alex. Thomson, Burnside
Charles Welsh, Crossgate

Dunfermline
Wm Bardner, High Street
John Douglas, St Margaret's Street
John Stenhouse, High Street

Kirkcaldy
Henry Fergus, Links
John Keddie & Son, Links
John Stocks Sr., Bridgetown
John Stocks, Jr., Links
Andrew Bridges, Mid. Street, Pathhead

Leven
David Ballingall, Back Street

Limekilns
Johnstone & Laing

St Andrews
George Berwick, South Street
Ireland & Halket, Argyll Brewery

St Monance
Andrew Mackie

FORFAR (ANGUS)
Arbroath
Jas. Anderson, South Grimstay
Robert Gilchrist, Market Gate
John Knight, Caroline Place
Robert Lindsay & Sons, St Vigeans

Barrie
Alex. Crighton, West Haven, brewer and baker

Brechin
Anderson & Co., Bridge End
George Reid, Back Street
David Scott, North Brewery

Dundee
Th. Miller, Perth Road
Pleasance Brewing Co., Pleasance

Forfar
Patrick Barry, Back Wynd
Blair, Skene & Co., High Street
Th. Morris, High Street
Wm Potter, Back Wynd
Alex. Stark, High Street

Montrose
John Alexander, Bridge Street
Wm Black, Bridge Street
Henry Farquharson, Castle Street
Jas. Potter, Back Street
Wm Ross & Co., Lochside

HADDINGTON (EAST LOTHIAN)

Athelstaneford
Walter Gibson

Dunbar
John Brown, Shore
John Dods, Dawell Brae
Dudgeon, Ellis & Co., Belhaven Brewery

Garvald
James Robertson, brewer and vintner

Haddington
Alex. Howden, Nungate
Catherine McBean, Back Street
Wm Shiells, Back Street

North Berwick
Henry Bertram
Wm Cunningham

Prestonpans
John Fowler, Robert Heslop, manager

INVERNESS

Inverness
Henry Wardlaw, Muirtown Brewery

KINCARDINE

Inverbervie
Robert Miller, brewer

Johnshaven
James Milne, brewer

Laurencekirk
Walter Adam, brewer and tavernkeeper

Stonehaven
Messrs Emry & Co., Carronside
Jas. Smart, Bridge of Cowie

KINROSS'

Kinross
John McCulloch
Thomas Morison, Milnathort

KIRKCUDBRIGHT

Castle Douglas
James Hewetson

Gatehouse
John McWilliam Jr, Front Street

Kirkcudbright
John McMillan, Mill Burn

LANARK

Airdrie
James Thomson, 30 South Bridge Street

Biggar
James Bell

Glasgow
Robert Aitken, Camlachie
Hugh Baird Jr, Canal Brewery
Jas. Bayne & Co., 399 Sugar House Close, Gallowgate
Wm Bryson, 8 Tureen Street
John Connal & Co., Finnieston Road
John Cowan & Co., Anderston Brewery
George Forest, Clyde Street, Anderston
Jas. Haig, Alston Street
Alex. Hedderwick, Clyde Terrace, Gorbals
John Hedderwick, Adelphi Brewery, Hutchesontown
John Hooper, 3 Thistle Street, Hutchesontown
Jas. and Robert Hunter, 16 Montrose Street
John Hutchison, New Street, Calton
Jas. Johnston, 16 Stirling Street
Jas. Paterson, Burnside
Andrew and John Robertson, 21 Struther Street, Calton
Wm Scott, Barrowfield Road
Jas. Stewart & Co., 84 King Street, Tradeston
Walter Stewart & Co., Haghill
Robert Struthers, Greenhead Brewery
Hugh and Robert Tennent, 22 Montrose Street
John and Robert Tennent, Well Park Brewery

Hamilton
James Forrest, Dovecoat Hall
Andrew Scott, Church Street

East Kilbride
James Robertson

Lanark
Muir & Brown, Wellgate
John Todd, High Street

Strathaven
Hugh Vallance

LINLITHGOW (WEST LOTHIAN)

Bathgate
Robert Boyd, Cochrane Street
Adam Dawson, Bathgate Brewery
Linlithgow
Adam & John Dawson, West End

Queensferry
Thomas Storrie

ORKNEY
Kirkwall
William Corston
Thomas Omond

PEEBLES

Peebles
Wm Aitchison, Kirkfield Brewery
Thomas Granger, Peebles Brewery

PERTH

Auchterarder
John Miller

Blairgowrie
John Anderson, Allan Street

Crieff
John Lindsay, Mitchell Street
David Porteous, Comrie Street

Dunblane
Andrew McLeich, Bridge End

Dunkeld
James Moncur, High Street

Dunning
Wm Eadie

Kincardine
Adam Murray, West Port

Methven
Daniel Paton

Perth
Hugh Cameron, 41 Watergate

Wm Muir, South Inch Brewery
Amelia Taylor, Bridgend
James White & Co., South Inch
John Wright, Methven Street

RENFREW

Greenock
Greenock Brewery Co., Nicholson Street
James Watt & Co., Carts Dyke

Paisley
James Chep & Co., Saw Hill
James Macfarlane, Lady Lane

Port Glasgow
Alex. Millar, Devils Glen

ROSS & CROMARTY

Cromarty
Wm Thomson

Tain
Tain Brewery Co., George Gallie, manager

ROXBURGH
Hawick
Adam Irvine

Jedburgh
Mark Briggs, Canongate
John Riddell, Abbey Place
Thomas Wright, High Street

Kelso
Wm Boyd, Roxburgh Street

Melrose
Francis Vanhegan

Yetholm
Robert Elliot

SELKIRK

Galashiels
Wm Brown

Selkirk
Agnes Haldane

STIRLING

Falkirk
James Aitken, High Street
Alex. Ballantyne
James Cowie, Roberts Wynd
John McKechnie
Robert Smith

St Ninians
Alex. Buchanan & Son

Stirling
James Burden
John Christie
John Henderson
William McEwan
Alex McLaren
George McQueen
John Stewart
Peter Stewart

WIGTOWN

Newton Stewart
James McLauren

Stranraer
Charles Angus, Strand
Wm Thorburn, Princes Street

Wigtown
James Frazer

Source: *Pigot's commercial directory of Scotland, 1825-1826.*

Appendix II

Scottish Brewery Valuations, 1793-1815

		Fixed Capital £	Stock £	Total £
1	Henry Abercrombie, Stirling (m&b)	320	280	600
2	Charles Addison, Bo'ness (b&mcht)	3195	4000	7195
3	Wm Ainslie, Duns (b) (1800)	780	1420	2200
	(1802)	1580	1620	3200
4	Jas Aitken, Glasgow (m)	—	500	500
5	John Aitken, Falkirk (m&b)	180	120	300
6	Allan, Cummine & Co., Aberdeen (m&b)	300	500	800
7	Jhn & Wm Anderson, Castle Douglas (b)	300	400	700
8	Th Anderson, Dunfermline (b&bker)	250	—	250
9	Anderson & Bardner, Dunfermline (b)	—	600	600
10	Jas Armstrong (b), Dalkeith	200	200	400
11	Henry Bardner, Dunfermline (writer)	750	550	1300
12	Geo Begbie, Dirleton (b&f)	120	—	120
13	Andrew Beveridge, Pathhead, Fife (b)	100	—	100
14	Wm Black & Co., Gilcomstone (b)	1700	1800	3500
15	Jas Blair & Co., Greenock (m&b) (1793)	970	1530	3700
	(1799)	1800	950	2750
16	Rbt Bowman & Co., Paisley, (f, b&m)	660	440	1100
17	Jas Brown, Haddington (b)	1980	1320	3300
18	Walter Brown & Co., Craigentinny (b)	400	500	900
19	Daniel Bruce, Ayr (m) (1800)	30	120	150
	Rbt Bruce, Ayr, (m) (1795)	—	250	250
20	Jhn Bryan, Ayr, (m)	40	80	120
21	Alex Buchanan, Stirling (b)	200	400	600
22	Wm Buchanan, Killearn (f&b)	300	500	800
23	Wm Burnett, Dunbar (f&b)	200	600	800
24	Jas Burns, Hamilton (m&b) (1795)	250	350	600
	(1800)	250	350	600
25	Alex Carfrae, Newbattle (b)	50	700	750
26	Rbt Cargill, Dunkeld (mcht)	100	50	150
27	David Cleghorn, Edinburgh (b)	160	290	450
28	Jas Cochrane, Lesmahagow (b) (1800)	120	—	120
	(1801)	180	—	180

29	Arch Colquhoun & Co, Falkirk (b)	2600	2000	4600
30	Matt Comb, Leith (b)	920	1150	2070
31	Jas Cooper, Dunfermline (b)	170	130	300
32	Wm Cooper, Rathen (m)	300	300	600
33	Rbt Cowan & Sons, Glasgow	1250	2500	3750
34	Jas Craig, Stirling (b)	65	115	180
35	Adam Dawson, Bonyton (m)	260	490	750
36	Jas Dobie, Dysart (b)	400	250	650
37	Jhn Drummond, Crieff (b)	200	200	400
38	Jhn Fergus, Linktown, Kirkcaldy (m)	85	120	205
39	Wm Ferrier, Cardross (m)	130	170	300
40	Jas Fleeming, London (mcht)	100	—	100
41	Th Foster, Coldstream (inn & b)	120	60	180
42	David Gardner, Strathmiglo (b)	95	205	300
43	Colin Gillies, Brechin (mcht) (1794)	135	765	900
	Wm Gillies, Brechin (b) (1815)	700	4000	4700
44	Jhn Glas, Snr, Stirling (mcht)	785	515	1300
45	Th Greenshields, Kilmarnock (b)	230	500	800
46	Jas Hadden, Montrose (mcht & m)	430	420	850
47	Jhn Handyside, Musselburgh (b)	400	—	400
48	Jhn Harvie, Yoker (f & m) (1796)	200	680	880
	(1801)	325	1495	1820
49	Jas Hoggart, Haddington (b)	290	300	590
50	Rbt Howden, Haddington (f&m)	200	500	700
51	Jas Hunter, Glasgow (b)	—	400	400
52	Jhn Hutton, Kinghorn (b)	90	310	400
53	Wm Johnston, Kirkcudbright (b)	300	—	300
54	Sam Lindsay, Dunkeld (b)	100	100	200
55	Geo Lowe, Markinch (f&b)	70	—	70
56	Wm Kay & Co., Crieff (b)	180	180	360
57	Rbt Kemp, Dalkeith (b)	220	450	670
58	Th Kidston, Stirling (b)	300	—	300
59	Jas King, Kirkcaldy (b)	300	250	550
60	Jas King Snr, Pt Glasgow (b)	900	400	1300
61	Jas Knox, Greenock (b dist & m)	1000	3100	4100
62	Th Littlejohn, Stirling (b)	900	550	1450
63	Jhn Logan, Ayr (bkr & m)	60	100	160
64	Jhn McKellar, Calder (b) (1793)	100	200	300
	(1801)	150	250	400
65	Wm McNie, Gargunnock (m)	50	90	140
66	Alex Malcolm, Pollockshaws (b&m)	150	100	250
67	Alex Manson, Thurso (b)	700	300	1000
68	Alex Masterton, Culross (mcht & m)	130	120	250
69	Rbt Meiklejohn, Alloa (m&b)	300	420	720
70	Jas Miller, Lasswade (f&b)	220	510	730

71 Jas Mitchell, Gladsmuir (f&b)	150	250	400
72 Jas Monteath, Stenhousemuir (b)	200	—	200
73 Pat Murison, Edinburgh (b)	340	500	840
74 Wm Murray, Tranent (coal grieve & b)	60	20	80
75 Wm & Hugh Murray, Edinburgh (porter dlrs)	1300	—	1380
76 Wm Murison, Edinburgh (b)	450	650	1100
77 David Neill, Kilmarnock (m)	100	—	100
78 Wm Naughton, Aberdeen (m)	30	—	30
79 Jas Peddie, Stirling (b)	140	20	160
80 Johnathan Pew, Edinburgh (b)	—	30	30
81 Alex Ponton, Inveresk (b)	100	100	200
82 Th Prentice, Lanark (b)	100	50	150
83 David Pringle, Dunbar (b&f)	200	580	780
84 And. Ramsay, Edinburgh (slater)	100	—	100
85 Jhn Ramsay, Perth (b)	1245	855	2100
86 Geo Reid, Ratho (b&f)	140	100	240
87 Arch Richardson, Newton Douglas (b) (1794)	300	—	300
(1795)	500	300	800
88 Sam Robertson, Ednam (b) (1795)	250	400	650
89 Peter Robertson, Ednam (b&f) (1815)	1390	2280	3670
90 Wm Ross, Ayr (m)	50	75	125
91 Is. Salter, Edinburgh (b)	700	—	700
92 David Scott, Johnshaven (mcht&m)	300	400	700
93 Arch Simpson, Dalkeith (b)	200	890	1090
94 Jas Smith & Co, Ayr (b)	350	250	600
95 Jhn Smith Jr & Co., Brechin (b)	400	700	1100
96 Pat Smith & Co., nr Aberdeen (b)	100	200	300
97 Frances Sprot, Edinburgh (widow) (b)	200	—	200
98 Alex Steele & And. Forgie, Bo'ness (b&m)	340	460	800
99 Jhn Stocks, Kinghorn (b&f)	150	300	450
100 Wm Strachan & Co., Newbridge (b)	900	1100	2000
101 Jhn Studart, Stirling (m)	395	10	405
102 Jhn & Rbt Tenant, Glasgow (b)	2000	2000	4000
103 Jhn Ure, Glasgow (m)	100	250	350
104 Hugh Wallace, Kilmarnock (b)		300	300
105 Th Wardlaw, Dunfermline (bker & b)	210	220	430
106 Jas Watson, Wallacetown (m)	80	70	150
107 Jas Watson, Musselburgh (m)	300	—	300
108 Jas Watt & Co, Greenock (b&m)	1400	1650	3050
109 Gilbert Waugh, Edinburgh (b)	300	—	300
110 Ch Welch, Cupar (bker & b)	175	—	450
111 Wm Welsh, Alloa (m)	950	—	950
112 Geo Whyllan, Glasgow (m)	—	250	250
113 Th Wilkie, Strathmiglo (b) (1794)	100	100	200
(1795)	150	150	300

114 Pat Wilson, Dunfermline (b)	250	700	950
115 Jhn Winton, Haddington (b)	140	360	500
116 Jhn Wright, Paisley (m)	—	300	300
117 A.C.Younger, Edinburgh (b) (1795)	1400	—	1400
(1801)	1000	—	1000
118 Alex Young & Co., Aberdeen (b)	2400	3600	6000
119 Jas Younger, Alloa (m)	80	70	150
120 Younger & Somerville, Edinburgh (b)	—	1600	1600

Note: b - brewer;   f - farmer;   m - maltster;
mcht - merchant; inn - innkeeper; bker - baker.

Appendix III

Beer and Ale Excise, 1707-1830 (Gross Produce)

Year	£		
		nd	2458
1707-08	43653	1726-27	48169
1708-09	51921	nd	2562
1709-10	48982	1727-28	46076
New Duty	253	nd	2451
1710-11	50847	1728-29	43669
nd	2704	nd	2321
1711-12	54355	1729-30	46994
nd	2887	nd	2492
1712-13	55722	1730-31	50510
nd	2964	nd	2687
1713-14	51496	1731-32	50930
nd	2733	nd	2710
1714-15	48130	1732-33	50803
nd	2559	nd	2700
1715-16	47810	1733-34	50183
nd	2543	nd	2668
1716-17	54606	1734-35	48068
nd	2904	nd	2547
1717-18	56747	1735-36	45840
nd	3021	nd	2437
1718-19	57805	1736-37	44223
nd	3076	nd	2351
1719-20	56476	1737-38	42670
nd	3061	nd	2269
1720-21	54407	1738-39	43758
nd	2898	nd	2327
1721-22	55506	1739-40	40865
nd	2959	nd	2175
1722-23	51768	1740-41	31264
nd	2756	nd	1667
1723-24	54573	1741-42	33925
nd	2904	nd	1808
1724-25	49097	1742-43	38301
nd	2615	nd	2037
1725-26	46165	1743-44	41244

nd		2192	a	13531
1744-45		40350	1772-73 o	26406
nd		2145	a	12433
1745-46		34795	1773-74 o	23217
nd		1858	a	11138
1746-47		38435	1774-75 o	23178
nd		2057	a	11022
1747-48		43034	1775-76 o	23853
nd			a	11194
1748-49		44509	1776-77 o	25657
nd			a	12090
1749-50		44887	1777-78 o	28226
nd			a	13402
1750-51		42206	1779-80 o	29182
1751-52		39539	a	13969
1752-53		35465	1780-81 o	31280
1753-54		35105	a	14486
1754-55		37233	1781-82 o	30836
1755-56		37787	a	13401
1756-57		33169	1782-83 o	25066
1757-58		34511	a	10642
1758-59		36700	1783-84 o	23391
1759-60		42704	a	10080
1760-61		43627	1784-85 o	23499
1761-62	Old Duty	39784	a	10007
	Add. Duty	21813	1785-86 o	24774
1762-63	o	36917	a	10599
	a	20029	1786-87 o	27606
1763-64	o	33942	a	9413
	a	17410	1787-88	38042
1764-65	o	32204	1788-89	42125
	a	16409	1789-90	47775
1765-66	o	29952	1790-91	48176
	a	14990	1791-92	55078
1766-67	o	28246	1792-93	58542
	a	13969	1793-94	50445
1767-68	o	29439	1794-95	50555
	a	14626	1795-96	69849
1768-69	0	31078	1796-97	75498
	a	15221	1797-98	73173
1769-70	o	30127	1798-99	76396
	a	14671	1799-1800	66946
1770-71	o	29331	1800-01	54723
	a	14109	1801-02 Consolidated	59391
1771-72	0	28395	New Duty	5866

1802-03 c	43924	1816-17	78696
n	35973	1817-18	74814
1803-04	70580	1818-19	85472
1804-05	75960	1819-20	80540
1805-06	84005	1820-21	84891
1806-07	84551	1821-22	87217
1807-08	80746	1822-23	86593
1808-09	81083	1823-24	84614
1809-10	86259	1824-25	88411
1810-11	83149	1825-26	76524
1811-12	83083	1826-27	79942
1812-13	78129	1827-28	72996
1813-14	87089	1828-29	78416
1814-15	93577	1829-30	72959
1815-16	86814	1830-31	51353

Appendix IV

Malt Excise, 1713-1807 (Nett Produce)

	£		
		1760-61	32218
1713-26	56838	61-62	26890
1726-27	22318	62-63	20635
1727-28	17180	63-64	26264
28-29	18564	64-65	24523
29-30	24206	65-66	18582
1730-31	25890	66-67	19921
31-32	25687	67-68	25859
32-33	25236	68-69	26309
33-34	23710	69-70	27237
34-35	21597	1770-71	26115
35-36	20458	71-72	26119
36-37	20129	72-73	21539
37-38	22362	73-74	21290
38-39	18289	1774-75	19767
39-40	15407	75-76	24858
1740-41	7247	76-77	28101
41-42	18112	77-78	29068
42-43	17400	78-79	33447
43-44	21562	79-80	47135
44-45	17984	1780-81	53781
45-46	14110	81-82	53715
46-47	21599	82-83	23774
47-48	21530	83-84	47801
48-49	22627	84-85	44444
49-50	22644	85-86	40299
1750-51	20669	86-87	53161
51-52	18124	87-88	44847
52-53	17477	88-89	41955
53-54	18483	89-90	37941
54-55	19340	1790-91	50946
55-56	16598	91-92	53870
56-57	8349	92-93	37591
57-58	11478	93-94	41019
58-59	17246	94-95	42221
59-60	30166	95-96	22460

96-97	51225	02-03	102233
97-98	46309	03-04	85668
98-99	60119	04-05	87510
99-1800	71657	05-06	94439
1800-01	62082	06-07	86512
01-02	97420		

Source of Appendix III and IV:E 904/3 Account of the Gross and Nett Produce of the Excise for Scotland, 1707-1807; also, E904/4 General Account of all Duties under the Management of the Commissioners of Excise, 1808-1832.